STUDY GUIDE
Business Today

Study Guide

Business Today

Seventh Edition

David J. Rachman
Michael H. Mescon
Courtland L. Bovée
John V. Thill

Prepared by:
Stanley Garfunkel
C.U.N.Y.– Queensborough Community College
Dennis Guseman
California State University, Bakersfield

McGraw-Hill, Inc.
New York   St. Louis   San Francisco   Auckland   Bogotá
Caracas   Lisbon   London   Madrid   Mexico City   Milan
Montreal   New Delhi   San Juan   Singapore
Sydney   Tokyo   Toronto

STUDY GUIDE
BUSINESS TODAY

3 4 5 6 7 8 9 0 SEM SEM 9 0 9 8 7 6 5 4 3

ISBN 0-07-051332-5

This book was set in Times Roman by Caliber/Phoenix Color Corp.
The editors were Bonnie K. Binkert, Jim Nageotte, and Bob Greiner;
the production supervisor was Annette Mayeski.
The cover was designed by Armen Kojoyian.
Semline, Inc., was printer and binder.

Contents

Introduction

The aim of the *Study Guide for Business Today, Seventh Edition*, is to enable you to obtain the maximum benefit from the time you spend studying business. You may already have developed efficient and satisfactory study techniques, or you may feel that you need some help in this respect. In either event, since you are not yet familiar with the subject, you will probably find the guidance offered here to be helpful. It will ensure that you will be able to discriminate between crucial and less important information, to check your memory and understanding of new concepts, and to broaden your knowledge of the subject by application.

Following this introduction is a section entitled "Approaching Your Introduction to Business Course—Study Hints and Test Strategies." This material will be of use to all students, for it outlines how to get the most out of a college textbook. Instead of memorizing endless pages, you'll learn to pick out the key points and terms. And if you've ever got a test question wrong, even though you understood the material (perhaps because you overlooked the words all or except, which gave a different meaning to the statement), you'll appreciate the test strategies material. This section discusses how to interpret test questions and answer them accurately, and discusses the best general approach to taking tests.

The *Study Guide* itself consists of the following items:

1. For each chapter:
   - Learning Objectives
   - Outline
   - Major Points to Remember
   - Key Terms
   - Key Terms Exercise (Answer keys included)
   - Self Test (Answers at the end of the *Study Guide*)
   - Projects
2. At the back of the *Study Guide*:
   - Answers to Self Tests
   - Supplemental Test Questions (Covering all chapters)

The *Learning Objectives* at the beginning of each *Study Guide* chapter are identical to those in the text; they succinctly state what you should know after studying the text chapter. If after reading the text you can do what the objectives ask, you have a good grasp of the material; if you can't, you should review those areas where your knowledge is weak. The *Outline* serves as a "road map" to the text chapter. It helps you to quickly get your bearings on what is covered and how the topics relate to each other. The *Major Points to Remember* expand on the *Outline* and highlight (with explanations) the important points you should know. The *Key Terms Exercise* thoroughly tests your knowledge of basic business terminology. Don't be tempted to look at the answers (inverted, following the exercise) before you complete the tests. The *Self Test* questions are similar to those you'll see in class exams. Take the tests and check your answers against those provided in the *Answers* section at the end of the *Study Guide*. These exercises and tests are designed to help you target your weak areas as well as to give you positive feedback. In the long run, this knowledge will help you use your study time more effectively.

The *Projects* show you how you can apply the concepts you're learning to specific, lifelike, situations, and give you some experience in problem solving and decision making in business. Many of the projects are research-oriented and require you to gather information from various sources. Some direct you to useful reference materials in your school library; others involve obtaining information directly from businesses in your community. You will find practicing research techniques is good experience for the future. The *Supplemental Test Questions* are similar to the *Self Tests* but appear without answers. Your instructor may choose to use these questions for quizzes or may make the answers available to you so you can test yourself further.

The *Study Guide* is designed to complement, not replace, *Business Today, Seventh Edition*. There is no substitute for reading the text; in any event, we feel that you will enjoy reading the text. We wish you much success as you begin your Introduction to Business course.

Approaching Your Introduction to Business Course: Study Hints and Test Strategies

You are about to begin a course in modern business practices. Maybe this is your first course in the subject. As you examine your copy of *Business Today* and this *Study Guide*, you may wonder how you will be able to digest all of the information they contain.

Keep in mind that no one expects you to memorize all of the information in a textbook that's more than 600 pages long. In fact, one of your first tasks as a student is to learn to identify the most important terms and concepts and to work on mastering them.

Mastering these concepts takes work. That's inevitable. However, there are techniques you can use to study more effectively. These techniques will help you increase your comprehension while you read, and they'll help you remember what you've read. Ultimately, they'll allow you to cut down on your study time.

You may find it helpful to understand a little of the theory about why this study method works. Research has shown that six factors increase your memory and comprehension:

1. Pattern recognition

2. Repetition

3. Multiple modality learning

4. Paraphrasing

5. Association

6. Understanding the purpose

PATTERN RECOGNITION   The human mind is designed and taught to organize information according to certain patterns. When you are faced with something that's completely new or unexpected, it's hard to understand until you know how to categorize it.

For example, suppose a group of people witness an accident. If you interview the witnesses, you will usually get a number of confusing and contradictory versions of what occurred. That's because an accident usually happens suddenly; the witnesses are not prepared for it. If you tell people that they are about to watch an accident and will be asked to give a report on it, you will get a much more uniform description. The witnesses know what kinds of things to look for. They have a pattern of events in mind.

Source: Prepared by Amy Roberts; updated by McGraw-Hill, 1992.

When you are studying, you are more likely to understand and retain information if you know what is coming and how it will be organized.

REPETITION   Repetition is easy to explain. From your own experience you know that the more often you see or hear something, the more likely you are to remember it.

MULTIPLE MODALITY LEARNING   This fancy term describes something very simple. We perceive things through all our senses. But the brain stores different kinds of memories in different places. Memories of what we see are stored in one place; memories of what we hear are filed in another.

Research has shown that your ability to recall something increases if you experience it through many senses simultaneously. You might have noticed that you tend to forget information that you hear a teacher say, but you remember it if the teacher also writes it on the board. That's because you see and hear it at the same time; your brain processes the information and stores it in several places. This is what is meant by multiple modality learning.

PARAPHRASING   Paraphrasing means putting something into your own words. Recent psychological studies have shown that in order to remember something for longer than a few hours, it must be stored in the long-term memory. In order to put an idea in the long-term memory, you must first translate the idea into your own words so that you really understand it.

ASSOCIATION   Our minds tend to group information so that we mentally connect one thing to another. For example, you might associate a song with a particular period in your life. Whenever you hear that song, you automatically remember that time. Associating an idea with a visual image or a concrete example increases your memory of it.

UNDERSTANDING THE PURPOSE   It's hard to put your heart and mind into something if you don't understand why you are doing it. This is also true when you read. How can you tell when you've found the right information when you don't know what you're looking for?

▶ HERE'S HOW TO READ *BUSINESS TODAY*

1. Before you start the chapter, read the "Outline" in the *Study Guide*. This will show you how the chapter is organized, which concepts are most important, and in what order they will be presented. (Pattern recognition)

Also read the list of key terms preceding the "Key Terms Exercise." Although you probably won't understand or remember them at this point, your mind will automatically focus on them when you see them again in the text. (Repetition)

Go back to the textbook. Look at the pictures and other visual aids, and read the captions. These captions emphasize many of the most important ideas in the chapter. (Repetition) You will begin to form an image to go along with these ideas. (Association)

Finally, read the "Learning Objectives" and the "Review Questions." (the "Objectives" appear in both the text and *Study Guide*; the "Review Questions" are at the end of each chapter in the text). These features tell you the questions you should be able to answer when you have finished reading the chapter. (Understanding the purpose)

2. Now estimate how long it will take you to read the chapter. Be realistic. When you read, try to keep up the pace so that you finish within your expected time. Most students find that slight pressure like a time-goal forces them to concentrate more.

3. Now begin reading, and keep your mind engaged. Reading is not a passive process. You should be duplicating the authors' thinking in your own mind and explaining the concepts to yourself so that you will remember them. (Paraphrasing)

Read to answer the review questions and learn the terms listed as key words. When you find a definition or an answer in the text, underline it. Then repeat the explanation out loud. That's right! Talk to yourself! That way you'll see, hear, and say the information you need to know. It goes into your memory through three different channels, and it will stick. (Multiple modality learning)

Here's an extra hint: After you have found and underlined an answer, you may want to write the number of the question in the margin. Then go to the review question at the end and write the number of the page that contains the answer. When it comes time to study for a test, you'll be able to find the information much more easily.

4. After you've read the chapter, carefully read the "Major Points to Remember" in the *Study Guide*. Everything in this summary should now be completely familiar to you. After reading each point, cover it up and repeat it to yourself in your own words. If you can't explain it, you don't really know it.

    If you're not satisfied with your own explanation, reread the concept or term you're trying to memorize, and this time write it down. This should plant it in your memory for good. (Multiple modality learning and Repetition)

5. Test yourself. Select one or two of the tests in the *Study Guide*. Check your answers. Write down anything that's still giving you trouble.

6. Retest yourself a week later. Take just ten minutes and try another quiz in the *Guide*. If you can answer the questions after that much time has elapsed, you really know your stuff. You'll find that you'll need much less time to study when you have to prepare for a major test.

One more study hint: Get to know your textbook. Examine the extra features, such as:

Glossary—Key ideas are briefly defined and page numbers are given for further information. Key terms are defined in the margins of the text as well.

Text References—This is a bibliography of the sources the authors used to gather information for *Business Today*. Do you have a research paper to write? This section lists the names of books and articles you may want to read.

These are just some of the features of your textbook. You paid for it—now take advantage of it!

▶ SELECTIVE READING

Good readers don't read at one steady rate. They speed up and slow down depending on the importance of a particular point. How do good readers know when to read faster or slower? They pay attention to certain signal words that the authors use to guide the readers.

Do you know how to use signal words effectively? Read the following passage and notice all the clues the authors have used.

Cause and Effect Signal. Extremely important in courses where you are supposed to know *why* something happens. *Slow down!* Other signals are *so, so that, because, consequently, therefore, thus.*

Summary Signal. An important point is restated or summarized. *Slow down!* Other signals are *finally, in sum, to summarize, in conclusion, in brief, looking back.*

The business that wants to sell a product and the customer that wants to buy it normally have a relationship based on healthy skepticism. The relationship is aptly captured in two familiar mottoes: "There's a sucker born every minute" and "Let the buyer beware." They reflect the traditionally and widely held view that people trying to sell things for profit are not necessarily to be trusted and conversely, that customers have only themselves to blame.

During the 1960s however, a growing number of people began to challenge the survival-of-the-fittest approach to business-customer relations. With increasing success, consumerists campaigned for greater frankness and accountability on the part of business. They demanded that consumers be protected from useless, inferior, or dangerous products, from misleading advertising, and from unfair pricing. As a result, producers and consumers alike became more aware of a variety of safety problems. Pill containers, for instance, were redesigned so that children could not open them. Television sets were made more shock resistant and radiation free. Plastic bags used by dry cleaners were made with holes so children could not suffocate themselves accidentally. In 1972, Congress created the Consumer Product Safety Commission, which took over the responsibility for implementing such existing laws as the Flammable Fabrics Act, the Federal Hazardous Substance Act, and the Refrigerator Safety Act of 1956. Recent important actions by the Commission include banning asbestos in certain items, like manufactured fireplace logs, and banning benzene in materials such as paint thinner and rubber cement. The Commission also has the authority to recall specific production batches and to develop uniform standards for consumer products. Ultimately, it plans to develop other safety standards for some ten to twelve thousand products.

Contrast Signal. Indicates a change of idea. *Slow down!* Other contrast signals are *but, unlike, in contrast to, in spite of, on the other hand, although, yet, nevertheless, even though, whereas.*

Example Signal. Examples are used to illustrate important points. If you understand the concept, *speed up!* Other signals are *one kind, for example, sometimes, in this case, especially.*

There is one other kind of signal that you should watch out for as you read *Business Today*. Business tends to evaluate a person, product, or system by how well or badly it performs. Throughout this text you will see the words *advantages* and *disadvantages*. They point out the good and bad aspects of the topic. Other signal words with a similar meaning are *pros* and *cons*, and *benefits* and *costs*.

▶ GENERAL RULES FOR TAKING TESTS

1. When you first receive a test, look it over thoroughly. How many sections are there? How long is it? How many points is each question worth?

2. Read the directions carefully so that you know which questions require more complete answers.

3. Next, mentally note which questions will be easy to answer and which will be harder. Take a minute to plan your attack. Decide the order in which you will answer the questions and budget your time accordingly.

4. If an exam offers you options and allows you to answer some questions and leave others out, make a tentative decision at the beginning. Mark the questions you plan to answer. If you have any doubts about which questions to answer, leave them till later when you can spare a moment to think about them more.

5. Always answer the questions you know first. This way you are sure to get all the easy points. It's not worth puzzling over the hard questions and running short of time for the easy ones.

6. Unless the instructor tells you otherwise, always choose an answer on an objective test and write something on a short answer or essay test. You cannot possibly get credit if you leave the question blank.

7. Be smart. Go to all of the classes the week before a big test. Most instructors will give you hints about what will be on the test. They don't want to see you fail. That makes it look like they aren't teaching you anything!

▶ HOW TO TAKE AN OBJECTIVE TEST— TRUE-FALSE AND MULTIPLE CHOICE

1. The first thing to remember is that you always have a 50 percent chance of getting a true-false question right even if you guess at the answer. Therefore, always choose an answer.

2. The same principle applies to multiple choice tests. If there are four questions, you have a 25 percent chance of guessing correctly. The odds are much better if you can eliminate one or two choices. Therefore, always make a guess.

3. The only time guessing is not a good strategy is on a national exam like the SAT or the GRE. Statistical methods used in scoring these tests reveal whether answers were chosen randomly. (Random answers result in a "guessing penalty.") If you are not sure whether guessing will hurt your score on a particular test, ask!

4. Most instructors are interested in measuring what you know rather than tricking you. Therefore, don't outsmart yourself by looking for a trick and ignoring the obvious answer.

5. The wording of objective tests is very important. Under the pressure of a test situation, it is especially worthwhile to read the questions carefully.

6. Watch for negatives (words that indicate the opposite of something), such as *not, never, except,* and for prefixes that indicate negatives, such as *in-, im-, ab-, anti-, dis-,* and *mis-*. For example:

> Which of the following is *not* one of the basic principles of pure capitalism?
> Which of the following is a *dis*advantage of continuous-process production?
> A promissory note *cannot* be transferred to collateral by anyone *except* the one to whom it is made out.

7. Watch out for words that indicate absolutes, such as *always, invariably, ever, never, all,* and *only*. For example:

> Money is the *only* motivation that can be used to increase productivity.
> *All* of the functions of marketing have to be performed in a marketing system.

8. Finally, watch for comparative statements and questions that require knowing how one thing is related to something else. These usually involve *comparison, frequency,* or *quantity*. The list of words that signal when a comparative judgment is needed is a long one. Some obvious ones are *greatest, least, less, often, more, better, generally, majority, primarily, probably,* and *few.* Evaluate the meaning of these words carefully before you try to answer the question. For example:

> Indexing is *probably* the *safest* approach to playing the stock market.
> The answer to the question "What business are we in?" is *usually* formulated in the
> _____.
> Packaging adds *little* value to the product.

9. If you're taking an objective test, you'll probably get the best results if you proceed in the following way.

    First, read an item through quickly and with high concentration. Answer the question on the basis of your first impression. Then reread the question asking yourself what it really means and express the thought in your own words. (Paraphrase)

    Now ask yourself if your original response still seems correct, even after your careful inspection of the wording. Do not change your answer if you're not sure. Change your answer only if you misread the question or if you are now positive that another response is better. When students change their answers, their new answers are incorrect in 70 percent of the cases.

▶ HOW TO ANSWER AN ESSAY QUESTION

1. Read the question carefully, paying particular attention to the words that indicate what your answer should include. For example:

    What types of goods are sold in the consumer market? What types of goods are sold in the business market? How are these goods different? Define each type of good for each market and give an example of each.

    This is a complicated question because it is really many questions. You are first asked to generalize and explain ("What types of goods"). You are asked to contrast ("How are they diferent?"). You are asked to define and then to give examples.

    Make sure you understand the directions before you do anything!

2. Before you start to write, do some brainstorming on a piece of scratch paper. Jot down specific details, such as facts and examples, that help answer the question. On an in-class essay, you don't have the time to tell everything you know about a subject, so choose the best examples.

3. Think before you write. Make a quick outline to force yourself to organize your thoughts and be sure that you've included everything necessary.

    Even if you don't write a formal outline, decide on the order of what you are going to say. For example, you may decide to discuss the causes of something and the results and then to give your opinion.

4. Now write out your answer, being sure that you stick to the topic and the plan you have made.

5. Always take a minute to reread what you've written. Leave enough room where you write so that you can add things later.

6. Spelling and punctuation may not count so much on an in-calss exam, but a clear, clean answer always makes a better impression than a sloppy one. It suggests that you are organized, confident, and in control of the situation.

STUDY GUIDE
Business Today

Chapter 1

....

Foundations of American Business

LEARNING OBJECTIVES

1. Explain what an economic system is.

2. List the four factors of production.

3. Name the three major types of economic systems and differentiate their identifying characteristics.

4. Describe the relationship between profit and sales, and explain how profit motivates entrepreneurs.

5. Discuss three ways companies compete.

6. Explain how supply and demand interact to establish prices.

7. List the four major economic roles of the U.S. government.

8. Identify six trends that will influence the economy in the years ahead.

OUTLINE

I. The ideal of economic freedom

    A. The nature of economic systems
        1. Factors of production
        2. Economic goals and measurements

    B. Types of economic systems
        1. Capitalism
        2. Communism
        3. Socialism

II. Economic forces affecting business

    A. The profit motive

    B. Scarcity and opportunity cost

    C. Competition
        1. Competition and price
        2. Competition, quality, and service
        3. Competition and innovation

    D. Supply and demand
        1. How prices are set
            a. Demand curves, supply curves, and equilibrium price
        2. How prices affect whole industries
        3. How prices affect labor decisions

    E.   Circular flow

    F.   The multiplier effect

III.   The role of government

    A.   Enforcing rules and regulations

    B.   Providing public goods and transfer payments

    C.   Fostering competition
        1.   Types of competition

    D.   Contributing to economic stability
        1.   Recession, business cycles, fiscal policy, and monetary policy
        2.   Employment and unemployment
            a.   Employment and the business cycle
        3.   Inflation and disinflation
            a.   The effects of inflation
        4.   High and low dollars
            a.   National monetary policy

IV.   Shifts in the economic climate

    A.   The history of the growth in the U.S. economy
        1.   Capital accumulation and increases in the power of business
        2.   Increases in foreign competition

    B.   The challenges ahead
        1.   The global economy
        2.   Accelerating technological development
        3.   Environmental concerns
        4.   The changing labor force
        5.   Participative management
        6.   The evolution of the service sector

MAJOR POINTS TO REMEMBER

1.   An **economic system** is a set of rules used to allocate a society's resources to satisfy its citizens' needs.

2.   The resources of a society are known as its **factors of production** and include natural resources (e.g., land, forest, minerals, water), labor, **capital** (money, machines, tools, and buildings), and **entrepreneurs** (people who develop new ways to use economic resources). In the United States, entrepreneurs are willing to risk their personal resources when they start a business because if it succeeds, they get to keep the rewards (i.e., profits).

3.   The dollar value of all the final goods and services produced by an economy in a year is known as **gross national product (GNP)**, and it is the traditional way that has been used to forecast trends, analyze economies, or compare two or more economies. The latest method used to track an economy is **gross domestic product (GDP)**. Like GNP, GDP measures the total output of goods and services, but GDP also includes profits from foreign-owned businesses operating within U.S. borders (excluded in GNP) and excludes receipts from the overseas operations of American companies (included in GNP). A rise in GNP or GDP is a sign of economic growth.

4. GNP and GDP may at times be misleading, due to differences in population size, so per capita GNP (a country's GNP divided by its population) is often calculated. But even per capita GNP fails to reveal anything about the way in which income is distributed among the people. Additionally, the **underground economy** is not included in GNP figures. The underground economy includes revenues from illegal activities (e.g., gambling, prostitution), under the table payments, and **bartering** (trading goods and/or services directly, rather than paying with money), and may have been worth as much as 15 percent of GNP in 1990.

5. The three main economic systems are **capitalism, communism,** and **socialism**. In the eighteenth century, Adam Smith described an economic system called **pure capitalism**, in which all production and allocation decisions would be made by private holders of property or money, on the basis of prices set by the free market. But in the United States, the government is allowed to use its power to affect prices or change the way resources are allocated. The U.S. system, therefore, may be called **mixed capitalism**.

6. Capitalist economies operate under a **free-market system** and are therefore often called **market economies**. This means that an individual with something to sell is free to charge any price and sell to anyone willing to pay this price. As buyers, we are free to purchase whatever we want and can afford.

7. Communism allows individuals the least degree of economic freedom. It is characterized by state ownership of the factors of production and by planned resource allocation. In this type of **planned economy**, social equality is a major goal and private enterprise is considered to be wasteful. Under communism, there is less of a gap between the rich and the poor, and unemployment and inflation can be more easily controlled. However, there is little incentive to develop more efficient and productive methods.

8. In the past few years, more and more communist countries have relaxed the central control of their economies and have encouraged individual initiative. In Eastern Europe, the shift away from communism has been especially dramatic, with many countries now embracing the principles of capitalism. East Germany (now reunited with West Germany), Poland, Hungary, Romania, Czechoslovakia, and Bulgaria are all moving to market-based economies. The former Soviet Union died in December 1991, as eleven republics formed the Commonwealth of Independent States (CIS) and pledged to move to a market-based economy, private ownership of property, and decentralized planning. Even businesspeople in China have made small but steady steps toward a more market-based economy (although people are fleeing Hong Kong in record numbers because the territory will revert to Chinese control in 1997).

9. Socialism also involves a high degree of government planning, as well as some government ownership of land and capital resources in industries viewed to be vital to the common welfare. Elsewhere, however, private ownership is permitted to exist. Citizens are typically taxed heavily in socialist states, because the government pays for medical care, education, housing, and other social services.

10. A number of socialist countries, like some communist countries, are presently moving toward capitalism. Mexico and Chile, for example, are selling off state-owned businesses, while some South and Central American nations are benefiting from the open-market economies they created in the 1980s. Around the world, both communist and socialist countries are becoming more capitalistic because they are impressed with the prosperity that seems to accompany the free-market system.

11. Economic forces affecting business include the profit motive, with **profit** (i.e., the difference between what someone is willing to pay for an item and its manufacturing and marketing costs) being the foundation of the United States' economic system. Scarcity (i.e., resources are scarce—for example, an individual or a business has only a certain amount of money) and **opportunity cost** (i.e., if you spend an amount of money in a particular way, that money is no longer available to be spent on something else) are also facts of economic life, as is competition.

12. An entrepreneur may wish to compete on the basis of price, quality, service, or innovation. An illustration of competition and price is when one gas station charges two cents less per gallon for unleaded regular gasoline than its competitor across the street. Rather than cutting price, though, a business may decide to attract customers by offering higher-quality goods or better services than its rivals. Yet another entrepreneur might compete by offering a more innovative product than the competitors.

13. Another economic force that can determine price levels is supply and demand. **Supply** refers to the quantities of a good or service that producers will provide on a particular date at various prices. **Demand** is the amount of a good or service that consumers will purchase on a given date at various prices. The theory of supply and demand states that people will be willing to pay a higher price for something they want very much, and, at this higher price, producers will be willing to provide more of the item (i.e., the more money a producer can get for a product, the higher the quantity he is willing to produce). Conversely, an item that is in abundant supply will be sold at a lower price. The forces of supply and demand, in conjunction with the profit motive, regulate what will be produced and the amount that will be produced in a free-market system.

14. The price that will make both the supplier and customer happy is set when the number of units of a product or service demanded equals the number supplied. The relationship between price and quantity demanded is often presented on a graph. A **demand curve** is the line showing the relationship between price and quantity demanded; a **supply curve** traces the relationship between price and the quantity supplied. The price at the point where the demand curve and the supply curve meet is known as the **equilibrium price** (the price at which the quantity demanded is equal to the quantity supplied).

15. The law of supply and demand also applies to labor. Individuals use the price of work, measured in salary or wages, to choose among different available jobs. Consequently, an industry must price its jobs properly if it is to attract workers.

16. While the law of supply and demand should, theoretically, operate just as well on a global scale as it does on a national scale, in reality it does not. Many major industries require huge facilities that can produce more than enough to meet domestic demand (because larger facilities are more efficient than smaller ones). To keep such plants in operation, some governments pass protective trade laws to keep out competing goods. Governments may also provide financial help to boost export sales.

17. Perhaps the most important economic concept affecting society as a whole is the **circular flow**, a term used to describe the movement of all resources within the economy. The economy carries goods and services one way and money the other. Goods and services flow from businesses or government to households (or other businesses), and households provide a return flow of money or taxes for these goods and services. Households also provide businesses with labor, in exchange for wages and salaries.

18. The process of saving and investing is also a part of this circular flow and is central to the economy's growth. Hence, it is feared that the decline in the household savings rate in the United States in the past few years may adversely affect the economy.

19. As companies do business on an international basis, they build factories in other countries, employ foreign labor, and obtain foreign capital. Consequently, what happens to the U.S. economy may depend on what happens in other countries.

20. Because the circular flow links each economic activity to all others, any change in one part of the economy creates some changes elsewhere. The pattern whereby all economic decisions ripple through the system is known as the **multiplier effect**.

21. Government is the final force affecting the economic system, and its laws help protect and enhance the economy, rather than just limit it. The government enforces rules and regulations, provides public goods and transfer payments, fosters competition, and contributes to economic stability.

22. The federal government creates new rules and regulations at the rate of 4,600 a year, with state and local governments adding even more. For example, you can't drive a cab without a license or open a restaurant without a certificate from the board of health. Companies and individuals must also share their profits with the government, whether they be in the form of wages, interest, or lottery winnings.

23. The government uses tax money to provide **public goods**. Examples of such public goods include roads and police protection. Additionally, from tax revenues, the government helps less self-sufficient individuals with

food stamps, Social Security, welfare, and unemployment compensation. These **transfer payments** do not require that the recipient provide anything in return.

24. Laws have been passed to foster competition (i.e., to see that a particular company does not become too powerful) because it is believed that competition benefits the economy. **Pure competition**, in which no single firm or group of firms in an industry is large enough to influence prices, is the theoretical ideal. Few industries, however, work this way, but it can work in industries in which economies of scale do not favor large manufacturers. **Oligopoly** exists when a few large companies dominate an industry (e.g., the U.S. auto industry). **Monopoly** is the situation in which one company dominates a particular industry or market, fixes prices, and keeps other companies from competing. Because this is contrary to the principle of competition, monopolies are prohibited by federal law (some monopolies, like utilities, are legal but closely regulated).

25. Where economies of scale provide an advantage, many foreign governments prefer having only one or two major companies in an industry. They believe that these large firms will be more competitive in the world marketplace.

26. The U.S. economy is constantly changing and may shift from periods of growth to **recession** (a period in which the economy contracts). These swings are known as the **business cycle**. The government attempts to influence the economy through its **fiscal policy** (i.e., juggling revenues and expenditures to stimulate or dampen the economy) and **monetary policy** (i.e., adjusting the nation's money supply) in an effort to lessen the impact of periods of economic decline.

27. Unemployment may become a major social problem during periods of economic downturns. By manipulating fiscal policy, the U.S. government spends money to keep businesses in operation and people working. However, recent economic conditions make it more difficult to intervene in the business cycle. Because the government is spending more than it takes in, any increase in government spending might actually make the situation worse.

28. **Inflation** exists when the prices of goods and services rise steadily throughout the economy; a reversal of this rise is **disinflation**. When inflation is high, people borrow money to buy goods and services before prices rise even further, and slowing high inflation becomes very difficult. Nevertheless, the federal government was able to bring about a period of disinflation during the 1980s. This was made possible by a weakening of the oil **cartel** (an association of producers that tries to control a market and keep prices high by limiting production), a deregulation of American industry, a decline in the power of labor unions, and a limit on the amount of money put into general circulation.

29. Another way the federal government tries to stabilize the economy is by juggling the value of the dollar relative to foreign currencies. A high dollar makes foreign goods relatively cheap for Americans and U.S. goods relatively expensive for foreigners. The nation's monetary policy helps determine the value of the dollar. For example, when the government tightens the supply of money, interest rates rise and inflation falls. Conversely, during the 1990–1991 recession, the government loosened up on the money supply and interest rates fell. This action pushed down the value of the dollar and resulted in a rise in U.S. exports to other nations.

30. The history of the United States has witnessed a number of shifts in economic growth. In prerevolutionary times, and for many years thereafter, the U.S. economic base was the small family farm. By the early nineteenth century, greater use of rivers, harbors, mineral deposits, and other natural resources allowed the accumulation of capital needed to increase production. This process of **capital accumulation** was aided by the fact that Americans believed in saving.

31. By the mid-nineteenth century, the United States was changing from an agrarian to an industrial economy, with independent artisans being replaced by large factories, mass production, and the division of labor. In the early 1900s, the government passed laws and regulations to stop the abuse of power by big business, and workers began to organize into labor unions. The Great Depression of the 1930s disenchanted Americans with the power of business to solve the country's economic problems.

32. World War II and the postwar reconstruction revived the economy, with the government exerting control over both the business sector and the economic situation. But as Western Europe and Japan strengthened, the United States entered a period of slowing growth, until finally inflation soared and the economy stagnated.

33. Competition from abroad has continued to increase during the 1980s, with entire industries in the United States abandoned and some giant companies either acquired by other firms or split into fragments. Some large firms have been forced to eliminate entire levels of management. During this period of turmoil, small firms began to play a larger role in the economy and were able to create enough new jobs to hire workers formerly employed by corporations.

34. The future seems to be in the direction of multinational corporations, which will grow through international joint ventures. Also, as more firms do business internationally, the lines between imports and exports will blur. U.S. companies will continue to face strong competition from Western Europe, Japan, and a number of newly industrialized Asian nations, while Third World countries will supply raw materials and basic commodities. The moves toward capitalism in Eastern Europe, the former Soviet Union, and Latin America will also provide American businesses with new opportunities and new challenges.

35. In the future, the United States will have to rely heavily on technology as its main competitive weapon. Because developments occur rapidly in such fields as robotics, lasers, and biotechnology, companies will have to respond quickly in order to obtain a profit before the technology becomes obsolete.

36. Environmental issues are among America's most important social concerns. As a result, companies are being pressured to handle and dispose of hazardous materials in an environmentally safe manner.

37. As "baby boomers" age and enter the ranks of middle and upper management, the U.S. labor force will change dramatically. Competition for top management jobs will increase, while employers may face a shortage of new workers. Management will have to alter its often paternalistic style to a more participative one (i.e., managers must become more flexible and people-oriented).

38. The past decade has witnessed the explosive growth of companies providing services, such as restaurants, retail stores, hotels, and theme parks. As the population ages, the services desired will shift to reflect changing interests (e.g., day care might decline, while financial investment services might increase).

KEY TERMS

economic system	demand curve
factors of production	supply curve
capital	equilibrium price
entrepreneurs	circular flow
gross national product (GNP)	multiplier effect
gross domestic product (GDP)	public goods
underground economy	transfer payments
bartering	pure competition
capitalism	oligopoly
communism	monopoly
socialism	recession
pure capitalism	business cycle
mixed capitalism	fiscal policy
market economies	monetary policy
free-market system	inflation
profit	disinflation
opportunity cost	cartel
supply	capital accumulation
demand	

KEY TERMS EXERCISE

Directions: On the line provided, place the letter of the statement on the right that most closely defines the key terms.

_O_   1.   Economic system

_B_   2.   Factors of production

_G_   3.   Gross domestic product

_K_   4.   Communism

_A_   5.   Socialism

_L_   6.   Pure capitalism

_P_   7.   Free-market system

_C_   8.   Profit

_H_   9.   Supply

_F_   10.   Demand

_R_   11.   Equilibrium price

_M_   12.   Circular flow

_D_   13.   Pure competition

_J_   14.   Oligopoly

_N_   15.   Monopoly

_E_   16.   Business cycle

_I_   17.   Inflation

_q_   18.   Fiscal policy

a.   An economic system in which there is both public and private ownership of the factors of production.

b.   A society's supply of natural resources, labor, capital, and entrepreneurs used to produce goods and services.

c.   The difference between what it costs to produce and market something and what someone is willing to pay for it.

d.   A competitive situation in which so many buyers and sellers exist that no single buyer or seller influences the price or number of units sold.

e.   Fluctuations that an economy experiences over a period of several years.

f.   The quantity of a good or service that consumers are willing to buy at a given time at various prices.

g.   The dollar value of all the goods and services produced by the economy over a given period of time, including profits from foreign-owned businesses within the nation's borders.

h.   The quantity of a good or service that producers are willing to provide at a given time at various prices.

i.   An economic condition in which prices increase throughout the economy.

j.   A competitive situation in which there are few producers.

k.   An economic system in which there is public ownership of the factors of production and planned resource allocation.

l.   A system that allows business firms to make and sell what they want, where they want, to whom they want, at a price they want.

m.   The movement of resources within an economy, such as the movement of goods and services from businesses to households in exchange for money.

n.   A competitive situation in which there are no direct competitors, so that one company controls the market.

o.   The process used by society to distribute resources to satisfy its citizens' needs.

p.   An economic system in which the factors of production and allocation decisions are made by private holders of property or money.

q. Use of government revenues and expenditures to stimulate or dampen the economy.

r. That price at which the quantity producers are willing to supply and the quantity consumers are willing to demand are equal.

ANSWERS TO KEY TERMS EXERCISE

5. a (p. 10)	10. f (p. 13)	15. n (p. 19)
4. k (p. 8)	9. h (p. 13)	14. j (p. 19)
3. g (p. 5)	8. c (p. 11)	13. d (p. 19)
2. b (p. 4)	7. l (p. 7)	12. m (p. 15)
1. o (p. 4)	6. p (p. 7)	11. r (p. 14)

18. q (p. 20)	
17. i (p. 20)	
16. e (p. 19)	

SELF TEST

True-False Questions

F   1. Every nation basically uses the same type of economic system to satisfy its citizens' needs.

F   2. Natural resources, as a factor of production, only include actual real estate and do not include any minerals, time, or water.

T   3. In communistic nations, private enterprise is generally regarded as wasteful and exploitative.

T   4. Yugoslavia, China, and Cuba would all be examples of communist nations.

T   5. Socialistic countries allow private ownership in the nonvital industries.

F   6. Taxes tend to be low in socialistic economies.

T   7. In the free-market system, business plays a major role in the society, in that it determines which goods and services will be produced.

T   8. The forces of supply and demand determine the profit potential of a product.

_____ 9. Changes in price levels can influence the amount supplied throughout the entire economy.

_____ 10. The labor market is subject to the forces of supply and demand.

_____ 11. Any change in one part of the economy tends to create changes elsewhere in the economic system.

_____ 12. The average length of expansion over the past eight business cycles has been three years.

_____ 13. The U.S. employment rate has historically been about 85 percent of the people willing and able to work.

_____ 14. The form of economic system in which there is a public ownership of the factors of production and a planned resource allocation is known as capitalism.

_____ 15. No force, not even the government, can completely control the course of the economy.

_____   16.   Technology is probably most responsible for the leap in the productivity of labor in the American economy during this century.

_____   17.   During periods of inflation, interest rates tend to increase.

_____   18.   When the value of the dollar is high, foreign goods are relatively cheap for Americans and American goods are relatively expensive for foreigners.

_____   19.   An extremely high value of the dollar is good for both the United States and foreign governments.

_____   20.   Predicting future shifts in the economy is fairly easy.

_____   21.   The U.S. economy has reached the limits of its potential and cannot support further growth.

_____   22.   A challenge for businesses is to find ways to safeguard the environment while still achieving economic growth.

_____   *23.   Rather than just being a problem caused by businesses, pollution exists wherever people live, regardless of their economic system or form of government.

Multiple Choice Questions

_____   1.   The factors of production are
   a.   raw materials used to produce goods.
   b.   the systems and processes used to produce goods.
   c.   the criteria to be evaluated in deciding which products to produce.
   d.   the resources of a society (i.e., natural resources, labor, capital, and entrepreneurship.)

_____   2.   Machines, tools, and buildings used to produce goods and services, as well as the money that buys other resources, are known as
   a.   natural resources.
   b.   labor.
   c.   capital.
   d.   assets.

_____   3.   The underground economy is thought to account for what percent of GNP?
   a.   less than 5 percent
   b.   15 percent
   c.   25 percent
   d.   over 25 percent

_____   4.   Which of the following is _not_ one of the major economic systems?
   a.   collectivism
   b.   capitalism
   c.   communism
   d.   socialism

_____   5.   The form of economic system in which there is public ownership of the factors of production and planned resource allocation is known as
   a.   collectivism.
   b.   capitalism.
   c.   communism.
   d.   socialism.

_____   6. The major goal of a planned economy is
a. maximization of production capacity.
b. social quality.
c. minimization of suffering.
d. redistribution of money from the wealthy to the poor.

_____   7. Which of the following countries has a capitalistic economy?
a. the United States
b. Germany
c. Japan
d. Canada
e. all of the above

_____   8. The incentive to take risks and exert effort to bring products to market is known as
a. the profit motive.
b. government legislation.
c. humanitarian principles.
d. innate characteristics.

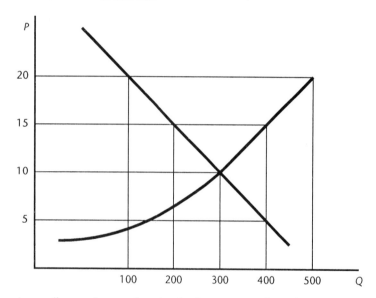

_____   9. According to the graph, what is the amount of product the producers will be willing to supply if the market price is $15?
a. 100
b. 200
c. 400
d. 500

_____   10. According to the graph, how much of the product would consumers demand at a price of $15?
a. 100
b. 200
c. 400
d. 500

_____   11. According to the graph, what should the market price be?
a. $5
b. $10
c. $15
d. $20

____   12.   Which force helps prevent the formation of oligopolies and monopolies?
a.   government intervention
b.   substitute products
c.   foreign competition
d.   all of the above

____   13.   The consumer attitude of "buy before the price goes up" is likely to exist during periods of
a.   high unemployment.
b.   high inflation.
c.   high deflation.
d.   high employment.

____   14.   Which of the following would *not* be an example of a public good?
a.   police protection
b.   military defense
c.   a smoke detector
d.   fire protection

____   15.   Changes in which of the following areas will present new problems and opportunities requiring businesses to experiment with management approaches?
a.   global competition
b.   technology
c.   environmental concerns
d.   demographic shifts
e.   all of the above

____   *16.   Pollution is a problem for
a.   capitalistic countries only.
b.   communist countries only.
c.   socialistic countries only.
d.   all countries—the form of government does not cause pollution, people do.

____   *17.   The index of leading economic indicators is
a.   a single variable used to predict future governmental activity.
b.   a scale used to determine the current level of economic activity.
c.   a composite of broad measures of economic activity used to predict changes in the business cycle.
d.   a set of variables used by a company to measure its financial wealth.

____   *18.   Which of the following would generally be considered an indicator in the index of leading indicators?
a.   prices on the stock market
b.   level of consumer confidence in spending
c.   number of new housing starts
d.   number of big-ticket business orders
e.   all of the above

Completion Questions

1.   In an economic sense, America is the land of opportunity because success or failure is largely the result of

_____.

2.   The factor of production used to develop new ways to use other economic resources more efficiently is known

as _____.

3. Increases in the gross domestic product (GDP) over time indicate that the economy is _____.

4. Economic activity that is not reported or calculated in the gross national product (GNP) is known as the

   _____.

5. The three major economic systems of _____ , _____ , and

   _____ can be distinguished by the amount of freedom given individuals to own the factors
   of production.

6. Adam Smith, the eighteenth-century philosopher, was one of the first proponents of _____
   as an economic system.

7. In _____ capitalism, the government is allowed to intervene in affecting prices and is
   allowed to change the way resources are allocated in order to ensure the best interest of everyone.

8. Businesses can compete in terms of price, quality, or _____.

9. The impact of change in one sector of the economy upon another sector is known as the _____.

10. _____ are goods or services that can more efficiently be supplied to all citizens by the
    government than by the individuals for themselves.

11. The ideal form of competition in a capitalistic economy is _____ competition.

12. Periods of contraction within the economy, known as _____, have averaged eleven
    months in length.

13. The theory of supply and demand holds that the supply of a product tends to _____ when

    demand is great and _____ when demand is low.

14. Manipulating the value of the dollar will stimulate or dampen _____ and

    _____.

15. Such things as acid rain, global warming, oil spills, pesticides, and polluted air make _____
    issues the top of America's social concerns.

PROJECT

Comparing Economic Systems

Chapter 1 has discussed three major economic systems: communism, socialism, and capitalism. The purpose of this exercise is to make a series of comparisons among these economic systems in order to gain insight into the nature of each system.

Go to your school's library and gather information on the following points for China, England, and the United States. (Use such sources as the *World Almanac*, the *Statistical Abstract of the U.S.*, *Europa Year Book*, and *Year Book of Industrial Statistics*.)

	China	England	U.S.
1. GNP (GDP) per capita			
2. Percent unemployment			
3. Rate of inflation			
4. Per capita spending on			
a. Education			
b. Health care			
c. Recreation			
d. National defense			
e. Advertising			

Based on this information, what observations and conclusions can you make about these three different economic systems? What are the advantages and disadvantages of each system?

Chapter 2

Forms of Business Enterprise

LEARNING OBJECTIVES

1. Identify the two broad sectors of the U.S. economy and the eight subsectors.
2. List four factors that have contributed to the growth of the service sector.
3. Discuss the three basic forms of business ownership.
4. List five advantages and four disadvantages of forming a sole proprietorship.
5. Explain the difference between a general and a limited partnership.
6. List the three groups that govern a corporation, and describe the role of each.
7. Cite four advantages of corporations.
8. Describe the four waves of merger activity.

OUTLINE

I. How to categorize a company by industry sector

    A. Service businesses versus goods-producing businesses

    B. Growth of the service sector
        1. Retailing and wholesaling
        2. Finance and insurance
        3. Transportation and utilities
        4. Other services

    C. Production's revival
        1. Manufacturing
        2. Construction
        3. Mining
        4. Agriculture

II. How to categorize companies by form of ownership

    A. Sole proprietorships
        1. Definition of sole proprietorship
        2. Advantages of sole proprietorships
            a. Ease of establishment
            b. Independence
            c. Privacy
            d. Tax advantages
        3. Disadvantages of sole proprietorships
            a. Limited profit potential
            b. Limited resources
            c. Managerial problems
            d. Unlimited liability
            e. Limited life

    B.   Partnerships
- 1.   Definition of partnership
  - a.   Types of partnerships
- 2.   Advantages of partnerships
  - a.   Ease of formation
  - b.   Tax advantages
  - c.   Pooling of talent
  - d.   Ability to add and/or replace partners
- 3.   Disadvantages of partnerships
  - a.   Unlimited liability
  - b.   Potential for interpersonal problems
  - c.   Potential for extreme competition among partners and aspiring partners

    C.   Corporations
- 1.   Definition of corporation
- 2.   Important characteristics of corporations
- 3.   Ownership of corporations
- 4.   Size of corporations
- 5.   Types of corporations
  - a.   Public corporations
  - b.   Private corporations
  - c.   S corporations
  - d.   Nonprofit corporations
  - e.   Subsidiary corporations, parent companies, and holding companies
  - f.   Alien, foreign, and domestic corporations
- 6.   Corporate structure and governance
  - a.   Shareholders
    - (1) Institutional investors
    - (2) Proxies
  - b.   Board of directors
  - c.   Officers
    - (1) CEOs
- 7.   Advantages of corporations
  - a.   Limited liability
  - b.   Liquidity
  - c.   Unlimited life span
- 8.   Disadvantages of corporations
  - a.   Public disclosure requirements
  - b.   Costs of incorporation
  - c.   Relatively high taxes

III. Mergers and acquisitions

    A.   Types of mergers
- 1.   Mergers and acquisitions
- 2.   Divestitures and leveraged buyouts
- 3.   Joint ventures and consortiums
- 4.   Cooperatives

    B.   How mergers occur
- 1.   Hostile takeovers
- 2.   Tender offers
- 3.   Proxy fights

C. The historical perspective
   1. History of merger activity in the United States
      a. Trusts, horizontal mergers, vertical mergers, and conglomerate mergers

D. Mergers and acquisitions today
   1. Reasons for merger and acquisition activity
   2. Problems with 1980s mergers
      a. The costs of mergers and acquisitions to individuals and communities
      b. Raiders and deal makers
   3. Benefits of 1980s mergers
   4. 1990s mergers

MAJOR POINTS TO REMEMBER

1. Almost all firms can be categorized by industry sector: (1) **service businesses**, which encompass transportation and utilities, wholesale and retail trade, finance and insurance, and other services; and (2) **goods-producing businesses,** such as manufacturing, construction, mining, and agriculture. However, the line between services and producers has blurred; for example, it is difficult to separate IBM products from IBM services.

2. Since World War II, the service sector has expanded more than the goods-producing sector and now accounts for about 72 percent of U.S. economic activity. Manufacturing today is only 23 percent of GNP (construction, agriculture, and mining accounts for the other 5 percent).

3. Services have accounted for at least half of all employment since 1940; however, the past ten to fifteen years have seen the service sector become even more vital. In fact, virtually all new jobs created in the United States in the 1980s have been in the service sector. Technology has improved the manufacturing process so that more goods may be produced with fewer workers, and some producers are now willing to let outside firms take over the services that they formerly performed themselves (e.g., data processing, advertising). Additionally, the inexpensive labor available to foreign producers has shifted much of the world's manufacturing out of the United States.

4. Although retailing and wholesaling may be the slowest growing service sector, it is the largest in terms of sales volume and total number of workers. While over the years many small family-run retail businesses have lost ground to their larger competitors, now many of the big chains are having financial problems.

5. The financial services sector includes both large and small firms—from giant insurance companies to local banks to neighborhood real estate brokers. About half of this sector's employment, and a little less than half of its sales, comes from firms with fewer than 500 employees. While this sector has expanded over the past decade, the savings and loan industry is in poor shape, many banks are suffering from bad real estate loans, and Wall Street brokerage firms reduced their work forces by 20 percent in the late 1980s.

6. Transportation and utilities have not grown much in the past ten years in terms of employment, and the performance of the airlines has been chaotic. Airlines, electric utilities, and telecommunications companies are all **capital-intensive** businesses, which means that they require large amounts of money to operate.

7. The service area with the most rapid growth has been the group of "other" services, such as beauty parlors, repair shops, private schools, health services, hotels, amusement parks, theaters, and business and professional services. Since the 1950s, the number of workers in these businesses has doubled. These service businesses are **labor-intensive,** with the labor usually supplied by the owner of the business (e.g., a plumber). The **barriers to entry** are relatively low, because to start a typical labor-intensive service business does not require a great deal of capital, facilities, or special knowledge.

8. The early 1980s were tough years for goods-producing businesses because of recession, the high dollar, heavy foreign competition, and lackluster productivity. Later in the 1980s, though, these same producers benefited from an upturn in the economy, a drop in the value of the dollar, and new government policies. Additionally, the managements of many firms cut costs by closing or modernizing factories, laying off superfluous workers, and eliminating layers of management. Such efforts increased **productivity** within the goods-producing sector, as measured in output per worker-hour. Manufacturing productivity in the United States is now growing by 3.6 percent a year, which is about three times as fast as in the 1970s.

9. The goods-producing sector typically has derived about 10 percent of its sales from foreign customers, versus 5 percent for the service sector. Today, though, both sectors want to increase their overseas sales. Sales swings in the goods-producing sector are more volatile than those for service businesses. In a weak economy, for example, a person may defer the purchase of a car but must still pay insurance premiums.

10. The greatest share of the goods-producing sector is manufacturing, and the performance of manufacturers has improved dramatically in recent years. While large companies dominate the manufacturing sector, smaller firms often serve as suppliers to large manufacturers and as pioneers of new technology.

11. Construction is a cyclical business, depending heavily on interest rates and the state of the economy. Most construction companies tend to have fewer than 100 employees. Mining is also a volatile business. It depends heavily on global supply and demand because it is a **commodity business** (i.e., there is little difference between one unit of production and another). Another commodity business depending on supply and demand is agriculture. U.S. farmers have seen their markets erode as more developing countries have become self-sufficient in food production, and farm profits have eroded as farming has become more capital intensive. These factors have forced many of the less successful farmers to sell out to larger companies, and this trend is expected to continue.

12. The three most common forms of business ownership are the sole proprietorship, partnership, and corporation.

13. A **sole proprietorship** is a business owned by just one person. It is the easiest and least expensive form of business to start. Most farms, retail stores, small service businesses, and part-time businesses run from the home have this type of ownership.

14. The advantages of the sole proprietorship include ease of establishment, independence (you work for yourself), and privacy (financial data can remain confidential). In addition, the sole proprietor has the advantage of paying taxes only on the personal income earned from the business.

15. Disadvantages of the sole proprietorship include the limited potential for profit. Government data show that only about 16 percent of sole proprietorships take in more than $1 million a year. Such businesses are typically started with modest resources, because there are limits to the amount of money an individual can raise. Managerial problems may also develop, because the owner may be too personally involved in the business to seek aid or may not be able to afford the help that's needed. Many sole proprietors also have difficulty delegating responsibility.

16. Sole proprietorships also suffer from **unlimited liability,** meaning that any damages or debt that can be attributed to the business can also be attached to the owner. For example, if the business were to lose money, the owner's home might be taken to satisfy a business debt. The business may also be disadvantaged by **limited life,** as it is usually hard for the business to outlive its owner.

17. A **partnership** is a legal association of two or more persons as co-owners of a business. The partners share profits, losses, and usually the management responsibilities. When all the partners are legally equal and equally liable for the firm's debts, the business is a **general partnership.** If, however, in addition to one or more partners acting as general partners and running the business, there are others whose liability is limited to the amount of their investment, the partnership is then said to be a **limited partnership.**

18. Partnerships are easy to form, and they often have a greater profit potential than sole proprietorships because several people are putting up money and pooling their talents. Additionally, partnership profits are taxed at

personal income-tax rates, rather than at the higher corporate rates. In some industries, the possibility of becoming a partner serves as an incentive for talented employees.

19. Partnerships may have better success than proprietorships in obtaining financing, since the partners are all legally responsible for paying off the debts of the group. Also, in contrast to sole proprietorships, partnerships may have an unlimited life span, as new partners can replace retiring ones.

20. Unlimited liability is a major disadvantage of the partnership (for general partners). This form of business ownership may also suffer from interpersonal problems among the partners and management difficulties resulting from too many partners having a say in the business's daily operations. Additionally, in large partnerships, employees may tend to be overly competitive because they aspire to become partners.

21. Corporations came into existence in the 1800s because huge sums of capital were needed to build railroads, coal mines, and steel mills. Since no one person or group of partners could afford to finance such an operation, the solution was to sell shares in the business to many investors, with each investor receiving a share of the profits. An investor's liability was limited to the amount of the investment.

22. In a corporation, ownership and management are separate, and owners of the company's **stock** (i.e., **shareholders**) can vote to oust managers. The firm's unlimited life span provides it with unlimited growth potential.

23. Even small companies can incorporate, and most corporations, like most businesses, are relatively small. In contrast, though, a huge corporation like General Motors employs about 775,000 people. Each year *Fortune* magazine publishes a list of the 500 largest corporations—"The Fortune 500."

24. A corporation whose stock is owned by public investors is called a **public corporation.** The stock of these firms can be purchased on the open market by anyone. Conversely, **private corporations** (or closely held corporations) do not sell stock publicly. This provides owners with complete control and protects a company from unwelcomed takeover attempts.

25. Other types of corporations include (1) the **S corporation** (or subchapter S corporation), which is permitted to have a maximum of thirty-five shareholders and offers the benefit of being taxed like a partnership; (2) the **nonprofit corporation,** such as the Public Broadcasting System (PBS); (3) the **subsidiary corporation,** which is entirely or partly owned by another corporation called a **parent company;** and (4) the **holding company**, which is a type of parent company that provides little control over the subsidiary and merely holds its stock as an investment.

26. Another criteria for classifying corporations is on the basis of where they do business. A corporation that is incorporated in another country but operates in the United States is an **alien corporation. A foreign corporation** is incorporated in one state but does business in several other states, while a **domestic corporation** does business only in the state where it is chartered.

27. Although in theory shareholders are the ultimate governing body in a corporation, in reality they most often accept the recommendations of management. Furthermore, not all corporate stock carries voting rights. In the past twenty years, **institutional investors** such as pension funds and insurance companies have become quite influential because they own large numbers of shares. Such investors want the value of the stocks they hold to increase, and they have begun to play a greater role in governing the corporations they invest in.

28. At least once a year, all owners of voting shares are invited to a meeting to choose directors for the company, select an independent accountant to audit the firm, and attend to other business. Most shareholders, however, do not attend and instead vote by **proxy** (i.e., they sign and return a slip of paper authorizing management to vote on their behalf).

29. The **board of directors,** which represents shareholders, has the job of guiding the corporation's affairs. Typically, the board consists of fifteen to twenty-five directors who vote on major management decisions. In some corporations, the board of directors merely acts as a "rubber stamp" in approving management's recommendations; in other firms, directors make major policy decisions.

30. The real power in a corporation usually rests with its **chief executive officer (CEO),** who is responsible for setting the policies of the company, under the direction of the board. The CEO typically appoints the other major corporate officers, who must also be approved by the board. The CEO may also serve as the chairman of the board, the president of the corporation, or both, and may also pick a slate of directors who will be loyal to him.

31. The significant advantages of the corporation are its **limited liability** (i.e., shareholders are liable only to the limit of their investment), **liquidity** (investment in a publicly held corporation can easily be converted to cash), and unlimited life span.

32. Disadvantages of corporations include the public disclosure requirements that corporations make some types of financial information public, the costs of incorporation and cost of making a public stock offering (for a public corporation), and the federal corporate tax rate, which taxes corporations at a higher rate than unincorporated businesses. Additionally, shareholders must pay taxes on the share of the company's profits that they receive as dividends, even though the corporation has already been taxed by the government (i.e., corporate profits are taxed twice).

33. Over time, companies may merge, divide, and/or restructure. Indeed, almost 40 percent of the companies to be found on a 10-year-old Fortune 500 list have disappeared, most being absorbed by other firms (e.g., R. J. Reynolds now owns Nabisco).

34. Businesses may combine or recombine in the following ways: (1) **merger**—two firms combine to create a new company, (2) **acquisition**—one company buys another company and remains the controlling firm, (3) **divestiture**—a company sells a portion of its business to another company, and (4) **leveraged buyout**—one or more individuals purchase a company with borrowed money, using the purchased company's assets to secure the loan.

35. Three less radical ways in which companies can combine are the **joint venture** (two firms work together on a project), the **consortium** (similar to a joint venture, but involving more than two companies), and the **cooperative** (an association of people or small firms that join together to obtain greater bargaining power and to benefit from economies of scale).

36. While 95 percent of all mergers and acquisitions are friendly deals, the two basic ways that **hostile takeovers** occur (i.e., one party fights to gain control of a company against the wishes of the existing management) are the **tender offer,** in which a raider offers to buy a certain number of shares at a price higher than the current stock price, and the **proxy fight,** in which the raider engages in a public relations battle for shareholder votes.

37. Mergers are not new to the American business scene. Between 1881 and 1911, "robber barons" created huge monopolistic **trusts.** These trusts were **horizontal mergers,** which are combinations of competing companies. In the 1920s, a second wave of mergers occurred, this time in the form of **vertical mergers.** These mergers combined companies that were involved in different phases of a particular business or industry. And again, in the late 1960s and early 1970s, another wave of mergers took place. This third wave consisted primarily of **conglomerate mergers,** in which companies acquired firms that operated in unrelated businesses.

38. The most recent wave of mergers occurred in the 1980s, during which $3.7 trillion was spent on mergers, acquisitions, and leveraged buyouts. During this period, many companies were worth more than the value of all their stock. As a result, a takeover artist could borrow money, buy enough stock to control the company, sell off one or more pieces of the company to repay debt, and still make a profit.

39. Many critics argue that the deals of the 1980s have created immense burdens of high-risk corporate debt and have diverted investment from productive assets. Indeed, some companies that assumed heavy debt loads to finance acquisitions subsequently went under. In sharp contrast, the mergers occurring in the 1990s do not involve a firm using debt to take over a company. Instead, large corporations are making deals for strategic purposes and financing them with cash and stock.

KEY TERMS

service businesses
goods-producing businesses
capital-intensive
labor-intensive
barriers to entry
productivity
commodity business
sole proprietorship
unlimited liability
limited life
partnership
general partnership
limited partnership
stock
shareholders
public corporation
private corporation
S corporation
nonprofit corporation
subsidiary corporation
parent company
holding company
alien corporation

foreign corporation
domestic corporation
institutional investors
proxy
board of directors
chief executive officer (CEO)
limited liability
liquidity
merger
acquisition
divestiture
leveraged buyout
joint venture
consortium
cooperative
hostile takeovers
tender offer
proxy fight
trusts
horizontal mergers
vertical mergers
conglomerate mergers

KEY TERMS EXERCISE

Directions: On the line provided, place the letter of the statement on the right that most closely defines the key term.

_____ 1. Sole proprietorship

_C_ 2. Unlimited liability

_____ 3. Partnership

_____ 4. Corporation

_____ 5. Private corporation

_A_ 6. Subsidiary corporation

_____ 7. Holding company

_____ 8. Shareholders

_____ 9. Proxy

_____ 10. Board of directors

_____ 11. Chief executive officer

_B_ 12. Merger

_____ a. A corporation whose stock is owned entirely or almost entirely by another corporation.

_____ b. Two companies combining to create a new company.

_____ c. The situation that exists when the debts of a company can be attached to the owner.

_____ d. An offer by one company to buy all or a great deal of another company's stock at a higher price than the market price in order to gain control of that company.

_____ e. An association of people with similar products, services, or interests formed to obtain greater bargaining power and other economies of scale.

_____ f. A parent company that does not actively participate in the management of the company it owns.

_____ g. The buying of one company's stock by another company with the intention of taking control of the board of directors to throw out the existing management.

_____ 13. Acquisition

_____ 14. Divestiture

_____ 15. Hostile takeover

_____ 16. Cooperative

_____ 17. Joint venture

_____ 18. Conglomerate mergers

_____ 19. Tender offer

_____ 20. Consortium

_____ h. A form of business organization with limited liability that is authorized by law to act as a private person.

_____ i. A slip of paper that stockholders sign to authorize management to vote on their behalf.

_____ j. An enterprise established by two or more companies to accomplish a specific task.

_____ k. Company owned by private individuals or companies.

_____ l. The officer of the company who is responsible for setting the policies of the company, under the direction of the board, and for supervising the officers who carry out those policies.

_____ m. The selling of a portion of a business to another business.

_____ n. The people who own a part of a corporation.

_____ o. A business owned by a single individual (the most common form of business ownership).

_____ p. The joining together of two corporations whose operations are unrelated.

_____ q. The purchase of one company by another company, with the purchasing company remaining dominant.

_____ r. A group that has the ultimate authority in guiding corporate affairs and in making general policy.

_____ s. A business organization of two or more persons who are co-owners of the business.

_____ t. A group of companies working jointly to promote a common objective or engage in a project of benefit to all members.

ANSWERS TO KEY TERMS EXERCISE

SELF TEST

True-False Questions

_____ 1. The environmental setting in which business must operate remains fairly stable.

_____ 2. The service sector of the economy has been growing, while the goods-producing sector has been declining.

_____ 3. Businesses are becoming more global in their orientation.

_____ 4. The sole proprietorship is the easiest form of business to start, particularly with limited funds.

_____ 5. One of the major disadvantages of partnerships is that conflicts between the partners can develop.

_____ 6. A corporation has the same rights as an individual.

_____ 7. A corporation has unlimited life.

_____ 8. In order to be considered a partnership, the co-owners must be actively involved in the management of the business.

_____ 9. All corporations must report their financial condition to the public.

_____ 10. A corporation must be a profit-making organization.

_____ 11. Theoretically, the voting shareholders are the ultimate governing body of a corporation, but in a large company they do not control the corporation.

_____ 12. As a practical matter, it is the board of directors that has the ultimate authority in guiding corporate affairs and making general policy.

_____ 13. The chief executive officer cannot also be the chairman of the board.

_____ 14. Incorporated businesses are taxed more heavily than unincorporated ones.

_____ 15. The purpose of a horizontal merger is to achieve economies of scale and to prevent cutthroat competition.

_____ 16. Mergers and acquisitions can enable a company to gain access to new technology or enter new markets without incurring the costs, risks, and delays of starting from scratch.

_____ 17. In the final analysis, mergers cause more good than harm.

_____ 18. The service sector offers only low paying dead-end jobs.

Multiple Choice Questions

_____ 1. Which of the following is _not_ part of the service business sector of the economy?
   a. transportation and utilities
   b. agriculture
   c. wholesale and retail trade
   d. professional, business, and personal service firms

_____ 2. Which of the following is *not* one of the common forms of business ownership?
   a. corporation
   b. sole proprietorship
   c. franchise
   d. partnership

_____ 3. Compared to other forms of business organization, the proprietorship enjoys the advantage(s) of
   a. more flexible organization and management.
   b. secrecy.
   c. less red tape in getting started and in operating.
   d. theoretical tax savings.
   e. all of the above.

_____ 4. All of the following are disadvantages of sole proprietorship *except*
   a. unlimited liability.
   b. the difficulty most people have in establishing them.
   c. high interest rates and difficulty owners confront in borrowing money.
   d. limited life and heavy dependence on a single person.
   e. tendency to be small in size and profit.

_____ 5. A corporation that is incorporated in one state but does business in several other states where it is registered is known as a(n)
   a. alien corporation.
   b. foreign corporation.
   c. domestic corporation.
   d. subsidiary corporation.

_____ 6. Partnerships have the following advantage(s) over sole proprietorships:
   a. the combining of several people's skills.
   b. usually higher credit ratings.
   c. the ability to raise money more easily.
   d. definite legal standing.
   e. all of the above.

_____ 7. Which of the following is *not* a characteristic of public corporations?
   a. limited life span
   b. ability to raise large sums of money quickly
   c. limited liability
   d. ability to attract high-quality personnel
   e. all of the above.

_____ 8. A merger in which a company involved in one phase of a business absorbs or joins a company involved in another phase of that business is known as a(n)
   a. horizontal merger
   b. vertical merger
   c. conglomerate merger
   d. amalgamation
   e. divestiture

Completion Questions

1. The two major sectors of the economy are _____ producing business and _____ businesses.

2. In a _____ partnership, all partners are legally equal and liable for debts, while under a

_____ partnership, some investors are only liable for the amount of their capital contribution.

3. _____ is the most common form of business ownership, yet _____ account for the most sales.

4. A business owned by just one person is a _____.

5. Most sole proprietorships are _____ in size and make _____ profits.

6. A legal association of two or more persons in a business, as co-owners of that business, is a

   _____.

7. A corporation is an artificial person with an unlimited _____.

8. The top officers of a corporation are elected by the _____.

9. When a company grows by purchasing another company and remains the dominant firm after the purchase,

   it has engaged in an _____.

10. A group of small companies or people with similar products, services, or interests banded together to

    achieve greater bargaining power is known as a _____.

PROJECT

Investigating Forms of Business Ownership

PART 1

The purpose of this project is to learn more about a particular form of business ownership. As you have learned from your text, a business can be a sole proprietorship, a partnership, or a corporation.

Select a type of business and go to your school's library to complete the following chart concerning the selected industry. (Consult such sources as the *Survey of Current Business* or census data.) The business may be a manufacturer, supplier, retailer, or service firm. Some examples of industries you might want to consider would be auto manufacturing, lawyers or attorneys, retail clothing stores, grocery stores, computer manufacturers, and advertising agencies.

Industry selected: _____

1. *Form of Ownership*
   Specify the number of companies currently operating under each form of ownership and also the percentage of each form within the industry.

	Number of Companies	Percent of Companies Within Industry
Sole Proprietorship	_____	_____
Partnership	_____	_____
Corporation	_____	_____

2. *Staffing*

List the total number of employees within the industry, according to form of company ownership. Also include the percentage of the total work force for the industry.

	Number of Employees	Percent of total Work Force
Sole Proprietorship	_____	_____
Partnership	_____	_____
Corporation	_____	_____

3. *Sales*

List the total annual sales for the industry, once again broken down by ownership type in both dollar values and percentages.

	Sales in Dollar Values	Percent of total sales for industry
Sole Proprietorship	_____	_____
Partnership	_____	_____
Corporation	_____	_____

PART 2

Select an individual company within that industry and interview a manager or owner. Discuss the company's form of ownership, attempting to pinpoint both the advantages and disadvantages of the form. Be certain to discuss the company's future, including any anticipated changes in the form of ownership. Based on both your interview and library research, does this company have the most appropriate business form? Why? What would the consequences be if the company were to change to one of the other two forms of business?

Chapter 3

Small Businesses, New Ventures, and Franchises

LEARNING OBJECTIVES

1. Differentiate between lifestyle businesses and high-growth ventures.
2. Discuss the demographic and economic factors that have affected small businesses in the 1980s and 1990s.
3. List four important functions of small business in the economy.
4. Identify three ways of getting into business for yourself.
5. Name ten topics that should be covered in a formal business plan.
6. List nine sources of financing available for new businesses.
7. Identify five managerial activities that are important to the success of a small business.
8. Explain the pros and cons of owning a franchise.

OUTLINE

I. The scope of small business

    A. The role of small businesses in our economy
       1. Types of small businesses

    B. Trends affecting small businesses
       1. Why the trend toward bigness has slowed

    C. The men and women who build businesses
       1. What it takes to start a business

    D. The economic role of small businesses
       1. Providing jobs
       2. Introducing new products and services
       3. Supplying the needs of large corporations
       4. Providing specialized goods and services

II. The job of building a business

    A. New business failures

    B. Finding an opportunity
       1. Starting a business, buying an existing business, and franchising

    C. Deciding on a form of ownership
       1. The choice of sole proprietorship, partnership, or corporation

    D. Developing a business plan

E. Obtaining financing
    1. Debt and equity funding sources
    2. Bank loans and other sources of debt
        a. Bank loans, the SBA, credit from suppliers
    3. Private investors
    4. Venture capitalists
    5. Corporate sources
    6. State and local government programs
    7. Public stock offerings

F. Managing the business
    1. Planning the activities of the business
    2. Marketing for the new business
    3. Monitoring and controlling operations
    4. Coping with red tape
    5. Adjusting to growth

III. The franchise alternative

A. Franchising facts
    1. Definition of franchising
    2. Types of franchises
    3. History of franchising

B. Advantages of franchising
    1. Risk reduction
    2. Instant name recognition and mass advertising
    3. Firm financial footing
    4. Training

C. Disadvantages of franchising
    1. No guarantee of wealth
    2. Monthly payment or royalty
    3. Very little independence for the franchisee
    4. Opportunities are occasionally fraudulent

D. Evaluating the franchise

MAJOR POINTS TO REMEMBER

1. The Small Business Administration officially defines a **small business** as an independently owned and operated firm, not dominant in its field, and relatively small in terms of annual sales and number of employees compared to other companies in the industry. In practical terms, any firm with fewer than 500 employees is usually considered small.

2. About 80 to 90 percent of small businesses in this country are **lifestyle businesses** (modest operations with little growth potential). Examples include neighborhood pizza parlors, local florists, and other mom-and-pop operations. The others are **high-growth ventures**, which are businesses trying to grow very quickly and therefore often needing large amounts of investment capital in order to introduce new products or services to a large market. Each year, *Inc.* magazine publishes a list of the most rapidly growing ventures. In 1990, the average company on this list was growing at an annual rate of 103 percent.

3. The benefits derived from **economies of scale** (i.e., the savings resulting from manufacturing, marketing, or buying large quantities of an item) helped turn the United States into a nation of employees. Today only 13 percent of men and 6 percent of women are self-employed, compared to 80 percent of the working population in 1800.

4.　However, the past fifteen to twenty years has seen a rebirth of self-employment and smaller companies, due to the economy's shift toward services and the advent of computer-aided manufacturing. Additionally, some baby boomers have left large corporations to start their own companies. Women today are starting businesses at twice the rate of men; if the present trend continues, they are likely to own as many businesses as men by the year 2000. All these factors contributed to three times as many new businesses being incorporated in the 1980s as in the 1960s.

5.　About 200,000 people start new businesses each year, with about half of them starting out with less than $20,000 in capital and operating informally from their homes. If the business is to succeed, the owner must be willing to work long hours. Additionally, about two-thirds of new businesses start from scratch, rather than by buying or inheriting a business.

6.　Small businesses play a number of very important roles in the economy, including (1) providing jobs—over half of the new jobs created in the United States in the past decade are in businesses with fewer than 100 workers (with 25 percent of these jobs part-time), (2) introducing new products and services—small businesses are often the ones to bring new ideas to the marketplace (a recent study indicates that 98 percent of "radical" new product developments spring from small firms), (3) supplying the needs of large corporations, and (4) providing specialized goods and services, such as watch repair or costume rental.

7.　Building a business is a difficult job. According to the Small Business Administration, about 40 percent of new businesses are still operating five years after they were begun.

8.　Starting a business from scratch is the most difficult method of going into business. However, the entrepreneur can reduce the risks somewhat by choosing a field where he or she has an advantage based on experience, contacts, knowledge, or interests. Alternatively, risks can be reduced by either purchasing an existing business or obtaining a franchise. A recent study, though, suggests that chances of success with a franchise may be no better than with a start-up.

9.　An entrepreneur must decide whether to organize as a sole proprietorship, partnership, or corporation. A sole proprietorship can be started very simply, but a partnership requires two legal instruments—a partnership agreement outlining the arrangements between the partners and a buy/sell agreement defining what happens if one partner dies. For a corporation, in addition to deciding on the state in which to incorporate, one must file incorporation papers, form a board of directors, name officers, and set up a stock redemption plan (similar to a buy/sell agreement in a partnership). Additionally, irrespective of the organization's form, all necessary licenses and permits must be obtained.

10.　The most important step in starting a new business may be planning, and the entrepreneur must develop a comprehensive written statement spelling out exactly what is to be done. Not only will the plan help focus the entrepreneur on how to turn his or her ideas into reality, but it will also help convince lenders and outside investors to provide financing. The plan should include information on the market and marketing strategy, identify problems that must be overcome, and provide financial background.

11.　The two basic sources of funds for financing a new business are **debt** and **equity**. Any debt must be paid back (with interest) from earnings, whereas equity makes the investor a part-owner of the company and entitles him or her to share in future profits. Most new firms are started with a mixture of both.

12.　The majority of new businesses are launched with less than $20,000 in capital. Most new businesses use the personal savings of the owner to start with. Bank loans are the second most common source of funds, and most banks expect the entrepreneur to put up 25 to 50 percent of the needed capital. Banks demand collateral and personal guarantees to pay back the loan and typically charge small businesses more interest than they would charge large corporations. If the owner is turned down by the banks, he or she may be able to qualify for an SBA-backed loan.

13.　Still another source of financing for a new business is credit from suppliers. This source is often overlooked, and many suppliers are agreeable to the extension of such credit because their risk is minimal (i.e., they can take back unsold merchandise).

14. Private investors (i.e., wealthy individuals) are sometimes willing to provide capital. One listing of private investors is provided by the nonprofit organization Venture Capital Network. **Venture capitalists**, who specialize in raising large amounts of capital to fund new high-growth ventures, are another source of funds. If a high-growth venture goes public, venture capitalists can sell their shares of stock at high prices and reap huge profits.

15. Other sources of funding for new businesses are (1) Small Business Investment Companies (SBICs) and Minority Enterprise Small Business Investment Companies (MESBICs), which, through the SBA, allow companies to borrow money at lower than ordinary interest rates; (2) corporations with formal programs to provide new ventures with financing in order to gain access to new technology; (3) state and local government programs designed to help businesses that would boost local employment; (4) "incubator" facilities, formed by states, local governments, and universities, which provide low-cost space and other support services; and (5) public stock offerings, which raise capital by **going public**, that is, selling the stock of the company on the open market.

16. Once a new business is financed, the difficult task of managing it begins. The entrepreneur must plan the activities of the business, including the development of strategies for coping with potential problems. Marketing is also especially important because the new firm will have to build a customer base, and the new businessperson will have to make decisions about prices, promotion, distribution, competition from bigger firms, and responding to the market. Small companies often have an edge over larger firms when it comes to product development because they can respond more quickly to the marketplace. But with respect to prices, small companies may be at a disadvantage because large firms may have lower costs per unit (due to their larger volume).

17. Other management tasks include monitoring and controlling operations (i.e., a record-keeping system), coping with red tape, such as government regulations and trademark requirements, and making changes in the business made necessary by its growth (e.g., hiring new people and arranging additional financing).

18. An alternative to starting a new business from scratch is to invest in a **franchise**, which permits a **franchisee** (you) to use the trade name and sell the products of the **franchiser** (e.g., Radio Shack). For this right, you must pay an initial fee and perhaps monthly royalties as well.

19. The three basic types of franchises are the **product franchise**, in which the franchisee pays for the right to sell trademarked goods (e.g., a car dealership); the **manufacturing franchise**, where the franchisee is licensed by the parent company to produce and distribute its products (e.g., a soft drink bottling plant); and the **business-format franchise**, in which the franchisee buys the right to open a business using the franchiser's name and format (e.g., Wendy's).

20. In the 1980s, service-oriented franchises catering to the needs of baby boomers grew rapidly (e.g., day-care centers, video rental stores). Also, instead of a franchisee owning and operating a single store, the 1980s saw more and more franchisees owning multiple units and delegating day-to-day operations to employees. It is expected that in the 1990s we will see an increase in corporate franchising.

21. Advantages of franchising include the reasonably low risk for the franchisee, as the franchiser's name is well known and is heavily advertised. Therefore, the franchisee can take advantage of the franchiser's proven business system. Franchisers also make sure that the franchisee is on firm financial footing before they'll approve the franchise request, and they provide training on how to run the business. The advantage to franchisers is that their business can be expanded without using very much of their own capital (some franchisers offer financial assistance to franchisees).

22. Purchasing a franchise, however, is no guarantee of wealth. Among the disadvantages of this form of business are the monthly payments or royalties that must be paid to the franchiser and the fact that franchisees are typically allowed very little independence. Additionally, investors must be cautious because franchises are occasionally fraudulent.

23. Prior to investing in a franchise, a prospective franchisee should study the operation carefully and talk to present franchisees.

KEY TERMS

small business
lifestyle business
high-growth venture
economies of scale
debt
equity
venture capitalist

going public
franchise
franchisee
franchiser
product franchise
manufacturing franchise
business-format franchise

KEY TERMS EXERCISE

Directions: On the line provided, place the letter of the statement on the right that most closely defines the key term.

_____ 1. Lifestyle business

_____ 2. High-growth ventures

_____ 3. Debt

_____ 4. Equity

_____ 5. Venture capitalists

_____ 6. Franchise

a. The funds obtained by selling shares of ownership in the company.

b. A business arrangement whereby an individual obtains rights from a larger company to sell a well-known product or service.

c. New businesses intended to achieve rapid growth and high profits on investments.

d. Groups of investment specialists who provide money to finance new businesses in exchange for an ownership interest in expectation of high returns.

e. The funds obtained by borrowing.

f. A small business whose primary goal is to provide a comfortable living for the owners.

ANSWERS TO KEY TERMS EXERCISE

2. c (p. 62)	4. a (p. 72)	6. b (p. 80)
1. f (p. 62)	3. e (p. 72)	5. d (p. 74)

SELF TEST

True-False Questions

_____ 1. Successful entrepreneurs, small business executives, and top managers from large companies have the same basic personality characteristics.

_____ 2. To be successful, small business owners need to be resilient.

_____ 3. Small businesses are actually less likely to fail than businesses in general.

_____ 4. Most small businesses rely only on equity financing to finance their business.

_____ 5. Managerial tasks are basically the same for small businesses as for large businesses.

_____   6.   Franchising as a means of doing business is on the decline.

_____   7.   The FTC requires franchisers to disclose information about their operation to prospective franchisees.

_____   8.   Growth in a small business is always desirable.

_____   9.   A company that provides unwanted products can be made successful by hard work.

_____   10. A good record-keeping system is crucial for a small business.

_____   11. Most banks are quite willing to lend money to a person to start a new business.

_____   12. Franchising is less risky than starting your own business.

_____   13. Most franchisers give their franchisees a great deal of control over the business.

_____   *14. Targeting a business to a specific segment of the market is better than trying to serve the entire marketplace.

_____   15. Given the popularity and success of franchising, it is not necessary to carefully evaluate a franchise agreement before purchasing a franchise.

Multiple Choice Questions

_____   1.   The majority of companies in America would be classified as
               a.   small independent businesses.
               b.   midsize companies.
               c.   large businesses.
               d.   conglomerates.

_____   2.   One of the first steps to take in starting a new business is
               a.   develop a business plan.
               b.   find sources of financing the new business.
               c.   form a corporation.
               d.   find a location from which to do business.

_____   3.   Which of the following is the most difficult, and riskiest, way of getting into business for yourself?
               a.   starting from scratch
               b.   buying an existing business
               c.   obtaining a franchise
               d.   inheriting a business

_____   4.   The two major categories of financing small businesses are
               a.   small business loans and family loans.
               b.   issuing stock and bank loans.
               c.   personal savings and loans from friends.
               d.   debt financing and equity financing.

_____   5.   Which of the following types of financing is usually not appropriate for lifestyle businesses?
               a.   personal savings or loans from friends and relatives
               b.   bank loans
               c.   money from venture capitalists
               d.   SBA loans
               e.   credit from suppliers

____   6.   The business plan can be used to
- a.   provide a course of action to turn an idea into reality.
- b.   help secure outside financing.
- c.   outline specific goals, objectives, and resource requirements.
- d.   force the business to consider important decisions about personnel, marketing, facilities, suppliers, and distribution before starting.
- e.   all of the above.

____   7.   Which of the following is not an advantage a small business can have over a large business?
- a.   stronger financial position
- b.   lower overhead
- c.   better response to local tastes and preferences
- d.   quicker response to market changes
- e.   provision of more specialized services

____   *8.   Which of the following is a common reason for failures of small businesses?
- a.   starting out with too little cash
- b.   setting the wrong price
- c.   taking too much money out of the business too soon
- d.   failing to detect bad credit risks early
- e.   all of the above are reasons

____   9.   In evaluating the decision to purchase a franchise, you should consider
- a.   the success of the franchiser in the past.
- b.   the acceptance of the product by consumers.
- c.   the reasonableness of the franchise contract.
- d.   the market area that the franchise covers.
- e.   all of the above.

Completion Questions

1.   A document designed to assist a new business in its start-up by reviewing the industry and markets, marketing strategy, operating plans, and financial situation is called a _____.

2.   A _____ business is a small, usually "mom-and-pop," company designed to provide a comfortable life for the owners.

3.   The steps involved in starting a new business are a. finding an opportunity, b. _____, c. developing a business plan, d. _____, and e. managing the business.

4.   The _____ is a comprehensive written statement of the company's goals and strategy for achieving those goals.

5.   _____ financing must be repaid with interest, while _____ financing does not accrue interest.

*6.   The _____ is the tendency of a small business owner to single-handedly run a company without ever seeking advice or help from others.

PROJECT

Part 1

Starting Your Own Business

Success as an entrepreneur requires finding a promising business opportunity in which you have some expertise and/or interest. This can involve finding some need that consumers have that is unmet or doing something that people don't like to do for themselves.

Think of some product or service that you could provide while attending school. This product could be to serve other students or the general public. Answer the following questions concerning your new business.

1. Description of the business.

2. What need does your business satisfy (i.e., why would people want to use your product or service)?

3. What type of person is most likely to use your business or product?

4. How do you propose to finance your new business?

5. What characteristics, experiences, and expertise do you have to help you in this new business?

6. From whom would you seek advice in starting your business?

7. Indicate an overall plan to help you start your new business.

Part 2

Based on your answer to question 6 of the first part of this project, interview someone to gain insight into starting the type of business you have suggested. (You may want to interview someone already in this line of business or a similar line of work.) Use the following questions to structure your interview.

1. What are the key factors contributing to success within this business?
2. What kind of person seems most successful in this line of work?
3. What are the major problems encountered in this type of work?
4. What does the future look like for this sort of business?
5. What suggestions would this person make for someone trying to start a new business in this field?

Based on this interview, would it be wise to start a new company in this field? Why?

Chapter 4

Ethical and Social Responsibilities of Business

LEARNING OBJECTIVES

1. Identify four groups to which business has a responsibility.

2. List and explain four philosophical approaches to resolving ethical questions in business.

3. Name three kinds of pollution, and outline actions to control each.

4. Specify the four rights of consumers.

5. State the responsibilities of the Equal Employment Opportunity Commission.

6. Identify four issues that are of particular concern to women in the workplace.

7. Delineate two general ways in which investors may be cheated of their rightful profits.

8. List six actions that companies are taking to encourage ethical and social responsibilities.

OUTLINE

I. Foundations of business ethics

    A. The evolution of social responsibility
        1. How the ethics of business have changed over time
        2. The impact of the Great Depression

    B. Philosophical bases for social responsibility
        1. Utilitarianism
        2. Individual rights
        3. Justice

II. Business and the environment

    A. The pervasiveness of pollution
        1. Air pollution
        2. Water pollution
        3. Land pollution

    B. Government and industry response
        1. Environmental protection legislation
            a. The role of the Environmental Protection Agency
        2. Progress toward cleaner air
            a. New cleaner air legislation
        3. The battle for cleaner water
            a. Legislation and industry assistance
        4. The war on toxic waste
            a. The Superfund

III. Business and consumers

    A. The right to safety
    B. The right to be informed
    C. The right to choose
    D. The right to be heard

IV. Business and workers

    A. The push for equality in employment
       1. Discrimination against minorities
       2. Government action
          a. Affirmative action
          b. The Equal Employment Opportunity Commission (EEOC)
          c. Voluntary affirmative action, mandatory affirmative action, quotas, and layoffs
       3. Business's response

    B. Women in the workplace
       1. Past discrimination and wage differentials
       2. The "mommy track"
       3. Sexual harassment

    C. People with disabilities
       1. Occupational health and safety
          a. The Occupational Health and Safety Administration (OSHA)
             (1) What OSHA does

V. Business and investors

    A. Cheating the investor
       1. Misrepresenting the investment
          a. Ponzi scheme
       2. Diverting earnings or assets
          a. Insider trading

    B. Overdoing the quest for profits
       1. "Questionable" business practices
          a. Bribing foreign officials
          b. Other unethical/illegal practices

VI. The effort to become more ethical

    A. How companies encourage ethical behavior
       1. Corporate codes of ethics
       2. Encouraging ethical behavior among employees

    B. Practical limitations of social responsibility
       1. The cost of ethical decisions

MAJOR POINTS TO REMEMBER

1. Every company functions as part of a system consisting of various **stakeholders**, such as managers, owners, consumers, workers, and society at large. If any of these groups are consistently shortchanged, the company will cease to exist. Because of this, most business executives try to be responsive to the needs of these groups.

2. Today the issue of business ethics is more complicated than in the past. The days of **caveat emptor** (let the buyer beware) are long gone, ever since President Franklin Roosevelt urged Congress to pass laws to protect workers, consumers, and investors.

3. At present, public confidence in business is low. Many people believe that business is not doing enough to help provide job security, keep the environment clean, and behave ethically.

4. While social responsibility means that each individual must think through the consequences of his or her actions and make the "right" choice, defining what is *right* remains elusive. Three philosophical approaches may be used to choose a course of action. The concept of **utilitarianism** states that the proper decision is the one that results in the greatest good for the largest number of people. The **individual rights** approach would reject any decision or plan that was felt to violate a person's rights (it emphasizes the importance of the rights of the individual). Finally, using **justice** as a criterion would mean that all individuals should be treated equally, rules should be applied consistently, and anyone who harms another should be held responsible. These three approaches are not mutually exclusive, and most people combine them to reach decisions.

5. One practical limitation to corporate social responsibility is the cost of such actions. Some companies find it less expensive to close their doors than to pay the costs of making their manufacturing processes environmentally acceptable to the government.

6. About two out of every three people in the United States breathe air that fails to meet the standards of the Environmental Protection Agency (EPA). The most noticeable form of air **pollution**, smog, is produced when sunlight interacts with hydrocarbons (the gas released when fossil fuels are burned). Another form of air pollution is **acid rain** (rain with a high acid content), which has been blamed for ruining lakes and forests in parts of Canada and the United States. The coal emissions that can cause acid rain also contribute to a **greenhouse effect**, in which a layer of warm air forms and prevents the earth's surface from cooling.

7. About 10 percent of river and lake water in the United States is polluted, due in part to runoff from municipal sewage plants and industrial facilities. While accidents like the Exxon Valdez oil spill contribute to water pollution, the main threat to water supply is the daily disposal of wastes from thousands of individual sources.

8. There are millions of tons of hazardous substances buried in the ground or dumped in inadequate storage sites. It has been estimated that more than $500 billion would be needed to clean up the sites.

9. When **ecology** (the balance of nature) became an important issue in the 1960s, federal, state, and local governments began to enact laws. Today, by a ratio of six to one, consumers want to reduce pollution even if it means paying higher prices.

10. The bedrock piece of legislation in the federal government's attempt to control pollution is the National Environmental Policy Act of 1969. In 1970, the Environmental Protection Agency (EPA) was founded to help regulate air and water pollution and to supervise pollution control efforts. In part, the effectiveness of the EPA over the past twenty years has been dependent on who has occupied the White House.

11. A promising new direction is to emphasize the prevention, rather than the correction, of pollution. Companies now spend over $35 million annually to fight air pollution, and it is hoped that by the year 2005, the new amendments to the Clean Air Act passed by Congress in 1990 will knock out 75 to 90 percent of the pollutants being released into the air.

12. The federal government has spent over $50 billion to fight water pollution since the Water Quality Act was passed in 1965. The National Pollutant Discharge Elimination System requires that any company pumping fluids into a river or lake must obtain a permit to do so. However, while this may stop "point-source" pollution, it does not control "nonpoint" pollution (i.e., the runoff from farms and streets) that accounts for 65 percent of stream pollution.

13. To help reduce the threat of land pollution, Congress established a "Superfund" in 1980 to clean up the 1,189 most hazardous waste dump sites. It has taken more than ten years to clean up sixty of these sites.

14. Business was awakened to its environmental and social responsibilities by the activism of the 1960s, which included the crusadership of Ralph Nader, who authored a book about poorly designed and unsafe products. Around the same time, President John F. Kennedy announced a new "bill of rights" for consumers.

15. Kennedy's new "rights" included the right to safety, primarily enforced today by the Consumer Product Safety Commission (CPSC), founded in 1972. Other "rights" include the right to be informed about products (i.e., labels must contain warnings), the right to choose, and the right to be heard.

16. Until the past few decades, many people in the United States had been targets of economic **discrimination**, most of which was aimed at **minorities**. While some individuals want the government to create special programs to help minority group members move up the economic ladder, others would prefer less government intervention. Supporters of **affirmative action** believe that equality can be achieved only if minorities are temporarily given special benefits. Such benefits would help make up for years of discrimination. Critics believe that the best way to achieve equality is through economic growth.

17. The Civil Rights Act of 1964 outlawed discrimination in employment and established the Equal Employment Opportunity Commission (EEOC). Job discrimination complaints are investigated by the EEOC, and the agency can also file legal charges against companies that have discriminated. But in the 1980s and early 1990s, the Reagan and Bush administrations attempted to soften the impact of prior civil rights legislation and guidelines. New appointees to the Supreme Court, for example, were conservatives, replacing a number of retiring justices who were considered to be liberals. This should continue the trend away from liberal support for civil rights.

18. Today, while companies can adopt **voluntary affirmative action** programs, federal courts can impose **mandatory affirmative action** programs. Where companies have clearly discriminated against minorities, **quotas** may be imposed, but white males with high seniority may not be laid off to save the jobs of minorities with less seniority.

19. While women have made significant strides in the workplace in the past twenty years, they often work for lower wages than men (about 68 percent of men's wages), in general because they are more likely to work part time or on a temporary basis. Discrimination has also been a factor, with women often being passed up for promotion. There appears to be a **glass ceiling** of discrimination that prevents women from moving into the highest ranks. Additionally, some companies have developed two separate career tracks for women—one for women who consider work to be their top priority, and one for women who want to balance their family and career (the "mommy track").

20. **Sexual harassment** is also sometimes suffered by employees, and includes both obvious requests for sexual favors and the more subtle creation of a sexist environment in which an individual is made to feel uncomfortable (e.g., off-color jokes and lewd remarks).

21. The Americans with Disabilities Act (ADA) of 1990 guarantees equal opportunities for the estimated 75 million people in the United States who have a condition that might handicap them. The law also requires companies serving the public to make their services and facilities accessible to people with disabilities.

22. The **Occupational Safety and Health Administration** (OSHA), established by the Occupational Safety and Health Act of 1970, has the task of preventing accidents and eliminating work-related diseases. Companies that do not abide by OSHA rules may be held criminally liable.

23. Every year, investors are cheated by individuals who either misrepresent the potential of the investment or divert the earnings or assets. For example, Operation Desert Storm resulted in telemarketing con artists touting phony oil and gas deals. This scam, known as a **Ponzi scheme**, pays off early investors with money raised from later investors. In other instances, a company's earnings may be diverted by an executive for personal gain, thereby reducing the profit returned to shareholders. Finally, recent cases of **insider trading** have exposed unfair stock market practices, as company executives used their knowledge of the firm's activities to benefit from fluctuations in stock prices.

24. The quest for profit can lead to problems other than insider trading. Activities such as spying on competitors and bribing foreign officials do occur.

25. Despite these abuses, the business community has become more responsible in its dealings with society. Today, 75 percent of all large companies have adopted a written **code of ethics** that defines the values and principles that employees should be guided by when making decisions. Some business firms also screen employees for honesty before they are hired. Additionally, companies are giving corporate responsibility an important place on the organization chart and have appointed environmental or community affairs executives to oversee companywide efforts to act responsibly. Companies like McDonald's have switched to biodegradable packaging, and Ben & Jerry's contributes a portion of profits to worthy causes.

26. There are practical limitations on the social responsibility demonstrated by businesses. Considering the fact that a firm cannot exist if it does not operate profitably, managers must often make hard choices with respect to whether a company's limited resources can afford a socially responsible action.

KEY TERMS

stakeholders
caveat emptor
utilitarianism
individual rights
justice
pollution
greenhouse effect
ecology
discrimination
minorities

affirmative action
voluntary affirmative action
mandatory affirmative action
quotas
glass ceiling
sexual harassment
Occupational Safety and Health Administration (OSHA)
Ponzi scheme
insider trading
code of ethics

KEY TERMS EXERCISE

Directions: On the line provided, place the letter of the statement on the right that most closely defines the key term.

_____ 1. Stakeholders

_____ 2. Utilitarianism

_____ 3. Individual rights

_____ 4. Justice

_____ 5. Pollution

_____ 6. Ecology

_____ 7. Discrimination

_____ 8. Insider trading

_____ 9. Ponzi scheme

_____ 10. Affirmative action

_____ 11. Code of ethics

a. The activities undertaken by business to recruit and promote minorities.

b. In a social and economic sense, denial of opportunities to individuals on the basis of some characteristic that has no bearing on the ability of these persons to perform.

c. A philosophy used in making ethical decisions that is aimed at protecting human dignity.

d. Form of fraud in which money received from later investors is used to pay off the earlier investors.

e. A written statement that sets forth an organization's principles for distinguishing between right and wrong.

f. Relationship among living things in the air, water, and soil, and the nutrients that support them.

g. A philosophy used in making decisions that aims to ensure equal distribution of burdens and benefits.

h. Employee's or manager's use of information gained in the course of his or her job that is not generally available to the public in order to benefit from fluctuations in the stock market.

    i. A philosophy used in making ethical decisions that strives to achieve the greatest good for the greatest number.

    j. All threats to the environment caused by human activities in an industrial society.

    k. Individuals or groups to whom business has a responsibility.

ANSWERS TO KEY TERMS EXERCISE

1. k (p. 90)	4. g (p. 94)	7. b (p. 104)	10. a (p. 106)
2. i (p. 92)	5. j (p. 94)	8. h (p. 113)	11. e (p. 114)
3. c (p. 92)	6. f (p. 95)	9. d (p. 112)	

SELF TEST

True-False Questions

_____ 1. Being socially responsible makes good sense for a business.

_____ 2. A business basically operates in a vacuum, in that the environment in which it operates has little or no impact upon it.

_____ 3. The needs and interests of the various groups that business must try to serve rarely, if ever, are in conflict.

_____ 4. Businesses have always perceived a need to be socially responsible.

_____ 5. Most companies today are socially responsible, regardless of the cost.

_____ 6. Rectifying the inequities in the past, women today find that they are paid the same as men and are promoted to higher ranks as frequently as men.

_____ 7. The majority of industrial waste disposal is done safely.

_____ 8. Off-color jokes and lewd remarks can be a form of sexual harassment.

_____ 9. There is a growing trend to use criminal charges and steep fines as tools in prodding companies to behave responsibly toward the environment.

_____ 10. The threat of a product liability suit has caused many companies to manufacture safe products.

_____ 11. In an attempt to meet their ethical and social responsibilities, some companies are reviewing their operations and products in an effort to minimize waste and protect the environment.

_____ 12. American business has assumed primary responsibility for ending patterns of discrimination.

_____ 13. Sexual harassment in the workplace is fairly uncommon.

_____ 14. The handicapped provide a good pool of talent from which to hire employees.

_____ 15. Most large companies do not have a written code of ethics.

_____ 16. Executives can be held criminally liable if they fail to provide adequately for the safety of their employees.

_____ *17. Many business situations present a moral dilemma in that it is not always clear-cut as to what is right or wrong.

_____ *18. You have a right to review any material contained in a credit bureau's file on you.

Multiple Choice Questions

_____ 1. At the turn of the century, the prevailing attitude of industrialists was that business had only one responsibility:
   a. to satisfy the needs of society at large.
   b. to provide a good working environment for employees.
   c. to maximize profits for shareholders.
   d. to maximize management's salaries.

_____ 2. Subtle discrimination against promoting women into the highest ranks within corporations is known as
   a. sexual harassment.
   b. a wall of discrimination.
   c. the Sally principle.
   d. the glass ceiling.

_____ 3. A shift by businesses to more favorable treatment of consumers and employees was basically brought on by
   a. the industrial revolution.
   b. the Great Depression.
   c. World War I.
   d. World War II.

_____ 4. Followers of the utilitarianism philosophy feel that
   a. protecting human dignity is most important.
   b. there should be equal distribution of benefits and burdens.
   c. the most satisfaction for the most people is the best alternative.
   d. everyone should be treated the same, regardless of race, color, creed, or station in life.

_____ 5. The equal treatment of people is the philosophy of
   a. individual rights.
   b. utilitarianism.
   c. justice.
   d. egalitarianism.

_____ 6. Smog, acid rain, the greenhouse effect, and airborne carcinogens are all examples of
   a. air pollution.
   b. water pollution.
   c. land pollution.
   d. noise pollution.

_____ 7. A "mommy track" is
   a. an organized baby-sitting program offered by a company for its employees.
   b. a company that hires only working mothers.
   c. an alternative career path for women who want to spend more time with family in exchange for slower career advancement.
   d. paying women lower wages for doing the same work as a man.

_____ 8. Knowing what is in a product, how to use it, and the costs of goods and services are a part of the consumers'
   a. right to safety.
   b. right to be informed.

c. right to choose.
d. right to be heard.

_____ 9. Which of the following is not one of the consumer's basic rights?
a. the right to safety
b. the right to be heard
c. the right to return merchandise
d. the right to choose
e. the right to be informed

_____ 10. A company can cheat its investors by
a. mismanaging the resources so as to reduce the return on investment.
b. misrepresenting the potential of the investment.
c. doing either of the above.
d. By definition, investors cannot be cheated.

Completion Questions

1. A business has an obligation to meet the needs of managers, owners, employees, consumers, and

_____ if it is to survive.

2. During the 1960s business activity was altered as a result of four basic activism movements:

(1)_____ , (2) _____ , (3) _____ , (4) _____ .

3. The _____ effect is the forming of a layer of gases around the earth as a result of air pollution.

4. The battle against air pollution from chlorofluorocarbons and toxic chemical emissions has _____ over the last few years.

5. A company with toll-free consumer information is facilitating the consumers' right to _____ .

6. _____ is an illegal means of misrepresenting the potential of an investment, while "creative accounting" is a legal means of doing the same thing.

7. Fetal protection, banning women of childbearing age from certain hazardous jobs, has been ruled to be an

illegal form of _____ discrimination.

PROJECT

Part 1

What Are You Going to Do?

Deciding between right and wrong is not always an easy task because of conflicting goals and pressures. The following paragraphs pose some difficult situations in which you must make a decision and then justify it.

1. You are aware of fellow workers in your office who are taking pencils, paper, tape, and other such items home for their own personal use. It probably amounts to less than $50 per year for each employee, but about half of the office workers are doing it. Should you inform management about this situation? Are you cheating the stockholders if you don't bring this to management's attention? How are you likely to be treated by the other employees if you do inform on them and they find out it was you who did so? What are you going to do?

2. You are the production manager for a regional chemical company and have just received a report indicating that one of the company's major products, representing 30 percent of the company's business, could cause cancer for the production workers as a result of exposure to the chemical over an extended period of time. If you stop production of the chemical until safety precautions can be instituted, estimated to take two years, 80 percent of the work force will have to be laid off, costing the company approximately 40 percent of its profits. If you continue with production and work on safety precautions, no layoffs or losses will be incurred, but some workers might contract cancer. What are you going to do? Justify your decision from both the employees' and investors' perspective.

3. You are a sales representative for a manufacturer of electric power drills, and you have an opportunity to close a big order, one that would put you 15 percent over quota and win you a big bonus. However, the purchasing agent is still wavering between your product and that of a competitor. Your marketing manager has suggested that you send the purchasing agent a gift of a stereo system that he wants. What would you do? Why? How would you justify your decision to your boss?

4. You are interviewing applicants for a position on the sales force. You have narrowed down the applicants to two—a woman and a man. The female applicant is more qualified than the male applicant and has had a higher degree of success. However, the rest of the sales force is male and would probably resent a woman. Hiring the woman, then, might hurt morale. You also know that your customers are prejudiced against women and are not likely to buy from one because they can buy similar products from competitors. The male applicant, although not as good as the woman, would probably do an adequate job. Which applicant would you hire? Why? How would you justify your decision to your boss?

5. Your company has just developed a new facial cream, which needs to be applied only once a day rather than twice, as is customary. Because consumers are in the habit of applying similar products twice a day, they will use two applications unless specifically told otherwise. Thus, if you omit the relevant instructions, consumers will use twice as much of your product as they need to. Would you inform consumers? Why? How do you justify your decision to your boss?

Part 2

Be prepared to defend in class your answers to the above situations. Your professor or a classmate may assume the role of your immediate supervisor or another superior and ask you to justify your decision.

Chapter 5

International Business

LEARNING OBJECTIVES

1. Differentiate between an absolute advantage and a comparative advantage in international trade.
2. Distinguish between the balance of trade and the balance of payments.
3. List and describe three international trade pacts.
4. Identify five techniques that countries use to protect their domestic industries.
5. Cite five drawbacks to protectionism.
6. Discuss the impact of a weaker dollar on U.S. companies.
7. List five common forms of international business activity.
8. Cite five things you can do to facilitate international business relationships.

OUTLINE

I. The dynamics of international business

    A. Why nations trade
        1. Absolute and comparative advantage
        2. The evolving role of the United States in the world economy
        3. The postwar boom
        4. The stimulus of foreign aid
        5. The rise of multinational corporations

    B. Where the United States stands today
        1. The balance of trade
        2. The balance of payments

II. Government actions relating to international business

    A. Protectionist measures
        1. Tariffs
        2. Quotas
        3. Subsidies
        4. Restrictive standards
        5. Retaliatory measures
        6. The pros and cons of protectionism

    B. International organizations
        1. The General Agreement on Tariffs and Trade (GATT)
        2. Trading blocs
            a. The European Community (EC)
        3. The International Monetary Fund (IMF) and the World Bank
        4. Economic summit meetings

    C. U.S. measures to encourage foreign trade
        1. The roles of federal agencies
        2. Federal legislation
        3. Government tax benefits
        4. Insurance

    D. Adjustments in currency values
        1. How foreign currency is traded
        2. Strong versus weak dollars

III. The global corporation from the employee's perspective

    A. Forms of international business activity
        1. Importing and exporting
        2. Licensing
        3. Franchising
        4. Joint ventures and strategic alliances
        5. Wholly owned facilities

    B. Foreign employers operating in the United States
        1. Working for a foreign corporation

    C. Cultural differences and how to handle them
        1. Techniques for improving intercultural interaction

MAJOR POINTS TO REMEMBER

1. Now that companies operate on a global basis, it is becoming difficult to separate imports from "Made in America" products. For example, the best-selling car for the past few years in America has been the Honda Accord. Can it be called a "Japanese import" when it is assembled in Marysville, Ohio?

2. No single country can do everything well. Some countries have special strengths that make them the best place in the world for certain industries. This gives them an **absolute advantage** relative to competitors in other nations. Some countries can produce products more efficiently than others, giving them a **comparative advantage.** However, such advantages may change over time; for example, Japan's cheap labor advantage has been somewhat replaced by its engineering expertise, production efficiency, and investment capital.

3. For about twenty years following World War II, the United States enjoyed more competitive advantages than any other country. Through the Marshall Plan, America helped its allies and former enemies rebuild, pouring $12 billion in aid into Europe. From 1945 to 1955, $2.5 billion in grants and trade credits were provided to Japan.

4. As U.S. companies increased their overseas sales, they began to open foreign branches and sales offices, and, eventually, shifted some production and assembly operations abroad. These companies became **multinational corporations,** with operations in several countries. Managers used the comparative advantages of several nations to increase the corporations' overall manufacturing efficiency.

5. The United States' lead in international business has gradually narrowed, and some industries have virtually disappeared (e.g., most TVs, and all VCRs and camcorders, are now imported). However, the U.S. worker is still the most productive in the world and enjoys the highest standard of living.

6. Buying from other countries is known as **importing;** selling to other nations is called **exporting.** The relationship between imports and exports is a nation's **balance of trade.** The U.S. **trade deficit** (a negative balance of trade, which is caused by importing more than is exported) peaked in 1987 when the value of the

dollar was very high against other currencies (making U.S. products expensive overseas). The Reagan administration worked to bring down the value of the dollar, and U.S. manufacturers went on a cost-cutting campaign to make their products more competitive. During the 1990–1991 recession, the gap between imports and exports narrowed (because a weak dollar made U.S. products less expensive overseas). While the balance of trade calculation considered as "exports" only products that are manufactured in the United States and sold overseas, American companies manufacture outside of the United States and sell abroad an additional $700 billion a year in products.

7. The broadest indicator of international trade is the **balance of payments**, which measures the total flow of money into and out of a country, including foreign aid by governments and direct investments. The U.S. balance of payments has been negative for most of the 1980s, despite the fact that foreign direct investment here has continued to increase. However, the United States is likely to attract less foreign money in the 1990s. In the first quarter of 1991 the United States had the first balance of payments surplus in nine years, due in part to a decline in U.S. interest rates.

8. Many countries, under the guise of **protectionism**, erect legal "fences" to shield their industries from foreign competition. Protectionist measures include **tariffs** (special levies against imported goods) and **quotas** (a limit on the number of a specific item that may be imported), which tend to raise the prices of both imported and domestic products, and **embargoes**, which prohibit trade in certain products or with certain countries (e.g., Cuban cigars may not be imported into the United States).

9. Other forms of protectionism include subsidies to domestic producers, which allow them to sell their products at lower prices than imported goods (e.g., the European Airbus), and the creation of restrictive standards, which give domestic firms an edge (e.g., Japan requires imported ski equipment to pass special tests). While the United States has relatively few trade barriers compared to other countries, it does tend to strike back against nations that engage in unfair practices. This is especially true in the case of **dumping**, which is when a company sells goods in a foreign market at a price lower than in their home market. While the United States tends to waffle between an open market and protectionism, studies have shown that in the long run protectionism hurts everyone.

10. Most international organizations created to encourage and assist world trade support the principle of **free trade**. After World War II, a worldwide trade pact was established. The General Agreement on Tariffs and Trade (GATT) is both a treaty and an organization to administer the agreement. GATT members, representing 111 nations, have reduced taxes on imports from an average of 40 percent to about 5 percent today.

11. While GATT members pay lip service to the notion of applying the same rules to all trading partners, they have been creating and strengthening regional **trading blocs**. Such blocs typically eliminate special taxes and other trade barriers among members and create barriers against goods entering the region from non-member nations. The European Community (EC), which includes most of Western Europe, is the oldest and best-known trading bloc; its member nations expect to reduce all trade barriers among themselves by the end of 1992. Elsewhere, the United States and Canada have agreed to phase out all tariffs and quotas between the two countries by 1999.

12. The International Monetary Fund and the World Bank deal with the financing of world trade and are especially helpful in channeling funds to the less-developed countries to assist them with their balance of payments. Both organizations are funded by the more industrialized members of the United Nations. A number of regional development banks also exist, such as the European Bank for Reconstruction and Development.

13. Nations also hold economic summit meetings with important trading partners to deal with such issues as exchange rates and trade imbalances. The United States has relied heavily on such meetings in recent years, either among the Group of Five (United States, Britain, France, Germany, and Japan), Group of Seven (Group of Five plus Canada and Italy), or the Group of Ten (Group of Seven plus Belgium, Netherlands, and Sweden; the group was later joined by Switzerland). One of the most unusual summit meetings occurred in

July, 1991, when the Soviet Union met with the Group of Seven to enlist support for moving the Soviet economy in the direction of capitalism.

14. The United States has established a number of domestic agencies and policies to help U.S. companies compete overseas. For example, the Export-Import Bank of the United States grants cheap financing to overseas purchasers of U.S. goods. The government also provides U.S. companies with incentives for exporting by permitting them to set up **foreign sales corporations**, which can exempt some of their export profits from U.S. income taxes.

15. The lowering of the value of the dollar relative to foreign currencies may be the strongest weapon used by the United States to help American companies compete overseas, because it makes U.S. products cheaper abroad. Every time a foreign company must pay for a purchase from the United States, it must exchange its country's currency for dollars at a bank that buys and sells **foreign exchange**. The number of yen or francs that must be exchanged for every U.S. dollar is known as the **exchange rate** between the two currencies. At present, there is a flexible or **floating exchange rate system**, controlled by the forces of supply and demand.

16. Over 100,000 U.S. firms are presently involved in international business in one or more of its various forms. One of the most common forms of international business activity is importing and exporting. Importing is very common in the U.S. retailing industry. To export, a firm may call directly on potential customers overseas or rely on intermediaries here or abroad. Many countries also have foreign aid offices to help importers and exporters; the International Trade Administration of the U.S. Department of Commerce offers such services.

17. Another low-risk approach is **licensing**, which entitles a firm to produce and/or market the product of another company in return for a royalty or fee. Franchising is yet another alternative, with the franchisee obtaining the rights to duplicate a product in return for a royalty fee. This is how McDonald's reaches overseas consumers.

18. Joint ventures, which allow two firms to share the investment costs and profits of a business venture, may also be used. The joint venture often implies a commitment to cooperate on future projects. In some countries, joint ventures are a must because a foreign company is not permitted to own facilities outright. Joint ventures often involve less risk than wholly owned facilities, where the company owns and operates a plant in another country. While some U.S. firms are opening their own factories overseas, foreign firms have been buying U.S. companies at a record pace. The number of U.S. workers on foreign payrolls is growing by nearly one million a year.

19. To be successful in doing business abroad, an American businessperson must allow for cultural differences. One of the biggest mistakes a person can make is to assume that "people are the same all over." Prominent differences exist with respect to decision-making habits, attitudes toward time, ideas of status, and so on. For example, cultural differences may result in a female executive finding some foreign businessman reluctant to deal with her.

KEY TERMS

absolute advantage
comparative advantage
multinational corporations
importing
exporting
balance of trade
trade deficit
balance of payments
protectionism
tariffs

quotas
embargoes
dumping
free trade
trading blocs
foreign sales corporations
foreign exchange
exchange rate
floating exchange rate system
licensing

KEY TERMS EXERCISE

Directions: On the line provided, place the letter of the statement on the right that most closely defines the key term.

_H_   1.   Multinational corporations

_E_   2.   Absolute advantage

_P_   3.   Comparative advantage

_K_   4.   Importing

_Q_   5.   Exporting

_C_   6.   Balance of trade

_N_   7.   Trade deficit ✓

_L_   8.   Balance of payments

_A_   9.   Licensing

_N_   10.   Free trade S

_____   11.   Foreign sales corporation g

_J_   12.   Protectionism F

_B_   13.   Tariffs J

_R_   14.   Quotas

_S_   15.   Embargo B

_M_   16.   Dumping

_i_   17.   Foreign exchange

_o_   18.   Exchange rate

_d_   19.   Floating exchange rate system

a.   An agreement to produce and market another company's product in exchange for a royalty or fee.

b.   The total ban on trade with a particular nation or in a particular product.

c.   The relationship between the value of goods and services a nation exports and those it imports.

d.   The world economic system in which the values of all currencies are determined by supply and demand.

e.   A nation's ability to produce a particular product with fewer resources (per unit of output) than any other nation.

f.   Government policies aimed at shielding a country's own industries from foreign competition.

g.   Tax-sheltered subsidiaries of U.S. corporations that engage in exporting.

h.   Firms with operations in more than one country.

i.   Foreign currency that is traded for domestic currency of equal value.

j.   Taxes levied on imports.

k.   Purchasing goods or services from another country and bringing them in one's own country.

l.   The sum of all payments a nation has made to other nations minus the payments it has received from other nations during a specific period of time.

m.   Charging less for certain goods abroad than at home.

n.   Negative trade balance.

o.   The rate at which the money of one country is traded for the money of another.

p.   A nation's ability to produce a given product at a lower opportunity cost than its trading partners.

q.   Selling and shipping goods or services to another country.

r.   Fixed limits on the quantity of imports a nation will allow for a specific product.

s.   International trade unencumbered by any restrictive measures.

ANSWERS TO KEY TERMS EXERCISE

1. h (p. 127)	6. c (p. 127)	11. g (p. 138)	16. m (p. 132)
2. e (p. 125)	7. n (p. 127)	12. f (p. 132)	17. i (p. 139)
3. p (p. 125)	8. l (p. 129)	13. j (p. 132)	18. o (p. 139)
4. k (p. 127)	9. a (p. 141)	14. r (p. 132)	19. d (p. 139)
5. q (p. 127)	10. s (p. 135)	15. b (p. 133)	

SELF TEST

True-False Questions

F   1.   If a country has relatively few natural resources and no absolute advantage, it cannot have a comparative advantage.

T   2.   The service account in the balance of trade has traditionally been positive for the United States.

F   3.   The International Monetary Fund and the World Bank are two agencies of the United Nations concerned with restricting free trade among nations.

F   4.   GATT works so well because it has legal power to enforce its rulings on international trade disputes among member nations.

_____   5.   Insurance against economic risk associated with doing business abroad is available through the Foreign Credit Insurance Association, but political risk insurance is not available anywhere.

_____   6.   Not much difference exists in the way foreign companies treat U.S. employees from the way U.S. companies treat their workers.

_____   7.   Protectionism is especially inappropriate, since our trading partners play by the same rules that we do and our companies enjoy equal access to their markets.

_____   8.   When foreign companies compete unfairly in the United States, the President can deny those firms access to U.S. markets.

_____   9.   By acting on monetary policy, the United States will lower the exchange rate of the dollar even more and not be concerned with the economic growth rates of its trading partners.

_____   10.   Despite recent slippages in U.S. business competitiveness, there are still several relative advantages U.S. businesses have in the world market.

_____   11.   The probability of an American reaching the upper management ranks in a foreign-owned company in the United States is quite high.

_____   12.   The best way to prepare yourself to do business with people from another culture is to study their culture in advance of any dealings with them.

_____   *13.   The devaluation of the peso has resulted in many U.S. companies moving manufacturing facilities to Mexico to take advantage of lower cost of land, labor, and materials.

_____   *14.   Proper market research may reduce or eliminate most international blunders, such as name problems, promotional requirements, and proper market strategies.

Multiple Choice Questions

_____   1.   Which of the following would be true of how foreign employers treat U.S. workers?
   a.   Foreign employers tend to treat blue-collar workers better and pay them higher wages than U.S. companies.
   b.   Foreign employers tend to pay white-collar workers higher wages than U.S. companies.
   c.   U.S. workers are likely to advance more rapidly into higher ranks of a foreign company than workers native to that company's country.
   d.   Foreign companies tend to have the same values and orientations as U.S. companies.

_____ 2. Which of the following statements concerning a comparative advantage is correct?
   a.   A multinational company may locate in a country to exploit that advantage.
   b.   A comparative advantage may change over time.
   c.   The United States also possesses comparative advantages.
   d.   All of the above are correct.

_____ 3. Probably the easiest form of international business activity to become involved in initially is
   a.   importing and exporting.
   b.   licensing.
   c.   franchising.
   d.   a joint venture.

_____ 4. The wholly owned facility seems to be especially popular in today's international business arena. Why?
   a.   It is the only method of entering most of the larger markets.
   b.   It ensures a profitable operation.
   c.   It allows for maximum control.
   d.   It is useful only for U.S. companies going overseas.

_____ 5. A U.S. agency that makes loans to exporters and grants credit to foreign buyers of American-made goods is
   a.   GATT.
   b.   the Group of Five.
   c.   the Export-Import Bank.
   d.   the Domestic International Sales Corporation.

_____ 6. Taxes levied against imports are
   a.   tariffs.
   b.   quotas.
   c.   embargoes.
   d.   subsidies.

_____ 7. Why are protectionist pressures mounting in the United States?
   a.   Trade barriers cost American consumers $50 billion a year.
   b.   Many people see foreign competition as causing loss of employment in the United States.
   c.   Protectionism usually leads to retaliation.
   d.   Pressures are mounting as a statement of support for U.S. industry.

_____ 8. The flexible or floating exchange rate system, which evaluates and prices various currencies, is governed by
   a.   the International Monetary Fund.
   b.   a loose coalition of major industrial countries that meet to decide what the various exchange rates should be.
   c.   the forces of supply and demand.
   d.   the policy of the Federal Reserve Board.

_____ 9. Which of the following statements accurately describes the situation of American businesses and their international competitiveness today?
   a.   They are decreasingly competitive, as American worker productivity continues to decline.
   b.   U.S. businesses have lost all relative advantages across all industries.
   c.   No U.S. companies seem able to compete internationally.
   d.   American companies are becoming increasingly internationally competitive.

_____   10.   The most comprehensive form of business operated on foreign soil is
            a.   a customs brokerage.
            b.   an export trading company.
            c.   a wholly owned subsidiary.
            d.   a franchise.

_____   11.   Which of the following is a measure a country can use to protect its industries from importers?
            a.   tariffs
            b.   quotas
            c.   subsidies
            d.   restrictive standards
            e.   All of the above are protective measures.

_____   12.   Experience has shown that in business dealings with a person of another culture it is best to
            a.   keep an open mind.
            b.   be alert to the other person's customs.
            c.   be aware that gestures and expressions mean different things in various cultures.
            d.   adapt your style to the other person's.
            e.   all of the above.

_____   *13. Doing business in another country can be extremely tricky because
            a.   colors on packaging can symbolize unintended messages.
            b.   advertising messages can be translated incorrectly.
            c.   promotional material may violate local customs.
            d.   language barriers may cause product names and advertising to give undesired meanings.
            e.   all of the above.

Completion Questions

1. _____ corporations are those businesses with operations in a variety of countries.

2. If a nation is able to produce a product with fewer resources than any other nation, it is said to have

    a(n)_____ advantage.

3. The relationship between imports and exports is referred to as the _____.

4. As an approach to reach consumers overseas, McDonald's and Kentucky Fried Chicken have used

    _____, which is similar to licensing but minimizes costs and risk of foreign expansion.

5. Exchanging goods and services between nations that produce them most efficiently is the basis

    of_____.

6. _____ are pacts among countries that are formed to encourage trade among member
    nations.

7. _____ are U.S. manufacturing plants located in Mexico.

8. A tax benefit to companies to encourage them to conduct international business by deferring some of their

    taxes on profits is available through a _____.

9. Barriers erected to shield domestic industry from foreign competition are known collectively as

    _____.

10. A _____ limits the number of items of a certain product that may be traded.

11. A firm sells its products in a foreign market at an unreasonably low price; this is called

    _____ the product.

PROJECT

Entering the International Market

In your community, there is sure to be some business involved in international trade. Some businesses export, others import; still others face direct competition from foreign manufacturers even if they don't engage directly in international trade. Interview a manager from one of these businesses and find out how he or she feels about international business and, more specifically, about the opportunities for that company to enter the international market or increase its activity if it is already involved. Use the following questions as guides:

1. At what level of activity is the firm currently engaging in international trade?

2. If involved, what form of market entry (export, joint venture, etc.) is used and why?

3. What is the company's five-year projection of the international market for its product?

4. Will the company increase, decrease, or keep its degree of international business the same? Why?

5. If the company plans any changes in international business, does that also mean it will be changing its market entry forms? Why?

Chapter 6

The Fundamentals of Management

LEARNING OBJECTIVES

1. Discuss the three categories of managerial roles.

2. Describe the three levels of management.

3. Distinguish among the three types of managerial skills.

4. List the four steps in the management process.

5. Distinguish strategic, tactical, and operational plans, and list at least two components of each.

6. Define staffing as a key component of the organizing function.

7. Cite three leadership styles, and explain why no one style is best.

8. Enumerate the four steps in the control cycle.

9. List five measures that companies can take to manage crises better.

OUTLINE

I. The scope of management

    A. Definition of management

    B. Why management is necessary

    C. Managerial roles
        1. Interpersonal roles
        2. Informational roles
        3. Decision-making roles

    D. Managerial hierarchy
        1. The different levels of management

    E. Managerial skills
        1. The job of managers at various levels
        2. Technical skills
        3. Human relations skills
           a. Oral communication
           b. Written communication
        4. Conceptual skills
           a. The five steps of decision making

II. The management process

    A. The planning function
        1. Goals and objectives
           a. Mission statements (statements of purpose)
           b. Goals versus objectives

      2. Levels of goals
         a. Strategic, tactical, and operational objectives
      3. Levels of plans
         a. Strategic, tactical, and operational plans

  B. The organizing function
     1. Definition of organizing
     2. Division of labor and staffing
       a. Replacing individuals with teams

  C. The directing function
     1. What directing involves
     2. Motivating and leading
     3. Leadership traits
       a. Trait theory
       b. Transactional and transformational leadership
     4. Leadership styles
       a. The autocratic style
       b. The democratic style
       c. The laissez-faire style
     5. Approaches to management
       a. Situational management
       b. Participative management

  D. The controlling function
     1. What controlling involves
     2. The establishment of standards
     3. Performance measurement
     4. Management by objectives

III. Crisis management

  A. Definition of crisis management
     1. Examples of proper and improper crisis management

  B. How to prepare for crises

MAJOR POINTS TO REMEMBER

1. **Management** is the coordination of an organization's resources (e.g., land, labor, and capital) to meet an objective. It is necessary in all organizations. Any time individuals are working together to achieve a common goal, some decisions must be made regarding who will have which job, and how and when other resources are to be used.

2. Managers have authority over others, and the relationships they maintain with their superiors, peers, and subordinates can be described as roles. The three categories of managerial roles are interpersonal roles (managers function as figureheads, leaders, and liaisons), informational roles (managers serve as monitors, disseminators, and spokespeople), and decision-making roles (managers serve as entrepreneurs, disturbance handlers, resource allocators, and negotiators).

3. The managerial staff usually consists of three levels of management. **Upper-level managers**, or **top managers**, have the most power and responsibility and take overall responsibility for the organization; **middle managers** have somewhat less power and responsibility and develop plans for implementing the broad goals set by top management; and **first-line managers**, or **supervisory managers**, oversee the work of operating employees and put into action the plans made at higher levels of management. These three levels form a management **hierarchy**, a structure with a top, middle, and bottom.

4. **Managerial skills** fall into three basic areas: technical skills, human relations skills, and conceptual skills. While all managers need human relations skills, conceptual skills are needed more as management levels increase, and technical skills are needed more as management levels decrease.

5. **Technical skills** are needed to perform the mechanics of a particular job and include some "technical" managerial skills known as **administrative skills** (e.g., the ability to make schedules and read computer printouts).

6. **Human relations skills** are those required to understand other people, to interact effectively with them, and to get them to work as a team. All managers need the human relations skill called **communication**, which is the ability to exchange information. Effective managers must also be able to select the most appropriate **communication media**, or channels of communication. **Oral communication** involves both speaking and listening and typically consumes a large portion of each business day. Additionally, **written communication** (business information in written form) must be suitable for its audience and be clearly presented. Effective communication involves gearing the message for the audience, writing simply and clearly, and being objective.

7. **Conceptual skills** are those that enable the manager to understand the relationship of the parts to the whole, that is, to see the "big picture." Managers must be able to imagine the long-range effects of their decisions. Decision making is a conceptual skill and involves (1) recognizing the need for a decision, (2) analyzing and defining the problem or opportunity, (3) developing alternatives, (4) selecting desired alternatives, and (5) choosing the most promising course of action.

8. Managers make two types of decisions. Programmed decisions are routine, recurring decisions that may be made according to previously established rules, while nonprogrammed decisions are unique and cannot be made according to any set of procedures or rules. Decisions are also made under conditions of certainty (where the manager has all the information necessary to feel confident about the success of the decision), risk (where good information is available, but there still exists a possibility of failure), uncertainty (the information is incomplete), and ambiguity (the objectives of the decision are unclear and there may be little or no information available).

9. The four functions of the management process are planning, organizing, directing, and controlling.

10. **Planning** is the first management function because all the others depend on it. It involves the establishment of goals for the organization and the attempt to determine the best ways to accomplish them. Planning fully utilizes a manager's conceptual skills.

11. An organization's overall purpose is called its **mission**, and the statement answering the question "What is this organization supposed to do?" is called its **mission statement**. It is through the planning process that the company's mission is supported by its goals (i.e., broad long-range targets of the organization) and objectives (i.e., specific short-range targets).

12. Organizational goals must be specific and measurable and may be divided into three categories. **Strategic goals** are set by top management and focus on broad issues, **tactical objectives** focus on departmental issues and are set by middle management, and **operational objectives** are set by first-line managers and deal with short-term issues.

13. As with goals, plans can also be divided into strategic, tactical, and operational categories. **Strategic plans** are actions that will allow strategic goals to be met, while **tactical plans** are actions designed to achieve tactical objectives and to support strategic plans. Finally, **operational plans** are developed by first-line managers and are the actions designed to achieve operational objectives.

14. **Organizing** is the process of arranging the company's resources (including people) to carry out its plans. Managers must determine a division of labor best suited to accomplishing the organization's objectives and then proceed with **staffing** the various positions (i.e., finding and selecting workers). Increasingly, companies are replacing individuals with **teams** (two or more people working together to achieve a specific objective).

15. Getting people to work effectively and willingly involves the activity of **directing**. This function of management involves **motivating** (the process of giving employees a reason to do the job and to try hard) and **leading** (showing employees how to do the job).

16. Although **trait theory** suggests that particular personality types (i.e., people with certain specific characteristics or **traits**) make better leaders, no conclusive evidence has been presented. In fact, whether a person will be successful as a leader often depends primarily on the situation. While identifying traits has been unsuccessful in identifying potential leaders, research has shown that management and leadership are not the same thing. The traditional management approach to leadership is called **transactional leadership** and involves getting workers to perform at an expected level. In contrast, **transformational leadership** involves motivating employees to perform better than expected. The traits of the transformational leader include charisma, individualized consideration, and intellectual stimulation. A true leader possesses both transactional skills and transformational traits, is able to focus his or her energies on a concrete objective, draws inspiration from visualizing a goal in great detail, and is able to share this vision with others. Additionally, a true leader is able to tolerate failure and to explore possibilities that might not work.

17. There are three basic **leadership styles**. The **autocratic leader** centralizes authority and personally makes all decisions. **Democratic leaders** emphasize group participation and a free flow of communication, although the leader still has the final say. In contrast to autocratic leaders, a democratic leader delegates authority. The **laissez-faire leader** takes the role of a consultant, offering opinions only when asked. Today, the move has been away from autocratic styles and toward more democratic and laissez-faire styles. This change is a result of workers being better educated and wanting more control over their working conditions.

18. There is no single leadership style appropriate for all occasions, and a manager should select the style best suited to the situation at hand. This is referred to as **situational management** or **contingency leadership**. It emphasizes adapting general principles to the actual needs of one's own business.

19. A firm that regularly involves its workers in decision making is using **participative management**. This approach has worked successfully for many companies.

20. **Controlling** is the process of ensuring that the company's objectives are actually being attained. It involves monitoring progress and, if necessary, correcting any deviations. This function serves to pinpoint flaws in the other three management functions and requires the use of a manager's technical skills. Managers set up **standards**, goals against which performance is later measured. These standards should be strongly linked to strategic goals and may be framed in terms of profitability, units produced or sold, employee turnover, and the like. Next, managers must measure performance, compare performance to standards and, if necessary, take corrective action.

21. One well-known method of controlling is **management by objectives (MBO)**. Introduced during the 1950s, an MBO program involves (1) communicating the overall strategic goals of the organization, (2) having middle managers meet with first-line managers to develop objectives, (3) periodically having middle managers assess the performance of first-line managers in relation to the previously established objectives, and (4) meeting periodically to assess whether strategic goals are being met.

22. The handling of unusual and serious problems is called **crisis management** and may determine whether the company will have a future. Experts caution that the first twenty-four hours of a crisis are critical. During this time, the company should explain the problem to both the public and the employees. The offending product should then be removed from stores and the source of the problem brought under control. Such an undertaking is made easier if management has prepared in advance for it. The best prepared companies hold drills, during which crisis conditions are simulated.

KEY TERMS

management
upper-level managers
top managers
middle managers
first-line managers
supervisory managers
hierarchy
managerial skills
technical skills
administrative skills
human relations skills
communication
communication media
oral communication
written communication
conceptual skills
planning
mission
mission statement
strategic goals
tactical objectives
operational objectives
strategic plans

tactical plans
operational plans
organizing
staffing
teams
directing
motivating
leading
traits
transactional leadership
transformational leadership
leadership styles
autocratic leader
democratic leaders
laissez-faire leader
situational management
contingency leadership
participative management
controlling
standards
management by objectives
crisis management

KEY TERMS EXERCISE

Directions: On the line provided, place the letter of the statement on the right that most closely defines the key term.

_____ 1. Management

_____ 2. Hierarchy

_____ 3. Planning

_____ 4. Goals

_____ 5. Objectives

_____ 6. Management by objectives

_____ 7. Operational plans

_____ 8. Strategic plans

_____ 9. Tactical plans

_____ 10. Programmed decisions

_____ 11. Mission statement

_____ 12. Nonprogrammed decisions

_____ 13. Organizing

a. A leader who emphasizes group participation in decision making.

b. Routine, recurring decisions made according to a predetermined system of decision rules.

c. The process of establishing objectives for an organization and determining the best way to accomplish them.

d. A type of long-range plan that answers the question "What is the overall purpose of the organization?" or "What business are we in?"

e. The process of getting people to work effectively and willingly.

f. Specific goals.

g. Actions designed to achieve tactical objectives and to support strategic plans, usually defined for a period of one to three years and developed by middle managers.

h. Management that emphasizes adapting general principles to actual needs.

i. The process of communicating the goals of the organization to subordinate managers and giving them the opportunity to structure personal goals to mesh with organizational objectives.

____ 14. Directing

____ 15. Autocratic leader

____ 16. Democratic leader

____ 17. Laissez-faire leader

____ 18. Situational management

____ 19. Controlling

____ 20. Crisis management

j. A system for minimizing the harm that might result from some unusually threatening situation.

k. The process of arranging resources, particularly people, to carry out the organization's plans.

l. Unique and often nonrecurring decisions that cannot be made according to any set of procedures or rules.

m. Pyramidlike structure comprising top, middle, and lower management.

n. A leader who emphasizes the use of authority.

o. The process of ensuring that organizational objectives are being met and of correcting deviations if they are not.

p. The process of coordinating resources to meet an objective.

q. Plans covering periods of up to a year and involving the kinds of situations that are likely to come up month by month, weekly, or daily.

r. Broad, long-term targets or aims.

s. A leader who basically lets the group make the decision.

t. Plans geared to a two- to five-year span, and sometimes longer.

ANSWERS TO KEY TERMS EXERCISE

1. p (p. 154)	6. i (p. 168)	11. d (p. 161)	16. a (p. 166)
2. m (p. 155)	7. q (p. 162)	12. l (p. 160)	17. s (p. 166)
3. c (p. 161)	8. t (p. 162)	13. k (p. 164)	18. h (p. 166)
4. r (p. 162)	9. g (p. 162)	14. e (p. 164)	19. o (p. 167)
5. f (p. 162)	10. b (p. 160)	15. n (p. 165)	20. j (p. 169)

SELF TEST

True-False Questions

____ 1. Every type of organization, regardless of size or purpose, requires management.

____ 2. Management skills are basically applied the same across various industries, organizations, and management levels.

____ 3. For most managers, a substantial part of any business day is involved with communication.

____ 4. The ability to communicate effectively on paper is only required of those managers at the upper levels.

____ 5. Every plan is based on a set of basic assumptions.

_____ 6. Businesses are only concerned with profit goals.

_____ 7. Top managers spend more time and energy in directing activities than operating managers.

_____ 8. Many think that the type and style of manager needed for a young company is different from the type needed for mature companies.

_____ 9. Under the proper circumstances, each style of leadership can be effective, but no style is effective in all situations.

_____ 10. Style of leadership must be geared to the situation.

_____ 11. The ability to communicate, both orally and on paper, is one of the most important human skills managers need to possess.

_____ 12. Each level of a management hierarchy performs the same four basic functions.

_____ 13. Supervisory management usually has a major role in designing the formal organization structure.

_____ 14. Technical skills are most needed by top-level managers.

_____ 15. More and more companies are using the team approach because it is a powerful management tool that can increase employee satisfaction, organizational productivity, and product quality.

_____ 16. The nature of a message, such as being routine or nonroutine, should influence a manager's choice of which communication media are used to convey that message.

_____ 17. The informational role of a manager requires that he or she give out information, without having to seek out any information.

Multiple Choice

_____ 1. For most organizations, management can be divided into
   a. top management, supervisory management, and operating management.
   b. top management, upper-level management, and lower-level management.
   c. top management, middle management, and supervisory management.
   d. upper-level management, middle management, and workers.

_____ 2. Supervisory managers are also known as
   a. middle managers.
   b. operating managers.
   c. upper-level managers.
   d. front-line managers.

_____ 3. Which of the following skills should a manager have?
   a. technical skills (i.e., the ability to perform the mechanics of the job)
   b. human skills (i.e., the ability to understand other people and interact effectivity with them)
   c. conceptual skills (i.e., the ability to understand the relationship of parts to the whole)
   d. all of the above

_____   4.   Which of the following is *not* a step in the decision-making process?
      a.   identifying the problem and pinpointing goals for the solution
      b.   finding possible courses of action
      c.   examining the options
      d.   choosing a course of action
      e.   All of the above are steps in the decision-making process.

_____   5.   Which of the following is *not* one of the functions of management?
      a.   planning
      b.   organizing
      c.   financing
      d.   directing
      e.   controlling

_____   6.   Which of the following statements is correct concerning the use of teams within a company?
      a.   Since employees' tasks are broadened, the organization becomes more flexible.
      b.   Teams encourage group spirit rather than a maverick attitude.
      c.   Teams may operate at any level within the organization.
      d.   Teams can range from formal and permanent to informal and temporary.
      e.   All of the above are correct.

_____   7.   Management by objectives (MBO) involves
      a.   establishing overall corporate goals.
      b.   developing personal goals consistent with corporate goals.
      c.   monitoring actual performance to goals on a routine basis.
      d.   evaluating the actual achievement of goals at periodic time intervals.
      e.   All of the above are a part of the MBO process.

_____   8.   Nonroutine messages would best be communicated through which of the following media?
      a.   memo
      b.   face-to-face conversation
      c.   letter
      d.   electronic mail

_____   9.   When a manager acts as a figurehead, leader, or liaison, he or she is playing what type of role?
      a.   interpersonal role
      b.   informational role
      c.   decision-making role
      d.   all of the above
      e.   none of the above

_____   10.   In maintaining relationships with others, managers are expected to fulfill which roles?
      a.   interpersonal roles
      b.   informational roles
      c.   decision-making roles
      d.   all of the above

_____   11.   The aspect of a manager's role concerning information would *not* include which of the following activities?
      a.   monitoring
      b.   disseminating
      c.   allocating resources
      d.   acting as spokesperson

_____ 12. Long-term goals and plans as developed by top management pertaining to broad, companywide issues are considered to be
   a.   strategic in nature.
   b.   tactical in nature.
   c.   operational in nature.
   d.   programmed in nature.

_____ 13. Goals and plans covering a one- to three-year period developed by mid-level managers to assist in obtaining broader companywide objectives are
   a.   strategic in nature.
   b.   tactical in nature.
   c.   operational in nature.
   d.   programmed in nature.

_____ 14. A true leader has
   a.   the ability to conceptualize and see less obvious problems and solutions.
   b.   the ability to inspire others to share their vision.
   c.   a high tolerance for failure.
   d.   all of the above.

_____ 15. A person who emphasizes the straightforward use of authority and who feels he or she should make all of the decisions is using which style of leadership?
   a.   autocratic
   b.   democratic
   c.   laissez-faire
   d.   dictatorial

_____ 16. If a leader talks things over first with followers and emphasizes group participation in decision making, he or she is using
   a.   autocratic leadership.
   b.   democratic leadership.
   c.   laissez-faire leadership.
   d.   no leadership.

_____ 17. The style of leadership in which the leader takes a hands-off approach and acts largely as a consultant, letting the group make most of the decisions, is known as
   a.   autocratic.
   b.   democratic.
   c.   laissez-faire.
   d.   bottom-up.

_____ 18. Decisions made under conditions of incomplete information so that the manager must make assumptions is known as decision making under
   a.   certainty.
   b.   risk.
   c.   uncertainty.
   d.   ambiguity.

_____ 19. Which of the following would be an example of a programmed decision?
   a.   certainty
   b.   risk
   c.   uncertainty
   d.   ambiguity

Completion Questions

1. _____ managers have the most power and take overall responsibility, _____ managers are chiefly responsible for implementing goals, and _____ managers are responsible for coordinating the work of all who are not managers.

2. The most important function of management is _____ .

3. _____ of the organization basically determine the direction the company takes.

4. _____ are actions taken to accomplish short-range goals.

5. _____ exists when a manager has all the information necessary to make a decision, so that he or she feels confident about the success of that decision.

6. Plans with a two- to five-year time span are known as _____ plans; those with a time span of a year or less are referred to as _____ plans.

7. _____ exists when a manager is expected to make a decision under unclear objectives, poorly defined alternatives, and little or no information.

8. The process of directing involves giving employees a reason to perform their best, referred to as _____ ; it also involves showing employees how to do the job or, _____ .

9. When managers act as entrepeneurs, disturbance handlers, resource allocators, and negotiators, they are fulfilling the role of being a _____ .

10. _____ is a system that prepares a company for unforeseen threats and prevents it from making mistakes during these situations.

11. Top management develops _____ goals, which focus on broad issues affecting the entire company; middle managers develop _____ objectives, which deal with departmental issues; first-line managers focus on short-term issues by developing _____ objectives.

PROJECT

Analyzing Style of Management

The purpose of this project is to investigate the nature of management and the style of a particular manager.
Answer the following questions concerning a particular manager. This manager may be at the top level, middle level, or supervisory level, and the information may be gathered by either personal interview or by reading articles on managers through such sources as the *Wall Street Journal*, *Fortune*, *Forbes*, and *Newsweek*.

1. Company name

2. Manager's name and title

3. Level (e.g., top, middle, or supervisory)

4. Technical skills required for the job

5. Human skills required for the job

6. Conceptual skills required for the job

7. Type of planning the manager does

8. Organizing duties

9. Motivating and directing activities

10. Controlling activities

11. Leadership style (e.g., autocratic, democratic, or laissez-faire)

12. What does a typical day for the manager involve? How does he or she spend his or her time?

Based on these responses, is this person an effective manager? (In developing your answer, you may want to consider the various tasks of managers at the various levels as listed in the text and compare those to the interviewed manager's actual duties.)
Would you want to have this person's job? Why?

Chapter 7

Organizing For Business

LEARNING OBJECTIVES

1. Discuss the three purposes of organization structure.

2. Describe the problems associated with specialization.

3. Explain how departmentalization facilitates goal achievement.

4. List five types of departmentalization.

5. Discuss how horizontal organization differs from vertical organization.

6. Explain three methods of horizontal organization.

7. Discuss the positive and negative aspects of the informal organization.

8. List six ways to define the culture of a company.

OUTLINE

I. Defining organization structure

    A. Definition of organization structure

    B. The importance of organizational structure
        1. The organization chart

II. Designing the formal organization

    A. Vertical organization
        1. Division of labor
        2. Authority, responsibility, and accountability
        3. Delegation
            a. The chain of command
            b. Line and staff authority
        4. Span of management
        5. Centralization versus decentralization

    B. Departmentalization
        1. Types of departmentalization
            a. Departmentalization by function
            b. Departmentalization by division
            c. Departmentalization by teams
            d. Departmentalization by matrix
            e. Departmentalization by network

    C. Horizontal organization
        1. Information systems
        2. Teams and task forces
        3. Managerial integrators

III. Understanding the informal organization

   A. How the informal organization functions

   B. Grapevines

   C. Office politics
      1. Networking

   D. Corporate culture
      1. Determining a company's culture

MAJOR POINTS TO REMEMBER

1. An **organization** is a group of people whose interactions are structured into goal-directed activities. **Organizational structure** is what managers use to (1) divide labor and assign jobs to individuals and to groups of workers, (2) define a manager's span of control and a firm's lines of authority, and (3) coordinate all the jobs of the organization. The visual presentation of this organizational structure is known as the **organization chart.**

2. Each firm has a different organizational structure, one that is best suited to allow it to accomplish its organizational goals.

3. A **formal organization** is a firm with an organizational structure designed to achieve the firm's strategic goals. When management develops a description of how the company is supposed to work and draws up an organization chart, the organizational plan has been formalized. In the development of a firm's organizational structure, managers must consider (1) vertical organization (creating jobs out of the tasks necessary to accomplish the planned work), (2) departmentalization (grouping jobs into departments and larger units), and (3) horizontal organization (coordinating all tasks so that the firm can operate as a single unit).

4. Linking the activities at the top of the organization to those at the middle and lower levels is the task of **vertical organization.** People responsible for others get their subordinates to do the work by exercising **authority,** which is power granted by the organization and acknowledged by the employees. A company's organization chart indicates who has authority over whom. Additionally, workers are assigned **responsibility** for their positions. This means that they are obligated to perform the duties and to achieve the goals associated with their jobs. The reporting of results to supervisors and justifying outcomes that fall below expectations is known as **accountability.**

5. Dividing tasks into distinct jobs is known as **division of labor** (also called work specialization). By having each worker concentrate on only one or a few tasks (rather than making the worker perform every task a company needs), overall organizational efficiency is improved. However, if specialization is overdone, workers may become bored with performing the same tiny, repetitive job over and over. Some firms have tried to balance specialization and employee motivation by having employees work in teams, with each team deciding how a complex task is to be broken down.

6. The assignment of the authority, responsibility, and accountability for work is known as **delegation.** While delegation may seem to be a fairly simple matter, it is often complicated when deciding how far down a chain of command those at the top will be held accountable for. A common problem in delegation is deciding how much authority an employee should be given; delegation will not work unless responsibility matches authority. Also, duties, responsibilities, and authority must be assigned to willing recipients. Part of the task of leadership involves getting employees to accept delegation and to understand clearly what is expected of them.

7. The flow of authority and communication within an organization is an unbroken line that connects each level of employee to the next. This is called the **chain of command,** and it establishes who has the authority to

give directions and who reports to whom. The two basic principles associated with the chain of command are that a worker is held accountable to only one supervisor, and that a firm's lines of authority are clearly defined and include every worker.

8. The simple chain-of-command system is known as **line organization,** because it establishes a clear line of authority flowing from the top downward through each subordinate position. Line organization is the simplest and most common structure for authority relationships, since everyone knows who is responsible to whom. It can speed decision making, provide for direct channels of communication, and may result in lower expenses.

9. Line organization has three important disadvantages. It concentrates most decision-making power at the top, even if those at this highest level may not have the specialized knowledge necessary to make the proper decision. Concentrating power at the top may also result in lower-level workers not developing the skills they will need to move higher in the firm. Lastly, the chain of command may grow so large that communication and decision making take too long.

10. The need to combine specialization with management control has resulted in the **line-and-staff organization.** This organizational form has a clear chain of command from the top downward, but it also includes various auxiliary groupings of people who come under the heading of staff. The **staff** supplements the line organization by providing advice and specialized services (e.g., a firm's legal department), but is not part of the line organization's chain of command.

11. **Span of management,** or **span of control,** refers to the number of employees a manager directly supervises. When a large number of people report directly to a manager, he or she has a wide span of management. A small number indicates a narrow span of control. In general, highly skilled workers normally require less supervision.

12. The span of management determines how many hierarchical levels a firm will have. A company with many levels in its managerial hierarchy (i.e., a narrow span of control) is known as a **tall structure.** In contrast, a **flat structure** has a wide span of control and fewer hierarchical levels. Tall structures cost more because they include many more managers, and their many levels may delay communication and decision making. Additionally, tall structures promote the creation of dull, routine jobs.

13. To improve effectiveness and to counteract the problems found in tall structures, companies have been **downsizing** (i.e., reducing their layers of middle management, widening spans of control, and reducing the size of their work force).

14. How centralized or decentralized authority is in an organization is determined by the hierarchical level at which decisions are made. **Centralization** focuses decision authority near the top of the firm, while **decentralization** pushes decision authority down to the lower levels of the organization. The advantages of centralization include simplified vertical coordination, the utilization of top management's experience and perspective, and the encouragement of strong leadership. But decentralization offers lower-level workers more challenge, eases the burden on top management, and also tends to speed decision making. In recent years, the trend has been toward decentralization.

15. **Departmentalization** is the first phrase of organizing, and involves grouping people into departments and then grouping departments into larger units to achieve goals. How the organization will operate is a function of how people working for the company are grouped. For example, the number of different groups dictates the number of supervisors that are needed.

16. Departments can be organized in a number of different ways. In **departmentalization by function,** employees are grouped according to similar skills, resource use, and expertise. For example, many firms have functional departments like marketing, human resources, finance, and accounting. While departmentalization by function permits the efficient use of resources and centralizes decision making, it also results in the slow response to environmental change.

17. Under **departmentalization by division,** departments are grouped according to similarities in product, process, customer, or geography. Each division is self-contained, with all the major functional resources it needs to achieve its goals (e.g., each division would include an accounting group). Under this organization structure, solutions to problems come lower in the hierarchy than they would under a functional organizational structure. A magazine publisher might use **product divisions,** with each magazine acting as a self-supporting, stand-alone unit; in contrast, a table manufacturer might use **process divisions,** with one department sizing and shaping the wood, a second department drilling and rough-finishing the pieces, and a third department assembling and finishing the table.

18. Other forms of departmentalization include **customer divisions** (e.g., a salesperson might specialize in selling to a particular type of customer or industry) and **geographic divisions** (e.g., a large magazine might have divisional advertising managers).

19. Division departmentalization allows a company to react quickly to changes and encourages customer service. However, it can lead to duplication of resources, and may result in one division competing with another.

20. A widespread practice today is **departmentalization by team,** which allows companies to push decision making to lower levels. Workers in functional departments may be permanently or temporarily assigned to a team in order to resolve mutual problems. Teams motivate workers to be more creative and to coordinate across functions. However, teams may also result in conflicts and dual loyalties. Under **project management,** workers assigned to a functional group temporarily abandon their position in the company's hierarchy and are assigned to a specific project. When the task is completed, workers return to their regular jobs. In contrast, under **departmentalization by matrix,** employees are permanently assigned to both a functional group and a project team.

21. Breaking major functions into separate companies that are electronically linked to a small headquarters organization is a more recent development known as **departmentalization by network.** Functional departments like marketing, engineering, and accounting are separate organizations working under contract, rather than part of one organization. This network approach is especially suitable for international operations, as it permits a firm to draw on resources worldwide. It is also extremely flexible, because the company can hire whatever services are needed. However, this approach lacks hands-on control and may also suffer from weak employee loyalty.

22. The system used to coordinate information and communication among employees in different departments is known as **horizontal organization.** It allows communication between and across departments without the need to go up and down the chain of command. Horizontal organization promotes innovation because it allows more views to be shared. The three methods typically used to achieve horizontal coordination are information systems, task forces and teams, and managerial integrators.

23. **Information systems** include all written and electronic forms of sharing information, processing data, and communicating ideas. Many firms today use electronic systems to quickly process and communicate vast amounts of information; such systems enhance horizontal coordination. Another technique is the **task force,** which is a group of people from different departments who are temporarily brought together to work on a specific issue or problem. Finally, a **managerial integrator** may be used to aid horizontal coordination. He or she is a manager who coordinates the activities of a number of functional departments but who is a member of none of them. This person may hold the title of project manager or program manager.

24. A company that emphasizes its vertical structure tends to have centralized authority, tight control over hierarchical levels, and routine jobs. One that stresses its horizontal structure allows tasks to be redefined to fit employee or environmental needs and uses decentralized decision making. Many firms try to strike a balance between vertical and horizontal structures so that they may benefit from the advantages of both.

25. The network of social interactions not specified by the formal organization, but which develops on a personal level among the workers, is known as the **informal organization.** The greatest positive impact of the informal organization comes from natural leaders who get things done. Other positive aspects include giving

workers an opportunity for social interaction, as well as an outlet for stress, tension, and anxiety. Informal organization also aids organizational communication and showcases future leaders.

26. However, not all aspects of informal organization are positive. It may create conflicting loyalties and rumors and can counteract a firm's values. The informal organization may also encourage resistance to management plans, complaints, poor-quality work, and absenteeism.

27. One of the best-known examples of the informal organization is the **grapevine,** an unofficial way of relaying news that bypasses the formal chain of command. A smart manager can make good use of the grapevine, as it can provide factual tips and feedback on both employee attitudes and outsiders' opinions of the company.

28. Other aspects of the informal organization include (1) **office politics,** which describes the complex power struggles that occur in companies; (2) **networking,** a term that describes the art of making and using contacts and involves the three elements of visibility, familiarity, and image; and (3) the use of **mentors,** or older workers who can guide younger employees through the corporate jungle.

29. The final element of the informal organization is **corporate culture,** which consists of the "feel" of the company and serves to let workers understand what the company expects from them. Although "cultures" vary greatly, understanding a corporation's culture makes it easier to get things done. Companies with strong, well-defined cultures are more likely to be successful.

KEY TERMS

organization
organizational structure
organization chart
formal organization
vertical organization
responsibility
accountability
division of labor
delegation
chain of command
line organization
line-and-staff organization
staff
span of management
span of control
tall structure
flat structure
downsizing
centralization
decentralization

departmentalization
departmentalization by function
departmentalization by division
product divisions
process divisions
customer divisions
geographic divisions
departmentalization by team
project management
departmentalization by matrix
departmentalization by network
horizontal organization
information systems
task force
informal organization
grapevine
office politics
networking
mentors
corporate culture

KEY TERMS EXERCISE

Directions: On the line provided, place the letter of the statement on the right that most closely defines the key term.

_____ 1. Departmentalization by division

_____ 2. Authority

_____ 3. Chain of command

_____ 4. Delegation

a. Specialization in or responsibility for some portion of an organization's overall task.

b. Grouping workers together according to their activities (e.g., production, finance, marketing).

c. The assigning of authority to others.

_____ 5. Division of labor

_____ 6. Departmentalization

_____ 7. Span of management

_____ 8. Tall structure

_____ 9. Flat structure

_____ 10. Departmentalization by function

_____ 11. Line organization

_____ 12. Line-and-staff organization

_____ 13. Project management

_____ 14. Informal organization

_____ 15. Networking

_____ 16. Mentor

_____ 17. Corporate culture

d. The number of people a manager directly supervises.

e. A typical organization with lines of authority but also various auxiliary groupings to supplement the line organization.

f. The organizational structure in which staff personnel work together as teams on specific projects.

g. Organizational structure where departments are grouped according to similarity in product, process, customer, or geography.

h. The network of social interactions that is not specified by formal organization.

i. The organizational climate and set of values that guide the organization.

j. An organization with a clear line of authority from top to bottom.

k. The grouping of people within an organization according to function, division, teams, matrix, or network.

l. A decentralized operation, characterized by relatively wide spans of management and delegation of authority to people in middle-management positions.

m. A highly centralized operation, with most of the authority and responsibility concentrated at the top.

n. The pathway for the flow of authority from one level of an organization's employees to the next.

o. The power granted by the organization and acknowledged by the employees.

p. The art of making and using contacts.

q. An older employee who acts as a guide and protector to a younger employee.

ANSWERS TO KEY TERMS EXERCISE

5. a (p. 180)
4. c (p. 181)
3. n (p. 183)
2. o (p. 181)
1. g (p. 189)

10. b (p. 188)
9. l (p. 185)
8. m (p. 185)
7. d (p. 184)
6. k (p. 187)

15. p (p. 197)
14. h (p. 196)
13. f (p. 194)
12. e (p. 183)
11. j (p. 183)

17. i (p. 198)
16. q (p. 198)

SELF TEST

True-False Questions

_____ 1. The goal of business is to organize the factors of production to produce products that can be sold at a profit.

_____ 2. Every organization relies on some sort of organizational structure.

_____ 3. For each industry, an ideal organizational structure for each company can be developed based on the environmental setting of that industry.

_____ 4. In actual practice, delegating authority is a complicated task.

_____ 5. Organizing is concerned with how best to divide labor and how to distribute authority and responsibility.

_____ 6. Each organization should be structured to best handle the situation in an appropriate manner.

_____ 7. Once developed, the organizational structure should not be changed.

_____ 8. Although a division of labor by task may be productive, it may create employee discontent due to the highly repetitive nature of the work.

_____ 9. Companies that operate on a nationwide basis are forced to organize according to geographic location.

_____ 10. The most widespread trend in organizational structure is to have departmentalization by team.

_____ 11. The most common error in delegation is failing to give the recipient enough authority to carry out assigned duties and responsibilities.

_____ 12. For delegation to be effective, people must be willing to accept authority as well as delegate it.

_____ 13. The span of management should be the same for all organizations and departments.

_____ 14. A line organization is the simplest and most common structure for authority relationships.

_____ 15. Line managers must accept the advice of staff.

_____ 16. An advantage of geographic location organization is greater responsiveness to local customs, styles, and product preferences.

_____ 17. The informal organization can be both beneficial and harmful.

_____ 18. Successful organizations tend to have strong, well-defined corporate cultures.

_____ 19. To be effective, top-level executives must believe in and exemplify the values of the corporate culture.

_____ 20. If the corporate culture is strong, it will directly influence every action and policy of a company.

_____ 21. For an organization to run smoothly, workers need to know not only what to do and when to do it but also who is monitoring them to make sure they do it right.

_____ 22. Most companies should strike a balance between the vertical and horizontal organization, rather than emphasizing one over the other.

_____ 23. The organization structure lets employees know where and how they fit into an organization, enabling them to work together toward company goals.

_____ *24. Intrapreneurs are employees who act as entrepreneurs within a company to develop new products.

_____ *25. Companies must learn to adapt to and manage change if they are to be successful.

Multiple Choice Questions

_____ 1. Before delegating authority, which of the following must be decided?
   a. How accountable will those at the top be for actions of those below them?
   b. How much authority should be delegated in order to perform the job?
   c. Will the person willingly accept the authority?
   d. All of the above must be considered in delegating authority.

_____ 2. Departmentalization by division can be according to similarities in
   a. product.
   b. process.
   c. customer.
   d. geography.
   e. all of the above.

_____ 3. A company that wants to have workers specialize in particular tasks and functions to bring about efficient production should organize according to
   a. product.
   b. process.
   c. customer.
   d. geography.

_____ 4. A company selling personal computers to both business and individual users would be best to organize according to
   a. product.
   b. process.
   c. customer.
   d. geography.

_____ 5. Which of the following is *not* an advantage of division departmentalization?
   a. Allows better coordination across different divisions.
   b. Offers a higher degree of flexibility.
   c. Provides a higher level of customer service.
   d. Allows a higher degree of focus on problem areas.
   e. Provides a good base for developing managers.

_____ 6. For delegation to be effective, a person should have
   a. more authority than responsibility.
   b. authority equal to responsibility.
   c. more responsibility than authority.
   d. neither responsibility nor authority.

_____   7. The number of subordinates a manager can supervise (span of management) depends upon
        a.   the manager's leadership ability.
        b.   the skill of the workers.
        c.   the motivation of the workers.
        d.   the nature of the job.
        e.   all of the above.

_____   8. A wide span of management would be _least_ suitable in which of the following situations?
        a.   managing a group of lawyers
        b.   managing a group of brain surgeons
        c.   managing a group of production-line workers
        d.   among top-level managers

_____   9. Which of the following is _not_ an advantage of the line organization?
        a.   Decisions can be made quickly.
        b.   It is a simple form of organization.
        c.   It sometimes lowers expenses.
        d.   Channels of communication are direct.
        e.   It diffuses decision-making authority.

_____   10. Networking, the art of making and using contacts, requires
        a.   visibility.
        b.   familiarity.
        c.   image.
        d.   all of the above.

_____   11. An organization's business environment, its values, its heroes, its day-to-day routines, and its network of communication are all reflected in the
        a.   organization chart.
        b.   formal organization.
        c.   informal organization.
        d.   corporate culture.

Use the chart below to answer questions 12 through 14:

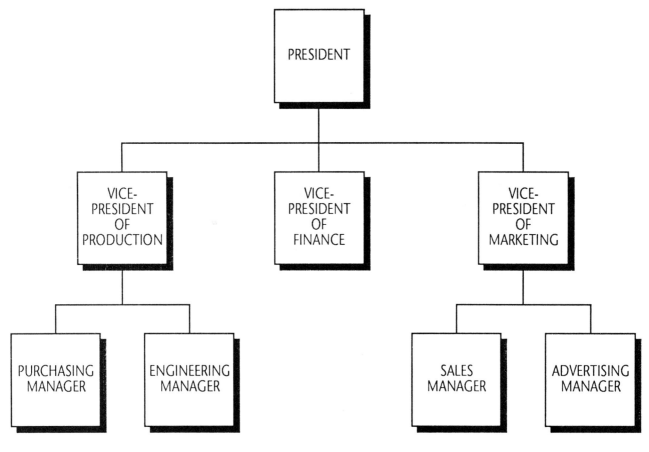

_____ 12. The vice president of marketing receives orders from the
        a. president.
        b. vice president of production.
        c. vice president of finance.
        d. sales manager.
        e. advertising manager.

_____ 13. Which of the following includes pairs that do *not* function on the same level?
        a. vice president of production and vice president of marketing
        b. engineering manager and sales manager
        c. purchasing manager and engineering manager
        d. purchasing manager and sales manager
        e. vice president of marketing and purchasing manager

_____ 14. The responsibility of hiring personnel is
        a. in the hands of the president.
        b. given to the vice president of production.
        c. given to the vice president of marketing.
        d. given to the purchasing manager.
        e. not clear from the chart.

_____ 15. A potential problem with a divisional departmentalization is
        a. duplication of resources across divisions.
        b. poor coordination across divisions.
        c. competition among divisions for resources.
        d. development of unhealthy rivalries across divisions.
        e. All of the above are potential problems.

_____ 16. Which of the following is *not* an advantage of departmentalization by team?
  a. It allows the organization to be more flexible and responsive.
  b. It motivates employees to be more creative.
  c. It pushes decision making down into the organization.
  d. It keeps everyone focused on overall corporate goals.

_____ 17. Breaking major functions into separate companies that are electronically connected to a small head-quarters organization is departmentalization by
  a. team.
  b. division.
  c. matrix.
  d. network.

_____ 18. Horizontal coordination within an organization can be achieved by
  a. developing efficient and effective information systems.
  b. creating interdepartmental teams and task forces.
  c. utilizing managerial integrators.
  d. all of the above.

_____ 19. The system that is used to coordinate information and communication among employees in various departments at various levels is the
  a. matrix organization.
  b. vertical organization.
  c. horizontal organization.
  d. network organization.

_____ 20. The organizational structure is used by managers to
  a. divide labor and assign formal tasks to individuals and groups.
  b. define a manager's span of control and lines of authority.
  c. coordinate all tasks so that the organization can act as a unit.
  d. all of the above.

Completion Questions

1. A person, at any point in the chain of command, is answerable to those _____ him or her and has responsibility for and authority over those _____.

2. Organizing is concerned with determining who will do each required task and also who will be _____ for seeing that the particular task gets done.

3. An organization in which a written description of authority and responsibilities exists is called a _____ organization.

4. Coordinating activity by facilitating communication and information exchange across departments without going up and down the vertical chain of command is achieved through the _____ organization.

5. A manager with a lot of people reporting to him or her has a _____ span of control.

6. A tall structure is highly _____ and has a narrow span of management; a _____ organization is decentralized and has a wide span of control.

7. Staff organizations supplement the line organization by providing _____ and specialized _____.

8. A company that needs in-depth skills in a functional department but also needs the flexibility to adapt to changes in environmental demands would be best to departmentalize according to _____.

9. Strategic planning defines what a company will do, while _____ defines how a company will do it.

*10. The most common ways organizations manage change are _____ and _____.

11. The _____ serves as a guidepost for employees to judge what is wanted, how to approach problems, and what types of solutions are acceptable.

PROJECT

Developing an Organizational Structure

This project is designed to give you additional insight into how companies are organized. Your task is to develop the organization chart for an organization and analyze it based on the concepts of Chapter 7 of your text.

Select an organization of your choosing—it may be a company, a nonprofit organization, or a campus group (perhaps some organization you are associated with)—and develop an organization chart showing the chain of command. (Information for this task can be obtained from personal interviews, annual reports, business literature, and other organizational reports.)

1. Draw the organization chart showing the chain of command.

2. What type of organizational structure is used? (e.g., line, line-and-staff, matrix)?

3. What type of departmentalization is used (e.g., function, territory, product, customer)?

4. Is the organizational structure tall or flat?

5. Is the span of control wide or narrow?

6. Evaluate the organizational structure in terms of its structure, use of departments, and span of control (i.e., indicate the good and bad points of the structure of the organization).

7. What changes or suggestions would you make?

8. What observations and comments can you make about the informal organization?

9. Can you draw any conclusions about the organization's corporate culture on the basis of its formal and informal organizational structure?

Chapter 8

The Production of Goods and Services

LEARNING OBJECTIVES

1. Diagram the conversion process.

2. Define the goal of most advances in production technology.

3. Cite the four technological advances that made mass production possible.

4. Explain three innovations in materials management.

5. Differentiate between quality control and quality assurance.

6. Define the five basic steps in production control.

7. Identify the three main production layouts.

8. Describe three techniques for improving scheduling.

OUTLINE

I. The quest for competitiveness

    A. Definition of production
        1. The conversion process
            a. Types of conversions
        2. What effectiveness means

    B. The industrial revolution
        1. Improving production efficiency
        2   Technological advances brought about by the industrial revolution
            a. Mechanization
            b. Standardization
            c. The assembly line
            d. Automation
            e. Mass production

    C. The second industrial revolution
        1. Advances in production technology
            a. Computer-aided design and engineering
            b. Computer-aided manufacturing
            c. Computer-integrated manufacturing
        2. New process designs
            a. Flexible manufacturing
               (1) The job shop
            b. The focused factory
            c. Just-in-time systems
        3. Materials management
            a. Inventory and inventory control
            b. Materials requirements planning (MRP)
            c. Manufacturing resource planning (MRP II)

   4. Quality assurance
       a. Quality control
       b. Statistical process control
       c. Statistical quality control
       d. Total quality management
   5. Improving human relations
       a. Methods improvement and ergonomics
       b. Job rotation, enlargement, and enrichment
       c. Quality circles

D. Competitiveness in service operations
    1. How service companies improve their services

E. Toward world-class manufacturing

F. Production and the natural environment

II. Production and operations management (POM)

   A. Definition of POM

   B. The issue of production facilities location

   C. Production forecasting

III. Production control

   A. Definition of production control

   B. Production planning
       1. The bill of materials

   C. Routing
       1. Definition of routing
       2. Process layout
       3. Assembly-line layout
       4. Fixed-position layout

   D. Scheduling
       1. Why scheduling is important
       2. Gantt chart
       3. Critical path method (CPM)
       4. Program evaluation and review technique (PERT)

   E. Dispatching

   F. Follow-up and control

MAJOR POINTS TO REMEMBER

1. The transformation of resources into goods or services that people want is known as **production.** At the core of production is the **conversion process**, in which resources are converted into products. The two basic types of conversions are (1) the analytic system, in which raw materials are broken down into one or more different products (e.g., meat packing), and (2) the synthetic system, which is the combining of two or more

materials into a single product (e.g., making steel). Smart businesspersons seek production **effectiveness,** that is, they want to increase competitiveness through efficiency, quality, and human relations.

2. The industrial revolution, which began in England more than 200 years ago, was brought about by a series of technological advances designed to lower costs by increasing production **efficiency.** The first advance associated with the industrial revolution was **mechanization,** the use of machines to do the work previously done by people. Next came **standardization,** or the production of uniform, interchangeable parts. The technology with the most wide-ranging influence was the **assembly line,** the manufacturing technique in which the item being put together progresses past a number of different workstations where each worker performs a specific task. Originated by Henry Ford, the assembly line reduced the time necessary to build his Model T chassis from 12 1/2 hours to 1 1/2 hours. Another technological advance was **automation,** or the process of performing a mechanical operation with the minimum human input.

3. Mechanization, standardization, the assembly line, and automation were all part of the development of **mass production,** which allows goods to be manufactured in very large quantities. It is this large-scale production that keeps the prices of the goods we purchase relatively low and thereby raises our standard of living.

4. Because they can dramatically increase efficiency, computer-controlled machines and robots are today helping to bring about a second industrial revolution. Industries wishing to remain competitive will have to pursue effectiveness through efficiency in production technology, process design, materials management, quality assurance, and improved human relations. Another benefit of operations effectiveness is time; companies that have learned to design and produce new products faster gain an advantage over their slower competition.

5. It is most desirable to use advanced production technologies when there is a large concentration of workers in one area of the factory, when employees are stuck in difficult or boring jobs that no one wants to do, or when there are many injuries in one part of the plant.

6. Computers play an important role in the design of new products. The use of computer graphics in the design of products is called **computer-aided design (CAD).** When used with **computer-aided engineering (CAE),** engineers are able to test products without building models, resulting in time savings and quality improvements.

7. **Computer-aided manufacture (CAM)** is the use of computers to control production machines (e.g., robots and inspection devices). The combination of computer-aided design and computer-aided manufacturing (CAD/CAM) is becoming an important factor in the design of many new products, and typically results in a reduction in the time and labor necessary to design and produce a product.

8. **Computer-integrated manufacturing (CIM)** represents the highest level of computerization in operations management. Using CIM, all the elements of design, engineering, and production are integrated into computer networks that communicate across departments. The "factory of the future" will have CIM as a key component.

9. Several new process designs that affect the way the production process is organized have emerged. One of these trends, **flexible manufacturing (FMS),** is an alternative to **hard manufacturing,** or the use of specialized equipment that is locked into place. Hard manufacturing is typically associated with **repetitive manufacturing** (doing the same thing over and over) and may result in reduced **setup costs** (the expense of initiating a production run). On the other hand, flexible manufacturing, also known as **soft manufacturing,** allows computer-controlled machines to adapt to different versions of the same operation. Changing from one product design to another under this system requires only a few different signals from the computer and increases a factory's flexibility. About 20 percent of U.S. factories currently employ FMS.

10. The flexible manufacturing layout may be most desirable for a **job shop,** which makes numerous items on such an irregular basis that repetitive operations are not feasible. Most small machine shops are job shops.

11. A **focused factory** concentrates on the manufacture of a limited number of products for a particular market. Flexible manufacturing is ideal for such factories because it allows plants to be smaller, more specialized, and closer to important markets.

12. In order to increase efficiency and profitability, companies can examine their methods for handling **inventory** (the goods they stock for the production process and for sales to customers). Firms need a system of **inventory control** to determine the proper quantities of supplies and finished products to have on hand. Another aspect of **materials management** involves trying to increase profitability by shortening **lead times,** the periods of time between the placement of a purchase order and the receipt of materials. By shortening lead times, companies can maintain lower inventory levels, thereby keeping inventory costs to a minimum.

13. One technique widely used to control inventory is called **materials requirements planning (MRP).** It is designed to get correct materials to where they are needed on time and without unnecessary stockpiling. A computer is typically used to coordinate this task.

14. For companies using flexible manufacturing, the parts and materials needed to produce products are always changing. But each part must be in the right place at the right time, or work at the factory comes to a halt. A new approach to materials management, the **just-in-time-system (JIT),** comes from the Japanese *kanban* system. It involves having only the right quantities of materials arrive at the exact times they are needed for use in production. The elimination of large inventories results in less required storage space, less accounting, and less investment. JIT places a tremendous burden on suppliers, who must be able to meet the production schedules of their customers. In this country, for example, JIT allowed St. Luke's Episcopal Hospital in Houston to save $1.5 million over three years by closing its supplies warehouse.

15. Inefficiencies may be reduced when factories install **manufacturing resource planning (MRP II),** a comprehensive computer system that integrates a company's activities and provides managers with information for decision making. MRP II, when linked with CAD, can even initiate automatically the process of ordering the parts and materials needed to produce a new product.

16. In recent years, American manufacturers have focused attention on improving the quality level of their products. The process of measuring quality against some standard after the good or service has been produced is known as **quality control.** A new watchword, however, is **quality assurance,** a term to describe a firm's practices and procedures to assure that the company's products satisfy customers. The proper design of tools, machinery, components, worker training programs, and the production process itself aid in this effort. Quality assurance includes **statistical process control,** which involves monitoring production through the use of control charts to permit management to determine whether the desired quality level is being met.

17. About thirty years ago, consultant W. Edwards Deming began helping companies employ a system known as **statistical quality control (SQC).** The concept involves random sampling to check the quality of production output.

18. **Total quality management (TQM)** is the highest level of quality awareness. TQM is a philosophy or management style that places quality at the center of everything the company does—it is the very reason for the company's existence. In the United States, the concept has been used successfully by both Hewlett-Packard and Motorola.

19. Companies can also increase effectiveness by improving human relations. Examining a job in order to increase its level of efficiency is known as **methods improvement.** This includes such considerations as changing operation sequences, balancing assembly-line tasks, installing worker aids, simplifying materials handling, and utilizing **ergonomics** (the study of human characteristics in designing and arranging the most effective and safest tasks, equipment, and environments). Companies have also attempted to increase workers' satisfaction and motivation with such techniques as job rotation, job enlargement (expanding a worker's tasks), and job enrichment (expanding a worker's tasks and responsibility).

20. Another method to increase job satisfaction is the **quality circle.** About five to fifteen workers meet regularly to identify and find solutions to problems of quality, safety, and production. These circles create a feeling of unity among employees. Ford Motor Company set up quality circles as part of its "Quality Is Job One" campaign. Quality is also an issue in the service sector, with many service organizations introducing quality circles.

21. Today, companies are realizing that if they want to compete globally they must be capable of **world-class manufacturing.** This means that they must offer a level of quality and operational effectiveness that puts the firm among the top performers worldwide.

22. The coordination of a firm's resources in order to manufacture its goods or provide its services is called **production and operations management (POM).** Because efficient production is no accident, POM has become one of the business world's most dynamic areas of specialization, and top business schools are now offering degree programs in manufacturing. Top managers must engage in **production forecasting,** the plan of how much to produce in a particular period of time. Estimating demand is no easy matter. Managers must also decide where production facilities should be located.

23. Another area of POM is **production control,** a set of steps that result in the efficient production of a high-quality product. The five steps usually involved in production control are (1) planning, (2) routing, (3) scheduling, (4) dispatching, and (5) follow-up and control. Once plans have been made (step 1), lists of all required parts and materials must be developed. Such a list, known as a **bill of materials,** also indicates whether parts are to be made or purchased.

24. The second step in the production control process is **routing,** the path through the factory that work will take and the sequence of operations to be performed. The three types of routing are process layout, assembly-line layout, and fixed-position layout.

25. A **process layout** concentrates, in one place, everything needed to perform a specific phase of the process and is frequently used in the service industries (e.g., a college has a language department). With the **assembly-line layout,** the production process occurs along a line, with the product flowing from one workstation to another (e.g., an automobile factory). In contrast, the manufacture of large, hard-to-move products (e.g., a Boeing 767 aircraft) necessitates a **fixed-position layout,** with the product remaining stationary as workers and production equipment come to it. Many services require a fixed-position layout as well. For example, the gardener must bring his lawn mower to the client's lawn.

26. Incorporating a time element into a routing plan and setting a time for each operation to begin and end is the task of **scheduling.** Managers, in coordinating the different steps of a project, may use a **Gantt chart,** which illustrates the amount of time it should take to finish each part of a manufacturing project or process.

27. Another tool for coordinating projects is the **critical path method (CPM),** which focuses on the sequence of tasks that is perceived to take the longest time and therefore determines when the project may be completed (the "critical path"). Also used in scheduling is the **program evaluation and review technique (PERT),** which is similar to CPM but employs statistical probabilities to estimate the likelihood that an activity will require a given amount of time. For each task to be performed, PERT requires the calculation of four separate time estimates: optimistic, pessimistic, most likely, and expected (an average of the first three).

28. The issuing of work orders and distribution of papers to department supervisors are a part of the **dispatching** process. Dispatches indicate the work to be done and the time frame for its completion.

29. The final element in the production control process is **follow-up and control.** A successful system is based on good communication between workers and the production manager. In addition, the control system must ensure that the products meet the necessary quality standards.

KEY TERMS

production
conversion process
effectiveness
efficiency
mechanization
standardization
assembly line
automation
mass production
computer-aided design
computer-aided engineering
computer-aided manufacture
computer-integrated manufacturing
flexible manufacturing
hard manufacturing
repetitive manufacturing
setup costs
soft manufacturing
job shop
focused factory
inventory
inventory control
materials management
lead times
materials requirements planning

just-in-time-system
manufacturing resource planning
quality control
quality assurance
statistical process control
statistical quality control
total quality management
methods improvement
ergonomics
quality circle
production and operations management
production forecasting
production control
bill of materials
routing
process layout
assembly-line layout
fixed-position layout
scheduling
Gantt chart
critical path method
program evaluation and review technique
dispatching
follow-up and control

KEY TERMS EXERCISE

Directions: On the line provided, place the letter of the statement on the right that most closely defines the key term.

O	1.	Production
P	2.	Conversion process
M	3.	Mechanization
R	4.	Standardization
I	5.	Assembly line
C	6.	Automation
U	7.	Mass production
S	8.	Computer-aided manufacture
N	9.	Computer-aided design
J	10.	Flexible (soft) manufacturing
F	11.	Focused factory
L	12.	Inventory

a. A continuous process of inventory control that through team work seeks to deliver a small quantity of materials to precisely where it is needed.

b. Regularly scheduled meetings of about five to fifteen employees to identify and suggest solutions to quality, safety, and production problems.

c. The process of performing a mechanical operation with the absolute minimum of human intervention.

d. Production planning, routing, scheduling, dispatching, and follow-up and control in the effort to achieve efficiency and high quality.

e. A companywide computer system that coordinates data from all departments in order to maintain minimum inventories and a smooth production process.

f. A manufacturing facility that deals with only one narrow set of products.

g. The period that elapses between placement of a purchase order and receipt of materials from a supplier.

h. The process of getting the correct materials where they are needed, on time, without stockpiling unnecessary materials.

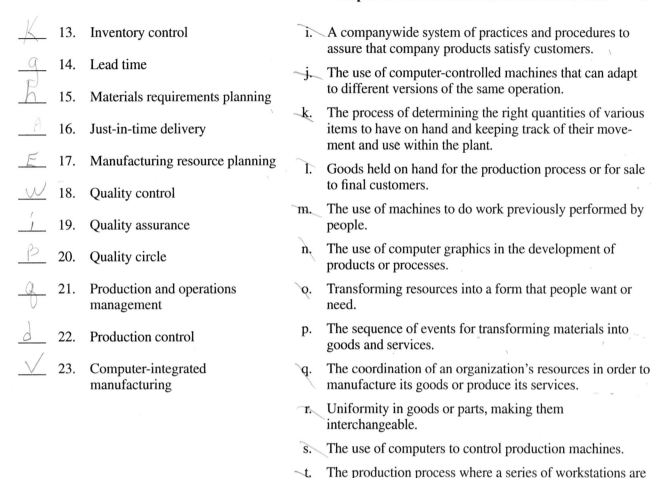

_K_ 13. Inventory control

_g_ 14. Lead time

_h_ 15. Materials requirements planning

_A_ 16. Just-in-time delivery

_E_ 17. Manufacturing resource planning

_w_ 18. Quality control

_i_ 19. Quality assurance

_p_ 20. Quality circle

_q_ 21. Production and operations management

_d_ 22. Production control

_v_ 23. Computer-integrated manufacturing

i. A companywide system of practices and procedures to assure that company products satisfy customers.

j. The use of computer-controlled machines that can adapt to different versions of the same operation.

k. The process of determining the right quantities of various items to have on hand and keeping track of their movement and use within the plant.

l. Goods held on hand for the production process or for sale to final customers.

m. The use of machines to do work previously performed by people.

n. The use of computer graphics in the development of products or processes.

o. Transforming resources into a form that people want or need.

p. The sequence of events for transforming materials into goods and services.

q. The coordination of an organization's resources in order to manufacture its goods or produce its services.

r. Uniformity in goods or parts, making them interchangeable.

s. The use of computers to control production machines.

t. The production process where a series of workstations are established at which workers perform certain tasks.

u. The manufacture of uniform products in great quantities.

v. Computer-based systems that coordinate and control all elements of design and production.

w. The routine checking and testing of a product or process for quality against some standard.

ANSWERS TO KEY TERMS EXERCISE

1. o (p. 206)	7. n (p. 207)	13. k (p. 211)	19. i (p. 215)
2. p (p. 206)	8. s (p. 209)	14. g (p. 212)	20. p (p. 216)
3. m (p. 207)	9. u (p. 208)	15. h (p. 212)	21. b (p. 218)
4. r (p. 207)	10. j (p. 210)	16. a (p. 212)	22. d (p. 219)
5. t (p. 207)	11. f (p. 210)	17. e (p. 213)	23. v (p. 209)
6. c (p. 207)	12. l (p. 211)	18. w (p. 214)	

SELF TEST

True-False Questions

_____   1.   Services require a production process.

_____   2.   Improved efficiency is a way for a company to remain profitable in the face of greater competition and slowing consumer demand.

_____   3.   Mass production has helped in giving the United States a high standard of living.

_____   4.   Mass production has made it possible for more products to be made available at lower prices.

_____   5.   The production manager wants to produce products as efficiently, quickly, and inexpensively as possible.

_____   6.   In a fully automated factory, there is no need for human beings at all.

_____   7.   Robots and computer-controlled machines are increasingly being used to improve production efficiency.

_____   8.   Computer-aided manufacture (CAM) increases an assembly line's output, speed, accuracy, and dependability.

_____   9.   Computer-aided engineering (CAE) allows engineers to test products without ever building preliminary models.

_____   10.   Advances in technology, such as CAM, have had little or no impact on the way the production process is organized.

_____   11.   With a focused factory approach, all of a company's products are produced at one location.

_____   12.   More companies prefer hard automation to soft automation.

_____   13.   Production and operations management (POM) requires setting objectives, developing strategies, and measuring performance.

_____   14.   A manufacturer that requires unskilled labor has more flexibility in locating a plant than one that requires skilled labor.

Multiple Choice Questions

_____   1.   Mass production is possible because of the technological advances of
   a.   mechanization.
   b.   standardization.
   c.   the assembly line.
   d.   automation.
   e.   all of the above.

_____   2.   Mass production
   a.   allows greater quantities of goods to be produced.
   b.   allows prices to be lowered because of economies of scale.
   c.   increases the standard of living.
   d.   made products available to more people.
   e.   all of the above.

_____ 3. Robots and computer-controlled machines are best used when
   a. the task is so difficult, tedious, or boring that no one wants to do it.
   b. many injuries occur in the performance of the task.
   c. there is an unusually high concentration of workers in one area of the plant.
   d. Robots and computer-controlled machines should be used for all of the above situations.

_____ 4. Another term for flexible manufacturing is
   a. variable manufacturing.
   b. hard manufacturing.
   c. soft manufacturing.
   d. automation.

_____ 5. Which of the following is _not_ a characteristic of flexible manufacturing?
   a. Plants must be larger.
   b. Plants can be more specialized.
   c. Plants can be located closer to important markets.
   d. Plants can be focused factories.

_____ 6. The steps involved in production control include all of the following _except_
   a. planning.
   b. routing.
   c. scheduling.
   d. handling.
   e. follow-up and control.

_____ 7. Selecting a site for a plant is influenced by
   a. the quantity and quality of labor.
   b. the closeness of resources.
   c. transportation and other available services.
   d. the desire of a community to have the plant.
   e. all of the above.

_____ 8. Which of the following is _not_ one of the main classifications of production routing?
   a. process layout
   b. service-line layout
   c. assembly-line layout
   d. fixed-position layout

_____ 9. Construction of a building is likely to use what type of production routing?
   a. process layout
   b. service-line layout
   c. assembly-line layout
   d. fixed-position layout

_____ 10. The factory of the future will integrate all the elements of design, engineering, and production into computer networks that communicate across departments. These networks are known as
   a. computer-aided design (CAD).
   b. computer-aided manufacturing (CAM).
   c. computer-integrated manufacturing (CIM).
   d. flexible manufacturing.

_____ 11. The conversion process of breaking raw materials into one or more distinct products in known as
   a. flexible manufacturing.
   b. analytic system.
   c. synthetic system.
   d. distillation process.

_____ 12. Steel manufacturing would be an example of
   a. flexible manufacturing.
   b. analytic system.
   c. synthetic system.
   d. distillation process.

_____ 13. World-class manufacturing refers to
   a. effectively producing quality products so that a company is among the top performers worldwide.
   b. viewing the world as your marketplace.
   c. achieving the quality standards established by the Committee on Quality Production Standards.
   d. adapting the quality of products to meet the needs of each individual country in which a firm operates.

_____ *14. For just-in-time inventory management to work, there must be
   a. close communication between suppliers and customers.
   b. attention to quality.
   c. adequate storage facilities and transportation options.
   d. reliable service from suppliers.
   e. all of the above.

Completion Questions

1. Production is made possible through the _____ process, which takes inputs and transforms them into an output.

2. The conversion process can be accomplished by _____ raw materials into one or more different products or by _____ two or more materials to form a single product.

3. Specifying the path that work takes through a plant and the sequence of operations is known as _____; the time required for each step from beginning to end is established by a _____.

4. Checking and testing the quality of products as they are produced is the task of _____.

5. The specific sequence of operations whose prompt completion is essential to the completion of the entire project is referred to as the _____.

6. The _____ process is the sequence of events in which resources are converted into products by either an analytic system or a synthetic system.

*7. _____ inventory management is the practice of having suppliers deliver items right before they are needed, rather than holding massive inventories of those items.

PROJECT

Service Production Processes

America is becoming a service-oriented society, with services accounting for an increasing proportion of consumer expenditures and employment. Thus, services deserve attention and study.

Production processes for services differ somewhat from those for products due to the intangible nature of services and the need to simultaneously produce a service as it is consumed.

This project is designed to increase your understanding of production processes in services. Select a service organization, such as a fast-food restaurant, dry cleaner, or auto repair, and answer the following questions.

1. Describe the conversion process being used to "produce" the service (i.e., What are the inputs, transformations, and outputs?).

2. Describe the type of production layout being employed (e.g., process, assembly line, fixed position).

3. Describe how the following concepts are applied:

    a. mechanization

    b. standardization

    c. assembly line

    d. automation

4. What evidence of quality control exists?

5. What evidence of production control exists?

6. How efficient and effective is this service operation? What suggestions would you offer to make it more efficient?

Chapter 9

Human Relations

LEARNING OBJECTIVES

1. List the three main components of good human relations within an organization.
2. Explain the five steps in Maslow's hierarchy of needs, as they relate to worker motivation.
3. Identify the two factors affecting worker motivation in Herzberg's motivational-hygiene theory.
4. List three basic assumptions of expectancy theory.
5. Describe three concepts linking motivation and management style.
6. Discuss the impact of three major trends in the work force.
7. Identify three approaches to motivating individual employees.
8. Name four job-oriented techniques for improving the motivation of workers.

OUTLINE

I. Human relations within an organization

   A. Definition of human relations

   B. The components of good human relations
     1. Leadership
     2. Communication
     3. Motivation

II. Motivation theory

   A. Nineteenth-century working conditions
     1. The role played by Robert Owen

   B. The classical theory of motivation
     1. Frederick W. Taylor
     2. Scientific management

   C. The Hawthorne studies
     1. Social pressure as a motivating force
     2. The power of the informal organization

   D. Maslow's hierarchy of needs
     1. Physiological, safety, social, esteem, and self-actualization needs

E. Motivational-hygiene theory
    1. Hygiene factors
    2. Motivators
    3. Relationship to Maslow's ladder

F. Expectancy theory
    1. Definition of expectancy theory
    2. How worker performance can be improved
    3. Addressing the "nine C's" of expectancy theory

G. Motivation and management style
    1. Theory X and Theory Y
        a. Assumptions of Theory X
        b. Assumptions of Theory Y
    2. Theory Z
        a. Theory Z and the U.S. worker

III. The challenge of motivating workers in the 1990s

A. The changing work force
    1. Work force characteristics
    2. The aging of the work force
        a. Baby boomers
    3. Women in the work force
    4. Cultural diversity

B. The changing economy
    1. Changes brought about by the service economy

C. The changing organizational culture
    1. How organizational cultures will have to change

IV. Motivational techniques

A. Common motivational methods

B. Employee-oriented techniques
    1. Goal setting
    2. Behavior modification
        a. How to reward people
    3. Retraining

C. Job-oriented techniques
    1. Job enrichment and redesign
    2. Flextime
    3. Telecommuting and home offices
    4. Work sharing and job sharing

D. Organization-oriented techniques
    1. Revamping the organization's objectives, strategies, or culture
        a. Employee empowerment (participative management)
            (1) The work team approach
            (2) Gain sharing
            (3) Employee stock options
            (4) Employee-owned businesses

MAJOR POINTS TO REMEMBER

1. The way individuals interact with one another is referred to as **human relations**. In business organizations, human relations are affected by the organization's culture, the practices of management, and other, more general forces.

2. Maintaining good human relations is important to any business, because satisfied workers tend to be more productive and less likely to leave or initiate a complaint.

3. The three components necessary for good human relations are leadership, communication, and motivation. **Leadership** is the ability to influence people to work toward accomplishing a goal. A leader's approach should be guided by the situation at hand, the needs and personalities of workers, and the organization's culture. Managers must learn the difference between authority (the ability to make someone do something) and leadership (the ability to inspire someone to do something) if they are to be effective.

4. A component of good organizational human relations is good **communication**, which is needed to build interpersonal networks and patterns of interaction. In one study, 90 percent of the people who reported good communication with their bosses were satisfied with their jobs. A third ingredient of good organization is **motivation**; the effective manager is able to persuade workers that their needs can be satisfied within the framework of the organization. Managers must also be sensitive to workers' **morale** (attitude toward the job and firm). Employees tend to work best in an environment of fairness, clarity, appreciation, responsiveness, and involvement.

5. During the nineteenth century, when most workers labored under horrendous conditions, a Scottish industrialist named Robert Owen pioneered modern business practices such as the merit system and the belief that the well-being of workers was as important as the upkeep of machinery.

6. The **classical theory of motivation** holds that on the job, money is the sole motivating force. A manager motivates workers by showing them that they'll earn more money by doing things the company way. Frederick W. Taylor, the "father of scientific management," was classical management's chief spokesperson. Believing strongly in the division of labor, he broke work down into small units that were efficient and easy to measure. Upon determining a reasonable productivity level, Taylor set a **quota** (minimum goal) for each worker. This **piecework system** paid workers a certain amount for each unit produced. When a worker exceeded the quota, he or she received a higher rate for all units produced. This created a very strong incentive for workers to increase their productivity. It should be emphasized that classical theory works well when workers are very poor, which is not necessarily the situation existing today.

7. The Hawthorne studies, conducted between 1927 and 1932, were designed to test the relationship between workers' physical surroundings and their productivity. Researchers discovered that social pressure (about what the proper output level should be) was much more important in determining productivity than the work environment; workers established their own **group norms**. The vast power of the informal organization in motivating workers and raising morale proved to be a stronger incentive than money, and this phenomenon came to be called the **Hawthorne effect**.

8. In 1943, Abraham Maslow organized into five categories the wide variety of needs that motivate workers. His hierarchy of human needs is commonly referred to as **"Maslow's ladder."** It is based on the notion that people have many needs and only unsatisfied needs cause people to act. When a lower-level need has been satisfied, at least in part, the individual begins to strive for the next rung on the ladder. The steps, from lowest to highest, are physiological needs (food, clothing, shelter), safety needs (security, insurance, money in the bank), social needs (love, sense of belonging), esteem needs (respect, sense of personal worth, integrity), and self-actualization needs (to become everything one is capable of). Usually, people are motivated by a combination of many different needs.

9. In the 1960s, Frederick Herzberg and his associates found that two entirely different sets of factors were associated with satisfying and dissatisfying experiences at work. Factors associated with potential dissatisfaction (if deficient within the work environment) were termed **hygiene factors** and include company policy, working conditions, and job security. Improving such factors, however, will not lead to greater employee

motivation. It is, instead, the **motivators**—such as achievement, responsibility, and recognition—that serve to increase productivity. Hygiene factors are a part of the job environment and resemble Maslow's lower-level needs, but motivators are part of human relations and closely resemble Maslow's higher-level needs.

10. **Expectancy theory** is another theoretical approach to motivation. It holds that the amount of effort people will expend on a task depends on the expected outcomes; people consider how well they think they might do on a task, whether they feel they will be rewarded for that performance, and whether the reward will be worth the amount of effort required. It must be noted, though, that each worker will view the task, its difficulty, and its rewards differently. As a consequence, managers must evaluate each worker in light of this theory and tailor the work and rewards accordingly.

11. According to Walter Newsome, the main issues that managers should address to implement expectancy theory can be referred to as the "nine C's." These are capability, confidence, challenge, criteria, credibility, consistency, compensation, cost, and communication.

12. Douglas McGregor believed that certain assumptions, which he called **Theory X**, underlie most managers' thinking. These assumptions include the beliefs that the average person dislikes and tries to avoid work; prefers to be directed; prefers to avoid responsibility; and must be forced, controlled, or threatened with punishment to put forth the level of effort required by the firm. But Theory X, McGregor felt, could not explain all work behavior, nor could it relate to the higher levels of Maslow's ladder. **Theory Y**, a second set of assumptions suggested by McGregor, emphasizes human growth and self-direction rather than the authority concepts behind Theory X. Theory Y states that people do not dislike work and that external control and threats of punishment are not the only way people can be motivated to meet an organization's goals. A Theory Y–oriented manager believes that workers can be motivated by giving them a chance to be creative or by allowing them to work hard for a cause they believe in. Theory Y, therefore, emphasizes human growth and direction, in contrast to Theory X's emphasis on strong authority.

13. A third alphabet theory has entered today's management vocabulary. **Theory Z**, developed by Professor William Ouchi of UCLA, assumes that the best management involves workers at all levels. It highlights the Japanese tradition of treating employees like family, and assumes that workers with a sense of identity and belonging will be more motivated to produce better products. Because the company looks after workers' welfare, Maslow's lower-level needs are satisfied; working through the group process satisfies middle-level needs; and allowing workers to take responsibility satisfies Maslow's higher-level needs.

14. Managers attempting to motivate employees are faced with a number of challenges. The three most significant trends that managers must deal with are the aging of the work force, more women in the work force, and the work force becoming more culturally diverse.

15. Baby boomers are approaching mid-career, raising the average age of the work force. Additionally, as baby boomers often decided to marry late and to have fewer children, there is a declining number of young people entering the labor force.

16. The growing number of women in the work force means that there are more two-career households, making it more difficult for companies to transfer workers from one part of the country to another. Firms today are increasingly offering child-care assistance, maternity/paternity leaves, flexible work schedules, telecommuting, and cafeteria-style benefit plans.

17. As the U.S. work force becomes more culturally diverse, some firms have developed programs to sensitize managers to this issue and give them tips on making the most of what employees from different backgrounds have to offer.

18. How business is conducted in the Unites States is evolving daily, with some past practices, like reciprocal loyalty between employees and the companies they work for, changing. For example, it is now estimated that the average person changes jobs every three to seven years. Still further, the shift to a service economy has displaced many manufacturing employees, and less-educated workers must compete with incoming foreign workers for entry-level jobs.

19. As the work force and the economy change, so too must organizational cultures. The importance of job advancement as the main source of job satisfaction will have to be downplayed, and organizational cultures will have to become more open in order to improve morale.

20. Employee-oriented motivational techniques include **goal setting**, in which workers participate in setting their own goals; **behavior modification**, which encourages desirable actions and discourages undesirable ones; and **retraining**, which teaches new skills to workers who would otherwise be let go because of cutbacks and layoffs.

21. Job-oriented motivational techniques include (1) quality circles; (2) **job enrichment** and redesign, in which dull jobs are made more interesting (less specialized) and employees are given a keener sense of where their job fits into the organization's objectives; (3) **flextime**, in which workers are permitted, within limits, to choose their own hours of work; (4) **telecommuting** and home offices, which tend to increase worker productivity by 15 to 20 percent; (5) **work sharing**, where a few hours are cut from everybody's work week in order to minimize layoffs; and (6) **job sharing**, a voluntary solution permitting two workers to share a single full-time job and to split the salary and benefits.

22. Organization-oriented motivational techniques may also be employed; these include revamping the firm's objectives, strategies, or culture. Most organization-oriented motivators fall under the category of employee **empowerment**, also known as participative management (i.e., giving workers more decision-making power). Self-directed work teams are the basic on-the-job approach to empowerment and to be successful must be accompanied by an appropriate compensation plan that is tied to team results. For example, under **gain sharing**, bonuses are tied to team performance. Additionally, workers may be given a share of the company (**employee stock options**), so that they have a direct stake in the organization's profitability. In an extreme instance, a firm might seek new owners: its own employees.

KEY TERMS

human relations
leadership
communication
motivation
morale
classical theory of motivation
quota
piecework system
group norms
Hawthorne effect
Maslow's ladder
hygiene factors
motivators
expectancy theory

Theory X
Theory Y
Theory Z
goal setting
behavior modification
retraining
job enrichment
flextime
telecommuting
work sharing
job sharing
empowerment
gain sharing
employee stock options

KEY TERMS EXERCISE

Directions: On the line provided, place the letter of the statement on the right that most closely defines the key term.

_____ 1. Human relations

_____ 2. Motivation

_____ 3. Morale

_____ 4. Classical theory of motivation

_____ 5. Hygiene factors

a. Giving employees greater involvement in the day-to-day workings of a company.

b. A scheduling system in which workers are given the option of arriving for work at any point within a given time span.

_____ 6. Theory X

_____ 7. Theory Y

_____ 8. Expectancy theory

_____ 9. Behavior modification

_____ 10. Job enrichment

_____ 11. Flextime

_____ 12. Work sharing

_____ 13. Job sharing

_____ 14. Empowerment

c. Theory of worker motivation based on the belief that the amount of effort that an individual will expend on a task depends on the expected outcomes.

d. People dislike work and therefore must be threatened with punishment in order to be motivated.

e. The way people interact with one another.

f. Slicing a few hours off everybody's workweek and pay in order to minimize layoffs.

g. Work is natural, and people work toward those things to which they are committed.

h. The view that money is the predominant motivator in the work force.

i. Giving employees a reason to do the job and put forth their best performance.

j. Dividing work in an organization so that workers have more responsibility for the total process.

k. Splitting a single full-time job between two workers for their convenience.

l. Factors in the job environment that, when absent, result in job dissatisfaction.

m. A person's attitude toward the job and the organization.

n. Motivational technique of applying rewards for desirable actions and punishing undesirable actions.

ANSWERS TO KEY TERMS EXERCISE

	12. f (p. 253)	8. c (p. 239)	4. h (p. 236)
	11. b (p. 252)	7. g (p. 241)	3. m (p. 235)
14. a (p. 254)	10. j (p. 251)	6. d (p. 241)	2. l (p. 235)
13. k (p. 253)	9. n (p. 249)	5. l (p. 238)	1. e (p. 234)

SELF TEST

True-False Questions

_____ 1. Recognition of an employee's performance is a powerful motivating technique.

_____ 2. Very few changes have occurred in the work force over the years.

_____ 3. The success of a business depends upon the people who work for the business.

_____ 4. The classical theory of motivation holds that money is the only motivator.

_____ 5. Under expectancy theory every worker can be motivated through the same basic set of rewards.

_____ 6. Most workers today will work for only one or two companies over their work career.

_____ 7. To keep pace with changes in the marketplace and technology, it is necessary for companies to continuously train and retrain employees.

_____ 8. Maslow's ladder is based on the premise that people have many needs and act to fulfill the needs that they have yet to be satisfied.

_____ 9. Money is effective in satisfying a person's social needs.

_____ 10. Improving hygiene factors tends to increase employee motivation.

_____ 11. Letting workers participate in making decisions increases the productivity and quality of work.

_____ 12. Theory Z management states that managers are the only ones capable of decision making.

_____ 13. Management should strive to develop a situation in which workers feel that they have something to gain by doing their jobs the way the organization wants them done.

_____ 14. According to Maslow's hierarchy of needs, once lower-level needs have been met, a person will strive to fulfill higher-level needs.

_____ 15. Esteem needs are the highest level of needs.

_____ 16. A good health insurance and pension plan helps workers meet their safety needs.

_____ 17. Theory Z tries to satisfy the employees' needs on all levels.

_____ 18. Given the growing percentage of the work force from diverse cultural and ethnic backgrounds, managers face a challenge of communicating with a more diverse group and facilitating cooperation and harmony among employees.

_____ 19. If goal setting is to be an effective motivational technique, workers should be allowed to participate in setting their own goals.

_____ 20. Motivational problems with all workers in a certain department or class of jobs are likely to be caused by the job structure itself rather than the employees.

_____ 21. Making the employees shareholders, or sharing the profits with them, can be an effective motivational technique.

_____ 22. Telecommuting is appropriate for almost any type of job.

_____ 23. Empowering work teams is not likely to succeed unless it is complemented by an appropriate compensation plan.

Multiple Choice Questions

_____ 1. The benefit of a good human relations program in a company is
   a. less employee turnover.
   b. more productive workers.
   c. fewer employee complaints.
   d. that managers receive spiritual or psychological reward for knowing they're treating their workers right.
   e. all of the above.

_____ 2. A good human relations program requires
           a. leadership.
           b. communication.
           c. motivation.
           d. all of the above.

_____ 3. Which of the following is *not* an effect of baby boomers on the work force?
           a. There is greater acceptance of authority by workers.
           b. Workers are more interested in meaningful participation on the job.
           c. Workers want to be considered as individuals.
           d. There is stronger competition for jobs and promotions.
           e. All of the above are correct.

_____ 4. Women in the work force have made
           a. transfers to other parts of the country more difficult.
           b. working overtime more difficult.
           c. child care a critical issue.
           d. employment decisions more complex.
           e. all of the above.

_____ 5. Which of the following is a change occurring within the economy that is affecting the manner in which businesses operate?
           a. the rate of technological advance
           b. work force demographics.
           c. the shift from an industry-based to a service-based economy
           d. all of the above

_____ 6. Which of the following presents the correct order of Maslow's hierarchy of human needs?
           a. physiological, safety, social, esteem, self-realization
           b. physiological, social, safety, esteem, self-realization
           c. social, physiological, safety, self-realization, esteem
           d. physiological, safety, esteem, social, self-realization

_____ 7. Which of the following is *not* a hygiene factor?
           a. company policy
           b. personal responsibility
           c. working conditions
           d. job security

_____ 8. To be successful, a company must convince its workers that
           a. the needs of the company are supreme.
           b. the needs of the individual are supreme.
           c. both needs of the company and of the person can be fulfilled.
           d. neither the needs of the company nor the individual can be completely met.

_____ 9. According to the classical theory of motivation, you motivate workers by
           a. providing them with a better work environment.
           b. showing them how to make more money by doing things the company way.
           c. showering them with a lot of psychic rewards.
           d. asking them politely to be more productive.
           e. doing none of the above.

_____ 10. The need for status and respect is
   a. a physiological need.
   b. a safety need.
   c. a social need.
   d. an esteem need.
   e. a need for self-realization.

_____ 11. Which of the following is *not* one of the characteristics of Theory X?
   a. The average person is creative.
   b. The average person has little ambition.
   c. The average person dislikes work and will try to avoid it.
   d. The average person must be forced to work toward organizational objectives.

_____ 12. According to Theory Y,
   a. work is a natural part of life.
   b. money is not the only motivation.
   c. people seek out responsibility.
   d. the rewards of achievement determine the amount of commitment a person has to achieving objectives.
   e. all of the above.

_____ 13. Which of the following is *not* one of the basic assumptions of expectancy theory?
   a. The amount of employee effort depends upon an individual's belief that he or she can do the task.
   b. The amount of employee effort depends upon the person's level within the organization.
   c. The amount of employee effort depends upon a belief of being rewarded for the effort.
   d. The amount of employee effort depends upon whether the reward is perceived as being worth the effort.

_____ 14. Determining the rewards valued by each worker, then establishing attainable performance levels and linking rewards to performance, is the premise of which motivational theory?
   a. Theory X
   b. Theory Y
   c. Theory Z
   d. expectancy theory

_____ 15. Which of the following is *not* an advantage of telecommuting to a company?
   a. Establishing workstations in the home office is fairly inexpensive.
   b. Office space costs are reduced.
   c. Disabled workers can be employed more easily.
   d. An employee who might otherwise leave can be retained.

_____ 16. One viable alternative to worker layoffs involves
   a. the promotion of employees to mid-level management.
   b. the retraining of employees for new positions.
   c. the formation of quality circles.
   d. the utilization of flextime.

_____ 17. Which of the following is an example of a job-oriented technique for motivating employees?
   a. quality circles
   b. job enrichment and redesign
   c. flextime
   d. work sharing and job sharing
   e. all of the above

____ 18. Empowerment, giving employees greater responsibility and greater accountability for the company's performance, has resulted in
   a.   reduced labor costs.
   b.   increased quality in products.
   c.   increased productivity.
   d.   improved morale.
   e.   all of the above.

____ 19. Rewarding workers with dollar bonuses given according to team effort in areas that employees can directly influence is known as
   a.   employee-owned business.
   b.   employee stock option.
   c.   gain sharing.
   d.   empowerment.

Completion Questions

1.   Effective human relations in an organization requires strong _____, effective _____, and

     _____.

2.   Expectancy theory states that a worker's motivation is a function of these questions: (1) "Can I do the task?"

     (2) _____ and (3) "Will it be worth my while?"

3.   _____ has created a need for companies to create a sensitivity toward ethnicity, cultural background, gender, age, race, disability, and sexual orientation.

4.   The classical theory of motivation holds that _____ is the sole motivator of a person in the work force.

5.   Increased productivity due simply to paying more attention to employees is known as the _____.

6.   Health Insurance, pension plans, and savings all help meet a person's _____ needs.

7.   Hygiene factors are a part of the job _____, while motivators are a part of _____.

8.   Theory X emphasizes _____, while Theory Y emphasizes _____ and self-direction.

9.   Behavior modification involves _____ desirable acts and _____ undesirable actions.

10. If many workers in a department or in a certain type of job are having motivational problems, the problem is

     probably not with the people but with the _____.

11. Worker motivation can be increased through _____, where an employee's job is expanded to have more responsibility over the total process.

12. Reducing the number of hours worked by everyone in order to minimize layoffs is known as

     _____, while two workers sharing the same job is known as _____.

13. Establishing an office in one's home with a computer link to the main office is known as _____.

14. The nine C's of expectancy theory are capacity (the individual needs the capacity to perform the job well), _____ (the individual must believe he or she can do the job well), challenges (the individual has to work hard to perform the job well), _____ (the individual knows the difference between good and bad performance), _____ (the individual believes that the manager will deliver on promises), consistency (the individual believes that effort is awarded appropriately), _____ (good perfor-mance is rewarded), cost (the effort needed to be rewarded, and communication (the manager communicates with employees).

15. Empowerment entails getting workers more involved in the actual workings of the company by forming self-directed _____, who set their own goals, solve problems, and manage their own work.

PROJECT

Employee Motivation

   Employee morale and motivation are important inputs into a successful operation as a company's employees tend to be its most valuable resource. Yet achieving and maintaining employee motivation is a difficult task that will not just happen, but rather requires a well thought out program. This project is designed to provide insight on how companies attempt to motivate their employees.
   Employee motivation is a function of the leadership style, communications, and motivation techniques employed. The type of motivational techniques that will be most effective will vary by the type of business and level within that business. For example, the military is more autocratic in style, while an advertising agency cre-ative staff requires a more laissez-faire approach. Likewise, the motivation approach for production workers is dif-ferent from that for top-level executives.
   For this project, interview a manager at a supervisory level and question him or her in terms of leadership style, communications, and motivation techniques employed. This supervisor may be at a local manufacturing company, retail store, or service firm, such as a fast-food outlet. Some examples of companies you might consider are Apple Computers, Avon, Domino Pizza, Famous Amos Chocolate Chip Cookies, Federal Express, Hallmark Cards, Hewlett-Packard, Holiday Inn, IBM, 3M Company, Nabisco, Pillsbury Co., WAL-Mart, and Xerox Corporation.
   You can use the following as a guide for your interview.

General Questions

   1. What is the current level of employee morale and motivation?

   2. What type of programs and activities does the company do to develop and maintain employee motivation?

Communication Questions

   1. How is communication with employees maintained?

   2. Are newsletters, bulletin boards, paycheck envelope stuffers, or other such devices employed?

   3. What mechanisms exist for employees to communicate with management?

Motivation Methods

   1. What techniques or methods are used to motivate employees? How effective are these techniques?

2. Are any of the following methods employed?
    a. goal setting
    b. behavior modification
    c. retraining
    d. quality circles
    e. job enrichment
    f. flextime
    g. job sharing

Based on your interview, evaluate the effectiveness of the company's employee motivation program. As part of the evaluation, address the following issues:

1. What type of leadership style does the manager seem to use (Theory X, Y, or Z)?

2. Which of Maslow's needs would seem to be most important to the employees? Are the motivational methods of the company fulfilling these needs?

3. To what extent are the hygiene factors being met?

4. To what extent are the motivators being employed?

5. Are there certain motivational techniques that should be applied but are not being used? Are there some techniques being used that should not be?

6. Would you want to work for this company under this manager?

Chapter 10

Human Resource Management

LEARNING OBJECTIVES

1. State the six main functions of human resource departments.

2. Identify six stages in the hiring process.

3. List at least three types of training programs.

4. Identify two general ways of compensating workers.

5. Describe the two possible components of employee pay.

6. Explain at least four standard employee benefits and services.

7. Describe three ways an employee's status may change.

8. Distinguish between the two reasons that employment may be terminated.

OUTLINE

I.   The process of human resource management

   A.   The scope of human resource management
      1.   What personnel management is
      2.   Why human resource management is becoming more complex
      3.   The job of the human resource manager
      4.   What human resource departments do

   B.   Human resource planning
      1.   Why planning is a critical step
      2.   Forecasting
         a.   Estimates of demand for workers
         b.   Estimates of supply of workers
         c.   The changing labor market
         d.   Strategic staffing techniques
            (1) The part-time labor force
      3.   Job analysis
         a.   What job analysis is
         b.   Methods of performing job analysis
         c.   The job description and job specification

   C.   Recruiting and selecting new employees
      1.   The job of recruiters
      2.   Stages in the hiring process
      3.   Interviewing
         a.   How to be a good interviewer
      4.   Testing
         a.   What tests are used for
         b.   Types of tests

     5. Hiring and the law
        a. What questions cannot be asked
        b. The issue of drug testing

  D. Training and development
     1. Orientation programs
     2. Training and retraining programs
        a. Specific company training programs

  E. Appraising employee performance
     1. Performance appraisal systems
        a. Problems with appraisal systems

II. Compensation

  A. Wage and salary administration
     1. Wages versus salaries
     2. Incentive programs
        a. Bonuses and commissions
        b. Profit sharing and goal sharing
           (1) Pay for performance
        c. Knowledge-based pay

  B. Employee benefits and services
     1. The scope of fringe benefits and perks
     2. Insurance plans and unemployment benefits
        a. Unemployment insurance
     3. Retirement benefits
        a. Social security
        b. Pension plans
        c. Pension guarantees
        d. Current pension issues
     4. Employee stock ownership plans (ESOPs)
     5. Family benefits
     6. Other fringe benefits
     7. Flexible benefits
     8. Health and safety programs
        a. Employee assistance programs

III. Changes in employment status

  A. Why workers leave their jobs

  B. Promoting and reassigning workers
     1. Pitfalls of promotion
     2. The issue of relocation
     3. Middle manager advancement

  C. Terminating employment
     1. Reasons for termination
        a. Restructuring
        b. Downsizing
     2. Layoffs
        a. Easing the pain of layoffs
           (1) Outplacement
        b. An alternative to layoffs
     3. Firings and "employment at will"
        a. Employee lawsuits

   D.   Retiring workers
      1.   Mandatory retirement
      2.   Early retirement
         a.   Worker buyout

MAJOR POINTS TO REMEMBER

1.   The specialized task of obtaining the workers a company needs and then overseeing their training, evaluation, and compensation is known as **human resource management,** formerly called **personnel management.** This new name better reflects the importance of the work force in helping a firm achieve its goals.

2.   Human resource management is becoming more complex as the work force, the economy, and corporate cultures are changing at an ever increasing pace. For example, changes in technology have resulted in mismatches between workers' skills and managements' needs.

3.   The first step in staffing a business organization is human resource planning. A miscalculation in planning, for example, might leave a firm without enough staff to produce a sufficient quantity of product to meet consumer demand. Therefore, the organization must forecast demand, then determine the numbers and types of workers that will be required to meet this demand. Factors to be considered include determining whether workers with the required skills can be found in the general work force (i.e., the firm must estimate the supply of available workers).

4.   Almost all new jobs created in the next ten years are expected to be for college graduates. But by the year 2000, the largest share of new workers may be minorities and immigrants with generally low levels of education.

5.   Today's rapidly changing business conditions have resulted in many firms turning to part-time and temporary workers when additional staffing is needed. Such usage allows companies to easily and quickly add workers when business picks up and let go workers when business slows down. Approximately 85 percent of all U.S. firms today use the services of temporary agencies.

6.   **Job analysis** is the process by which jobs are studied to determine the tasks and dynamics involved. Questions that must be asked include the qualifications and skills required to do the job, as well as the actual tasks to be performed. The information needed for job analysis may be obtained by interviewing employees or supervisors, by direct observing of employees, or by asking workers to keep diaries describing their work.

7.   After completing the job analysis, the human resource manager may develop a **job description,** which is a specific statement of the tasks involved in the job and the conditions under which the holder of the job will work. A **job specification** may also be devised, that is, a statement describing the kind of person who would be best for the job, including skills, education, and previous work experience.

8.   Using the job specification, **recruiters** (specialists on the human resource staff responsible for obtaining candidates) try to match it to a person. The person may be found within the organization or outside.

9.   Although the actual stages of the hiring process may vary from one firm to another, most companies go through certain basic processes. A small number of qualified candidates may be chosen on the basis of a standard application form and/or on the basis of their **résumés** (summary of education, experience, interests, and other personal data compiled by an applicant). It should be noted that questions on an application form that are not directly job-related are illegal in some states because they might be used to discriminate. Each candidate would then be interviewed and may be asked to take a test or series of tests. An in-depth interview with the most likely candidates may follow; then the candidates would be interviewed by the individual who, if they were hired, would be their supervisor. Reference checks and a physical examination may also be required.

10. Good interviewers are able to build an atmosphere of trust and rapport between themselves and the interviewee. They keep the conversation focused on job-related issues, so that the interviewee's qualifications for the job can be determined.

11.   While testing is a much-debated aspect of the hiring process, companies are increasingly using preemployment testing to determine which applicants are suited to the job and will be worth the expense of hiring and training. Three types of testing are common today: job-skills testing, psychological testing, and drug testing.

12.   Job-skills tests are designed to determine the competency or specific abilities needed to perform a job. A typing test given to an applicant for a secretarial position would be an example of a job-skills test. In contrast, psychological tests usually take the form of pencil-and-paper questionnaires filled out by applicants.

13.   An increasing number of companies are requiring that job applicants (and current employees) be tested for the presence of illegal substances. According to the American Management Association, more than 60 percent of U.S. firms now conduct drug testing, and 96 percent of these firms will not hire an applicant who tests positive. The legal aspects of drug testing vary from state to state and continue to change. Even the government requires some federal workers and employees of federal contractors to undergo drug screening.

14.   Regulations and guidelines currently exist to ensure that application forms, interviews, and tests are fair to minority members and women. The information sought from applicants must not violate EEOC regulations; however, questions about marital status, age, religion, or credit status may be asked if they relate to a bona fide occupational qualification (BFOQ).

15.   Firms have **orientation** programs for new workers to ensure that they understand the company's goals, policies, and procedures. Most often, such programs include information about the company, its employment policies, standards of employee conduct, company benefit programs, and job duties and responsibilities.

16.   Many firms also conduct training and retraining programs. Training may take place at the work site or in a classroom setting. Additionally, as the pool of qualified entry-level workers continues to shrink, companies are finding it necessary to provide new workers with remedial education (e.g., basic reading and math skills). Some firms contribute money to educational institutions and then let the schools provide education and training to employees.

17.   Companies today are developing highly structured **performance appraisal** systems to provide the necessary objective worker evaluations. Such systems include standards, in writing, so that both supervisors and workers understand what is expected of them. The biggest problem with such systems, however, is finding a way to measure performance, as it is not always an easy criterion to judge.

18.   In return for their services, workers receive **compensation,** which can include payments, benefits, and employer services. For many blue-collar and some white-collar workers, compensation takes the form of **wages,** a payment based on a calculation of the number of hours worked or the number of units produced. Other workers are paid a **salary,** which bases compensation on a unit of time such as a week, a month, or a year, rather than an hour. Salaried workers typically receive no pay for working overtime.

19.   To increase productivity, firms often offer workers **incentives** linked to levels of production or profitability. Both salaried and wage-earning workers may receive a **bonus,** a payment in addition to the regular wage or salary. Some companies, for example, pay an annual Christmas bonus. **Commissions,** payments made to an employee based on sales made, may also be used as an addition to a worker's salary or as an employee's sole method of compensation.

20.   **Profit sharing,** whereby employees receive a portion of the company's profits, is used by many firms today. If the rewards are tied not to overall profits but to cost savings resulting from meeting goals for quality, safety, and customer service, the program is called **goal sharing.** One goal-sharing approach, **pay for performance,** asks workers to accept a lower base pay in return for being well rewarded when production goals are met.

21.   A compensation approach being considered by some firms today is **knowledge-based pay** (or skill-based pay). Under this system, a worker's pay is keyed to his or her knowledge and abilities, rather than the job per se.

22. Financial benefits other than wages, salaries, and incentives that are provided for workers are called **fringe benefits.** Executives, for example, may receive company cars or country club memberships as **perks.** Companies may also provide health and safety programs for workers. Fringe benefits may account for well over a third of total pay.

23. The most common fringe benefit is insurance. Firms negotiate with insurance companies for group insurance plans for workers and then pay all or most of the costs. Employers also pay the costs of **unemployment insurance** and contribute to company-sponsored **pension plans.** Because of the importance of pensions, the Employee Retirement Income Security Act was passed by Congress in 1974 to guarantee that workers receive their retirement benefits regardless of what may happen to the company they worked for. However, in the uncertain economy of the 1990s, companies became creative about substituting other assets for cash payments to retirees (e.g., stocks and bonds). Unisex legislation may further strain pension programs.

24. Another fringe benefit program is the **employee stock ownership plan (ESOP),** in which a firm places some stock in trust for all or some of its workers. This plan has worked well in some companies and poorly in others.

25. Working parents are increasingly looking for such "family" benefits as unpaid leaves to take care of new babies, day-care assistance, and care for aging parents. Other fringe benefits given to employees include paid holidays, sick pay, overtime pay, and paid vacations.

26. A newer concept in providing fringe benefits is the flexible "cafeteria" approach, in which a worker may pick benefits up to a certain dollar amount to meet his or her particular needs, rather than having to accept a single benefit package provided to all workers. About 25 percent of large firms offer this approach, and it seems to be gaining in popularity.

27. Many firms have developed health and safety programs in order to take a more active role in maintaining employee health. Such programs attempt to keep health-related losses to a minimum and encourage workers to exercise, to eat the right foods, and to give up smoking. Some companies have also instituted **employee assistance programs** for workers with personal problems, like drug and alcohol dependence.

28. When a worker decides to leave the job, the vacancy may be filled from outside or from within the company. Promotion from within aids employee morale because workers see that they have a chance for advancement. However, the biggest pitfall is that people may be given jobs that are beyond their abilities, as the new position may require a set of skills different from those needed for the former job.

29. Another important issue today is relocation. Increasingly, workers are unwilling to be relocated because they belong to two-career families or are committed to community activities and quality-of-life issues. Also, selling a home and purchasing a new one in another locale is often an expensive undertaking. To offset these objections, companies today often help spouses find jobs in new locations and soften the financial ordeal of selling and buying homes.

30. Middle managers are often finding fewer opportunities for advancement, as companies tend to employ a flatter organizational structure. Some firms are offering these managers "lateral transfers" or suggesting challenging tasks in unfamiliar areas to help them broaden their experience.

31. Sometimes employees must either be laid off because of cutbacks or fired for poor performance. This is known as **termination.** Some companies faced with decreasing business have avoided mass layoffs through **restructuring** (e.g., cutting administrative costs and freezing wages) and **downsizing** (reducing the size of the work force).

32. In the past, a firm was free to lay off whomever it wished. However, recent lawsuits by workers have claimed that the layoffs were based on age, gender, religion, or other discriminatory factors. Additionally, layoffs based on **seniority** (which was thought to be a discrimination-free system) have also been challenged in court, as women and minorities have usually been the last workers hired and the first to be let go. Many firms now provide **outplacement** services (job-hunting and other assistance for laid-off workers).

33. There are businesses that have adopted a no-layoff policy, also known as guaranteed employment. Workers in such firms are often highly motivated to be productive because they know they will not work themselves out of a job.

34. Employees not covered by a contract may be fired "at will," except in cases of discrimination or as punishment for union activity. However, several recent court cases have ruled that any such firing must be done "fairly." To avoid lawsuits over firings, some firms today have statements on their application forms or in company handbooks that affirm the "employment at will" notion. Some employees, though, have won **wrongful discharge** suits against former employers, claiming that documents issued by the company stated that employees may not be fired without proper warning and an opportunity to remedy whatever problems may exist.

35. Retirement is also an issue today, as the U.S. population ages rapidly. Some firms have **mandatory retirement** policies that require a worker to retire when he or she reaches a certain age. Workers have gone to court to put an end to such policies, and the 1986 Age Discrimination in Employment Act prohibits mandatory retirement for most employees. The Federal Age Discrimination Act of 1987 makes it illegal to discriminate against anyone between the ages of forty and sixty five.

36. Some firms attempt to cut labor costs by offering employees nearing retirement an incentive to leave the firm. Usually the program, known as a **worker buyout,** involves financial incentives. Early retirement programs are also on the rise.

KEY TERMS

human resource management
personnel management
job analysis
job description
job specification
recruiters
résumés
orientation
performance appraisal
compensation
wages
salary
incentives
bonus
commissions
profit sharing
goal sharing

pay for performance
knowledge-based pay
fringe benefits
perks
unemployment insurance
pension plans
employee stock ownership plan
employee assistance programs
termination
restructuring
downsizing
seniority
outplacement
wrongful discharge
mandatory retirement
worker buyout

KEY TERMS EXERCISE

Directions: On the line provided, place the letter of the statement on the right that most closely defines the key term.

____d____ 1. Human resource management

____E____ 2. Job analysis

____L____ 3. Job description

____a____ 4. Résumé

____r____ 5. Performance appraisal system

a. Payments to employees for their work.

b. A payment to workers who achieve a certain level of sales.

c. The stock placed in trust for employees, with each employee entitled to a share.

d. The specialized function of planning how to obtain employees, prepare them for work, oversee their performance, and provide compensation.

_A_ 6. Compensation

_N_ 7. Wage

_I_ 8. Salary

_K_ 9. Bonus

_B_ 10. Commission _B_

_J_ 11. Profit sharing

_M_ 12. Production sharing

_g_ 13. Fringe benefits

_C_ 14. Employee stock ownership plan

_P_ 15. Knowledge-based pay

_O_ 16. Employee assistance program

e. The process by which jobs are studied to determine the tasks involved in performing them.

f. Evaluaton of an employee's work according to specific criteria.

g. Compensation other than wages, salaries, and incentive programs.

h. A summary of a person's education, experience, interests, and other personal data compiled by the applicant for a job.

i. Compensation based on time worked for a week, month, or year rather than for an hour.

j. A system whereby employees receive a portion of the company's profits.

k. A cash payment in addition to regular wages or salary.

l. A specific statement of the tasks involved in a job and the working conditions.

m. Plan for rewarding employees not on the basis of overall profits but in relation to cost savings resulting from increased output.

n. Cash payments for services based on the number of hours worked or the number of units produced.

o. Company-sponsored counseling or referrals for employees with personal problems.

p. Pay that is keyed to employees' knowledge and abilities rather than to their jobs per se.

ANSWERS TO KEY TERMS EXERCISE

16. o (p. 283)	12. m (p. 277)	8. i (p. 276)	4. h (p. 267)
15. p (p. 277)	11. j (p. 277)	7. n (p. 276)	3. l (p. 266)
14. c (p. 231)	10. b (p. 277)	6. a (p. 275)	2. e (p. 265)
13. g (p. 275)	9. k (p. 277)	5. f (p. 274)	1. d (p. 262)

SELF TEST

True-False Questions

_T_ 1. The success of a business depends upon the people who work for the business.

_T_ 2. Changes in technology and in the business environment are creating a mismatch between workers' skills and employers' needs.

_F_ 3. Forecasting the supply of workers is a fairly easy job for human resource managers.

_T_ 4. Most companies use more than one source when recruiting.

_F_ 5. Employment tests have been proven to be flawless in selecting employees.

_T_ 6. The biggest problem of a performance appraisal system is finding a way to measure performance.

_F_ 7. Employees are more willing to accept transfers to other parts of the country today than in the past.

_F_ 8. Deciding who to lay off during a business downturn is usually an easy decision.

_F_ 9. For the most part, a company has a right to fire employees "at will."

_T_ 10. Worker buyouts, even though expensive, are more effective than layoffs because of the increased employee morale.

_F_ 11. Profit sharing is best suited for production workers, and production sharing is best suited for executives.

_F_ 12. A salaried employee earns overtime pay for the extra time he or she works.

_F_ 13. Fringe benefits usually make up a small portion of an employee's total compensation.

_F_ 14. Employers are required by law to provide pensions for their employees.

_T_ 15. Strong employee health and safety programs make economic sense as well as being good from a humanitarian perspective.

_T_ *16. Finding a balance between employer and employee rights is a difficult matter.

_T_ 17. Employee assistance programs should be voluntary and confidential.

Multiple Choice Questions

_____ 1. The human resources manager is responsible for
   a. forecasting the personnel needs of the company.
   b. hiring new workers.
   c. training and evaluating employees.
   d. administering wages, salaries, and employee benefits.
   e. all of the above.

_____ 2. Which of the following is *not* a problem for human resource managers?
   a. retaining good workers in the face of pay freezes
   b. laying off workers equitably
   c. dealing with complex employee benefits
   d. meeting the challenge of equal opportunity in employment
   e. all of the above

_____ 3. Questions such as, "What tasks are involved in the job?" "What qualifications and skills are needed?" and "What kind of setting does the job take place in?" would be part of a job
   a. analysis.
   b. description.
   c. specification.
   d. evaluation.

____   4.   A job analysis is a statement of
     a.   the task to be performed in a job.
     b.   the skills, education, and previous experience required of a person to do a job.
     c.   the duties and responsibilities involved in a job, and the skills required to fulfill those duties and responsibilities.
     d.   none of the above.
     (e.) all of the above.

____   5.   Recruiters look for potential employees
     a.   among employees.
     b.   through private employment agencies.
     c.   through schools.
     d.   through newspaper advertising.
     (e.) through all of the above sources.

____   6.   The Equal Employment Opportunity Commission handles complaints concerning discrimination on the basis of
     a.   religion.
     b.   national origin.
     c.   sex.
     d.   race.
     (e.) all of the above.

____   7.   Employment tests can be used to measure a person's
     a.   ability.
     b.   intelligence.
     c.   aptitude.
     d.   personality.
     (e.) all of the above

____   8.   Which of the following is *not* an advantage of promoting from within?
     a.   lower recruiting costs
     b.   less orientation needed
     c.   higher morale
     d.   more success in getting the best employee

____   *9. Being a good employee requires
     a.   being a professional.
     b.   using time wisely.
     c.   using discretion.
     d.   having respect for your job.
     (e.) all of the above.

____   10. Paying employees according to the new knowledge and abilities they acquire, rather than their jobs per se, is a(n)
     a.   pay for performance system.
     (b.) knowledge-based system.
     c.   job rotation pay system.
     d.   information-based pay system.

____   11. Paying workers a lower base pay but rewarding them if they reach production targets, or some other goal, is a(n)
     (a.) pay for performance system.
     b.   knowledge-based pay system.
     c.   bonus payment plan.
     d.   commission.

Completion Questions

1. Human resource planning involves forecasting _____ and _____ of the numbers and kinds of workers at various points in the future.

2. After conducting a job analysis, the _____ can be developed, which lists tasks to be performed in the job, and the _____ can be written, which indicates the skills required to perform the job.

3. _____ is the process of finding potential employees to fill positions.

4. The hiring process consists of soliciting applicants, collecting _____ forms and/or resumes, interviewing, conducting _____ checks, evaluating candidates, and selecting one candidate for the job.

5. Providing information on the company's history, general policies, and standards and describing various employee benefits is a part of the _____ process.

6. Employees can be terminated either by _____ due to business downturns or by _____ because of poor performance.

7. Companies that provide financial incentives to employees to encourage their leaving are engaging in an _____.

8. Sales representatives are most commonly paid by _____.

9. Health and life insurance are a common type of _____.

PROJECT

Selecting Applicants

   Finding qualified personnel is not always an easy task. Before seeking applicants, it is important to know what you are looking for. This project is designed to provide insight into the selection process.
   Assume you have just been appointed the sales manager of a newly formed computer company. Your company sells personal computers and software to small businesses. Your first task as the sales manager is to recruit a sales force. You have broken down the task into several steps which you must complete.

1. Preparation of a job description.
2. Preparation of a job specification.
3. Development of sources of applicants.

   After you have completed the above activities, assume the following four individuals have applied for a position. Which of the four, if any, will you hire? Provide complete justification for your reasons for hiring or not hiring each individual. (Relate your reasons back to your job description and specifications.)

Applicant 1:
   Name: Jeff Stanley
   Age: 38
   Experience: Managed a computer operation while in the military, from which he has just retired. No previous selling experience.
   Education: High school and technical training in computers.

Applicant 2:

Name: Linda Bartel

Age: 23

Experience: Retail sales clerk at local department store. Active in school clubs and organizations.

Education: Just completing a bachelor's degree in business with a 3.75 GPA.

Applicant 3:

Name: Tom Downs

Age: 52

Experience: Over twenty-five years of experience in selling office equipment and supplies to small businesses.

Education: Bachelor's degree in business.

Applicant 4:

Name: Janet Allen

Age: 25

Experience: No previous sales experience. Has held several odd jobs while attending school. Extremely active in various school organizations and community projects.

Education: Master's degree in political science.

Each of the four applicants has a pleasant personality and should have no trouble interrelating with the customers. Only two people are needed right now. Which, if any, should be selected?

Chapter 11

Union-Management Relations

LEARNING OBJECTIVES

1. Identify two main types of labor unions.

2. Outline the organizational structure of unions.

3. Identify the two main steps unions take to become the bargaining agent for a group of workers.

4. Describe the four main stages in collective bargaining.

5. Identify four options that unions have if negotiations with management break down.

6. Identify five options that management has if negotiations with the union break down.

7. List five general issues that may be addressed in a labor contract.

8. Describe four major practices that management and unions are using to respond to changes in the structure of the economy.

OUTLINE

I. Labor organizations in the U.S. economy

    A. Why workers form labor unions

    B. A history of unions
       1. Craft unions
       2. The development of nationwide unions
          a. The Knights of Labor
          b. The American Federation of Labor (AFL)
          c. The growth of industrial unions
             (1) The Congress of Industrial Organizations (CIO)

    C. The labor movement today
       1. The erosion of union strength
       2. The shift in American industry
       3. New union directions
       4. Why workers join
          a. Conditions under which workers seek out unions
       5. How unions are structured
          a. The composition of national unions
             (1) Locals (or local unions)
             (2) Labor federations
          b. The labor union hierarchy
             (1) Shop stewards and business agents
       6. How unions organize
          a. The use of authorization cards
          b. The role of the National Labor Relations Board
             (1) Certification elections

   7. Why unions are challenged or removed
       a. How companies try to head off unionization
       b. Decertification elections
           (1) Possible reasons for union losses

II. The collective bargaining process

   A. Preparing to meet

   B. Meeting and reaching an agreement
       1. The negotiating process
           a. Permissive and mandatory subjects
           b. Mediation and arbitration

   C. Voting and ratifying a contract

III. When negotiations break down

   A. The yellow-dog contract and the blacklist

   B. Labor's options
       1. Slowdown
       2. Strikes and picket lines
       3. Boycotts
           a. Secondary boycotts
       4. Financial and political influence
       5. Publicity

   C. Management's options
       1. Strikebreakers and management-run operations
       2. Lockouts
       3. Injunctions
       4. Industry pacts and organizations

IV. The collective bargaining agreement

   A. Basic contract issues
       1. Union security and management rights
           a. Types of "shops"
       2. Compensation
           a. Wage rates
               (1) Pattern bargaining
               (2) Two-tier wage plans
               (3) Cost-of-living adjustment (COLA)
               (4) Profit sharing
               (5) Employee benefits
       3. Job security
           a. The lifetime security issue
           b. Automation as an issue
       4. Work rules and job descriptions
       5. Worker safety and health

   B. Administration of the agreement
       1. Grievances and due process
           a. Arbitration and grievance mediation

V. Union-management relations in a changing environment

  A. Plant shutdowns and bankruptcy
    1. Advantages of filing for bankruptcy

  B. Employee rights without unions
    1. The changing role of government

  C. Worker ownership
    1. The employee stock ownership plan (ESOP)

  D. New directions for unions
    1. How unions might remain healthy

MAJOR POINTS TO REMEMBER

1. Because owners of businesses wish to use resources as they see fit and because workers feel they should have job security and rewards commensurate with their contributions, the potential for conflict is always present. Therefore, workers join together to form **labor unions**, which are organizations of workers established to advance their members' interests. A labor union changes the supply-and-demand equation by representing a firm's supply of labor (i.e., workers). While a single worker might be easily replaced, a whole group of workers (i.e., union members) cannot.

2. The first union in the United States was formed in 1792 by shoemakers in Philadelphia to discuss matters of common interest. Other unions appeared during the next several decades, and like the shoemaker's union, they were **craft unions** (i.e., made up of skilled artisans belonging to a single profession or craft and concerned only with trade-related matters).

3. As better transportation reduced shipping costs and helped create national markets, local craft unions joined together to form national craft unions. In 1869, several of these national organizations banded together as the Knights of Labor. However, several member unions became dissatisfied with this organization because its leadership stressed moral betterment rather than improvements in wages and working conditions. The 1886 Haymarket Riot in Chicago also turned public opinion against the union. By 1890, the union movement in the United States was controlled by the American Federation of Labor (AFL), which had been founded in 1886.

4. Labor union membership expanded greatly in the 1930s, especially among unskilled workers. Legislation passed during the presidency of Franklin D. Roosevelt helped, as did the work of an unofficial Committee for Industrial Organization, which was established by the AFL in 1935 for the purpose of organizing **industrial unions** (i.e., unions representing both skilled and unskilled workers). Eventually, this committee developed into the Congress of Industrial Organizations (CIO), an independent federation of industrial unions.

5. Unions also grew during World War II, as they won concessions from management in return for no-strike pledges. However, after the war, labor's demands resulted in a number of severe strikes, and Congress reacted in 1947 by passing legislation to restrict some union practices.

6. In 1955, the AFL and CIO merged their 16 million members, and union membership began to level off. In the late 1950s, alleged corruption and links to organized crime hurt the image of unions, and Congress passed new laws to regulate union activities. Union membership has been declining since this time (although through the late 1970s unions did continue to have considerable clout in the U.S. economy).

7. In the past decade, union strength has badly eroded as a result of its tarnished image, a leadership sometimes out of touch with the changing work force, deregulation, and unsympathetic administrations. Whereas unions represented over 40 percent of U.S. workers in 1955, today they represent only 16 percent.

8. The large shift in American industry has also hurt unions. Older blue-collar "smokestack" industries have been on the decline as a result of inefficient production methods and lower-cost foreign competitors. Consequently, one-fifth of all large unionized companies have gone bankrupt since 1980. Furthermore, the newer high-technology service industries are often harder to unionize. Unions are not giving up, however,

and are trying to obtain members among professionals, white-collar workers, women, and youth groups. Unionized public employees are also on the rise.

9. Companies that have most successfully resisted unionization appear to practice a participative management style and feel a sense of responsibility toward workers. But workers want to be unionized if they are deeply dissatisfied with their current job and working conditions, believe that unionization can improve job conditions, and are willing to overcome the generally negative stereotype of unions. Recent studies indicate that women, minorities, and low-wage workers are most likely to be interested in unionization.

10. **National unions** (whose members are employed in a particular craft or industry) usually consist of several **locals** (or local unions), each representing workers in a certain geographic area or facility. The national union organizes new areas or industries, negotiates industrywide contracts, provides strike aid, and helps each local negotiate individual contracts. Local unions provide financial support to the national union (i.e., dues), submit contracts for approval, and send representatives to national conventions.

11. Groups consisting of a variety of national unions (and local unions not affiliated with a national union) are known as **labor federations**. The AFL-CIO is the premier example; its two main jobs are promoting the labor movement's political objectives and assisting its member unions in their collective bargaining efforts.

12. Both national unions and federations have officers and staffs of experts. The "rank and file" members of each local union elect a president, and each department or facility also elects a **shop steward**, who acts as an intermediary between a supervisor and a union employee when a problem develops. In large locals and in locals representing workers in several locations, an elected full-time **business agent** visits the sites to handle member problems.

13. Unions organize by finding a group of dissatisfied workers and convincing them that unionization will solve their problems. Such workers are mailed **authorization cards**, which designate the union as their bargaining agent. When such cards have been signed by 30 percent or more of a company's workers, the union may ask management to recognize it (more typically, the union waits until 50 percent of employees have signed authorization cards). If management is unwilling to recognize the union, the union asks the National Labor Relations Board (NLRB) to supervise a **certification** election. If a majority of workers vote for the union, the union becomes certified. Employees can also ask for a **decertification** vote, which would sever their relationship with a particular union. During the 1980s, unions lost 75 percent of all decertification elections, due in part to higher wages and better employer-employee relations. Sometimes, unions cause their own decertification by allowing too many **givebacks** (deletions from the contract resulting in a reduction in union members' pay and/or benefits).

14. Once certified, a union's main task is to negotiate employment contracts with management. This process is known as **collective bargaining**. Most labor contracts are compromises between the desires of union members and those of management. Each tries to see how far it can go before the other wants to break off negotiations. Neither side really wants a strike. The union's negotiating team must understand the needs and desires of the employees it represents, and management must determine the point at which labor's proposals are likely to cost the company less than a strike. Unions may call for a strike vote prior to negotiations, just to demonstrate to management that their members stand united.

15. When actual labor contract negotiations get under way, each side states its opening position. Labor typically wants additions to the current contract, and management may ask for givebacks. If one of the parties refuses to discuss a particular issue, the other side may ask the NLRB to rule if the subject matter (1) may be omitted, (2) is a **permissive subject** (e.g., health insurance for retiring workers), or (3) is a **mandatory subject** (e.g., wages and hours).

16. If management and the union cannot reach an agreement, outside help may be necessary. **Mediation** is the most common alternative (bringing in an impartial third party to make recommendations), although **arbitration** (in which the third party's judgment is binding on both sides) may also be used.

17. After the contract has been agreed to by both management and the union, it goes to the union members for **ratification.**

18. The majority of contract negotiations are settled in a timely and businesslike manner. However, in the early days of unions, managements used such practices as the **yellow-dog contract** (an agreement that forced workers, as a condition of employment, to promise not to join or remain in a union) and the **blacklist** (secret lists circulated among employers to keep union organizers from getting jobs), while unions attempted sabotage, violence, and property damage.

19. Organized labor's most powerful (and best-known) weapon is the **strike,** a temporary work stoppage aimed at forcing management to accept union demands. An important part of a strike is **picketing**, in which union members, known as pickets, are positioned at entrances to the firm. They try to persuade nonstriking workers and others not to do business with the company. Since the early 1980s, the number of strikes in the United States has decreased, as companies have been able to operate throughout a strike either because they are highly automated or because they are able to put managers and temporary employees to work in the union jobs. Workers may also engage in a **slowdown**, in which they do their jobs, but at a very slow pace.

20. Other union tactics include the **boycott** (union members and sympathizers refuse to buy or handle the firm's products), financial influence (unions and their members have huge financial assets), political influence (unions can support and raise funds for candidates), and the waging of a publicity battle. Additionally, in 1988 the Supreme Court declared that **secondary boycotts** (boycotts of companies doing business with the targeted union employer) are legal if they do not involve coercive tactics or picketing.

21. Management has the right to replace striking workers with **strikebreakers** (people who cross picket lines to work). Often, however, supervisory and other white-collar personnel can keep the company functioning, or the company may depend on its computers to function. A second weapon, the **lockout**, prevents workers from entering a struck business in order to pressure a union to accept management's last contract proposal.

22. Management may also be able to obtain an **injunction,** a court order directing someone to do something or to refrain from doing it. Whereas the issuance of injunctions was commonplace in the past, today they may be issued only in certain cases. The President, under the Taft-Hartley Act, has the right to obtain an injunction to halt a strike harmful to the national interest. As a final weapon, some industries have formed mutual-assistance pacts, which are agreements to abandon competition in order to assist a competitor singled out for a strike. Some industries have also formed national organizations to counterbalance the powerful national unions. These organizations coordinate industrywide strategy and lobby against pro-labor legislation.

23. The collective bargaining agreement lays the groundwork for the discussions that continue between management and labor throughout the life of the contract. Unions would like to see all workers they represent working in a **closed shop**, but this arrangement in which workers must join the union as a condition of employment was outlawed by the Taft-Hartley Act. The **union shop** is the next best alternative for unions, because after a probationary period, the worker must join the union. Other alternatives are the **agency shop**, which requires nonunion workers who benefit from union-management agreements to pay service fees to the union, and the **open shop**, in which nonunion workers pay no dues. Some states have passed **right-to-work laws,** which give workers the right to get a job without having to join a union.

24. Until recently, new contracts between labor and management have traditionally contained wage increases. However, due to economic recessions and foreign competition, many unions have engaged in "concession bargaining." Such contracts agree to keep wages at their present levels, or may even specify a number of givebacks in return for job-security guarantees. This type of bargaining replaced **pattern bargaining**, in which similar wages and benefits were negotiated with all firms in an industry or all plants within a company. Still further, a number of concessionary contracts have specified a **two-tier wage plan**, in which newly hired workers receive a lower starting wage. This scheme, though, often creates morale problems among the lower-paid newcomers. While union workers today still average 36 percent higher wages than nonunion workers, their wage gains are at the lowest point in the past few decades.

25. Still popular are **cost-of-living adjustments (COLAs)**, which guarantee that a worker's pay will keep pace with inflation. While in 1976 over 60 percent of workers covered by labor contracts benefited from COLA provisions, only 38 percent had COLAs in 1987. Another technique, **profit sharing**, may provide workers with deferred income to be claimed upon retirement or cash payments each time a company's profits are determined. It is estimated that 16 percent of all full-time workers in medium and large private companies benefit from some type of profit-sharing plan.

26. One way that management can avoid wage increases in labor contracts is by providing additional benefits. However, huge increases in medical insurance costs, as well as increases in Social Security taxes and unemployment insurance, have resulted in management often asking for givebacks in the area of employee benefits.

27. In return for the concessions that managements have won from unions on wages and work rules, some unions have asked that their members be granted **lifetime security**. This is an arrangement giving workers some protection against temporary layoffs and the closings of outmoded factories. Automation has been an especially acute problem area, as firms introduce new equipment that results in the need for fewer workers.

28. In industries like the automobile industry, unions tend to focus on job guarantees. However, they are often willing to accept "income" guarantees and better retirement packages in lieu of jobs. Under the 1990 United Auto Workers contract with the Big Three American automakers, workers will receive 85 percent of their regular take-home pay for three years if they opt for "pre-retirement leave" or are laid off.

29. **Work rules** define the types of work union members may do and the working conditions they must have. Both management and unions realized that practices such as "featherbedding" were unprofitable and that productivity could be increased through changes in work rules. Union contracts typically include provisions covering employees' safety and health.

30. Throughout the life of the union-management contract, both parties will have to deal with **grievances** (complaints of management violating some aspect of the contract). Difficulties usually arise when a union member feels that he or she is not being treated fairly. The contract gives the employee the right to **due process**, a system of procedures and mechanisms to ensure equity and justice on the job.

31. Typically, grievances are first referred to the shop steward, who discusses the issue with the worker's immediate supervisor. If not successfully resolved, the chief steward meets with the department head. As a next step, the union grievance committee discusses the issue with the company's human resource (or personnel) manager. If the dispute still cannot be settled, the union business agent (a full-time union staff member) and the plant manager attempt to settle the conflict.

32. If the problem cannot be resolved using the above steps, the worker's complaint goes to an arbitrator, whose powers are defined in the contract and whose ruling, in most cases, is final. Because this arbitration process is considered a last resort and can be complicated and expensive, there has been a shift to grievance mediation, where a neutral third party meets with both sides and attempts to steer them toward a solution to the problem.

33. A changing economic environment is having an effect on union-management relations. Because labor costs are often much lower in foreign nations, unions and managements have begun working together to keep plants in operation. Sometimes, however, inefficient factories must be closed. A new law went into effect in 1989 requiring firms to give workers at least sixty days' notice of a plant closing or layoff.

34. If the situation is bad enough, a company may file for bankruptcy. There have even been cases of firms declaring bankruptcy, then reopening as nonunion companies (e.g., Continental Airlines). Or a company may rid itself of a union by closing a plant and selling it to a supposedly independent company that it actually controls. The plant then reopens with a nonunion work force.

35. As a new weapon to reduce union influence, management may grant to nonunionized employees the same benefits enjoyed by union members. Such a practice makes workers reluctant to join a union. Further, many benefits such as safety in the workplace and pension plans, which were achieved mainly through union battles in the past, are now mandated by law.

36. As unions have become concerned with mounting job losses from mergers and plant closings, they have taken a number of steps to ensure their survival. Givebacks have been granted in exchange for employee ownership programs, allowing workers to have more say in how a firm is run. Representatives of labor now sit on many boards of directors. ESOPs have allowed workers to gain partial or complete ownership of companies. Some unions have even tried to buy companies outright.

37. In order to remain healthy, unions must (1) win job guarantees, (2) make imaginative pay deals that exchange a piece of the profits for traditional wages and benefits, (3) do a better job of communicating with members, (4) accept new technologies that make employers more competitive, and (5) attract new members from the service industries.

KEY TERMS

labor unions	strike
craft unions	picketing
industrial unions	slowdown
national union	boycott
locals	secondary boycott
local union	strikebreakers
labor federations	lockout
shop steward	injunction
authorization cards	closed shop
certification	union shop
decertification	agency shop
givebacks	open shop
collective bargaining	right-to-work laws
permissive subject	pattern bargaining
mandatory subject	cost-of-living adjustments
mediation	profit sharing
arbitration	lifetime security
ratification	work rules
yellow-dog contract	grievances
blacklist	due process

KEY TERMS EXERCISE

Directions: On the line provided, place the letter of the statement on the right that most closely defines the key term.

_____ 1. Labor unions

_____ 2. Craft unions

_____ 3. Industrial unions

_____ 4. Due process

_____ 5. Labor federations

_____ 6. Shop steward

_____ 7. Collective bargaining

_____ 8. Lifetime security

_____ 9. Work rules

_____ 10. Strike

_____ 11. Picketing

_____ 12. Boycott

_____ 13. Strikebreakers

_____ 14. Lockout

_____ 15. Injunction

a. The policies set during collective bargaining that govern the types of work union members may do and the working conditions they must have.

b. Union activities in which members and sympathizers refuse to buy products made by a company.

c. Unions made up of skilled artisans belonging to a single profession.

d. A management activity in which union members are prevented from entering a business during a strike to force union acceptance of management's last contract proposal.

e. The process used by unions and management to negotiate work contracts.

f. People who cross picket lines to work.

g. Umbrella organizations of national unions and unaffilliated local unions that undertake large-scale activities on behalf of their members.

h. A temporary work stoppage by union workers to force management to accept union demands.

i. A court order directing someone to do something or to refrain from doing something.

j. Organizations of workers formed to protect and advance their members' interests.

k. A union member and worker who is elected to represent other union members and who attempts to resolve employee grievances with management.

l. Unions representing both skilled and unskilled workers from all phases of a particular industry.

m. An arrangement that gives workers some protection against temporary layoffs due to economic slowdowns and job loss during a downsizing or plant closing.

n. System of procedures and mechanisms for ensuring equity and justice on the job.

o. Strike activity in which union members march before company entrances to persuade nonstriking workers to walk off the job and to persuade customers and others to cease doing business with the company.

ANSWERS TO KEY TERMS EXERCISE

1. j (p. 296)	5. g (p. 300)	9. a (p. 313)	13. f (p. 307)
2. c (p. 296)	6. k (p. 300)	10. h (p. 305)	14. d (p. 308)
3. l (p. 296)	7. e (p. 303)	11. o (p. 305)	15. i (p. 309)
4. n (p. 314)	8. m (p. 312)	12. b (p. 305)	

SELF TEST

True-False Questions

_____ 1. Workers who band together have more bargaining power than they would have as individuals.

_____ 2. Labor prices are influenced by demand and supply.

_____ 3. Unions cannot influence the level of supply of labor.

_____ 4. Our economic system produces certain unavoidable differences of interests between workers and management.

_____ 5. The needs of management and workers can never be met simultaneously.

_____ 6. Close to 50 percent of all workers are union members, and the rate is growing.

_____ 7. White-collar workers are more likely to be union members than blue-collar workers.

_____ 8. Unions are becoming more popular among professionals.

_____ 9. Most workers feel that unions are not necessary and that they make it difficult for companies to stay in business.

____ 10. At the start of negotiations, both management and union negotiators are likely to withhold their realistic estimates from the other party.

____ 11. In tough negotiations, using outside negotiators is usually better than using inside negotiators.

____ 12. Most labor contracts that are ratified are a compromise between the desires of union members and the desires of management.

____ 13. Signing a contract marks the end of negotiations between the union and management.

____ 14. Calling in an arbitrator is usually one of the first steps in resolving a grievance.

____ 15. Union members may now resign from the union during a strike so they may continue working.

____ 16. No one usually wins during a strike.

____ 17. Most labor-management disputes end in a strike.

____ 18. Either management or unions may refuse to discuss certain issues in collective bargaining if they are permissive subjects.

____ 19. Unions have shown little interest in gaining membership in the high-tech industries.

____ 20. Good management-employee relations reduce the need for unionization.

____ 21. Unions can provide some useful functions for management.

____ 22. Foreign competition is forcing unions and management to work together more closely to achieve common goals.

____ 23. The current U.S. work force shows a growing interest in joining unions.

Multiple Choice Questions

____ 1. Under which of the following circumstances would the needs of management and workers most likely be met simultaneously?
   a. during periods of economic downturn
   b. during periods of economic prosperity
   c. during periods of intense competition
   d. during periods of high unemployment

____ 2. The declining power of unions can be attributed to
   a. more white-collar workers in the labor force.
   b. increased foreign competition.
   c. a social and political climate somewhat against unions.
   d. deregulation of industries.
   e. all of the above.

____ 3. Which of the following is a nontraditional goal (i.e., a new goal) unions are now seeking for their membership?
   a. higher wages
   b. better benefits and working conditions
   c. greater involvement in decision making
   d. more job security
   e. greater safety

_____   4.   In its preparation for negotiations, management attempts to
   a.   calculate the point at which labor's proposals are likely to cost the company more than a strike.
   b.   select an arbitrator.
   c.   recruit nonunion workers in the event there is a strike.
   d.   select a mediator.
   e.   do all of the above.

_____   5.   Which of the following issues is an example of a permissive subject in negotiations?
   a.   wages
   b.   working hours
   c.   health insurance for retired workers
   d.   pension benefits

_____   6.   Decisions made by a mediator in negotiations are
   a.   binding to management.
   b.   binding to the union.
   c.   binding to both management and the union.
   d.   not binding to either party.

_____   7.   What action will union members likely take if they feel they have been unfairly passed over for promotion or aren't receiving a fair share of overtime?
   a.   file a grievance with the shop steward
   b.   walk out on a strike
   c.   picket
   d.   quit

_____   8.   Bargaining issues between labor and management would include
   a.   union security and management rights.
   b.   compensation.
   c.   working time.
   d.   job security and promotion.
   e.   all of the above.

_____   9.   Which of the following did the Taft-Hartley Act outlaw?
   a.   closed shop
   b.   union shop
   c.   agency shop
   d.   open shop
   e.   all of the above

_____   10.   Which of the following weapons can unions legally use?
   a.   a strike
   b.   a boycott
   c.   financial influence
   d.   political influence
   e.   all of the above

_____   11.   Management *cannot* employ which of the following tools against unions?
   a.   strikebreakers
   b.   a lockout
   c.   a blacklist
   d.   injunctions
   e.   mutual-assistance pacts

____ 12. The most commonly used method of resolving labor-management disputes is
   a. a strike.
   b. collective bargaining.
   c. an injunction.
   d. a boycott.
   e. the employment of strikebreakers.

____ 13. In a conflict between employees and management, the basic issue is to determine
   a. who is right in the dispute.
   b. if the disagreement can be resolved.
   c. if the National Labor Relations Board should be called in to resolve the conflict.
   d. the appropriate strategy to win the negotiations in the dispute.

____ 14. Which of the following is the *most* powerful weapon that labor unions can use to achieve demands?
   a. a strike
   b. a boycott
   c. picketing
   d. political influence
   e. collective bargaining

____ 15. Which of the following is likely to suffer economic damage during a union strike (work stoppage)?
   a. the striking workers
   b. the company's management that is being struck
   c. the industry in which the strike occurs
   d. the country as a whole
   e. All of the above suffer to some extent during a strike.

____ 16. The success of unions in the future will depend on their ability to
   a. win job guarantees for their members.
   b. establish effective lines of communication.
   c. accept new technologies in companies.
   d. attract new members from the service industries.
   e. do all of the above.

____ 17. Having a grievance procedure whereby an employee can have an opportunity to present his or her side of the story ensures the employee's
   a. arbitration rights.
   b. mediation rights.
   c. due process rights.
   d. injunction rights.
   e. all of the above.

Completion Questions

1. The basic conflict between management and workers is that management wants to maximize _____, while workers want job security, safe and comfortable working conditions, and high pay.

2. _____ have the power to resolve disputes between competing unions.

3. Grievances a worker has with management would be taken to the _____.

4. At least _____ percent of the workers must sign authorization cards before a union can request management to recognize it as the official bargaining unit for the workers.

5. The National Labor Relations Board has the right to conduct a _____ election to officially recognize a union as the bargaining agent for workers.

6. A _____ shop is where every employee must join the union, a _____ shop is where every worker must join the union after a probationary period, and a _____ shop is where nonunion members must pay union dues if they benefit from negotiated union contracts.

7. Putting new employees on a lower wage scale than senior employees is known as _____ .

8. A guarantee that worker's pay will keep pace with inflation is known as _____ .

9. The tactic whereby management prevents workers from entering a struck business in order to pressure a union to accept a contract proposal is known as a _____ .

10. The negotiation process involves preparing to meet, meeting and reaching agreement, and voting and _____ .

11. A _____ is an attempt by management to have the union delete an item in a current contract.

12. Rather than using an arbitrator to solve grievances, many companies are using _____ because it is less expensive and just as effective.

13. To assist a company in its fight with a union, some industries have formed _____ , where they temporarily agree to abandon competition with that company.

PROJECT

PART 1

Negotiating a Contract

Being able to negotiate effectively is a desirable skill. To develop a better understanding of how the negotiating process works, engage in the following role-playing situation involving a collective bargaining process.

Assume you are part of the management of the regional telephone company and have been assigned to negotiate a new contract with the union. The basic issues of the contract deal with pay and job security. The union wants a 10 percent increase in pay, along with a 5 percent increase in fringe benefits. Workers feel that this is necessary to meet the increased costs of living. Management, however, feels that if this demand is met, it will make the company uncompetitive with private phone service providers and thus cost them business. The union also wants a guarantee that no workers will be replaced because of the increased use of computers and advances in technology. Management feels that these technologies are necessary to remain competitive and to provide the service customers expect, and that fewer employees will be needed to provide higher levels of service.

You have been assigned the responsibility of developing the company's initial position and overall strategy for negotiating with the union. Provide the reasoning that you will use to persuade the union to accept your position. What will you do if the union rejects your initial position?

PART 2

Now assume you are the representative of the union in this situation. Management has offered to provide a 5 percent increase in pay with a 1 percent increase in fringe benefits. Management is not willing to make any guarantees about retraining workers displaced by technology. What is your reaction to management's offer? What is your strategy and counteroffer from this point?

You should be prepared to take either management's or the union's position in this exercise, as your instructor may assign you to a group for a role-playing situation.

Chapter 12

....

Marketing and Consumer Behavior

LEARNING OBJECTIVES

1. Explain what marketing is.

2. Describe the four forms of utility created by marketing.

3. Discuss the three major eras in the evolution of marketing.

4. Identify and contrast the two basic types of markets.

5. Specify the four basic components of the marketing mix.

6. Outline the four steps in the strategic planning process.

7. Describe the five steps in the buyer's decision process.

8. Define market segmentation, and list the four bases most often used to segment markets.

OUTLINE

I.   Marketing fundamentals

    A. Definition of marketing
        1. What marketing includes

    B. The role of marketing in society
        1. Needs and wants
        2. Exchanges and transactions
            a. The exchange process
            b. Transactions
        3. The four utilities
            a. Form, place, time, and possession utility

    C. The evolution of marketing
        1. The production era
        2. The sales era
        3. The marketing era
            a. The "marketing concept"
        4. Competitive marketing
            a. How to establish a competitive advantage
            b. Product differentiation

II. Marketing management and planning

    A. What marketing strategy is

B. Types of markets
   1. The consumer market versus the organizational market
       a. Types of organizational markets
   2. Market segments and target markets

C. The marketing mix (the four P's)
   1. Product
   2. Price
   3. Place
   4. Promotion

D. The marketing planning process
   1. Strategic marketing planning
   2. Analyzing the external environment
       a. Economic forces
       b. Social trends
       c. Technology
       d. Competition
       e. Legal and regulatory climate
       f. Natural environment
   3. Setting objectives
   4. Analyzing internal capabilities
   5. Selecting the strategy
       a. The leader's options
       b. The challenger's options

E. The role of market research
   1. Approaches to marketing research

III. Buying behavior

A. Consumer buying behavior
   1. The purchase-decision process
       a. The steps of the purchase decision process
   2. Factors that influence buyer behavior
       a. Culture
          (1) Subculture
       b. Social class
       c. Reference groups
       d. Self-image
       e. Situational factors

B. Organizational buying behavior
   1. Differences in products and purchasing
   2. Differences in buyer-seller relationship

IV. Market segmentation

A. Definition of market segmentation

B. Bases of segmentation
   1. Demographic segmentation
   2. Geographic segmentation
   3. Behavioral segmentation
   4. Psychographic segmentation

    C.   Target-market alternatives
        1. Undifferentiated
        2. Concentrated
        3. Differentiated
        4. Customized

MAJOR POINTS TO REMEMBER

1. According to the American Marketing Association (AMA), **marketing** may be defined as planning and executing the conception, pricing, promotion, and distribution of ideas, goods, and services to create exchanges that satisfy individual and organizational objectives. Note that while we most often think of marketing in connection with the sale of products for a profit, the definition covers services and ideas as well (e.g., a candidate for political office has to be marketed to the voting public).

2. Marketing helps people satisfy their needs and wants. **Needs** are basic to your physical, psychological, and social well-being. When your needs are not being met, you feel deprived and are motivated to change the situation.

3. **Wants** are more specific than needs. While you may need food, what you "want" may be a hamburger or pasta, depending on your experiences, your culture, and your personality.

4. In a free-market economy like ours, the mechanism that allows marketers to know what to produce is known as the **exchange process.** It permits consumer preferences to be identified. For example, when you purchase an item (i.e., pay money for a product or service), you are casting a vote for that item and encouraging producers to supply more of them. A **transaction** is when an exchange actually occurs, usually involving money exchanged for an item.

5. Of the four types of **utility,** one is created by production (**form utility**) and three are created by marketing activities. Having a product available to consumers at a convenient place is **place utility**; having it available when a customer wants it is **time utility**; when the purchaser takes possession of the item by paying for it, the product has **possession utility**.

6. Marketing has changed greatly during the twentieth century. Until the 1930s, many businessmen viewed marketing as an offshoot of production. Then the production era evolved into the sales era as production capacity increased and it became necessary to work harder to sell all the goods a business could manufacture. To stimulate demand, manufacturers spent more on advertising. The marketing era developed after World War II and takes the view that the buyer should have a say in what goods or services the firm sells. In other words, a firm should identify consumers' needs and then create goods and services to satisfy them. Today's **marketing concept** stresses not only customer needs, but also long-term profitability to the firm and the integration of marketing with other parts of the company.

7. Firms must also pay more attention to their competition and therefore attempt to gain a **competitive advantage** (something that will make their products more appealing to customers than their competitors' products). This may be accomplished by lower prices or by doing a better job of meeting customer needs (to offset an equal or higher price). If quality or features are to be stressed (rather than a lower price), a firm must communicate to the buying public exactly what its competitive advantage is. This approach is known as **product differentiation**.

8. Because marketing is so important to an organization, the firm should develop a **marketing strategy** (i.e., an overall plan) for its products and services. The first step would be to identify the particular group of customers the firm will try to satisfy. Then the firm must decide on the combination of ingredients that will be employed in the marketing program.

9. A group of people who might want or need a firm's products and have the money to buy them is known as a **market.** Generally, the two broad categories of markets are the **consumer market** and the **organizational market.** The organizational market has three main subgroups: the industrial/commercial market (firms buying goods and services to produce their own goods and services), the reseller market (wholesalers and retailers), and the government market (federal, state, and local).

10. Both the consumer market and the organizational market may consist of many different **market segments,** which are subgroups with particular needs and interests. Since all such subgroups typically cannot be satisfied, a company must focus on specific **target markets.**

11. The **marketing mix** (also known as the **four P's**) is the blend of product (ideas, goods, services), price, place (distribution), and promotion that satisfies the demands of the chosen market segment. A businessperson's first marketing decision concerns the products or services to offer. Social trends may provide an indication of what products consumers want, and changing conditions require changes in marketing programs. Decisions must also be made whether to price the product low or high in order to maximize profits. Next, place decisions must be made regarding the number and types of outlets the product should be sold in, as well as how the product is to be transported to the customer. Finally, a determination must be made regarding the most effective ways to communicate information about the product or service to prospective customers. Many firms rely heavily on advertising, while others may prefer to emphasize personal selling. The range of promotional possibilities is huge.

12. Marketers must combine the elements of the marketing mix in a way that can increase profits. **Strategic marketing planning** examines a firm's market opportunities, allocates resources to make the most of these opportunities, and then predicts the market and financial performance that is likely to occur. The steps of the marketing planning process are (1) analyzing the external environment, including economic forces, social trends, technology, competition, legal and regulatory climate, and natural environment; (2) setting objectives, often expressed in terms of sales growth, profitability, and increases in **market share,** (3) analyzing internal capabilities (e.g., financial resources and production capabilities); and (4) selecting the strategy.

13. The proper marketing strategy is often dependent upon a firm's relative position in the industry. Leaders generally have one primary goal—to stay on top. They must defend against attackers and may also try to strengthen their advantage. In contrast, challengers can assault the leader directly, play a "me too" game, or carve out a special niche.

14. Firms today spend over $2 billion annually on **marketing research** to find out what products and services customers want, what forms, colors, packaging, prices, and retail outlets customers prefer, and how to best sell them (e.g., advertising, public relations, selling practices). The two basic approaches to marketing research are (1) interview or survey methods and (2) observational methods. Even small firms have the resources to gather information that would be useful in guiding their marketing decisions. By talking to customers, a company can identify its marketing problems, fine-tune its products and services, learn about competitors, and analyze alternative marketing strategies.

15. A simple formula to sum up the consumer decision-making process is *choice = want + ability to buy + attitude* toward the brand.

16. The first stage in the buying process is when you become aware of a problem. In looking for a solution, you consider a number of possibilities based on past experience (prior use of products) and the marketing messages to which you have been exposed. If the problem is complex, you will want to seek more information (e.g., from friends, by reading articles in magazines, or through comparison shopping). You may finally make a choice, postpone the decision, or decide against making any purchase at all. If you are satisfied with the item after buying it, you may eventually develop a loyalty to the brand. Often after a major purchase, however, you will suffer from **cognitive dissonance** or buyer's remorse; that is, you will wonder if you made the proper choice.

17. Factors that influence buyer behavior include culture, subculture, social class, reference groups, self-image, and situational factors. As part of the American culture, we share a number of common values, such as

admiration for George Washington. We are also members of many subcultures. For example, citizens in the South often admire Robert E. Lee; he is part of the Southern subculture. Social class also affects our attitudes and buying behavior, with upscale consumers preferring golf and downscale buyers bowling.

18. Reference groups consist of people who have a lot in common; we are all members of many such groups. We use the opinions of group members to determine what is appropriate to purchase. In every group, the opinions of "influentials" carry a lot of weight. Self-image is also important, because we reinforce the image we have of ourselves through our purchases. Finally, situational factors often determine our purchase decisions, such as having a cents-off coupon for a particular brand of coffee.

19. Products sold to organizational markets include raw materials (e.g., steel and grain), highly technical and complex products (e.g., telecommunications systems), and products that are also sold in consumer markets (e.g., food, ballpoint pens, cleaning supplies). Some products are designed specifically for individual customers, such as production machinery. Purchases are often made in huge quantities (e.g., by the ton or truckload) and have large dollar values. The motivations behind organizational purchases are economic in nature and involve much greater risks to the buyer than consumer purchases do (i.e., a wrong decision can be a multimillion-dollar mistake).

20. Relationships in the organizational market between buyers and sellers tend to be stable and long term. Source loyalty develops because of the amount of time and effort that goes into choosing a supplier (i.e., Why risk trying a new source?), and benefits the buyer by improving the communication flow and giving him or her preferred status in case of shortages. Finally, organizational buying decisions involve many more people than consumer buying decisions.

21. **Market segmentation** is an attempt to subdivide the overall market into smaller groups of potential customers who share some common need or characteristics. The most common bases for segmenting the consumer market are demographic, geographic, behavioral, and psychographic.

22. Factors such as age, gender, occupation, and income are **demographic segmentation** factors. **Geographic segmentation** may be appropriate when customers in different areas have different needs (e.g., you can't sell snow shovels in Miami, Florida).

23. Segmenting a market based on consumers' knowledge of, attitude toward, use of, or response to products or product characteristics is known as **behavioral segmentation.** For example, a hotel might tailor its services and promotion for either vacationers or business travelers. Also, under this classification, the market would be divided into nonusers, former users, potential users, occasional users, and frequent users.

24. **Psychographics** identifies consumers in terms of their psychological makeup, including attitudes, interests, opinions, and lifestyles. A common psychographic model is called Values and Lifestyle (VALS). While the original version of VALS categorized each consumer into one of nine types, the latest version, VALS 2, identifies eight consumer groups. The promotional message that might be effective in reaching one of these groups may not work well for the others.

25. The four alternative approaches to target marketing are (1) undifferentiated, (2) concentrated, (3) differentiated, and (4) customized. In **undifferentiated marketing** (also known as "mass marketing"), the firm does not subdivide the market but instead feels that all buyers have similar wants that can be met with the same product (e.g., salt and sugar). **Concentrated marketing,** in contrast, aims the firm's entire effort at a single market segment, its target customer group.

26. If **differentiated marketing** is employed, the company selects a few target customer groups and varies the marketing mix elements to appeal specifically to each segment (e.g., Nike has footwear for basketball, baseball, running, and so on). Finally, **customized marketing** views each customer as a separate segment and tailors the four P's to this buyer's needs (e.g., interior design and home repairs). Customized marketing has been showing up in some surprising places, due to **database marketing,** which uses information collected about customers to fine-tune marketing programs.

KEY TERMS

marketing
needs
wants
exchange process
transaction
utility
form utility
place utility
time utility
possession utility
marketing concept
competitive advantage
product differentiation
marketing strategy
market
consumer market
organizational market
market segments

target markets
marketing mix
promotion
four P's
strategic marketing planning
market share
marketing research
cognitive dissonance
market segmentation
demographic
geographic segmentation
behavioral segmentation
psychographics
undifferentiated marketing
concentrated marketing
differentiated marketing
customized marketing
database marketing

KEY TERMS EXERCISE

Directions: On the line provided, place the letter of the statement on the right that most closely defines the key term.

___G___ 1. Marketing

___J___ 2. Competitive advantage

___L___ 3. Product differentiation

___R___ 4. Form utility

___F___ 5. Place utility

___N___ 6. Time utility

___8___ 7. Possession utility

___M___ 8. Marketing mix

___S___ 9. Four P's

___d___ 10. Marketing strategy

___0___ 11. Marketing research

___b___ 12. Market

___c___ 13. Market segments

___P___ 14. Target markets

___I___ 15. Consumer market

a. Using computer databases to collect information about individual customers in order to customize marketing programs for each one.

b. People who need or want a product and who have the money and authority to buy it.

c. Groups of individuals or organizations within a market that share certain common characteristics.

d. The overall plan for marketing a product.

e. The classification of customers on the basis of their psychological makeup.

f. The consumer value added by making a product available in a convenient location.

g. The process of planning and executing the conception, price, promotion, and distribution of ideas, goods, and services to create exchanges that satisfy individual and organizational objectives.

h. The categorization of customers according to their relationship with products or responses to product characteristics.

i. Individuals who buy goods or services for personal use.

j. A quality that makes a product more desirable than those offered by the competition.

___T___ 16. Organizational market

___A___ 17. Database marketing

___U___ 18. Market segmentation

___K___ 19. Demographics

___H___ 20. Behavioral segmentation

___e___ 21. Psychographics

k. The study of the statistical characteristics of a population.

l. Features that distinguish one company's product from another company's similar product.

m. The blend of elements that satisfies a chosen market.

n. The consumer value added by making a product available at a convenient time.

o. The process of gathering information about marketing problems and opportunities.

p. Specific groups of customers to whom a company wants to sell a particular product.

q. The consumer value created when someone takes ownership of a product.

r. The consumer value created by transforming inputs into products.

s. The marketing elements—product, price, promotion, and place.

t. Customers who buy goods or services for resale or for use in conducting their own operations.

u. The division of a market into subgroups.

ANSWERS TO KEY TERMS EXERCISE

	18. u (p. 344)	12. b (p. 333)	6. n (p. 329)
	17. a (p. 350)	11. o (p. 338)	5. f (p. 329)
	16. t (p. 333)	10. p (p. 332)	4. r (p. 329)
21. e (p. 347)	15. i (p. 333)	9. s (p. 333)	3. l (p. 332)
20. h (p. 346)	14. d (p. 333)	8. m (p. 333)	2. j (p. 332)
19. k (p. 345)	13. c (p. 333)	7. q (p. 329)	1. g (p. 328)

SELF TEST

True-False Questions

___T___ 1. By paying the retailer the retail price for the product, the customer gains possession utility.

___T___ 2. Marketing techniques must differ when marketing to the consumer and to industrial markets.

_____ 3. For any given market, there may actually be more than one successful segmentation strategy.

___T___ 4. Marketing goals are derived from corporate goals.

___F___ 5. Most companies today operate in the production era.

_____ 6. A company that focuses its resources on customers is operating in the marketing era.

_____ 6. A company that focuses its resources on customers is operating in the marketing era.

_____ 7. The type of purchases made by consumers is influenced by the economy's condition.

_____ 8. Changes in technology will always result in a better situation for companies.

_____ 9. The key to selecting a marketing strategy is to maximize the firm's strengths while capitalizing on the opponent's weaknesses.

_____ 10. The goal of a market leader is to stay on top.

_____ 11. Members of different social classes will tend to buy different goods, shop in different places, and react to different media.

_____ 12. The buying process for organizations is quite similar to the buying process for individuals.

_____ 13. Because of the greater risk involved, organizational buyers are more likely to select their suppliers carefully.

_____ 14. Organizational buyers prefer to develop a loyalty toward a few good suppliers rather than a larger number of suppliers.

_____ 15. The marketing concept emphasizes long-term profitability.

Multiple Choice Questions

_____ 1. Companies seek something that sets them apart from their rivals and makes their product more appealing to customers. This something is referred to as
    a. a monopolistic advantage.
    b. a competitive advantage.
    c. a significant difference.
    d. "me too" marketing.

_____ 2. The market of households that purchase goods for personal use is classified as
    a. a consumer market.
    b. an industrial market.
    c. an organizational market.
    d. a market segment.

_____ 3. The type of market an organization decides to serve (e.g., consumer versus organizational) will influence
    a. the product design.
    b. the hours of operation.
    c. the needs satisfied.
    d. all of the above.

_____ 4. The steps in marketing research and analysis are
    a. asking customers where they buy products.
    b. planning how the product should look.
    c. analyzing advertising preferences of customers.
    d. all of the above.

_____ 5. Developing different types of gasoline, which take different climatic variations into account in order to provide the proper amount of power, is an example of what type of segmentation?
   a. geographic
   b. psychographic
   c. behavioristic
   d. demographic

_____ 6. A company that feels that success depends upon having a strong sales force and effective advertising is operating in the
   a. production era.
   b. sales era.
   c. marketing era.
   d. competitive era.

_____ 7. Operating in the marketing era involves
   a. focusing on improving technology.
   b. striving to meet the needs of the entire society.
   c. stressing promotion in order to increase sales.
   d. developing a marketing mix to satisfy the customer's needs.
   e. offering the customer many different products.

_____ 8. Developing a marketing strategy involves
   a. developing a marketing mix.
   b. defining a target market.
   c. segmenting a market.
   d. both a and b.

_____ 9. A market leader will most likely attempt to
   a. carve out a special niche.
   b. defend against attackers.
   c. strengthen its advantage.
   d. both a and b.
   e. both b and c.

_____ 10. Which of the following variables influences buyer behavior?
   a. a person's culture and social class
   b. a person's reference groups
   c. a person's self-image
   d. situational variables in which the purchase occurs
   e. all of the above

_____ 11. Treating yourself to a special purchase because you are "feeling down in the dumps" is an example of what type of purchase influence?
   a. culture
   b. reference group
   c. situational
   d. social class
   e. family

_____ 12. Which of the following is not true about the organizational buying process?
   a. It is more likely to involve customized product design.
   b. It involves larger quantities.
   c. It takes less time to plan the purchase.
   d. It involves higher dollar amounts on average.

_____ 13. When a company wants to serve the mass market, it is following what type of approach to market segmentation?
   a. undifferentiated
   b. concentrated
   c. differentiated
   d. customized

_____ 14. Appealing to several target customer groups and developing a marketing mix for each segment is what type of market segmentation strategy?
   a. undifferentiated
   b. concentrated
   c. differentiated
   d. customized

_____ 15. The process of examining market opportunities, allocating resources to capitalize those opportunities, and predicting the success of these actions is known as
   a. target market definition.
   b. market segmentation
   c. strategic marketing planning
   d. marketing mix development.

Completion Questions

1. Either offering the lowest possible price for a product or developing a unique product for which a higher price may be charged is known as a (n) _____ .

2. The _____ of a good or service is its value to a customer.

3. Having a product in the store when the customer wants it is an example of _____ utility.

4. A _____ is the group of people who might need your product and who have the money to buy it.

5. The key to product decisions is to determine customer _____ and _____ and translate them into desirable products.

6. Individual consumers are more likely to be driven by desire for personal satisfaction, while organizational buyers are more driven by _____ motives.

7. Developing a marketing strategy consists of two steps: defining a _____ and developing a _____ .

8. A market _____ has several strategy options: it can attack the leaders, use a "me too" approach, or carve out a niche.

9. _____ is the process of having many people involved in making the buying decision in an organization.

10. The marketing concept states that a firm should meet customer needs and wants, have a _____ perspective on profitability, and integrate marketing with other parts of the company.

PROJECT

Developing Marketing Mixes

Marketing is crucial for all organizations that wish to achieve their objectives (profit for business organizations). Develop a marketing mix by filling in the grid below for four different organizations, all of which use marketing in their day-to-day operations.

	UNITED AIRLINES	THE YMCA	USX	PROCTER & GAMBLE
Product				
Price				
Promotion				
Place				

Chapter 13

Product and Pricing Decisions

LEARNING OBJECTIVES

1. List three types of consumer products and two types of organizational products.

2. Cite the three levels of brand loyalty and explain the concept of brand equity.

3. Discuss the functions of packaging.

4. Describe the five stages of product development.

5. Specify the four stages in the life cycle of a product.

6. Identify four ways to expand a product line.

7. List seven common pricing objectives.

8. Distinguish between two methods for setting prices.

OUTLINE

I. Products: The basis of commerce

    A. Definition of "product"

    B. Types of products
        1. Tangible and intangible products
            a. The product continuum
            b. Special characteristics of service products
        2. Consumer products
            a. Convenience products
            b. Shopping products
            c. Specialty products
        3. Organizational products
            a. Capital item buying behavior
            b. Expense item buying behavior
            c. Classifying organizational products by intended usage

    C. Product brands and trademarks
        1. Brands, brand names, and brand symbols
        2. National brands, private brands, and generic products
        3. Trademarks
        4. Brand loyalty
            a. Degrees of brand loyalty
        5. Brand equity
        6. Brand strategies
            a. Individual branding versus family branding
            b. Licensing

   D. Packaging
       1. The purpose of the package

   E. Labeling
       1. Federal regulation of labeling

II. Product development and the product life cycle

   A. The product development process
       1. The scope of new product development
       2. Generation and screening of ideas
           a. Feasibility studies and concept testing
       3. Business analysis
       4. Prototype development
       5. Product testing
           a. Test marketing
       6. Commercialization

   B. The product life cycle
       1. Introductory
       2. Growth stage
       3. Maturity stage
       4. Decline

III. Product mix and line decisions

   A. Width and depth of product mix

   B. Product-line strategies
       1. Full-line versus limited-line strategy
           a. Line filling
           b. Line extensions
           c. Brand extensions
           d. Line stretching

IV. Pricing

   A. Factors that affect pricing decisions
       1. Marketing objectives
           a. Return on investment
           b. Other pricing goals
               (1) Pricing goals and the product life cycle
       2. Costs
           a. Fixed and variable costs
           b. The experience curve
       3. Government regulations
           a. Price fixing
           b. Price discrimination
           c. Deceptive pricing
       4. Price and demand
           a. Elastic and inelastic demand
       5. Competitive conditions
           a. Pricing above, below, and with the market
               (1) Price leaders

B. Pricing methods
1. Markup pricing
    a. How markups are calculated
    b. How markups vary by type of store
    c. The relationship between markup and turnover
2. Break-even analysis
    a. Calculating the break-even point
    b. Why it is important to know the break-even point

C. Pricing strategies
1. Price lining
2. Odd-even pricing
3. Discount pricing
    a. Trade discount
    b. Quantity discount
    c. Cash discount

MAJOR POINTS TO REMEMBER

1. While we most often think of products as tangible objects that we can touch and possess (e.g., automobiles and televisions), intangible services like a basketball team or a TV program are also products. From a marketing perspective, a **product** is anything that is offered for the purpose of satisfying a want or need in a marketing exchange.

2. Nearly all products are combinations of tangible and intangible components, and the product continuum can graphically illustrate a product's relative amounts of each. While products like salt and sugar represent the tangible extreme, political ideas are at the intangible extreme, and a restaurant meal falls somewhere in the middle. Service products, due to the fundamental intangibility of services, must be marketed differently than more tangible products. You usually cannot show service in an ad or demonstrate it prior to purchase. Services also cannot be created in advance and stored until people want to buy them. It is this "perishability" that leads movie theaters to offer less expensive tickets during the day.

3. Consumer products may be divided into three categories. **Convenience products** and services are things that people purchase often, without much thought; examples include inexpensive items such as toothpaste and razor blades. For such products, advertising and packaging are used to create an easily recognizable image. In contrast, purchases that require more thought may be classified as **shopping products.** Such goods and services (e.g., a new dress or a tax service) are purchased after the consumer has shopped around and compared brands, models, and prices. For such merchandise and services, personal selling is often an important promotional tool.

4. If a person is shopping for items for which there are no acceptable substitutes and if the shopper knows which brands will be purchased in advance, these items are said to be **specialty products,** the third category of consumer products. The consumer will seek out these items regardless of price or location.

5. Organizational buyers tend to use more objective criteria in making purchases. The two basic types of organizational products are **expense items** (inexpensive goods and services used within a year of purchase) and **capital items** (more costly than expense items and with a longer useful life). Expense items are often purchased with little advanced notice, or ordered automatically by computers that monitor inventory and supply levels. In contrast, the purchase of capital items is somewhat similar to the way consumers purchase shopping goods, with the organizational buyer educating himself or herself about the alternatives before making a decision. For very expensive or complicated capital items, the purchase decision is often made on the basis of written, competitive bids.

6. Organizational buyers and sellers often classify products according to their intended usage, as follows: (1) raw materials, (2) components, (3) supplies, (4) equipment, (5) installations, and (6) business services.

7. A **brand** is a unique name or design used to identify a product. Pepsi and Sony are **brand names,** whereas McDonald's golden arches or the Pillsbury doughboy are **brand symbols.** Brands owned by national manufacturers are **national brands;** brands owned by retailers (e.g., The GAP, A&P) and wholesalers are **private brands.** In contrast, **generic products** are offered by some retailers as alternatives to branded products and are usually packaged in plain containers. They may cost up to 40 percent less than brand-name products because of their lower quality, plain packaging, and lack of promotion.

8. A **trademark** is a brand that has been given legal protection; its owner has the exclusive rights to use it. Both brand names and brand symbols may be registered with the U.S. Patent and Trademark Office.

9. The degrees of brand loyalty move from brand recognition, to brand preference, and finally to brand insistence.

10. The term that indicates a brand's overall strength in the marketplace is **brand equity,** and it is a notion of the value of a brand. Some companies buy established brand names in order to obtain brand equity. For example, Cadbury Schweppes calculated that out of the $220 million it paid for the Hires and Crush brands, $20 million was for physical assets and $200 million was for "brand value."

11. The traditional brand strategy has been to create a separate identity for each of a company's products; this practice is called individual branding. In recent years, however, **family branding** has gained popularity. When adding a new product to a product line, family branding allows the new item to capitalize on the reputation of the established product whose name it shares (e.g., the Snickers name is now found on ice cream bars, not just on candy bars).

12. Another method of reducing the cost of building a new brand is **licensing.** This is when a company buys the rights to specific names and symbols that are already established. For example, a children's pajama manufacturer might license a popular cartoon character to put on its garments.

13. Packaging is a $55 billion a year industry (it is the third largest industry in the United States) and is particularly important when you consider that 80 percent of all purchasing decisions are made in the store. The package protects the product, communicates the product's benefits, makes the item easier for the retailer to display, attracts customers' attention, reduces the temptation to steal, and provides convenience. The color of a package also communicates to customers; for example, dishwashing liquid in a yellow container connotes a lemony scent.

14. A label identifies a brand, may provide ingredient information, and can be used by a manufacturer or retailer to monitor product sales (i.e., through electronic bar codes). The Food and Drug Administration (FDA) regulates the labeling of foods, drugs, cosmetics, and health products; the Fair Packaging and Labeling Act of 1966 specifies what information a label must contain.

15. The **product development** process involves an analysis of the marketplace, the buyer, the firm's capabilities, and the economic potential of new ideas. Typically, a five-step process is employed. Generation and screening of ideas is the first step. A firm may get ideas from within the company or from outside sources. For industrial or technical products, the screening of ideas is often called a feasibility study. **Concept testing** (asking potential customers about the new product idea) may also be used as part of the screening process for both consumer and industrial products.

16. The second stage of the product development process is business analysis, which is used to determine if the company can generate enough profit with the item to justify the investment. Generally, the next step is prototype development, in which a few **prototypes** (samples) are developed and tested. Now, a few consumers may be asked to try the product and test it against other brands (the product-testing stage). **Test marketing** may also be conducted, which means that the product will be sold in selected areas and consumers' reactions will be monitored. This process is usually both expensive and time-consuming and gives competitors a look at the firm's newest idea. For these reasons, an electronic minimarket may be held, in which the purchases of several thousand consumers are monitored by computers. Finally, **commercialization** occurs, at which time the product is distributed for sale on a large scale. Some firms introduce new products gradually, going from

one part of the country to another. In this way, the costs of launching a new product are spread out over a longer time period, and product strategy can be refined as the rollout proceeds.

17. Products go through a **product life cycle,** which represents the stages of growth and decline in sales and earnings from the time an item is introduced into the marketplace until the time it is withdrawn from the marketplace. While the life cycle for some products may last only a year or two (e.g., electric hot dog cookers), for the others it may last for decades (e.g., baking soda and safety pins).

18. The four stages of the product life cycle are introductory, growth, maturity, and decline. In the introductory stage, the manufacturer must try to make the public aware of the product's existence. The extensive promotional campaign that is usually involved at this stage may mean that the manufacturer will not be making a great deal of profit. A rapid upswing in sales characterizes the growth stage, and usually other companies now enter the market. Sales tend to level off (or may even shown a slight decline) in the maturity stage, which is typically the longest-lasting product life cycle phase. A company must try to broaden the product's appeal and/or make minor improvements in this stage. Finally, as sales and profits begin to decrease, the product is in the decline stage and will eventually be withdrawn from the market.

19. A **product mix** is the collection of goods or services that a firm offers for sale. Some companies sell only a single product, while others offer a **product line,** which is a group of products within the product mix that are similar in terms of use or characteristics. A number of firms also offer several widely diversified product lines. For example, in addition to its retail outlets, Sears offers real estate, investment, insurance, and credit services.

20. Companies offering a narrow product mix hope to benefit from economies of scale (i.e., lower production costs per unit). A broad product mix, however, may guard against shifts in taste, technology, or economic circumstances.

21. Product lines tend to grow over time as firms look for ways to increase sales. Growth in product lines may come from (1) line filling—developing items to fill gaps in the market, (2) line extension—offering a new variation of the basic product (e.g., Tartar Control Crest), (3) brand extension—a current brand name extending to a new category (e.g., Jell-O Pudding Pops), and (4) line stretching—adding higher- or lower-priced items at either end of the product line.

22. A number of internal and external factors influence a firm's pricing decisions. The first step in setting price may be to determine what the company is trying to accomplish with a particular good or service. Some common objectives, for example, would be to achieve a certain profit target, to increase sales, to increase market share, and to promote a certain product image.

23. Most firms have overall profit targets as their major goal, and they use **return on investment (ROI)** to measure their success. The life cycle stage may also determine pricing objectives. In the introductory stage, the firm may use **skimming** (charge a high initial price that can be lowered when competition increases) or **penetration pricing** (charge a low price to discourage competitors). During maturity, attracting additional customers or maximizing the cash provided by the product might be the goal. And in decline, a firm may wish to charge a low price in order to clear out inventory so it can get out of the business quickly.

24. Two types of costs involved with producing a product are **fixed costs** (costs that do not change with volume, such as rent) and **variable costs** (costs that depend on the volume sold, including such items as raw materials and components). In general, costs decline as volume increases because as a company produces more units, it experiences economies of scale in production. This is referred to as the **experience curve.**

25. The U.S. government plays a big role in pricing because of price-related legislation that has been enacted over the years. For example, specifically outlawed are **price fixing** (competing companies agree with one another on prices) and **price discrimination** (attractive prices offered to some customers but not to others). Additionally, the Federal Trade Commission (FTC) can investigate and stop cases of **deceptive pricing** (misleading pricing schemes).

26. The relationship between price and demand may vary from one product or service to another. If people will buy a product regardless of its cost (within reason), the product is said to have an **inelastic demand.** However, if the market is highly responsive to price changes (i.e., lowering price greatly increases demand), the product is said to have an **elastic demand.** Undifferentiated goods and services typically have an elastic demand.

27. Competitive conditions can also determine price. Some firms price their products above the market; that is, they charge higher prices than their competitors (e.g. Sony). Other companies, though, price either below the market (e.g., Goldstar) or with the market. When pricing with the market, firms generally follow the pricing policy of a major company in the industry, known as the **price leader.**

28. A popular pricing method is markup pricing. **Markup** is the difference between the cost of an item and its selling price. It is normally expressed as a percentage (i.e., the **markup percentage).** Many businesses that carry a vast number of items use an **average markup** in setting prices. This means that the same markup percentage is used for each item in a given product line. **Turnover** (the number of times average inventory is sold during a given period) must also be considered, because the lower the turnover rate, the greater the profit that must be made on each item sold.

29. A second pricing technique, **break-even analysis,** allows a firm to determine the number of units of an item that it must sell at a particular price in order to break even. This minimum sales volume is referred to as the **break-even point.** It can be computed by dividing fixed costs by the selling price per unit minus the variable cost per unit.

30. Companies may use a variety of strategies to optimize their pricing decisions. Some firms follow a policy of **price lining,** in which merchandise is offered at a limited number of set prices. Other companies use **odd-even pricing** and price the product slightly below the next dollar figure, (e.g., $3.98, $9.95). Finally, **discount pricing** occurs when firms offer price reductions, such as **trade discounts** (offered by the producer to a wholesaler or retailer), **quantity discounts** (given to purchasers of large quantities of a product), and **cash discounts** (a reduced price to people who pay cash or who pay promptly).

KEY TERMS

product	skimming
convenience products	penetration pricing
shopping products	fixed costs
specialty products	variable costs
expense items	experience curve
capital items	price fixing
brand	price discrimination
brand names	deceptive pricing
brand symbols	inelastic demand
national brands	elastic demand
private brands	price leader
generic products	markup
trademark	markup percentage
family branding	average markup
licensing	turnover
product-development process	break-even analysis
prototypes	break-even point
test marketing	price lining
commercialization	odd-even pricing
product life cycle	discount pricing
product mix	trade discounts
product line	quantity discounts
return on investment	cash discounts

KEY TERMS EXERCISE

Directions: On the line provided, place the letter of the statement on the right that most closely defines the key term.

_____ 1. Product

_____ 2. Convenience products

_____ 3. Shopping products

_____ 4. Specialty products

_____ 5. Expense items

_____ 6. Capital items

_____ 7. Product mix

_____ 8. Product line

_____ 9. Product life cycle

_____ 10. Product-development process

_____ 11. Concept testing

_____ 12. Prototypes

_____ 13. Test marketing

_____ 14. Commercialization

_____ 15. Brand

_____ 16. National brands

_____ 17. Private brands

_____ 18. Generic brands

_____ 19. Trademark

_____ 20. Family branding

_____ 21. Licensing

_____ 22. Return on investment

_____ 23. Skimming

_____ 24. Penetration

_____ 25. Fixed costs

_____ 26. Variable costs

a. Offering a reduction in price.

b. A complete list of all products that a company offers for sale.

c. Charging a high price for a new product during the introductory stage, then lowering the price later on.

d. Products that are readily available, low-priced, and heavily advertised and that consumers buy quickly and often.

e. The working samples of a proposed product.

f. The sales volume at a given price that will cover all of a company's cost.

g. The amount added to the cost of an item to create a selling price that produces a profit.

h. The stages of growth and decline in sales and earnings.

i. Giving rights to a company to use a well-known name or symbol in marketing its products.

j. Brands owned by a manufacturer and distributed nationally.

k. Anything that is offered for the purpose of satisfying a want or need in a market exchange.

l. Products for which a consumer spends a lot of time shopping in order to compare prices, quality, and style.

m. Using a brand name on a variety of products that are related.

n. A constant markup percentage used in setting prices for all products in a product line.

o. Setting a "suggested retail price" before distribution to wholesalers and retailers.

p. A major producer in an industry that tends to set the pace in establishing prices.

q. Relatively inexpensive industrial products that are consumed within a year of their purchase.

r. A method of calculating the minimum volume of sales needed at a given price to cover all costs.

s. Introducing a new product at a low price in hopes of building sales volume quickly.

____ 27. Markup

____ 28. Markup percentage

____ 29. Average markup

____ 30. Turnover

____ 31. Break-even analysis

____ 32. Break-even point

____ 33. Price leader

____ 34. Price lining

____ 35. Odd pricing

____ 36. Suggest pricing

____ 37. Discount pricing

____ 38. Trade discount

____ 39. Quantity discount

____ 40. Cash discount

t. The discount offered buyers of large quantities.

u. The stages through which a product passes from initial conceptualization to actual appearance in the marketplace.

v. Business costs that must be covered no matter how many units of a product a company sells.

w. Products of minimum quality in plain packaging that bears only the name of the item, not of its producer.

x. Setting a price at an odd amount slightly below the next highest dollar figure.

y. A group of products that are physically similar or that are intended for similar markets.

z. Products that a consumer will make a special effort to locate.

aa. The large-scale production and distribution of a product.

bb. A profit equal to a certain percentage of a business's invested capital.

cc. The number of times that average inventory is sold during a given period.

dd. Relatively expensive industrial products that have a long life and are used in the operations of a business.

ee. The process of getting reactions about a proposed product from potential customers.

ff. Any name, term, sign, symbol, design, or combination of these used to identify the products of a firm and to differentiate them from competing products.

gg. Brands that carry the label of a retailer or wholesaler rather than a manufacturer.

hh. Business costs that increase with the number of units produced.

ii. The product development stage in which a product is sold on a limited basis.

jj. A discount offered to a wholesaler or retailer.

kk. A reduced price to people who pay cash or pay promptly.

ll. The difference, in percentage terms, between the cost of an item and its selling price.

mm. A brand that has been given legal protection so that its owner has exclusive rights to its use.

nn. Offering merchandise at a limited number of set prices.

ANSWERS TO KEY TERMS EXERCISE

10.	n	(p. 368)	20.	m	(p. 375)	30.	cc	(p. 378)	40.	kk	(p. 380)
9.	h	(p. 370)	19.	mm	(p. 363)	29.	n	(p. 378)	39.	t	(p. 380)
8.	y	(p. 372)	18.	w	(p. 363)	28.	ll	(p. 378)	38.	jj	(p. 380)
7.	b	(p. 372)	17.	gg	(p. 363)	27.	g	(p. 378)	37.	a	(p. 380)
6.	dd	(p. 362)	16.	j	(p. 363)	26.	hh	(p. 374)	36.	o	(p. 380)
5.	q	(p. 362)	15.	ff	(p. 363)	25.	v	(p. 374)	35.	x	(p. 380)
4.	z	(p. 361)	14.	aa	(p. 370)	24.	s	(p. 374)	34.	uu	(p. 380)
3.	l	(p. 361)	13.	ii	(p. 369)	23.	c	(p. 374)	33.	p	(p. 377)
2.	d	(p. 361)	12.	e	(p. 369)	22.	bb	(p. 374)	32.	f	(p. 379)
1.	k	(p. 358)	11.	ee	(p. 369)	21.	i	(p. 365)	31.	r	(p. 379)

SELF TEST

True-False Questions

_____   1. For all consumer and industrial goods, price is the primary consideration in the purchase decision.

_____   2. A product line is composed of the physically similar products offered by a company.

_____   3. The sales of generic products seem to be increasing in recent years, as consumers become familiar with the generally high quality of the products.

_____   4. Packaging's only role is to protect the product from damage or tampering.

_____   5. Most products have a combination of tangible and intangible features.

_____   6. Turnover is the number of times that a company sells its inventory during a given time period.

_____   7. Break-even analysis will provide a company with the exact price it should charge for a product.

_____   8. A company would almost always prefer to compete by attracting customers by unique product features rather than by engaging in a price war.

_____   9. Because of the intangibility, services need to be marketed differently than tangible products.

_____   10. The maturity stage of the product life cycle is the longest stage for most products.

_____   11. It is illegal for companies to agree with one another to set a certain price in order to reduce competition.

Multiple Choice Questions

_____   1. Convenience products
   a. have no acceptable substitute.
   b. are purchased after considerable thought.
   c. have an easily recognizable image developed by advertising.
   d. are purchased infrequently.

_____   2. Disneyland, a baseball game, and a car repair would all be classified as
   a. tangible products.
   b. intangible products.
   c. industrial goods
   d. none of the above.

_____ 3. Which step in the new product development process is concerned with the financial analysis of whether the product can make enough to justify the investment?
a. idea generation
b. idea screening
c. business analysis
d. product testing

_____ 4. Products that have survived the test stage and have been produced and distributed are in what step of the new-product development process?
a. test marketing
b. commercialization
c. business analysis
d. prototype development

_____ 5. Building on the name recognition of an existing brand to help introduce a new product is termed
a. illegal.
b. licensing.
c. brand bundling.
d. family branding.

_____ 6. A company's pricing goals for a product may vary over time. An example of such changes would be
a. following a penetration pricing strategy in the introductory and growth stages
b. charging a high price during the decline stage to keep competition honest.
c. pricing to maximize cash flow during the maturity phase.
d. all of the above.

_____ 7. An average markup is often used by businesses because
a. they are, on average, meeting the competition.
b. they charge average prices in the marketplace.
c. they handle too many products to calculate easily the proper markup percentage for each.
d. they are profit maximizers.

_____ 8. A company following a market-based pricing strategy may
a. price the same as the competition.
b. price higher than the competition.
c. price lower than the competition.
d. any of the above.

_____ 9. Organizational products that are classified as being capital items tend to be purchased
a. with a great deal of planning.
b. after a long time is taken to make the decision.
c. with a written, competitive bid.
d. all of the above.

_____ 10. Organizational products that involve large outlays of capital and are major pieces of equipment and buildings used to make other products are know as
a. components.
b. equipment.
c. installations.
d. raw materials.
e. supplies.

_____ 11. Inexpensive, frequently purchased items often bought out of habit are classified as
a. convenience products.
b. shopping products.
c. specialty products.
d. unsought products.

_____ 12. Most consumers would classify stereos, cars, and washing machines as
   a. convenience products.
   b. shopping products.
   c. specialty products.
   d. unsought products.

_____ 13. In which stage of the product life cycle will there be the largest increase in sales, but also the largest number of competitors?
   a. introduction
   b. growth
   c. maturity
   d. sales decline

_____ 14. The action in which companies supplying the same types of products agree to sell those products at a certain price in order to reduce competition is known as
   a. price fixing.
   b. deceptive pricing.
   c. price discrimination.
   d. predatory pricing.

_____ 15. Offering different customers who buy the same basic product under the same basic circumstances different prices is the illegal pricing practice of
   a. price fixing.
   b. deceptive pricing.
   c. price discrimination.
   d. predatory pricing.

_____ 16. The highest level of brand loyalty exists for
   a. convenience products.
   b. shopping products.
   c. specialty products.
   d. unsought products.

_____ 17. Using the same brand name for a group of related products, such as for Green Giant corn, peas, etc., is known as
   a. individual branding.
   b. family branding.
   c. national branding.
   d. private branding.

_____ 18. The stage of the product life cycle in which the company tries to stimulate demand, build distribution channels, and expend large amounts of money on promotion is known as
   a. introduction.
   b. growth.
   c. maturity.
   d. decline.

_____ 19. Promoting the price of a product in an unfair way, such as making phony price comparisons or having strings attached for a bargain, is known as
   a. price fixing.
   b. deceptive pricing.
   c. price discrimination.
   d. predatory pricing.

_____ 20. The increasing number of product liability suits and the large amount being awarded in lawsuits has resulted in
   a. some new products not being introduced to the marketplace.
   b. the removal of some potentially dangerous products from the marketplace.
   c. safer product designs.
   d. the provision of specific instructions and warnings on product use.
   e. all of the above.

Completion Questions

1. Products bought by consumers on a frequent basis, without too much formal thought, are called

    _____ products.

2. The overall strength of a brand in the marketplace and its value to the company that owns it is known as

    brand _____.

3. The _____ is the collection of goods and services offered to the market by an organization.

4. A process of growth and decline in sales and earnings for a product is termed a _____.

5. A _____ is a way of identifying a product through a unique name or design.

6. A brand owned by a national manufacturer is a _____ brand.

7. A _____ is a legally protected brand name.

8. _____ is profit expressed as a percentage of capital investment.

9. During the introductory stage of the product life cycle, a company may follow a _____ price practice, charging a high initial price.

10. _____ is the difference between the cost of an item and its selling price.

11. Capital items for organizational buyers tend to use the same process as consumers do when buying

    _____, while expense items are similar to how consumers purchase _____.

12. Products whose demand is relatively insensitive to changes in price have _____ demand, while

    products with high responses to price changes have _____.

PROJECT

Product Packaging

   Packaging is becoming increasingly important to marketers because of both competitive pressures and regulations. In fact, as your text describes, packaging can even help "create a new product." Evidence of the importance of packaging in a promotional sense as well as a protective sense can be seen easily on a trip to a supermarket. Go to a local supermarket and observe the various functions packaging performs. To help guide your observations, select one product category and answer the questions listed below.
   Examples of product categories are soft drinks, laundry detergents, and pet foods.

1. Give three examples of how packaging provides physical protection for products.

2. How does packaging make products easier to promote? Give three examples.

3. What are some examples of how packaging can become part of the product itself? What are some additional uses for packaging?

4. Did you find any packages that seemed ecologically unsound? What arguments might businesses make to counter your complaints?

5. Did you find the information on the labels helpful or valuable? Why or why not? What additional information would you like to see on the labels? What information now appearing on labels would you like to see removed?

Chapter 14

Distribution

LEARNING OBJECTIVES

1. List nine functions performed by marketing intermediaries.

2. Name the alternative distribution channels for consumer goods, organizational goods, and services.

3. Differentiate among intensive, selective, and exclusive market-coverage strategies.

4. Describe the three types of wholesalers.

5. Name at least ten types of retailers.

6. Explain what is meant by the "wheel of retailing."

7. Specify the activities included in physical distribution.

8. List the five most common ways of transporting goods.

OUTLINE

I. The distribution mix

    A. What a channel of distribution is
       1. The distribution mix

    B. The role of marketing intermediaries
       1. The utility intermediaries help create
       2. Functions performed by intermediaries

    C. Channel alternatives
       1. Channels for consumer goods
       2. Channels for organizational goods
       3. Channels for services

    D. Reverse channels

    E. Channel selection
       1. Market coverage
          a. Intensive, selective, and exclusive distribution
       2. Cost
       3. Control
       4. Other factors
          a. The use of multiple channels
          b. How the optimum distribution system for a product may change over time

    F. Channel conflicts
       1. Vertical and horizontal conflicts

    G. Vertical marketing systems
       1. The corporate vertical marketing system

      2. The administered vertical marketing system
          a.   Channel captains
      3. The contractual vertical marketing system

   H.   International distribution

II.   Types of intermediaries

   A.   Wholesalers
      1. Merchant wholesalers
          a.   Rack jobbers
      2. Agents and brokers
          a.   Manufacturer's agents
          b.   Brokers
      3. Producer-owned wholesalers
          a.   Branch offices and sales offices

   B.   Retailers
      1. The status of the U.S. retailing industry
      2. Department stores
          a.   History of department store retailing
          b.   How department stores deal with competitors
              (1)   Scrambled merchandising
      3. Bargain stores
          a.   Discount stores
              (1)   The wheel of retailing
          b.   Off-price stores
          c.   Warehouse clubs
          d.   Factory outlets
      4. Specialty shops
      5. Supermarkets
          a.   The hypermarket
      6. Convenience stores
      7. Nonstore retailers
          a.   Telemarketing
          b.   Mail-order firms
          c.   Vending machines
          d.   Door-to-door retailers

III. Physical distribution

   A.   The scope of physical distribution

   B.   In-house operations
      1.   Forecasting
      2. Order processing
      3. Inventory control
      4. Warehousing
          a.   Distribution centers
      5. Materials handling

   C.   Transportation
      1. The importance of transportation
      2. Modes of transportation
      3. Ground transport
          a.   Trucks

   b. Rail
   c. Water
   d. Air
   e. Pipelines
   4. Environmental impact of transportation
       a. The *Exxon Valdez* incident
       b. Problems with trucking

MAJOR POINTS TO REMEMBER

1. The systems used to move goods and services from producer to the ultimate user are called **distribution channels** (or marketing channels). There are many distribution alternatives, and a company's decisions regarding which combination of channels to use are known as its **distribution mix**.

2. For about 97 percent of what individuals buy, **marketing intermediaries** are relied on to simplify transactions between consumers and producers. Intermediaries help create place, time, and possession utility by simplifying the exchange process and by having goods and services available for consumers at the proper time and place. In addition, intermediaries may (1) provide a sales force; (2) provide market information; (3) provide promotional support; (4) sort, standardize, and divide shipments; (5) carry stock; (6) deliver the product; (7) assume risks; (8) provide financing; and (9) buy.

3. One channel for consumer goods is producer to consumer. This is the most direct way to market an item and is used, for example, by artisans who sell their leather goods or jewelry at crafts fairs. Producer to retailer to consumer is another channel that is used often in the clothing business and in automobile sales. The most common channel, producer to wholesaler to retailer to consumer, is best for the small producer unable to afford its own sales force. Finally, producer to agent/broker to wholesaler to retailer to consumer is found in agriculture, where specialists are needed to negotiate the sale or to sort or grade merchandise.

4. For organizational goods, the most common channel is for the product to go directly from the producer to the user. However, if there are many small producers or if buyers are geographically scattered, then one or more levels of intermediaries may be employed.

5. Services are most often distributed directly by the producer to the user, because the nature of most services requires such direct contact (e.g., hair stylist or lawyer). Some service businesses, though, like the travel industry, do rely on intermediaries.

6. While most channels move products from producers to consumers, **reverse channels** flow in the opposite direction. Examples of reverse channels include those used for recycling and product recalls.

7. Every producer must decide whether to sell directly to end users or rely on intermediaries. Determining which distribution channel or channels to use involves trade-offs concerning the number of outlets where the product will be available, the cost of distribution, and control over the product. With respect to market coverage (i.e., the availability of the product), inexpensive convenience goods or organizational supplies may be distributed using **intensive distribution** (i.e., the product is to be sold in as many outlets as possible), which makes long distribution channels necessary. When **selective distribution** is considered proper (i.e., the product is to be sold in a limited number of outlets), the distribution chain can be shorter; shopping goods are sold this way. Specialty goods and technical products may be marketed using either direct sales or **exclusive distribution,** which restricts the number of outlets in a particular area that sell the item.

8. Cost plays a role in a firm's distribution decision. Firms that cannot afford to build large warehouses and distribution centers or to hire large sales forces need the help of intermediaries. But dealing with intermediaries means giving up some control. For example, manufacturers cannot force intermediaries to promote their products aggressively. Other factors (e.g., geographic concentration of customers, buyers' need for service, or the importance of rapid delivery) may also influence the distribution decision. Often, in fact, the best solution is to employ multiple channels to reach different target markets. Additionally, the "best" distribution arrangement for a product is likely to change over time (i.e., it may change as the product goes through different stages of the product life cycle).

9. Channel conflicts are common in the business world, especially when participants have different objectives. The two basic types of channel conflict are vertical and horizontal. **Vertical conflict** occurs between channel members at different levels in the distribution chain, whereas **horizontal conflict** is between channel members at the same level.

10. **Vertical marketing systems** are a way to reduce channel conflict. In the **corporate vertical marketing system,** the same company owns both the production and distribution operations. A more informal arrangement is the **administered vertical marketing system,** in which one member of the distribution chain has enough power to influence the others. This dominant firm is called the **channel captain.** Finally, the **contractual vertical marketing system** is a cross between the corporate and administered versions, with channel members bound by contractual agreement. An example of this type of system is the franchise.

11. The international distribution of products and services adds an additional set of problems to the management of marketing channels. For example, exporting a product to India would require abiding by U.S. export laws and the import and general business laws of India. Additionally, the transaction would have to adhere to the legal requirements in any and all countries the goods passed through on the trip from the United States to India.

12. The two main types of intermediaries are wholesalers and retailers. **Wholesalers** sell to retailers, other wholesalers, and organizational users, whereas **retailers** sell to people who purchase the item for their own use.

13. There are 300,000 wholesale businesses in the United States. About 80 percent of all wholesalers are **merchant wholesalers,** who take title to merchandise and then resell it to retailers or organizational users. While some merchant wholesalers provide a great many services to customers, others offer less. **Rack jobbers,** for example, set up displays, stock inventory and mark prices.

14. **Manufacturer's agents** never actually own what they sell; they receive a commission for any transaction they handle. One very common type of agent is the sales representative, who calls on customers in a specified territory. Special types of agents who concentrate on selling a particular commodity (e.g., coffee or soybean oil) are known as **brokers.** They may arrange for a sale and thereby earn a commission. Brokers also operate in the financial field, real estate, insurance, and securities.

15. The two types of producer-owned wholesaler businesses are the **branch office,** which carries inventory and performs many marketing functions, and the **sales office,** which limits its activities to selling.

16. The United States is presently "overstored." While retail space in suburban malls has almost doubled over the past twelve years, the population has increased only 13 percent. As a result, there is now about 40 percent more retail capacity than is needed. Large chain stores account for over half of all retail sales, but about a third of all retail sales are made in small operations with no paid employees other than the owner.

17. **Department stores** are large retail establishments that bring together a wide range of merchandise under one roof. They have a reputation for quality, fashion, and service. Within the past thirty years, most department stores have established branches in suburban areas. Today, these retailers are having problems because identical merchandise is often available at lower prices in other types of stores. To fight back, department stores are having more sales and are trying to sell items that generally are not available elsewhere. They are also trying to increase sales by using **scrambled merchandising** (i.e., carrying products ordinarily handled by other types of outlets), by eliminating unprofitable lines to maximize profit per square foot of selling space, and by emphasizing service.

18. Bargain stores can offer nationally advertised and private-brand goods at low prices. **Discount stores** like Wal-Mart and K-Mart started the discounting movement after World War II by offering inexpensive merchandise in bare-bones outlets at cheap locations. However, many such discounters have upgraded their chains and become more like traditional department stores. This evolutionary process is called the **wheel of retailing.** It allows such retailers to be replaced with lower-priced competitors when they upgrade their offerings.

19. There are three other types of bargain stores: off-price stores, warehouse clubs, and factory outlets. **Off-price stores** sell name-brand items at below-department-store prices. **Warehouse clubs** are large, bare out-

lets stacked floor to ceiling with merchandise; usually customers must purchase an annual membership in order to shop there. A **factory outlet,** on the other hand, is a store owned and operated by a single manufacturer selling only its own goods.

20. **Specialty shops** carry only a limited number of product lines but offer a large selection of brands, styles, and variations. Many are owned and operated by chains (e.g., The Limited, B. Dalton, and Baskin Robbins). Franchising is also popular.

21. **Supermarkets** are large departmentalized food stores, often with annual sales in the millions. They carry nationally branded merchandise, private brands, and generic products. Although there has been a trend to include a separate delicatessen or bakery department, self-service is still an important characteristic. In recent years, some supermarkets have become "hypermarkets," which combine a discount store with a supermarket. A bit smaller than hypermarkets, superstores or combo stores also stock a great many nonfood items.

22. **Convenience stores** are food stores whose chief stock in trade is time and place convenience (e.g., 7-Eleven). They are typically open seven days a week, twenty four hours a day, and can operate in an area that does not have a large enough population to support a supermarket. Convenience stores carry a limited selection of brands and sizes and charge higher prices than other stores, but their customers avoid long lines at checkout counters.

23. Nonstore retailers include **telemarketing** (telephone retailing), **mail-order firms** (e.g., L. L. Bean, Lands' End), vending machines, and door-to-door retailers (including party plans). The latest innovations in nonstore retailing include selling via computers and cable TV.

24. **Physical distribution** involves all the activities required to move finished products from the producer to the consumer. The in-house operations include forecasting, order processing, inventory control, warehousing, and materials handling.

25. A firm must have an accurate estimate of demand if it is to control the flow of products through the distribution system. **Order processing** includes checking the buyer's credit, recording the sale, making the proper accounting system entries, arranging for shipping, adjusting inventory records, and billing customers. Most firms try to ship orders within a specific period of time. **Inventory control** is also important and involves the attempt to have the right amount of goods on hand to fill orders.

26. Products are physically stored in a **warehouse** prior to being shipped to buyers. Such facilities may be owned by the company, by an intermediary, or by a private firm that leases warehouse space. Some firms have **distribution centers** that serve as command posts for moving items to customers.

27. The movement of goods within and between physical distribution facilities is called **materials handling.** It involves choosing a storage method and keeping track of inventory.

28. Normally, the largest single item in the overall cost of physical distribution is transportation. The two major types of ground transportation are trucks and railroads. Trucks are the most frequently used form of transportation, because they offer both door-to-door delivery and the ability to operate on public highways. Railroads can carry heavier loads and actually transport a larger volume of goods than any other form of transportation.

29. Water is the cheapest form of transportation and is widely used for bulk items despite its slowness and infrequent service. Air transport is limited by the location of airports, as well as by cargo size and shape limitations. It is therefore the least dependable and most expensive mode of shipment, although it is the fastest. Pipelines are used almost exclusively to ship liquids and gases. They are expensive to build but economical to operate.

30. Transportation has an impact on our environment. The *Exxon Valdez* oil spill in Alaska's Prince William Sound resulted in a call for double-hulled tankers. Segments of our interstate highways are in poor shape because of the damage caused by 80,000-pound trucks. Trucks also generate four times as much pollution per ton hauled as railroads.

KEY TERMS

distribution channels
distribution mix
marketing intermediaries
reverse channels
intensive distribution
selective distribution
exclusive distribution
vertical conflict
horizontal conflict
vertical marketing systems
corporate vertical marketing system
administered vertical marketing system
channel captain
wholesalers
retailers
merchant wholesalers
rack jobbers
manufacturer's agents
brokers
branch office

sales office
department stores
scrambled merchandising
discount stores
wheel of retailing
off-price stores
warehouse clubs
factory outlet
specialty shops
supermarkets
convenience stores
telemarketing
mail-order firms
physical distribution
order processing
inventory control
warehouse
distribution centers
materials handling

KEY TERMS EXERCISE

Directions: On the line provided, place the letter of the statement on the right that most closely defines the key term.

_____ 1. Distribution channels

_____ 2. Distribution mix

_____ 3. Marketing intermediaries

_____ 4. Intensive distribution

_____ 5. Selective distribution

_____ 6. Exclusive distribution

_____ 7. Wholesalers

_____ 8. Retailers

_____ 9. Merchant wholesalers

_____ 10. Rack jobbers

_____ 11. Manufacturer's agents

_____ 12. Brokers

_____ 13. Branch office

_____ 14. Sales office

_____ a. Producer-owned operation that carries stock and sells it.

_____ b. Food stores that offer convenient locations and hours but that stock a limited selection of goods.

_____ c. Functions involved in receiving and handling an order.

_____ d. The policy of carrying merchandise that is ordinarily sold in a different type of outlet.

_____ e. Systems for moving goods and services from producers to consumers.

_____ f. Stores that carry only particular types of goods.

_____ g. Companies that sell products through catalogs and ship them directly to customers by mail.

_____ h. Producer-owned operation that does not carry stock but takes orders.

_____ i. Combination of intermediaries and channels that a producer uses to get a product to end users.

_____ 15. Department stores

_____ 16. Scrambled merchandising

_____ 17. Discount stores

_____ 18. Wheel of retailing

_____ 19. Off-price stores

_____ 20. Warehouse clubs

_____ 21. Specialty stores

_____ 22. Supermarkets

_____ 23. Convenience stores

_____ 24. Mail-order firms

_____ 25. Physical distribution

_____ 26. Order processing

_____ 27. Warehouse

_____ 28. Distribution centers

_____ j. Firms that sell products to other firms for resale or for organizational use.

_____ k. Business people and organizations who channel goods and services from producers to consumers.

_____ l. Retailers that sell a variety of goods below the market price by keeping their overhead low.

_____ m. An approach to distribution that involves placing the product in nearly every available outlet.

_____ n. Merchant wholesalers that are responsible for setting up and maintaining displays in a particular store area.

_____ o. A facility for storing backup stocks of supplies or finished products.

_____ p. Approach to distribution in which intermediaries are given the exclusive right to sell a product within a given market.

_____ q. Low-priced stores that sell memberships to small retailers and consumer members.

_____ r. Firms that sell directly to the public.

_____ s. Large retail stores that carry a wide variety of high-quality merchandise.

_____ t. Large departmentalized food stores.

_____ u. Wholesalers that do not take title to products but that receive a commission for selling products.

_____ v. The evolutionary process by which stores that feature low prices are gradually upgraded until they forfeit their appeal to price-sensitive shoppers and are replaced by competitors.

_____ w. An approach to distribution that relies on a limited number of outlets.

_____ x. Warehouse facilities that specialize in collecting and shipping merchandise.

_____ y. Retailers that offer bargain prices by maintaining low overhead and acquiring merchandise at below-wholesale costs.

_____ z. Agents that specialize in a particular commodity.

_____ aa. Independent wholesalers that take legal title to products.

_____ bb. All the activities required to move finished products from the producer to the consumer.

ANSWERS TO KEY TERMS EXERCISE

28. x (p. 407)	21. f (p. 402)	14. h (p. 398)	7. j (p. 397)
27. o (p. 407)	20. q (p. 401)	13. a (p. 398)	6. p (p. 392)
26. c (p. 406)	19. y (p. 401)	12. z (p. 398)	5. w (p. 392)
25. bb (p. 405)	18. v (p. 400)	11. n (p. 398)	4. m (p. 392)
24. g (p. 404)	17. l (p. 400)	10. u (p. 398)	3. k (p. 388)
23. b (p. 404)	16. d (p. 399)	9. aa (p. 398)	2. i (p. 388)
22. t (p. 403)	15. s (p. 399)	8. r (p. 397)	1. e (p. 388)

SELF TEST

True-False Questions

_____ 1. Franchising is the most common type of contractual vertical marketing system.

_____ 2. Most services are distributed through an indirect distribution channel.

_____ 3. Market and buyer behavior-related factors are the only variables of concern in making distribution decisions.

_____ 4. For a company considering distribution alternatives, the best solution often is to use multiple channels to reach different target markets.

_____ 5. Vending machines lend themselves to the efficient sale of most consumer goods.

_____ 6. Once a customer orders a product, all of the physical distribution activities occur after the product leaves the producer's facilities.

_____ 7. For any business, the largest single cost in physical distribution is the cost of transportation.

_____ 8. A manufacturer is always best served by using the cheapest available form of transportation.

_____ 9. Because it is inexpensive, shipment by water is attractive and suitable for most products.

_____ 10. Companies that sell products requiring maintenance and repair need to develop reverse distribution channels.

_____ 11. Distributing products to foreign countries is basically the same as distributing products domestically.

_____ 12. The environmental impact of transportation is of increasing importance to businesses and consumers.

Multiple Choice Questions

_____ 1. Intermediaries simplify the transactions between consumer and producer. Which utilities do intermediaries help create?
   a. place, time, and form
   b. place, ownership, and form
   c. place, time, and ownership
   d. time, ownership, and form

____ 2. Conflict between channel members of different levels, such as manufacturers and retailers, is known as
   a. vertical conflict.
   b. horizontal conflict.
   c. interchannel conflict.
   d. power conflict.

____ 3. Which of the following is an example of a vertical marketing system?
   a. corporate
   b. administered
   c. contractual
   d. all of the above
   e. none of the above

____ 4. The most direct way to market a consumer good is
   a. producer to wholesaler to retailer to consumer.
   b. producer to retailer to consumer.
   c. producer to agent/broker to wholesaler to retailer to consumer.
   d. All of the above are equally direct in terms of providing a consumer good to the buyer.

____ 5. In general, when an organization chooses one distribution channel over another, it is assessing
   a. the size of the middlemen in each channel.
   b. trade-offs between cost and control.
   c. the number of functions performed by wholesalers in the alternative channels.
   d. all of the above.

____ 6. Under what circumstance is an organization more likely to use a direct distribution channel?
   a. when customers are concentrated in a limited geographic area
   b. when each order is relatively small
   c. when the product is relatively inexpensive
   d. when there is no competition

____ 7. An agent or organization who never takes title to the merchandise, is owned by the producer, and conducts only the selling activities for the producer is called a
   a. broker.
   b. sales representative.
   c. branch office.
   d. sales office.

____ 8. Stores that specialize in buying other people's mistakes and offering national brands at low prices (because they bought at below wholesale prices) are called
   a. discount stores.
   b. bargain stores.
   c. off-price stores.
   d. gray market outlets.

____ 9. A store that carries a limited line of products, but an extensive selection within each line, and that may offer highly personalized service is called a
   a. factory outlet.
   b. variety store.
   c. specialty store.
   d. supermarket.

_____ 10. The physical distribution activity of order processing includes
  a. recording the sale.
  b. checking the customer's credit.
  c. adjusting inventory records.
  d. all of the above.

_____ 11. As a form of ground transportation, trucks have what characteristics?
  a. They can carry all types of cargo.
  b. They offer door-to-door delivery.
  c. They are the fastest form of transportation.
  d. They are the cheapest form of transportation.

_____ 12. Some distributors never actually own the merchandise they sell. These distributors are known as
  a. retailers.
  b. rack jobbers.
  c. agents.
  d. none of the above.

_____ 13. When distributing products internationally from the United States to foreign countries, a company must
  a. abide by U.S. export laws.
  b. abide by the import laws of the destination country.
  c. abide by applicable laws of all countries through which the product passes.
  d. all of the above.

Completion Questions

1. The system used to move goods and services from producers to customers is called the _____.

2. When one participant in the distribution channel is stronger than the others in that channel, _____ is likely to occur.

3. _____ are a way of organizing and controlling a channel of distribution to reduce channel conflict.

4. The channel member who makes the decisions within an administered vertical marketing system is known as the _____.

5. _____ sell to individuals who buy the product for their own use.

6. A merchant wholesaler that sets up displays in retail outlets is known as a _____.

7. When a department store, or any other retailer, adds products ordinarily handled by another type of outlet, it is attempting to build traffic by _____.

8. The evolutionary process by which stores that feature low prices are gradually upgraded until they lose their appeal to price-sensitive shoppers is known as the _____.

9. Mail-order catalogs, vending machines, or door-to-door sales forces are all examples of _____ retailers.

10. With _____ distribution, the market is saturated with a product.

11. Product recalls and product recycling require that _____ distribution channels be developed to move products from consumers to producers.

12. A retail facility owned and operated by a manufacturer to sell the company's discontinued merchandise, irregulars, closeouts, and canceled orders at reduced prices is known as a _____.

PROJECT

PART 1

Comparing Retail Stores

Retailers have different mixes and offer different services to their customers. To analyze this point, complete the following table, comparing the stock, display, and pricing of three different kinds of products by a convenience grocery store, such as 7-Eleven, and a national chain supermarket, such as a Safeway.

Dry Breakfast Cereal

	CONVENIENCE GROCERY STORE	NATIONAL CHAIN STORE
1. Number of different brands carried		
2. Number of different sizes of packages		
3. Number of linear feet of exposure		
4. Average prices		

Potato Chips and Snacks

	CONVENIENCE GROCERY STORE	NATIONAL CHAIN STORE
1. Number of different brands carried		
2. Number of different sizes of packages		
3. Number of linear feet of exposure		
4. Average prices		

Canned Fruit

	CONVENIENCE GROCERY STORE	NATIONAL CHAIN STORE
1. Number of different brands carried		
2. Number of different sizes of packages		
3. Number of linear feet of exposure		
4. Average prices		

PART 2

What major conclusions can you draw about the marketing strategy of a convenience grocery store and a national chain? Is there a need for both types of stores?

Chapter 15

Promotion

LEARNING OBJECTIVES

1. Describe the four basic categories of promotion.

2. Distinguish between "push" and "pull" strategies of promotion.

3. Explain the concept of positioning.

4. List the seven steps in the personal-selling process.

5. Define institutional, product, and competitive advertising.

6. List the five main types of advertising media and at least three lesser-known types.

7. Explain the role of public relations in marketing.

8. Distinguish between the two main types of sales promotion, and give at least two examples of each type.

OUTLINE

I. The promotional mix

    A. Definition of promotion

    B. Promotional goals
        1. The three basic goals of promotion

    C. Promotional ethics
        1. Public concern over the potential misuse of promotion
        2. Regulation of Advertising
            a. The Federal Trade Commission (FTC)
            b. Other federal agencies
            c. State regulation of promotion
            d. Self-regulation
                (1) The National Advertising Review Board

    D. Four elements of promotion
        1. The promotional mix
            a. Personal selling
            b. Advertising
            c. Public relations
            d. Sales promotion

    E. Promotional strategies
        1. Product-related factors
            a. Type of product
            b. Price of product
            c. PLC stage of product

2. Market-related factors
    a. Push strategy
    b. Pull strategy
    c. Size and concentration of the market
3. Positioning
    a. What positioning is
    b. Positioning and the promotional mix

II. Personal Selling

  A. Types of sales personnel
    1. Order getters
    2. Order takers
    3. Sales support personnel
      a. Missionary salespeople
      b. Technical salespeople
      c. Trade salespeople
    4. Telemarketing

  B. The creative selling process
    1. Prospecting
    2. Preparing
    3. Approaching the prospect
    4. Making the presentation
    5. Handling objections
    6. Closing
    7. Follow-up

III. Advertising

  A. What advertising is

  B. What advertising does
    1. Per capita spending on advertising

  C. Types of advertising
    1. Product advertising
    2. Institutional advertising
      a. Advocacy advertising
    3. Competitive advertising
    4. Comparative advertising
    5. National advertising
    6. Local advertising
      a. Cooperative advertising

  D. Advertising appeals
    1. Logic and emotion
    2. Celebrity appeal
    3. Sex appeal
    4. The power of novelty

  E. The elements of advertising
    1. Ad copy
      a. Five purposes of ad copy
    2. Artwork

F.   Advertising media
     a.   The media mix
     b.   Media buying
        (1) How to evaluate cost
        (2) Reach, frequency, and continuity
1.   Characteristics of advertising media
     a.   Recent shifts in the distribution of media spending
     b.   Newspapers
     c.   Television
     d.   Direct mail
        (1) Database marketing
     e.   Radio
     f.   Magazines
     g.   Other media

IV. Public relations

    A.   What the public relations job involves

V.   Sales promotion

    A.   Consumer promotions
       1.   Couponing
       2.   Point-of-purchase displays
       3.   Special event sponsorship
       4.   Other sales promotion techniques

    B.   Trade promotion
       1.   Trade allowances
       2.   Trade shows

MAJOR POINTS TO REMEMBER

1.   Of the four elements in the marketing mix, the one most often associated with marketing is **promotion,** a term that may be defined as persuasive communication that motivates individuals to buy whatever the organization is selling (i.e., goods, services, or ideas).

2.   Most promotional activities have three basic goals: (1) informing the customer about the item, (2) persuading a customer to purchase the item, and (3) reminding the customer about the product.

3.   Public concern about potential misuse of promotion has been responsible for the growth of government regulations. The Federal Trade Commission (FTC), the government's advertising watchdog, has created regulations for the industry (e.g., all statements of fact must be supported by evidence, and advertisers must not create an overall impression that is incorrect). The Food and Drug Administration and the U.S. Department of Agriculture recently developed a set of guidelines and policies for ad claims and product-label wording. Many states also regulate promotional practices by particular industries, such as liquor stores and small loan companies.

4.   There are many examples of self-regulation of advertising. For instance, the National Advertising Review Board—whose members include ad agencies, advertisers, and the public—has a full-time staff to investigate complaints.

5.   The combination of activities that are put together to promote a particular product, service, or idea is called the **promotional mix.** It consists of personal selling, advertising, public relations, and sales promotion. **Personal selling** is direct, person-to-person communication, either in person or over the telephone. It is the only form of promotion that permits the seller to adjust the message to the exact needs and wants of the buyer. Personal selling's main drawback, however, is its high cost.

6. **Advertising** is any paid form of nonpersonal presentation made through a mass communications medium on behalf of goods, services, or ideas. While it has the ability to reach large numbers of people economically, it is often very expensive and difficult to personalize. **Public relations** consists of all nonsales communications that businesses have with their various publics. In addition to responding to journalists' requests for information, public relations also seeks to generate favorable news coverage for the firm in the media. The final element of promotion, **sales promotion,** includes the many promotional activities not considered to be personal selling, advertising, or public relations (e.g., coupons, rebates, contests, in-store demonstrations, free samples, trade shows, and point-of-purchase displays).

7. Promotional strategies must consider a number of product-related factors. Certain types of products or services lend themselves to different forms of promotion, and the item's price may also be a factor (i.e., low-priced products sold to a mass market are usually heavily advertised, while high-priced items lend themselves to personal selling). The nature of the promotional mix is also dependent upon the product's position in the life cycle (i.e., advertising usually dominates the mix in the maturity stage).

8. The promotional mix also depends upon a number of market-related factors, such as whether the effort will focus on intermediaries or final users. Producers use a **push strategy** to convince wholesalers and retailers to carry the item; this necessitates heavy personal selling and sales promotion. Conversely, if the focus is on the end user, the producer is employing a **pull strategy** and uses advertising, direct mail, contests, coupons, and so on to stimulate consumer demand. The size and concentration of buyers in the market also influence the promotional mix. Advertising is generally used with many widely dispersed buyers, and personal selling may be most appropriate in markets with relatively few customers located in a limited area.

9. We all have a place in our mind for each product category that we are aware of. Marketers attempt to have their products achieve certain positions in our minds via a combination of product attributes, advertising, public relations, and other marketing mix aspects. **Positioning** is the process used by manufacturers to achieve a desired position in the mind of the market.

10. Almost 10 percent of the work force is involved in some type of personal selling, and for some companies it is a major activity. The three categories of salespeople are order getters, order takers, and sales support personnel. **Order getters** have the job of generating new sales and increasing sales to present customers. Their job is sometimes called **creative selling,** especially if the salesperson must first determine the customer's needs, then devise a way to convince the customer that the product or service can meet those needs. In contrast, **order takers** do little creative selling but may "suggest" the purchase of additional items (e.g., a McDonald's counter person might ask if you would like fries with your hamburger).

11. **Sales support personnel** usually do not sell products; they facilitate the overall selling effort by providing a number of services. **Missionary salespeople** work for manufacturers and disseminate information about new products to present customers (intermediaries) and try to motivate them to sell the product. **Technical salespeople** offer technical assistance to customers and may accompany salespeople to answer the highly technical questions that may be asked by prospects. **Trade salespeople** sell to and offer support to marketing intermediaries (e.g., they may give in-store demonstrations or set up displays).

12. As the cost of a personal sales call continues to rise, many organizations are turning to **telemarketing** (i.e., selling over the telephone). A company making cold calls on potential customers is using outbound telemarketing; inbound telemarketing establishes telephone lines that are used by customers to call in and place orders.

13. There are seven steps in the creative selling process. Step one, prospecting, involves generating sales leads, identifying prospects, and qualifying prospects. The ones with the authority to buy and the available money to buy are known as **qualified prospects.** In the next step, preparing, the salesperson must create a prospect file and decide how to best approach the prospect. While cold calling might be used for a first call, a salesperson typically either drops by unannounced or calls ahead for an appointment when trying to sell to existing customers.

14. The third step, approaching the prospect, concerns the initial contact between the salesperson and the prospect. Positive first impressions are the result of appropriate appearance, correct attitude and behavior,

and the salesperson's opening lines. The salesperson then goes from the approach directly into step four, making the presentation. Either a **canned approach** (a memorized presentation) or a **need-satisfaction approach** (identifying the customer's needs and addressing them in the presentation) might be used.

15.   **Handling objections** is step five of the creative selling process. The three basic approaches to overcoming objections are asking the prospect a question, giving a response to the objection, or telling the prospect that you will look into the matter and address it later. After objections have been handled, the salesperson can move to step six, **closing.** Some of the more popular closing techniques are the alternative proposal close (the salesperson asks the prospect to choose between some minor details), the assumptive close (the salesperson assumes the prospect has decided to buy), the silent close (the salesperson finishes the presentation and sits quietly), and the direct close (the salesperson asks for the order).

16.   The final step in the creative selling process is follow-up. During this phase, the salesperson makes sure that the product was delivered properly and that the customer is satisfied. Keeping a customer satisfied involves handling complaints promptly and pleasantly, maintaining contact with customers, keeping the customer served, and showing appreciation.

17.   The greatest advantage of advertising is its ability to reach mass audiences quickly and at a low per-person cost. A firm has more control over this form of promotion than any other, because the media does not rewrite or edit advertisements. Business spending on advertising is over $400 a year for every woman, man, and child in this country, with some firms spending up to 30 percent of total earnings to promote their products (most companies spend 2 to 5 percent of income on advertising).

18.   Advertising can be classified according to its promotional goal. **Product advertising** aims at getting purchasers to use a particular brand of product. **Institutional advertising** (also called corporate advertising) is designed to create goodwill and to build a desired image for a company rather than sell specific goods. It is often used by a firm to help its public image; when used to address hotly debated public issues, it is referred to as **advocacy advertising.**

19.   Ads that specifically emphasize how a product is better than its competitors is known as **competitive advertising;** when two or more brands are directly compared in an ad, it is called **comparative advertising.** Companies must be careful to ensure that their comparative advertising remains within legal and ethical boundaries.

20.   Advertising may also be categorized according to sponsor. When sponsored by a company selling its products on a nationwide basis, it is called **national advertising.** If sponsored by a local merchant, it is **local advertising.** A cross between national and local advertising is **cooperative advertising,** where the cost of the local advertising is shared by the national manufacturer and the local merchant (or wholesaler).

21.   The "best" appeal to use in advertising depends on the target audience; as a consequence, advertisers try to identify which groups of people can be reached with various types of appeals. For example, the decision must be made whether the appeal should be predominantly rational or predominantly emotional. Emotional appeals that might be employed in advertising include fear, anger, how good it will feel to use the product, and humor. The celebrity appeal is another approach that is used frequently, although the public does not always find such ads to be convincing.

22.   Another type of appeal, sex appeal, is an old standby of the advertising world. Today, though, the tendency is to keep the clothes on the models and to just hint about sex. Still further, novelty is an approach that has taken hold in recent years. The idea is to grab the audience's attention by making the ad really strange.

23.   The two elements all advertisements contain are **copy** (the verbal part of the ad) and **artwork** (the visual part of the ad). The arrangement of copy and artwork is called the layout. The job of the copy is to get the prospect's attention, stimulate interest, build credibility, heighten desire for the product, and motive the prospect toward action. Sometimes artwork is even more prominent than the copy in an ad.

24.   After the message has been developed, the firm must select the **media,** or communication channels, that are suitable to carry the message. The **media plan** specifies how the advertising budget is to be allocated among

media alternatives, and when the ads are to be scheduled. The critical task of the media planner is to select a **media mix,** which is a combination of print, broadcast, and other media for the advertising campaign. An increasingly popular approach is the "concentration" strategy, which appropriates most of the budget for a single media type. This permits the advertiser's message to dominate the medium in its product class.

25. Next, specific vehicles in each of the chosen media categories must be selected (i.e., which TV programs, which magazines). Four important pieces of information are relied upon for media buying: **cost per thousand** (the cost for reaching a thousand people with the ad in a particular advertising medium), **reach** (the total number of households that will be exposed to a given message at least once in a time period), **frequency** (the average number of times each household is exposed to the message), and **continuity** (the period spanned by the media schedule and the timing of the ad messages).

26. Advertising media include newspapers and television, which each account for about a quarter of total media spending. Direct mail, radio, and magazines together account for about another third of the total, with billboards, signs, and yellow pages accounting for the remaining fifth. The distribution of media spending has been shifting in recent years as advertisers are putting more of their budgets into specialized media directed at selected audiences. Alternative media such as shopping cart and elevator advertising are also gaining ground.

27. The strengths of newspapers as an advertising medium include extensive market coverage, low cost, short lead time for placing ads, and selection of topic areas to place ads (e.g., sports section, financial section). However, newspapers have a short life span, poor graphic quality, and suffer from lots of visual competition from other ads. TV offers the combined impact of sight, sound, and motion, and reaches a massive audience (the average TV set is turned on for six hours a day). But TV advertising is very expensive, and commercials may get zapped by viewers' remote controls.

28. The third largest advertising medium is **direct mail,** which offers the ability to deliver large amounts of information to narrowly selected audiences. The use of **database marketing,** in which the advertiser collects, stores, and uses data about customers' needs, purchase habits, and so on, promises to permit the precise targeting of advertising messages. However, direct mail suffers from its "junk mail" image.

29. Radio advertising recently has received a boost from the resurgence of network radio. Additionally, the cost of radio advertising has grown more slowly than that of advertising on network TV. Radio is used primarily by advertisers as a reminder tool to stimulate the purchase and use of products the consumer is already familiar with.

30. Magazines can offer highly targeted audiences, as many publications are aimed at narrow market niches. They also offer high-quality reproduction, long message life, and the opportunity for a single ad to be read by a number of people.

31. In addition to other media like the Yellow Pages, outdoor, and transit advertising, new advertising media are continually being tried. These include in-flight advertising, supermarket shopping cart advertising, and electronic advertising through such services as CompuServe and Prodigy.

32. For many companies, **public relations** is the fastest growing component of the marketing mix. **Press relations** is the process of communicating with the media (e.g., newspapers and magazines) and is an important part of public relations. The usual tools of press relations are the **press release** (or news release) and the **press conference** (or news briefing).

33. The term **sales promotion** includes a wide range of activities. Promotions directed at the consumer are known as **consumer promotions;** the most common types are specialty advertising, point-of-purchase advertising, coupons, rebates, games and sweepstakes, special events, and premiums. **Couponing** is the biggest category of consumer promotions. Over 200 billion coupons are distributed each year in the United States. Coupons help stimulate trial of new products and reach out to nonusers of mature products, but they also encourage delayed purchase and help encourage consumers to adopt a bargain-hunting mentality. Another effective sales promotion device is the **point-of-purchase display (POP),** which displays a product in such a way as to stimulate immediate sales. Other techniques include rebates, free samples, **premiums**

(free or bargain-priced items offered to encourage product purchase), contests and sweepstakes, and **specialty advertising,** which is advertising on coffee mugs, pens, calendars, and so on.

34. The major element of most **trade promotions** (i.e., promotions aimed at distributors or retailers) is the **trade allowance,** which permits a price reduction to be passed along to consumers. In some product categories, up to 100 percent of the merchandise sold to retailers offers a trade deal. Trade allowances create the controversial practice of **forward buying,** in which the retailer stocks up when the price is low. Another trade promotion is the **trade show,** which allows a company to demonstrate and explain its products to prospects. In some industries, a firm can reach a high percentage of its prospects by trade show participation.

KEY TERMS

promotion
promotional mix
personal selling
advertising
public relations
sales promotion
push strategy
pull strategy
positioning
order getters
creative selling
order takers
sales support personnel
missionary salespeople
technical salespeople
trade salespeople
telemarketing
qualified prospects
canned approach
need-satisfaction approach
closing
product advertising
institutional advertising
advocacy advertising
competitive advertising

comparative advertising
national advertising
local advertising
cooperative advertising
copy
artwork
media
media plan
media mix
cost per thousand
reach
frequency
continuity
direct mail
press relations
press release
press conference
consumer promotions
couponing
point-of-purchase display
premiums
specialty advertising
trade allowance
forward buying
trade show

KEY TERMS EXERCISE

Directions: On the line provided, place the letter of the statement that most closely defines the key term.

_____ 1. Promotion

_____ 2. Promotional mix

_____ 3. Pull strategy

_____ 4. Push strategy

_____ 5. Advertising

_____ 6. Product advertising

a. Advertising sent directly to potential customers, usually through the U.S. Postal Service.

b. Ads that present a company's opinion on issues such as education and health.

c. Particular blend of advertising, personal selling, public relations, and sales promotion that a company uses to reach potential customers.

d. Cost of reaching 1,000 people with an ad.

_____   7.   Cooperative advertising

_____   8.   Institutional advertising

_____   9.   Advocacy advertising

_____   10.   Media

_____   11.   Positioning

_____   12.   Direct mail

_____   13.   Media plan

_____   14.   Media mix

_____   15.   Cost per thousand

_____   16.   Reach

_____   17.   Frequency

_____   18.   Continuity

_____   19.   Missionary salespeople

_____   20.   Trade promotion

_____   21.   Trade allowance

_____   22.   Trade show

_____   23.   Specialty advertising

_____   24.   Point-of-purchase display

_____   25.   Couponing

_____   26.   Premium

e.   The process of achieving a desired position in the consumer's mind.

f.   Distribution of certificates that entitle buyers to a discount on a particular item.

g.   The average number of times that each audience member is exposed to the message (equal to the total number of exposures divided by the total audience population).

h.   Advertising on various items such as coffee mugs, pens, and calendars designed to help keep a company's name in front of customers.

i.   Communication channels, such as newspaper, radio, and television.

j.   Encompasses a wide variety of persuasive techniques used by companies to communicate with their target markets and the general public.

k.   The pattern according to which an ad appears in the media; it can be spread evenly over time or concentrated during selected periods.

l.   Paid, nonpersonal communication to a target market from an identified sponsor utilizing mass communication channels.

m.   Joint efforts between local and national advertisers, in which producers of nationally sold products share the costs of local advertising with local merchants and wholesalers.

n.   Advertising or display materials set up at a retail location to encourage sales of an item.

o.   Industry gathering in which producers set up displays and demonstrate products to potential customers.

p.   Promotional approach designed to motivate wholesalers and retailers to push a producer's products.

q.   Advertising that seeks to create goodwill and to build a desired image for a company rather than to sell specific products.

r.   A written plan that outlines how a company will spend its media budget, including how the money will be divided among the various media and when the advertisements will appear.

s. The total number of audience members that will be exposed to a message at least once in a given period.

t. Discount offered by producers to a wholesaler or retailer.

u. Free or bargain-priced item that encourages consumers to buy a product.

v. Advertising that tries to sell specific goods or services generally by describing features, benefits, and occasionally, price.

w. Salespeople who support existing customers, usually wholesalers and retailers.

x. Promotional strategy that stimulates consumer demand, which then exerts pressure on wholesalers and retailers to carry a product.

y. Sales promotion efforts aimed at inducing distributors or retailers to push a producer's products.

z. Combination of various media options that a company uses in an advertising campaign.

ANSWERS TO KEY TERMS EXERCISE

1. j (p. 418)
2. c (p. 420)
3. x (p. 422)
4. d (p. 422)
5. l (p. 420)
6. v (p. 430)
7. m (p. 430)
8. q (p. 430)
9. b (p. 430)
10. i (p. 435)
11. e (p. 422)
12. a (p. 438)
13. r (p. 435)
14. z (p. 435)
15. d (p. 436)
16. s (p. 436)
17. g (p. 436)
18. k (p. 436)
19. w (p. 423)
20. y (p. 441)
21. t (p. 441)
22. o (p. 441)
23. h (p. 440)
24. n (p. 440)
25. f (p. 440)
26. u (p. 440)

SELF TEST

True-False Questions

_____ 1. Effective promotion can guarantee success of a product in the marketplace.

_____ 2. Promotion can be used effectively only in the sales of physical goods, not in the marketing of services.

_____ 3. For most products, a blend of the four promotional elements is desirable.

_____ 4. In general, promotion of consumer products tends to be pull-oriented, while promotion of industrial products is more often push-oriented.

_____ 5. Advertising is as useful in the promotion of ideas, such as prevention of drunk driving, as it is in the promotion of a physical good.

_____   6.   Advertising's only regulation is from the FTC.

_____   7.   As an advertising medium, telephone directories are very low in importance and decreasing in use every day.

_____   8.   Although advertising is an effective marketing tool and is actually an important part of society, there is little formal regulation of the advertising industry.

_____   9.   Order takers do little creative selling; they primarily process orders.

_____   10.   Technical salespeople are usually engineers, scientists, or other people with specialized technical training.

_____   11.   Preparation is essential in making an effective sales presentation.

_____   12.   The absence of objections by a prospect during a sales presentation should be taken as a sign of agreement by the salesperson.

_____   13.   The Federal Trade Commission encourages companies to use comparative advertising.

_____   14.   The type of appeal to use (e.g., logic or emotion) depends largely on the target audience being appealed to.

_____   15.   Advertisers who use celebrities in their advertising believe that consumers are inclined to use products that celebrities use.

_____   16.   Public relations play a major role in creating a good reputation for a company.

Multiple Choice Questions

_____   1.   Which of the following is *not* one of the major objectives of promotion?
     a.   informing
     b.   entertaining
     c.   persuading
     d.   reminding
     e.   All of the above are major promotional objectives.

_____   2.   Which of the following is a criticism levied against advertising?
     a.   It convinces people to buy unnecessary or undesirable goods.
     b.   It manipulates the consumer on a subconscious level.
     c.   It exploits stereotypes.
     d.   It encourages materialism at the expense of worthwhile values.
     e.   All of the above are criticisms.

_____   3.   A basic aim of promotional activities is
     a.   to increase product sales.
     b.   to stabilize sales so demand does not fluctuate widely.
     c.   to provide information to the market.

_____   4.   An advantage of advertising over other types of promotion is
     a.   it is the form of promotion over which the organization has the greatest control.
     b.   it is available at a very low cost.
     c.   it can force people to buy an organization's product, which assures success in the market-place.
     d.   an advertiser can say anything it wants, as advertising is protected under the rights of free speech in the U.S. Constitution.

____ 5. An institutional ad used to present the company's position on a social topic would be an example of the use of
  a. brand advertising.
  b. cooperative advertising.
  c. generic advertising.
  d. advocacy advertising.

____ 6. In analyzing radio as an advertising medium for purchase, which of the following statements is correct?
  a. Network TV audiences are increasing, while network radio audiences are decreasing.
  b. Radio is a highly flexible medium, with specialized programming attracting specific audiences.
  c. The fact that radios can be easily switched from one station to another is an advantage, in that listeners are certain to hear a commercial on one station or another.
  d. All of the above are correct.

____ 7. The process of creating a desired position in the mind of the market is known as
  a. branding.
  b. advertising.
  c. public relations.
  d. positioning.

____ 8. The standardized ratio that is especially useful for comparing media that reach similar audiences is
  a. cost per thousand.
  b. reach.
  c. frequency.
  d. continuity.

____ 9. An advantage of personal selling compared to other types of promotion is
  a. flexibility.
  b. completion of the sale on the spot.
  c. product demonstration.
  d. all of the above.

____ 10. A salesperson who uses creative selling to generate new sales and increase sales to existing customers would be classified as a(n)
  a. order getter.
  b. order taker.
  c. sales support.
  d. technical salesperson.

____ 11. A sales promotion effort that attempts to generate interest in the product on the part of wholesalers is
  a. trade promotion.
  b. a relatively long-term pull emphasis.
  c. illegal under anti-trust legislation.
  d. a trade show.

____ 12. Salespeople who are responsible for building relationships with wholesalers and retailers by setting up displays, giving in-store demonstrations, and the like are known as
  a. order takers.
  b. order getters.
  c. missionary salespeople.
  d. trade salespeople.
  e. technical salespeople.

_____ 13. Generating sales leads, identifying prospects, and qualifying prospects are a part of which step of the creative selling process?
   a. prospecting
   b. preparing
   c. approaching
   d. presenting

_____ 14. Asking for the order during the sales presentation is which stage of the creative selling process?
   a. prospecting
   b. making the presentation
   c. handling objections
   d. closing
   e. follow-up

_____ 15. Competitive advertising that compares the features and benefits of a product to a competitor's products is
   a. institutional advertising.
   b. advocacy advertising.
   c. comparative advertising.
   d. national advertising.

_____ 16. Advertising is using a predominantly emotional appeal when it promotes
   a. fear.
   b. anger.
   c. celebrities.
   d. sex.
   e. all of the above

_____ 17. The purpose of advertising copy is to
   a. get a prospect's attention.
   b. stimulate interest in the product.
   c. build credibility for the product and the company.
   d. heighten desire for the product and motivate action.
   e. all of the above.

Completion Questions

1. The regulatory body that acts as a watchdog over the truthfulness of advertising is the _____.

2. The advertising medium that has as its strength the combination of sight and sound is _____.

3. _____ is the medium used to sell products through the U.S. Postal Service.

4. The size and concentration of consumers are _____ factors that influence the promotional mix.

5. The combination of print, broadcast, and other media that is selected in the promotional plan is the _____ mix.

6. The amount of time the media schedule covers is the _____ element of the media plan.

7. Missionary salespeople, trade salespeople, and technical salespeople are all examples of _____ personnel, who generally do not sell products, but facilitate the overall selling effort by providing a variety of services.

8. Telemarketing can be either _____, when the company calls potential customers, or

    _____, when customers call the company.

9. A discount on the price of the product offered to a distributor or retailer is a _____.

10. The creative selling process involves these steps: (1) _____, (2) preparing, (3) _____,

    (4) making the presentation, (5) handling, (6) closing, and (7) _____.

11. The two basic elements of an advertisement are the _____, which is the verbal part, and the _____, which is the visual part of the ad.

12. Direct-mail marketers are using _____ marketing to collect, store, and use data about each customer's needs and purchasing habits.

PROJECT

Media Mix for Pizza Delivery

In order to meet expenses, you've been working part-time for Pronto Pizza. On a slow evening the owner asks you about the courses you are taking. When he learns that you are interested in business, he asks you for some ideas about how to improve Pronto's advertising.

Design a media mix that might be effective in selling more Pronto pizzas. Be sure to examine all the alternatives available in designing the mix. Think about who Pronto's current customers are and what other groups you might be able to attract. Remember, the library has resources that could tell you more about the current as well as potential customers and the media alternatives available to Pronto.

1. Why is your selection the best?

2. Besides advertising, what other elements of the promotional mix would be useful? Why?

Chapter 16

Computers and Information Technology

LEARNING OBJECTIVES

1. Distinguish between data and information and explain the characteristics of useful information.

2. Identify the five generations of computer hardware.

3. Describe the five categories of computer systems.

4. Identify the major elements of a computer system.

5. List the main categories of applications software.

6. Describe the four generations of computer languages.

7. Explain the purpose of computer networks.

8. Discuss the social and business concerns caused by extensive computerization.

OUTLINE

I. Computers in today's business environment

    A. From data to information to insight
        1. Data, databases, and information usage
        2. The chief information officer (CIO)

    B. Making information useful
        1. The five criteria needed to make information useful

    C. Information systems
        1. Transaction processing systems (TPS)
        2. Office automation systems (OAS)
        3. CAD and CAM systems
        4. Management information systems (MIS)
        5. Decision support systems (DSS)
        6. Executive information systems (EIS)
        7. Other information systems
        8. Can computers really think?
           a. Artificial intelligence
               (1) Expert systems
               (2) Natural language processors

II. Information-processing technology

    A. The evolution of computer systems
        1. Five generations of computer technology
        2. From batch processing to real time

        a.   Batch processing
        b.   Time-sharing system
        c.   Real-time processing

B.   Types of computer systems
    1.   Microcomputers
    2.   Workstations
    3.   Minicomputers
    4.   Mainframe computers
    5.   Supercomputers

C.   Hardware
    1.   Input devices
    2.   Central processing unit
    3.   Output devices
    4.   Storage

D.   Software
    1.   Types of software
    2.   Systems software
        a.   Utilities
        b.   Shells
    3.   Application software
        a.   Accounting/finance
        b.   Word processing
        c.   Publishing
        d.   Business graphics
        e.   Communications
        f.   Drafting and CAD
        g.   Production and process control
        h.   Project management
        i.   Database management
        j.   Industry-specific solutions
        k.   Integrated software

E.   Computer languages
    1.   Machine language
    2.   Assembly language
    3.   High-level language
    4.   Fourth-generation languages

F.   Computer networks
    1.   Long-distance networks
    2.   Local area networks
    3.   Micro-to-mainframe links
    4.   Communications networks

III.   Computers and society

A.   The benefits of computerization

B.   The drawbacks of computerization

C.   Ethical questions

D.   Computer security versus computer convenience

MAJOR POINTS TO REMEMBER

1. Recorded statistics, facts, predictions, and opinions that flow into a firm everyday are **data.** A collection of related computer files that can be cross-referenced to extract information is known as a **database.** **Information** is a specific collection of data that is relevant to a particular problem or decision. Because information is so vital to companies, many firms now employ a top-level executive with the title of **chief information officer (CIO).**

2. To be useful, information must be (1) accurate, (2) timely, (3) complete, (4) relevant, and (5) concise.

3. Information systems can be categorized according to the type of information they handle and the people in the firm that they serve. A **transaction processing system (TPS)** is a computerized information system that handles much of the daily flow of data in and out of a business firm. In contrast, an **office automation system (OAS)** helps people perform office tasks more efficiently (e.g., a PC with word processing software or a computer network). CAD (computer-aided design) and CAM (computer-aided manufacturing) systems help automate the work of architects, engineers, and other technical personnel. A firm's **management information system (MIS)** supplies periodic, predefined reports to assist managers with decision making, while a **decision support system (DSS)** goes beyond the MIS by providing managers with the tools and data needed for decision making. An **executive information system (EIS)** is similar to a DSS but is customized to the strategic needs of executives. Other types of information systems include geographic information systems, which are computerized maps that allow firms to identify markets.

4. The attempt to create computers that parallel the human thought process falls under the heading of **artificial intelligence.** A computer system that mimics the thought process of a human expert in a particular area of knowledge is known as an **expert system;** such systems are typically built to solve a fairly narrow range of problems. Another advance in artificial intelligence is the **natural language processor,** which lets a computer user "speak" with a computer in English (or another language), rather than using a computer language. Natural language processing makes many computer tasks easier.

5. Thus far we have experienced five generations of computer technology. First-generation systems include the ENIAC, the first electronic computer (developed in 1946), and the UNIVAC, the first truly programmable computer (1950). These machines relied on vacuum tubes, and **programming** (giving a computer the instructions needed to perform a task) had to be performed using strings of ones and zeros.

6. In second-generation computers of the 1950s, the **transistor** replaced the vacuum tube; programming was accomplished through the use of a language that could be read by human beings. By the early 1960s, third-generation systems offered greater power and affordability and used more advanced programming languages. Transistors were replaced with **integrated circuits,** which were collections of multiple transistors on a silicon chip. Fourth-generation systems (1971) incorporated **microprocessors,** which combined the basic functions of a computer onto a single chip. These machines gave rise to the Apple I and the IBM Personal Computer. The state of the art in computer technology is the fifth-generation system, used for artificial intelligence and other sophisticated tasks. Such a machine employs **parallel processing,** which means that multiple processors in a single computer unit increase the speed at which complex calculations can be completed.

7. Until the 1960s, computer use was characterized by **batch processing,** in which users prepared data and programs and submitted these "jobs" to the computer center. These jobs were then fed to the computer in batches, while computer users waited for results. **Time-sharing systems,** in which a number of independent terminals (keyboards and monitors) were attached to the computer, replaced batch processing and allowed users to interact with the computer simultaneously. While time-sharing systems work well, they do slow down the time it takes the computer to provide a terminal with an answer (i.e., the more terminals that share the computer, the slower the response time).

8. **Real-time processing** is a method of information processing in which the computer's files are updated as soon as new information arrives. The availability of today's more powerful computers have allowed real-time processing to replace time-sharing systems.

9. The computers available today can be grouped into five classes: microcomputers, workstations, minicomputers, mainframes, and supercomputers. **Microcomputers,** also called personal computers, include the IBM PC and the Apple Macintosh. They are the smallest and least-expensive type of computer and are manufactured in a number of sizes, including desktop, laptop, notebook, and palmtop. In contrast, **workstations** marry the speed of minicomputers with the convenience of microcomputers. They are used primarily by engineers, scientists, and designers who need fast computing and powerful graphics capabilities. Computer-aided design (CAD) work is most often accomplished with workstations.

10. **Minicomputers** were first developed in the 1960s and offer many of the same capabilities as mainframes, but they are smaller and less expensive. **Mainframes** were the most popular type of computer until the arrival of microcomputers. These are large, powerful systems capable of handling vast amounts of data. Users typically access mainframes from dumb terminals (devices that look like a microcomputer but do not operate on their own). Finally, **supercomputers** are able to handle the most complex processing jobs. Some are capable of performing over a billion calculations per second.

11. Computer **hardware** is the physical equipment used in a computer system, while **software** includes the instructions, or **programs,** that tell the hardware what to do. The four basic groups of hardware are input devices, the central processing unit, output devices, and storage devices.

12. Input devices include the keyboard, the mouse (which issues commands based on a pointer's position on the computer screen), the computer pen (which lets a user write on special tablets that can translate writing into computer-compatible data), the scanner (which "reads" what is on a piece of paper and sends the image to the computer), and the bar code reader (similar to a supermarket check-out scanner).

13. A computer's **central processing unit (CPU)** performs the three functions of arithmetic, logic, and control/communications. In microcomputers and workstations, there is a single microprocessor, while in minicomputers, mainframes, and supercomputers there can be either a single processing unit or multiple processing units operating in parallel. Even complex electronic circuits are really only switches that can be either off or on (representing a zero or a one). Each switch represents one **bit** of information. A package of eight bits makes up a **byte** of information.

14. Output devices include the display (or monitor), the printer, and the plotter (used by scientists and engineers to draw images on paper).

15. **Primary storage devices** store data and programs while they are being used by the computer. They include **random access memory (RAM),** which is a set of semiconductor devices that allow the computer to access any piece of data in such memory at random, and **read only memory (ROM),** which are special circuits that store data and programs permanently but do not allow users to record their own data or programs. **Secondary storage** is for data and programs that are not needed at all times; it also provides a permanent record of such information. The **disk drive** is the most common secondary storage medium; it can take the form of a hard disk drive or a floppy disk drive.

16. Computer software includes systems software such as **operating systems,** which control the computer's operations, and **application software** (programs that perform specific functions for users, such as word processing). Operating systems unique to one type of computer are known as **proprietary operating systems** (e.g., the Apple Macintosh), while those that will run on computers from various manufacturers are called **open systems** (e.g., UNIX). Microsoft's **disk operating system (DOS),** called MS-DOS, lies between these two extremes. In addition to operating systems, systems software includes utilities, shells, and languages.

17. Application software can be either custom (developed for a single user or set of users) or commercial (sold to anyone). Software products are usually referred to as "packages" (e.g., a word-processing package). Popular applications packages include (1) accounting/finance, (2) **spreadsheets** (allows users to manipulate data in a row-column matrix), (3) word processing (often with mail merge, which lets a single generic letter be merged with a list of names at printing time), (4) publishing (including **desktop publishing**), (5) business graphics, (6) communications (including **electronic mail** and **bulletin board systems**),

(7) drafting and CAD, (8) production and process control (e.g., computer-aided manufacturing), (9) project management (Gantt and PERT charts), (10) database management (**database management software** creates, stores, maintains, rearranges, and retrieves the contents of databases), (11) industry-specific solutions (i.e., software for specific industries, such as a package to help real estate agents track sales leads), and (12) integrated software (a single package that performs several functions, such as word processing, spreadsheet, and business graphics). The Business Software Database currently lists over 10,000 software application products.

18. A **computer language** is a set of rules and conventions for communication with a computer. The lowest-level language is **machine language,** which allows a computer to use ones and zeros. First-generation computers understood only machine language. An improved computer language was **assembly language,** which was composed of mnemonic code words that people could read and write more easily. Assembly-language programs were converted into machine language automatically with a software tool called an assembler, but it still required a lot of instructions to perform even a simple task.

19. **High-level languages** were introduced in the late 1950s and 1960s and permitted programmers to use a single command to accomplish the equivalent of several assembly-language commands. A compiler or an interpreter converts a high-level language into assembly language so that the program can be run.

20. The term **fourth-generation languages (4GLs)** applies to software tools that allow users to give instructions to computers in a language similar to English (or any other natural language). Such capabilities have become common in today's database management software.

21. Connecting multiple computers to one another and allowing them to send information back and forth is known as **data communications.** The first of the three categories of data communications is the long-distance network. A **network** is hardware and software that permits multiple computers to communicate. In a long-distance network, computers at different locations are linked through regular telephone lines. The ability to use telephone lines is made possible by equipping each computer with a **modem.**

22. In contrast, a **local area network (LAN)** addresses data communications needs within a small area, such as an office or university. The LAN might have a special computer called a file service provide common storage facilities for the network. The rise of LANs has resulted in **workgroup computing,** which allows teams of workers to work together easily on projects.

23. **Micro-to-mainframe links** are the final type of network. Here, the company's central mainframe computer handles important tasks, while microcomputers may be used by individual workers for such work as word processing. Employees can use the microcomputers to tap into the mainframe system.

24. In a centralized communications network, the mainframe has all the processing power, with terminals acting only as communications ports. However, with **distributed processing,** some of the processing power is spread among the computers attached to the network.

25. An important change made possible by computer networks is electronic data interchange (EDI). This system permits computers in one firm to communicate directly with computers in another firm for the purpose of placing orders and tracking shipments.

26. Society can both benefit from and be hurt by computers. While computers may make it possible for individuals to receive their Social Security checks more quickly, they also generate more junk mail. Furthermore, unethical data processing or database use may lead to invasion of privacy. Then there is the issue of data security. There are well-publicized stories of "hackers" gaining electronic access to the computer systems of banks, hospitals, even government agencies, and of "viruses" that have crippled computer systems by corrupting data and programs.

KEY TERMS

data
database
information
chief information officer
transaction processing systems
office automation systems
management information system
decision support system
executive information system
artificial intelligence
expert system
natural language processor
programming
transistor
integrated circuits
microprocessors
parallel processing
batch processing
time-sharing systems
real-time processing
microcomputers
workstations
minicomputers
mainframes
supercomputers
hardware
software
programs
central processing unit

bit
byte
primary storage devices
random access memory
read only memory
secondary storage
disk drive
operating systems
application software
proprietary operating systems
disk operating system
open systems
spreadsheet
desktop publishing
electronic mail
bulletin board systems
database management software
data communications
network
modem
local area network
workgroup computing
micro-to-mainframe links
distributed processing
computer language
machine language
assembly language
high-level languages
fourth-generation languages

KEY TERM EXERCISE

_____ 1. Mainframe computer

_____ 2. Management information system

_____ 3. Transaction processing system

_____ 4. Work station computer

_____ 5. Data

_____ 6. Operating systems

_____ 7. Software

_____ 8. Minicomputer

_____ 9. Microcomputer

_____ 10. Network

a. Recorded statistics, facts, predictions, and opinions.

b. A specific collection of data that are relevant to a particular decision or problem.

c. A computerized information system that processes the daily flow of customer, supplier, and employee transactions, including inventory, sales, and payroll records.

d. Computer system that assists with the tasks that people in a typical business office face regularly, such as drawing graphs or processing documents.

e. A system that supplies periodic, predefined reports to assist in managerial decision-making.

f. Extensions of management information systems that provide managers with the tools and data they need for decision-making.

g. Personal computers, such as desk tops and lap tops.

_____   11.   Office automation system

_____   12.   Hardware

_____   13.   Supercomputer

_____   14.   Application software

_____   15.   Computer language

_____   16.   Decision support systems

_____   17.   Information

h.   Computer the size of a microcomputer but with the speed of a minicomputer.

i.   Smaller, cheaper, less powerful mainframe computer.

j.   With the exception of supercomputers, the largest and most powerful computers.

k.   Highest level of computer.

l.   Physical equipment used in a computer system.

m.   Programs that direct the activities of a computer's hardware.

n.   Software which controls the computer's overall operation.

o.   Software that performs specific functions, such as word processing.

p.   A collection of hardware and software that allows multiple computers to communicate.

q.   Sets of programmable rules and conversations for communicating with a computer.

ANSWERS TO KEY TERMS EXERCISE

	15. q (p. 469)	10. p (p. 472)	5. a (p. 452)
	14. o (p. 466)	9. g (p. 460)	4. h (p. 461)
	13. k (p. 462)	8. i (p. 461)	3. c (p. 455)
17. b (p. 452)	12. l (p. 462)	7. m (p. 462)	2. e (p. 456)
16. f (p. 456)	11. d (p. 455)	6. n (p. 466)	1. j (p. 461)

SELF TEST

True-False Questions

_____   1.   Manipulating data produces information which can be used to develop insight.

_____   2.   To be helpful, information must be useful.

_____   3.   Managers normally have perfect information with which to base decisions.

_____   4.   Decision support systems can be programmed to make decisions for a manger.

_____   5.   Natural language processors allows a person to communicate with a computer without having to use a computer language.

_____   6.   Each new generation of computers has produced faster, more reliable, smaller computers.

_____ 7. The central processing unit of a computer can perform arithmetic, logic, and control/communication functions.

_____ 8. Electronic mail and bulletin board systems are examples of how one computer can exchange information with other computers.

_____ 9. Machine language communicates using 1's and 0's.

_____ 10. High-level language focuses on what the user wants done, rather than what the computer should do.

_____ 11. Computers are both a help and a hinderance to society's goals.

_____ 12. The high degree of computerization has produced social and ethical issues of the proper use of computers.

Multiple Choice Questions

_____ 1. To be useful information must be
   a) accurate and timely.
   b) complete and relevant.
   c) concise.
   d) all of the above.

_____ 2. Airline reservation systems, sales processing, and handling library loans would be examples of what type of computer systems?
   a) transaction processing system
   b) office automation system
   c) management information system
   d) decision support system
   e) executive information system

_____ 3. Computer systems which help people perform typical office tasks more efficiently, such as word processing, are known as
   a) transaction processing systems.
   b) office automation systems.
   c) management information systems.
   d) decision support systems.
   e) executive information systems.

_____ 4. The difference between a decision support system (DDS) and an executive information system (EIS) is that
   a) EIS organizes the necessary information to assist decision-making, while DDS does not.
   b) EIS has a more strategic focus than DDS in order to handle executive decisions.
   c) EIS makes decisions, while DDS cannot.
   d) EIS is used for complex, one-of-a-kind decisions, while DDS is used for routine decisions.

_____ 5. Which of the following is the correct progression of computer systems from the first computers to modern times?
   a) transistor; vacuum tubes; integrated circuits; microprocessor; parallel processing
   b) vacuum tubes; transistor; microprocessor; integrated circuits; parallel processing
   c) vacuum tubes; transistor; integrated circuits; microprocessor; parallel processing
   d) vacuum tubes; transistor; integrated circuits; parallel processing; microprocessor

____   6. The first generation of computers was developed in the
        a) late 1940's, early 1950's.
        b) mid 1950's.
        c) late 1950's.
        d) late 1950's, early 1960's.

____   7. What is the correct order of computers in terms of their processing power, from least to most powerful?
        a) microcomputer; work station; minicomputer; mainframe; supercomputer
        b) microcomputer; minicomputer; work station; mainframe; supercomputer
        c) minicomputer; microcomputer; work station; mainframe; supercomputer
        d) minicomputer; microcomputer; work station; supercomputer; minicomputer

____   8. Computer-aided design (CAD) and other such applications used by designers, engineers, and scientists are likely to use which type of computer system?
        a) microcomputer
        b) work station
        c) minicomputer
        d) mainframe
        e) supercomputer

____   9. That part of the computer's hardware which "reads" the data, such as a keyboard, mouse, or computer pen, is the
        a) input device.
        b) central processing unit.
        c) computer program.
        d) storage.

____   10. Which of the following is *not* normally considered a category of application software?
        a) accounting/finance
        b) spreadsheets
        c) word processing
        d) business graphics
        e) All of the above are categories of application software.

____   11. Which computer language uses mnemonic code words, such as "M" for multiply, to communicate?
        a) machine language
        b) assembly language
        c) high-level language
        d) fourth-generation language

____   12. Fourth-generation computer languages
        a) use 1's and 0's to communicate.
        b) use mnemonic codes to communicate.
        c) use words similar to the function to be performed to communicate.
        d) communicate in terms of what the computer is to do rather than what the user wants done.

Completion Questions

1. The successful collection, storage, and application of data and information is the primary responsibility of

    the _____ officer.

2. The computer system which is typically used by middle management to generate reports and statistics to

    convert data into useful information is a _____ system.

3. Computer systems which mimic the thought processes of a human are known as _____,
    with examples being expert systems and natural language processors.

4. Minicomputers are basically a smaller, cheaper, less powerful _____ computer.

5. The two major components of a computer are the _____, the physical equipment in a com-
    puter system, and the _____, the instructions or programs.

6. _____ software create, store, maintain, rearrange, and retrieve the contents of databases.

7. Computers are capable of communicating with each other through _____, which can be
    either long distance or local in nature.

8. The high utilization of computers has raised two basic ethical concerns: 1) _____ and
    2) _____.

PROJECT

Management Information Systems (MIS)

   A management information system is a means of structuring people, machines, and procedures to generate an
orderly flow of relevant information for use in decision-making. This exercise is designed to help you understand
the role and importance of such a system. Either on your own after reviewing the material in Chapter 16, or,
preferably, through interviewing a management information systems manger for a business in your area, answer
the following questions.

1. What types of information are needed to make management decisions?
2. What are the sources of data that make up a firm's database?
3. What is the difference between data and information?
4. How does a management information system convert data into information?
5. What are the basic data-processing manipulations that such a system can perform?

Chapter 17

Accounting

LEARNING OBJECTIVES

1. Describe the importance of accounting to managers, investors, creditors, and government.

2. Distinguish between public and private accountants.

3. State the basic accounting equation.

4. Explain the purpose of the balance sheet and identify its three main sections.

5. Explain the purpose of an income statement and identify its three main components.

6. Explain the purpose of the statement of cash flows.

7. Identify five areas in which accountants may exercise considerable discretion in their methods and assumptions.

8. List the four main categories of financial ratios.

OUTLINE

I. The nature of accounting

    A. Functional areas of accounting
        1. Financial accounting
            a. Generally accepted accounting principles (GAAP)
        2. Management accounting
            a. Budgets

    B. Types of accountants
        1. Public accountants
            a. Audits
            b. Certified public accountants (CPAs)
            c. Public accounting firms
                (1) Management advisory services (MAS)
                (2) Personal financial planning (PFP)
        2. Private accountants
            a. Certified management accountants (CMAs)
            b. The in-house accounting staff
                (1) Bookkeepers
                (2) Controllers

    C. The reliability of accounting information

II. Key accounting concepts

    A. The accounting equation
        1. Assets, liabilities, and owners' equity

    B. Double-entry bookkeeping
        1. Two-part entries for all transactions

III.   Financial statements

    A.   The balance sheet
        1.   What a balance sheet contains
            a.   Calendar years and fiscal years
        2.   Assets
            a.   Current assets
                (1)   Types of current assets
            b.   Fixed assets
                (1)   Types of fixed assets
            c.   Intangible assets
                (1)   Types of intangible assets
                    (a)   Goodwill
        3.   Liabilities
            a.   Current liabilities
                (1)   Types of current liabilities
            b.   Long-term liabilities
                (1)   Types of long-term liabilities
        4.   Owners' equity
            a.   What owners' equity is

    B.   The income statement
        1.   What an income statement is
        2.   Revenues
            a.   Two methods of recording revenues
                (1)   Accrual basis
                (2)   Cash basis
            b.   Gross sales versus net sales
        3.   Expenses
            a.   Cost of goods sold
                (1)   How cost of goods sold is calculated
            b.   Operating expenses
                (1)   Selling expenses
                (2)   General expenses
        4.   Net income or loss
            a.   How net income or loss is calculated

    C.   The statement of cash flows
        1.   What the statement of cash flows represents

IV.   Financial analysis

    A.   Reviewing the economic and competitive context

    B.   Allowing for different accounting methods
        1.   When are revenues recorded?
        2.   Which depreciation method is used?
        3.   How is cost of goods calculated?
            a.   FIFO versus LIFO
        4.   Are reserves adequate?
        5.   What are the effects of extraordinary or unusual items?

    C.   Calculating trends and ratios
        1.   Trend analysis
        2.   Ratio analysis
            a.   Profitability ratios

          (1)   Return on investment (ROI)
          (2)   Return on sales (net profit margin)
          (3)   Earnings per share
    b. Liquidity ratios
          (1)   Working capital
          (2)   Current ratio
          (3)   Quick ratio
    c. Activity ratios
          (1)   Inventory turnover ratio
    d. Debt ratios
          (1)   Debt-to-equity ratio
          (2)   Debt-to-total-assets ratio

MAJOR POINTS TO REMEMBER

1. **Accounting** is the system business uses to measure its financial performance. It does this by recording and classifying sales, purchases, and other transactions and by providing ways to present these data so that company performance can be evaluated.

2. There are two distinct types of accounting: financial accounting and management accounting. **Financial accounting** deals with preparing information for the outside world (e.g., suppliers, banks, and shareholders). Since users of such information must compare it to similar data from other sources, financial accounting statements are prepared according to **generally accepted accounting principles (GAAP).** In contrast, **management accounting** deals with the internal needs of a particular business firm and helps managers evaluate results and make decisions. The job of management accounting includes the preparation of **budgets** (a financial plan for a given time period) and the analysis of production costs.

3. Accountants can be divided into two basic groups: public accountants and private, or corporate, accountants. **Public accountants** operate independent of the businesses, individuals, and other organizations they serve. They prepare financial statements and report on the fairness of such statements, often performing an **audit** to evaluate the accuracy. Their reports indicate whether the statements have been prepared in agreement with GAAP, and their detached position obligates them to be objective and, if necessary, critical.

4. Public accountants who meet a state's requirements for education and experience and pass an examination become **Certified Public Accountants (CPAs).** About half of all CPAs are in private practice, working in one of the 40,000-plus accounting firms in the United States. The industry is dominated by a small number of large firms that together audit over 95 percent of all Fortune 500 companies. There has been a trend for the largest accounting firms to merge. Today the six largest firms (the "Big Six") dominate the industry and provide their global customers with both auditing and consultation services. Some of the "Big Six" firms recently have been in the news for failure to identify client fraud during their audits. Additionally, as company mergers provide public accounting firms with a shrinking pool of clients, some have begun offering management advisory services (MAS) to small and mid-size businesses. Accountants are also expanding their services to include personal financial planning (PFP).

5. **Private accountants** (also called corporate accountants) are employed by a business, government agency, or nonprofit corporation to supervise the accounting system and bookkeeping staff. Although many private accountants are CPAs, a growing number are also **certified management accountants (CMAs),** a comparatively new designation indicating that the individual has passed a test comparable in difficulty to the CPA exam. The job of the in-house accounting staff ranges from routine **bookkeeping** to the high-level decision making of the **controller** (or financial vice president), the firms's highest-ranking financial officer.

6. Accounting is not an exact science; using the same data, different accountants could legitimately come up with a range of results. Some firms maintain two sets of records: one for shareholders and one for tax purposes. However, most accountants do adhere to the generally accepted accounting principles.

7. Accounting theory is based on the **accounting equation. Assets** (what the firm owns) must equal **liabilities** (what the firm owes) plus **owners' equity** (the owners' claim on the assets).

8. The system used in accounting is known as **double-entry bookkeeping** and dates back to 1494. Two entries are required for every transaction; in this way, the accounting equation is always kept in balance. If, for example, a business borrowed $20,000 from a bank, $20,000 would be added to assets (cash) on the left side of the accounting equation and $20,000 would also be added to liabilities (bank loans) on the right side. One of the terms used in double-entry accounting is **retained earnings.** This refers to the net increase in assets for an accounting period and is part of owners' equity.

9. The **balance sheet** is a statement of a firm's financial position at one moment in time and includes all the elements in the accounting equation. It is a "snapshot" of a company's financial condition. At least once a year, all companies prepare balance sheets. This is commonly done at the end of the **calendar year,** but some firms use a **fiscal year,** which may be any twelve consecutive months.

10. Assets on a balance sheet are usually divided into three types—current, fixed, and intangible—and are listed in order of the ease with which they can be converted into cash. **Current assets** include cash and other items that can or will become cash within the following year, including marketable securities (temporary cash investments like stocks and bonds), accounts receivable (amounts due from customers), notes receivable (signed and written promises to pay a definite sum, plus interest, usually on a certain date and at a certain place), inventories, and prepaid expenses (supplies on hand and services paid for but not yet used).

11. **Fixed assets**—sometimes called property, plant, and equipment—consist of permanent investments in buildings, equipment, furniture and fixtures, transportation equipment, land, and any other tangible property used in running a business. They have a useful life of more than a year and are not expected to be converted into cash. With the exception of land, fixed assets depreciate yearly. **Depreciation** (or **amortization** for intangible assets) is the allocation of the cost of a long-lived asset to the periods in which it is used to produce revenue. When a balance sheet is prepared, fixed assets are depreciated so that their current value, not their original value, is portrayed. In this way, the cost of an asset is spread over a number of years.

12. **Intangible assets** include patents on a process or invention, the costs of starting a business, copyrights to written or reproducible material, and trademarks. Least tangible of all, but no less valuable an asset, is **good-will,** consisting mainly of the firm's reputation, especially in its relations with its customers.

13. An organization's liabilities (debts that a company has incurred) may be either current or long-term. **Current liabilities** are debts that will have to be paid within a year of the date of the balance sheet. These include accounts payable (which are generally due in thirty days or less), notes payable, and accrued expenses incurred but for which bills have not yet been received or recorded). Debts falling due a year or more after the date of the balance sheet are **long-term liabilities,** such as leases and mortgages.

14. Owners' equity is the investment of the owners in the business. Sole proprietorships list the owner's equity under the owner's name, and partnerships list each partner's share of the business separately. In the case of a corporation, owners' equity is the amount of common stock outstanding plus retained earnings.

15. The **income statement** shows how a firm's **revenues** (sales) compare with **expenses** over a given period of time. When expenses are subtracted from revenues, the resulting profit or loss of a company is known as **net income** —the "bottom line." Revenue may be recorded on either an **accrual basis** (recorded as soon as the sale is made) or on a **cash basis** (recorded only when money from a sale is actually received). Companies generally prefer recording revenue on a cash basis to avoid being taxed on monies not as yet collected.

16. **Gross sales** is the total dollar amount of goods sold. When returns and discounts are deducted from gross sales, the result is termed **net sales.** Companies must also calculate their expenses. A manufacturer, for example, would calculate **cost of goods sold** differently from a retailer. The manufacturer would consider the costs of producing the goods, including labor, raw materials, and factory operations. These costs would be added to the value of the finished goods inventory at the beginning of the year; the value of the inventory at the end of the year would be subtracted. In contrast, a retailer totals the inventory on hand at the beginning of the year, adds purchases made during the year, and then subtracts the year-end inventory.

17. Companies must also account for two types of **operating expenses** (or overhead): selling expenses and general expenses. **Selling expenses** are the costs of marketing and distributing products, including advertising and the salaries of sales personnel. In contrast, **general expenses** arise from the overall administration of a business and include office salaries, professional services (e.g., accounting and legal fees), and depreciation of office equipment.

18. Deducting the cost of goods sold from net sales equals **gross profit** (or gross margin). When total operating expenses are then deducted, the result in called **operating income.** By adding other income (e.g., interest income) and subtracting other expenses (e.g., income taxes), you arrive at a figure referred to as **net income.**

19. All public companies and many privately owned firms prepare a **statement of cash flows** in addition to the income statement and balance sheet. This statement summarizes the company's receipts and disbursements for the areas of operations, investments, and financing. It also serves to indicate a firm's liquidity (i.e., its ability to pay short-term obligations).

20. The various financial statements of a firm are used to spot both problems and opportunities, but they tell only part of the story. Because the state of the economy affects the financial health of companies (e.g., people delay purchases when times are tough), uncontrollable economic forces should be taken into consideration when assessing the quality of a firm. It is important to examine how the firm responds to economic forces, compared to its competitors.

21. One problem that arises when comparing one firm to another is the fact that each company may use different accounting techniques. For example, sales may be recorded when all potential returns can be reasonably projected, or they may be recorded well before a payment is due. On the other hand, assets may be depreciated unrealistically so that company profits look higher.

22. Earnings can also be raised or lowered by manipulating how cost of goods sold is calculated. **FIFO** (first in, first out) treats inventory as if costs were on a conveyor belt, whereas **LIFO** (last in, first out) is like stacking inventory costs in a box. The costs at the bottom can't be reached until all the layers above it are removed. LIFO, in times of high inflation, increases cost of goods sold and thereby lowers profits. The result would be a reduction in the taxes the firm would have to pay.

23. An individual examining the financial health of a company must also determine if the firm's reserves are adequate. Businesses need reserves to cover bad debts (uncollectible accounts receivable) and **unfunded pension liabilities** (the difference between what a company has put aside to meet pension expenses and how much it estimates it will actually need). Also to be examined are the extraordinary items, such as whether a firm's profitability stems from its basic operations or from, for example, selling off assets (an extraordinary measure).

24. Comparing financial data from year to year to detect changes is known as **trend analysis.** The examiner must consider both changes in the economy and how other firms in the same industry have fared. Trends may also be distorted by changes in the value of the dollar. For this reason, the Securities and Exchange Commission in 1979 began requiring the largest public companies to show what their costs would look like when adjusted for inflation.

25. **Ratio analysis** compares two elements from the same year's financial figures and shows how a firm is performing compared to other companies in the industry. For example, **profitability ratios** indicate how well a company is conducting its ongoing operations. The three most common ratios of this type are (1) **return on investment (ROI),** also known as return on equity, which is the income a firm earns for every dollar of owner or stockholder investment; (2) **return on sales** (or net profit margin), which is before-tax income per unit of sales; and (3) **earnings per share,** which compares how much profit a company earns for each share of outstanding stock.

26. **Liquidity ratios** indicate how well a company can pay its bills. One indicator of liquidity is a firm's **working capital,** because it represents the amount of current assets remaining after payment of all current liabilities. Current assets divided by current liabilities is known as the **current ratio.** A firm with a current ratio of

at least 2.0 is considered a safe short-term credit risk. But some analysts consider the **quick ratio** (or acid-test ratio) a better indication of a company's ability to pay immediate debts. In calculating the quick ratio, inventories are not included under the category of current assets. A quick ratio of 1.0 is considered to be reasonable.

27. How well a firm is managing its assets can be determined by **activity ratios.** The **inventory turnover ratio** is calculated by dividing cost of goods sold by the average value of inventory for a period. This tells a potential investor how quickly a firm's inventory is turned into sales. The "ideal" ratio varies with the type of operation.

28. **Debt ratios** (or coverage ratios) indicate how well a company can pay its long-term debts. The **debt-to-equity ratio** (total liabilities divided by stockholders' equity) shows the extent to which a firm is financed by debt: the lower this ratio, the safer the firm is, from a lender's viewpoint. Another debt ratio is the **debt-to-total-assets ratio** (total liabilities divided by total assets), which is a simple measure of a firm's ability to carry long-term debt. As a general rule, debt should be no more than half the size of total assets.

KEY TERMS

accounting
financial accounting
generally accepted accounting principles
management accounting
budgets
public accountants
audit
certified public accountant
private accountants
certified management accountants
bookkeeping
controller
accounting equation
assets
liabilities
owners' equity
double-entry bookkeeping
retained earnings
balance sheet
calendar year
fiscal year
current assets
fixed assets
depreciation
amortization
intangible assets
goodwill
current liabilities
long-term liabilities
income statement
revenues
expenses

net income
accrual basis
cash basis
gross sales
net sales
cost of goods sold
operating expenses
selling expenses
general expenses
gross profit
operating income
net income
statement of cash flows
FIFO
LIFO
unfunded pension liabilities
trend analysis
ratio analysis
profitability ratios
return on investment
return on sales
earnings per share
liquidity ratios
working capital
current ratio
quick ratio
activity ratios
inventory turnover ratio
debt ratios
debt-to-equity ratio
debt-to-total-assets ratio

KEY TERMS EXERCISE

Directions: On the line provided, place the letter of the statement on the right that most closely defines the key term.

E   1.   Accounting

S   2.   Financial accounting

J   3.   Management accounting

L   4.   Generally accepted accounting principles

N   5.   Budget

B   6.   Public accountants

O   7.   Audit

C   8.   Private accountants

U   9.   Accounting equation

Q   10.   Assets

H   11.   Liabilities

F   12.   Owners' equity

K   13.   Double-entry bookkeeping

M   14.   Balance sheet

T   15.   Goodwill

P   16.   Income statement

A   17.   Revenues

R   18.   Expenses

I   19.   Cost of goods sold

D   20.   Working capital

G   21.   Return on investment

a.   The amount of sales of goods or services and inflow from miscellaneous sources such as interest, rent, and royalties.

b.   Independent outsiders who provide accounting services for businesses and other organizations.

c.   In-house accountants employed by organizations and businesses.

d.   Current assets minus current liabilities.

e.   The process of recording, classifying, and summarizing financial activities of an organization.

f.   That portion of a company's assets that belongs to the owners after obligations to all creditors have been met.

g.   Ratio between the income earned by a firm and total owners' equity.

h.   Debts or obligations a company owes to other individuals or organizations.

i.   The cost of producing or acquiring a company's products for sale during a given time period.

j.   The area of accounting concerned with preparing information for use by managers within the organization.

k.   A method of recording financial transactions that requires two entries for every transaction so that the accounting equation is constantly in balance.

l.   Professionally approved standards used by the accounting profession to prepare financial statements.

m.   A financial statement that shows assets, liabilities, and owners' equity on a given date.

n.   A financial plan for a company's future activities that estimates revenues and proposed expenditures and forecasts how expenditures will be financed.

o.   An accountant's evaluation of the fairness and reliability of a client's financial statements.

p.   A financial statement showing how a business's revenues compare with expenses for a given period of time.

q.   Physical objects and intangible rights that have economic value to the owner.

r. Costs created in the process of generating revenue.

s. The area of accounting concerned with preparing information for outside users.

t. The value assigned for a business's reputation calculated
as the difference between the price paid for the business
and the underlying value of its assets.

u. Assets equal liabilities plus owners' equity.

ANSWERS TO KEY TERMS EXERCISE

1. e (p. 482)	7. o (p. 484)	13. k (p. 487)	19. i (p. 494)
2. s (p. 482)	8. c (p. 486)	14. m (p. 489)	20. d (p. 504)
3. j (p. 482)	9. n (p. 487)	15. t (p. 491)	21. g (p. 503)
4. l (p. 482)	10. b (p. 487)	16. p (p. 492)	
5. u (p. 483)	11. h (p. 487)	17. a (p. 492)	
6. b (p. 484)	12. f (p. 487)	18. r (p. 492)	

SELF TEST

True-False Questions

_____ 1. Accounting provides ways to present information, thus making it possible to evaluate a company's past performance, present condition, and future prospects.

_____ 2. Financial accounting practices tend to be tailor-made for each individual company.

_____ 3. Budgets are both a planning and a controlling tool.

_____ 4. The method of accounting can influence the profitability of the firm.

_____ 5. Accounting is an exact science.

_____ 6. The owners have first claim on the assets.

_____ 7. With a double-entry bookkeeping system, the accounting equation will always be in balance.

_____ 8. The balance sheet is a snapshot of where the company is financially at a given moment in time.

_____ 9. Companies generally prefer to avoid the accrual method of recording revenue.

_____ 10. Working capital is an important indicator of a company's financial health.

_____ 11. The state of the economy as a whole has little impact on most companies and industries.

_____ 12. Profits on a current-cost basis (LIFO) tend to be lower than profits computed on a historical-cost basis (FIFO).

_____ 13. Inflation can affect both the balance sheet and the income statement of a firm.

_____ 14. Inflation tends to overstate "true" profits.

_____ 15. Liquidity ratios measure a company's ability to pay its bills as they come due.

_____ 16. A firm desires to have a debt-to-equity ratio above 1.0.

_____ 17. A firm's total assets should be about twice as much as its debt.

_____ 18. In evaluating an annual report, you should start in the back with the accountant's report and footnotes.

_____ 19. Footnotes are a valuable source for evaluating an annual report.

Multiple Choice Questions

_____ 1. Which type of accounting is concerned with providing information for internal use?
   a. financial accounting
   b. management accounting
   c. public accounting
   d. certified accounting

_____ 2. The person in charge of virtually every aspect of a company's financial affairs is the
   a. bookkeeper.
   b. private accountant.
   c. certified public accountant.
   d. certified management accountant.
   e. controller.

_____ 3. The accounting equation can be kept in balance by
   a. increasing both assets and owners' equity by the same amount.
   b. increasing both assets and liabilities by the same amount.
   c. exchanging one asset for another.
   d. doing all of the above.

_____ 4. Retained earnings are
   a. current assets.
   b. fixed assets.
   c. intangible assets.
   d. current liabilities.
   e. owner's equity.

_____ 5. If a firm has assets of $500,000 and liabilities of $200,000, then the owners' equity must be
   a. $700,000.
   b. $300,000.
   c. $200,000.
   d. $500,000.
   e. none of the above.

_____ 6. The system that requires two entries for every transaction so that the accounting equation is constantly in balance is known as
   a. a dual accounting system.
   b. checks and balances.
   c. double-entry bookkeeping.
   d. cross-balance bookkeeping.

_____ 7. Which of the following is not a type of asset?
   a. current
   b. fixed

     c.   intangible
     d.   retained earnings

    8.   Cash, accounts receivable, inventories, and marketable securities are all examples of
     a.   current assets.
     b.   fixed assets
     c.   intangible assets.
     d.   current liabilities.
     e.   long-term liabilities

    9.   Which of the following is *not* a commonly used profitability ratio?
     a.   return on investment
     b.   net profit margin
     c.   current ratio
     d.   earnings per share

    10.   Which of the following are liquidity measures?
     a.   current ratio and quick ratio
     b.   accounts receivable and notes receivable
     c.   earnings per share and net profit margin
     d.   return on investment and cash flow

    11.   A company's ability to pay its long-term debts is measured by its
     a.   profitability ratios.
     b.   liquidity ratios.
     c.   activity ratios.
     d.   debt ratios.

    12.   How well a company is managing its assets is measured by its
     a.   profitability ratios.
     b.   liquidity ratios.
     c.   activity ratios.
     d.   debt ratios.

    13.   Accountants can exercise discretion in
     a.   the timing of revenue recognition.
     b.   their choice of depreciation method.
     c.   their choice of inventory evaluation.
     d.   the determination of allowance amounts.
     e.   all of the above.

    14.   What is the best advice in evaluating an annual report?
     a.   Ignore the footnotes, as they are unimportant.
     b.   Make comparisons with previous years and other companies in the industry.
     c.   Pay attention only to the net income figure.
     d.   Ignore the "subject to" clause.

Completion Questions

1.   Financial accounting is concerned with preparing information for _____.

2.   Financial accounting records must be _____, consistent over time, and comparable to
information supplied by other companies.

3. An accountant who has met certain state education, experience, and examination requirements is known as a

   _____.

4. Private accountants are also known as _____ accountants.

5. A double-entry bookkeeping system requires that there be _____ entries for every transaction.

6. The amount of total earnings minus any amounts distributed as dividends is referred to as the

   _____.

7. A snapshot of where a company is financially at one moment in time is indicated on the

   _____.

8. The actual profit of the firm after expenses are subtracted from revenue is called _____.

9. Manufacturers and retailers tend to record sales and expenses in the same period in which they are incurred,

   which is known as the _____ basis of recording revenues.

10. Service firms tend to record revenues and expenses in the period in which they are received or paid. This is

    known as the _____ method of recording revenues.

11. Gross sales minus returned goods and cash discounts equal _____.

12. The process of comparing financial data from year to year to see how they have changed is known as

    _____, while _____ is a comparison of figures within the same year.

PROJECT

Developing a Balance Sheet and Income Statement

From the following information, prepare a balance sheet and income statement in proper form. Use the forms provided on pages 203 and 204.

Item	Amount
Gross sales	$2,000,000
Returns and discounts on sales	50,000
Cash	100,000
Purchases	1,400,000
Purchase returns and discounts	200,000
Equipment	1,000,000
Building and land	2,000,000
Mortgage on building and land	1,500,000
Beginning merchandise inventory	200,000
Accounts receivable	250,000
Accounts payable	200,000
Office supplies	25,000
Selling expenses	200,000
Advertising expenses	400,000
General administration expenses	200,000
Retained earnings	1,500,000
Owners' equity	375,000
Accrued wages payable	100,000

BROWN MANUFACTURING COMPANY

BALANCE SHEET

December 31, 19__

Assets

Liabilities and Owners' Equity

BROWN MANUFACTURING COMPANY

INCOME STATEMENT

For Year Ending December 31, 19__

_____

_____

Chapter 18

Money and Banking

LEARNING OBJECTIVES

1. Name three functions of money.

2. Distinguish M1 from the total money supply.

3. Differentiate between demand deposits and time deposits.

4. Identify nine members of the banking system.

5. Explain how deregulation has affected the financial system.

6. Explain the responsibilities and insurance methods of the FDIC.

7. Describe the organization of the Federal Reserve System.

8. Cite the four ways the Federal Reserve System regulates the money supply.

OUTLINE

I. The nature of money

    A.   Functions and characteristics of money
        1.   Money as a medium of exchange
        2.   Money as a measure of value
        3.   Money as a store of value
        4.   Characteristics of money

    B.   The money supply
        1.   The "M1" and "M2" measures of money
        2.   Currency
        3.   Demand deposits
        4.   Time deposits
        5.   Plastic money

II. The banking system

    A.   Members of the system
        1.   Commercial banks
            a.   National banks and state banks
        2.   Thrift institutions
            a.   Savings banks and savings and loan associations
        3.   Credit unions
        4.   Finance companies

5. Other financial institutions
   a. Limited-service banks
   b. Large brokerage houses
   c. Insurance companies
   d. Pension funds
   e. Investment banks
B. What banks do
   1. Deposit functions
      a. Interest rates
      b. Customer accounts
         (1) Regular checking
         (2) NOW and Super NOW accounts
         (3) Money-market accounts
         (4) Certificates of deposit (CDs)
         (5) Individual Retirement Accounts (IRAs)
         (6) Keogh accounts
      c. Loan functions
         (1) How banks create new money
         (2) Reserve requirements
      d. Other services
         (1) Discount brokerage
         (2) Electronic banking
            (a) Electronic funds transfer systems (EFTs)
            (b) Automated teller machines (ATMs)
            (c) Debit cards

C. Today's banking environment
   1. Bank failures
      a. Causes of the financial system's plight
      b. The commercial paper market
   2. Banks
      a. The condition of U.S. banking at the start of the 1990s
      b. Federal bank rescues
      c. Banking industry consolidation
   3. Thrifts
      a. The S&L debacle

D. Bank safety
   1. The FDIC

III. The Federal Reserve System

A. The Federal Reserve's structure and mission
   1. How the Fed is organized

B. The Federal Reserve's functions
   1. Regulating the money supply
      a. Reserve requirements
      b. The discount rate
      c. Open-market operations
      d. Selective credit controls
   2. Supplying currency
      a. Clearing checks

MAJOR POINTS TO REMEMBER

1. Anything that is generally accepted as a means of paying for goods and services can be called **money**, and it functions as a "medium of exchange" because it simplifies transactions between buyers and sellers. Money also functions as a "measure of value"; a buyer does not have to negotiate relative worth to make a purchase, as would be necessary if you were bartering milk for airline tickets. Also, because money will keep, it serves as a "store of value" (i.e., money is not perishable). Any society's money (whether in the form of dollars, cattle, or salt) has the characteristic of liquidity, which means that it can be converted quickly into other forms of wealth.

2. The U.S. money supply comes in many forms, including currency, demand deposits, time deposits, and plastic money. **M1**, the narrowest commonly used measure of money, consists of currency and demand deposits. A broader measure, **M2**, includes time deposits as well.

3. Bills and coins, the most obvious form of money, are referred to as **currency**. Cashier's checks, money orders, and traveler's checks, which can be purchased from a bank for their face value plus a small fee, are also considered currency.

4. Each check a person writes and signs is an order for the bank to release the amount of money specified on the check, "on demand," to the **payee**. This was the origin of the term **demand deposit**.

5. A huge portion of the money supply is held in **time deposits** such as saving accounts, money-market funds, and certificates of deposit (CDs). All time deposits pay interest, but they restrict the owner's right to withdraw funds on short notice and cannot be used as a medium of exchange.

6. On average, adults carry about seven credit cards (plastic money). Institutions that issue credit cards typically charge annual fees ranging from $20 to $250, in addition to charging 17.5 to 20 percent interest on unpaid balances. These high fees and high interest rates make credit cards a huge money-maker for the banks that issue them.

7. **Commercial banks** accept deposits and use these funds to make loans. There are two types of commercial banks: national banks and state banks. **National banks** are chartered by the federal government, and **state banks** are chartered by state governments. These banks are a prime source of capital for business; they also provide loans and checking and savings accounts to consumers. All national banks and about 90 percent of state banks are members of the Federal Reserve System.

8. Both **savings banks** and **savings and loan associations** are **thrift institutions**. They perform many of the same functions as commercial banks (e.g., checking and savings accounts, loans) but use the majority of their assets for financing home mortgages. Changes in the banking laws and the S&L crisis of the 1980s have resulted in an industrywide consolidation, and experts believe that thrifts will merge into banks within this decade.

9. **Credit unions** are member-owned cooperatives that offer checking and savings accounts, credit cards, and consumer loans. Most of the 15,600 credit unions in the country serve employee groups.

10. While not accepting deposits, **finance companies** offer short-term loans to businesses or individuals. They typically serve high-risk customers and charge high rates of interest. However, finance companies formed by automobile companies (e.g., GMAC and Ford Motor Credit) and other large manufacturers (e.g., IBM) have been taking market share from banks; today finance companies provide 25 percent of all commercial business loans.

11. Nonbank banks, more popularly known as **limited-service banks**, mix other businesses with banking functions (e.g., insurance, real estate). They may accept demand deposits, or they may make commercial loans, but they may not do both. Types of limited-service banks include large brokerage houses, insurance companies, pension funds, and investment banks (which help corporations raise capital).

12. Most financial institutions operate on the principle of attracting deposits and then lending some of this money to other customers. Often, they offer other money-handling services (for a fee). Banks attract depositors by offering interest and a host of other services, such as deposit insurance, convenient local branches, and free or low-cost checking.

13. Banking deregulation has lifted interest rates on savings accounts from the former mandated ceilings to whatever percentage rate the bank wishes to offer. Although regular checking accounts typically pay little or no interest, a new form of hybrid account, the **NOW account**, pays interest and allows unlimited check writing (as long as a sizable minimum balance is maintained). **Super NOW accounts** pay even higher interest and require even larger minimum balances. Another alternative, the **money-market account**, earns the highest interest but often limits the number of checks that may be written.

14. Savings and checking accounts have no restrictions regarding when money can be withdrawn. However, if a person invests at least $500 and is willing to leave the money in the bank for a specified period of time, a higher rate of interest can be earned with the purchase of a **certificate of deposit** (CD).

15. Under the present law, a consumer may also invest up to $2,000 yearly in an **Individual Retirement Account** ($2,250 for married, single-income couples), and self-employed individuals can put money into a **Keogh account**, which has a maximum contribution ceiling of $30,000 a year. While IRAs and Keoghs pay high interest that is not taxed until retirement, there are financial penalties for withdrawing money prematurely (i.e., prior to retirement).

16. Banks create new money as part of the process of making loans. This is permitted as long as sufficient reserves are on hand. According to present requirements, between 3 and 12 percent of all demand deposits must be kept in reserve, depending on the total amount of demand deposits a particular bank has.

17. A number of other functions are provided by banks: most operate trust departments, provide safe deposit boxes, issue traveler's checks, wire money to other places, exchange currency, and issue credit cards. Banks also offer discount brokerage services and electronic banking.

18. While the Glass-Steagall Act of 1933 prohibits banks from underwriting stocks and from giving customers advice on stocks, discount brokers do neither of these things. In 1986, the Supreme Court ruled that banks have the right to expand their discount brokerage operations.

19. Electronic banking is one of the financial industry's newest services. For example, **electronic funds transfer systems (EFTs)** offer customer convenience and permit companies to transfer wages directly into employees' accounts. **Automated teller machines (ATMs)** allow consumers to make deposits and get cash twenty-four hours a day without the need for tellers. And **debit cards** permit a point-of-sale terminal to transfer money from a customer's account to the store's account to pay for a purchase.

20. Today's banking environment is vastly different from that of just a decade ago, as our entire financial system has undergone change. Over 1,200 banks failed during the 1980s, with much of the thrift industry saved by the largest taxpayer-financed bailout in history. During this period, the loan-deposit insurance fund for savings and loan associations (FSLIC) collapsed, and the fund for banks (FDIC) was close to insolvency. By 1990, banks' after-tax profits had dropped drastically, while the amount of bad loans soared. These problems were caused by inflation, deregulation, growth in commercial building, and competition in the industry from both domestic and foreign banks. Banks and thrifts often invested heavily in real estate, but overbuilding in the 1980s caused the U.S. real estate market to collapse (and left financial institutions with unrepaid loans). Additionally, banks kept their interest rates high even when inflation began to subside (in order to keep profits high), forcing U.S. businesses to turn to foreign banks or to issue **commercial paper** (an IOU from corporations to raise short-term capital). While banks were often reluctant to purchase commercial paper, the finance companies (e.g., GMAC and GE Credit) thrived in this market.

21. By 1990, the U.S. banking system was in its worst shape since the Depression, and some experts predicted that industry consolidation would reduce the top 125 banks to 15. When the Bank of New England collapsed (losing $450 million in one quarter alone), the cost to the Federal Deposit Insurance Corporation (FDIC) was $3 billion. Presently, the largest U.S. banks favor reforms, including the legalization of interstate banking, the ability to offer a broader range of financial services, and industrial ownership of banks. It has been estimated that banking industry consolidation could also trim $10 billion a year from the industry's operating costs.

22. It is estimated that the bailout of the thrift industry will ultimately cost taxpayers $500 billion. While savings and loans were created in the 1930s for the sole purpose of providing home loans, deregulation permitted them to invest directly in real estate. The bailout bill passed by Congress in 1989 requires thrifts to meet more stringent financial requirements.

23. There is concern today that the FDIC may not be able to insure all deposits, due to (1) the solvency of the so-called fund that insures deposits in FDIC banks, (2) the unwritten "too big to fail" doctrine, and (3) the amount of insurance available on each deposit. While the FDIC was in the black in 1990, it was expected to be in the red by 1992. And while the FDIC might be able to bail out a small bank, a bailout of a money-center bank would bankrupt the fund.

24. The Federal Reserve System (or Fed) consists of twelve regional banks and has the task of controlling the nation's banking system. Its powers were enhanced in 1980 by the Depository Institutions Deregulation and Monetary Control Act, which extended some of the Fed's regulatory powers to nonmember banks. Policies are established by the seven-member board of governors, who are appointed by the President to fourteen-year terms. The organization's main task is to set and implement **monetary policy**, which is a set of rules for handling the economy and the money supply. It does this by regulating the money supply, supplying currency, and clearing checks.

25. The Fed regulates the money supply because too much money can lead to inflation and too little may raise interest rates. As the official banker of the government, the Fed must also raise money to offset budget deficits. To do this, the Fed might either borrow from the public or decide to lend money to the Treasury itself.

26. The Federal Reserve Board has four basic tools at its disposal for regulating the money supply and expanding the economy: it may change reserve requirements, it may change the discount rate (the interest rate that member banks must pay to borrow from the Fed), it may engage in open-market operations (i.e., the buying and selling of government securities), and it may set the terms of credit for certain types of loans (selective credit controls). The Fed can change the **reserve requirements**, that is, the sum of money (called **reserves**) equal to a certain percentage of deposits that a bank must keep on deposit with the Federal Reserve Bank in its district. When reserve requirements are increased, banks have less money to lend their customers. Conversely, the Fed can lower these requirements to stimulate business. When one bank has excess reserves, it can lend some of these funds to another bank at the **Fed funds rate** (the rate allowed for overnight loans).

27. The rate that the Fed charges member banks for loans is called the **discount rate**. Such loans are attractive to commercial banks if they can charge their customers a higher interest rate. By varying the discount rate, the Fed can alter the **prime interest rate**, which is the lowest rate at which banks will make loans to their most creditworthy business customers.

28. The tool the Fed uses most frequently to carry out monetary policy is its power to buy and sell government bonds on the open market. These are known as **open-market operations**. Selling government bonds to the public and to banks reduces the amount of money available and can help fight inflation. To get the economy moving again, the Fed buys back the bonds, thereby putting cash into the economy.

29. The last tool employed by the Federal Reserve Board is **selective credit controls**, or the setting of credit terms on various kinds of loans. For example, the Fed sets the **margin requirements** that limit the amount of money financial institutions can lend customers for the purpose of buying stock.

30. Other functions performed by the Fed include supplying banks with adequate amounts of currency and clearing checks. Banks can use the Federal Reserve's check-clearing service to clear checks drawn on banks outside their Federal Reserve districts. Checks drawn on commercial banks are usually forwarded to the closest Federal Reserve bank, which then collects the funds from the Federal Reserve bank that services the commercial bank upon which the check is drawn. Some rural banks pay larger banks to perform this service for them, and transactions within the same Federal Reserve district are handled locally and then reported to the Fed.

KEY TERMS

money
M1
M2
currency
payee
demand deposit
time deposits
commercial banks
national banks
state banks
savings banks
savings and loan associations
thrift institutions
credit unions
finance companies
limited-service banks
NOW account
Super NOW account

money-market account
certificate of deposit
Individual Retirement Account
Keogh account
electronic funds transfer systems
automated teller machines
debit cards
commercial paper
monetary policy
reserve requirements
reserves
Fed funds rate
discount rate
prime interest rate
open-market operations
selective credit controls
margin requirements

KEY TERMS EXERCISE

Directions: On the line provided, place the letter of the statement on the right that most closely defines the key term.

_____ 1. Money

_____ 2. M1

_____ 3. M2

_____ 4. Currency

_____ 5. Payee

_____ 6. Demand deposit

_____ 7. Time deposits

_____ 8. Commercial banks

_____ 9. National banks

_____ 10. State banks

_____ 11. Savings banks

_____ 12. Savings and loan associations

_____ 13. Credit unions

_____ 14. Finance companies

a. Unregulated companies that specialize in making loans.

b. The lowest rate of interest charged by banks for loans to their most creditworthy customers.

c. Banks offering savings, interest-bearing checking, and mortgages.

d. Savings accounts that restrict withdrawals to a specified time.

e. A note issued by a bank that guarantees to pay the depositor a relatively high interest rate for a fixed period of time.

f. Funds a financial institution keeps on tap to meet projected withdrawals.

g. That portion of the money supply consisting of currency, demand deposits, and time deposits.

h. An interest-bearing checking account with a relatively high minimum-balance requirement.

i. Anything used by a society as a token of value in buying and selling goods and services.

_____ 15. Investment banks

_____ 16. NOW account

_____ 17. Super NOW account

_____ 18. Money-market accounts

_____ 19. Certificate of deposit

_____ 20. Individual Retirement Account

_____ 21. Keogh account

_____ 22. Electronic funds transfer systems

_____ 23. Automated teller machines

_____ 24. Debit card

_____ 25. Commercial paper

_____ 26. Monetary policy

_____ 27. Reserves

_____ 28. Reserve requirement

_____ 29. Fed funds rate

_____ 30. Discount rate

_____ 31. Prime interest rate

_____ 32. Open-market operations

_____ 33. Selective credit controls

_____ 34. Margin requirements

j. The interest rate charged for overnight loans between banks.

k. The percentage of a bank's deposits that must be kept on hand.

l. A type of retirement savings account for the self-employed that provides tax and interest-rate advantages.

m. Banks chartered by a state government.

n. An IOU issued by corporations to raise short-term capital.

o. Tactics for expanding or contracting the money supply as a means of influencing the economy.

p. Person or business to which a check is made out.

q. Electronic terminals that permit people to perform simple banking transactions without the aid of a teller.

r. Limits set by the Federal Reserve on the amount of money that stockbrokers and banks may lend customers for the purpose of buying stocks.

s. Traditional banks offering checking, savings, and loan services.

t. Financial institutions that specialize in helping companies or government agencies raise funds.

u. Banks chartered by the federal government.

v. An interest-bearing checking account with a minimum-balance requirement.

w. The Federal Reserve's power to set credit terms on various types of loans.

x. Cooperative financial institutions that provide loan and savings services to their members.

y. A type of savings account that provides tax and interest-rate advantages to depositors who are building a fund for retirement.

z. Bank accounts that pay money-market interest rates and permit depositors to write a limited number of checks.

aa. Bills and coins that make up the cash money of a society.

bb. That portion of the money supply consisting of currency and demand deposits.

cc. Computerized systems for performing financial transactions.

dd. Mostly in New England, banks offering interest-bearing checking, savings, and mortgages.

ee. The interest rate charged by the Federal Reserve on loans to member banks.

ff. Money in a checking account that can be used by the owner at any time.

gg. A form of plastic money that automatically decreases a person's bank account when used.

hh. The activity of the Federal Reserve in buying and selling government bonds on the open market.

ANSWERS TO KEY TERMS EXERCISE

	27. f (p. 531)	18. z (p. 521)	9. u (p. 517)
	26. o (p. 531)	17. h (p. 521)	8. s (p. 517)
34. r (p. 533)	25. n (p. 525)	16. v (p. 521)	7. d (p. 516)
33. w (p. 533)	24. gg (p. 523)	15. t (p. 520)	6. ff (p. 516)
32. hh (p. 533)	23. q (p. 523)	14. a (p. 518)	5. p (p. 516)
31. b (p. 532)	22. cc (p. 523)	13. x (p. 518)	4. aa (p. 516)
30. ee (p. 532)	21. l (p. 521)	12. c (p. 517)	3. g (p. 515)
29. j (p. 532)	20. y (p. 521)	11. pp (p. 517)	2. bb (p. 515)
28. k (p. 531)	19. e (p. 521)	10. m (p. 517)	1. i (p. 514)

SELF TEST

True-False Questions

_____ 1. The most obvious form of money is currency.

_____ 2. All the money supply of a country like the United States is held by definition within that country.

_____ 3. Time deposits can be used as a medium of exchange.

_____ 4. Credit cards not only function as a medium of exchange but also are officially included in the measure of the money supply.

_____ 5. Commercial banks can be either national banks or state banks.

_____ 6. Corporations issue commercial paper to solve their long-term capital needs.

_____ 7. In the process of making loans, a financial institution actually creates new money.

_____ 8. The impact of the reserve requirement is to safeguard demand deposits for consumers.

_____ 9. In the 1990s, the U.S. banking system was in its worst condition since the Depression.

_____ 10. All checks written in the United States are sent through the Fed for clearance.

Multiple Choice Questions

_____ 1. The ability to transport money easily, and keep it safe from one day to another, illustrates which function of money?
a. medium of exchange
b. measure of value
c. store of value
d. all of the above

_____ 2. The business or person to whom a check is written is known as the
a. payer.
b. payee.
c. drawer.
d. demand depositor.

_____ 3. Organizations that use the bulk of their funds to finance home mortgages but still provide checking and savings accounts are called
a. thrift institutions.
b. national banks.
c. commercial banks.
d. all of the above.

_____ 4. An underwriter that helps corporations raise capital is also known as
a. an investment bank.
b. an insurance company.
c. a pension fund.
d. a finance company.

_____ 5. Which of the various accounts offered by a financial institution offers the highest interest rate?
a. regular checking accounts
b. money-market accounts
c. NOW accounts
d. basic savings accounts

_____ 6. A point-of-sale terminal transfers the money for a purchase from a customer's account to the seller's account after the customer has used
a. a debit card.
b. an automated teller machine.
c. an asset management system.
d. a credit card.

_____ 7. A type of Individual Retirement Account for self-employed people is the
a. Super NOW account.
b. Keogh account.
c. brokerage account.
d. securitized account.

_____ 8. The institutions that could fare the best during the banking industry's consolidation are
a. thrifts.
b. small community banks.
c. regional banks.
d. major money-center banks.

_____ 9. The Federal Reserve System's major function is
a. regulating the money supply.
b. supplying currency.
c. clearing checks.
d. All of the above are major functions of the Federal Reserve System.

_____ 10. The discount rate, when changed by the Fed, is most likely to influence the
      a. reserve requirements.
      b. prime interest rate.
      c. margin requirements.
      d. stock market gains.

Completion Questions

1. Anything that is generally accepted as a means of paying for goods and services is _____.

2. Bills and coins, or _____, constitute the most obvious form of money.

3. _____ hold the major portion of the money supply. Examples include money-market funds, government bonds, and certificates of deposit.

4. A commercial bank chartered by the federal government is a _____ bank.

5. A _____ does not accept deposits but does provide short-term loans to businesses or individuals.

6. A _____ account allows unlimited check writing, pays interest on the account, but requires a sizable minimum balance.

7. _____ are free-standing, self-service terminals that provide convenience for customers of a bank.

8. The Fed sets _____, which is a set of guidelines for handling the nation's economy and money supply.

9. _____ includes the money supply as defined in M1 plus time deposits.

10. The _____ is in charge of keeping an adequate amount of currency in circulation.

PROJECT

Money and Banking

Form a team with fellow students. Assign part of the team to interview a traditional banker. Assign another part of the team to interview an official of a nonbank bank. Address the following questions (and others you may have) to each. Compare the responses. Give your assessment of how nonbank banks are affecting the money supply and banking system.

Questions to ask:

1. In what ways are nonbank banks changing the money and banking system?

2. From a customer's point of view, what are the advantages of dealing with a bank as opposed to a nonbank bank?

3. In what ways do current regulations affect the functions performed and the services offered by a traditional bank and a nonbank bank?

4. How do the needs of customers of banks and nonbank banks differ?

5. How are the assets of customers of each type of bank protected?

Chapter 19

Financial Management

LEARNING OBJECTIVES

1. List the five steps involved in the financial-planning process.
2. State the matching principle.
3. Explain the chief advantage of debt versus equity.
4. Define the objective of the capital-budgeting process.
5. Name three major types of short-term debt.
6. List four major long-term financing options.
7. Explain the guiding principle of cash management.
8. State the financial manager's primary goal in handling receivables and payables.

OUTLINE

I. Finance: A company's lifeblood

    A. The goals of financial management
       1. The use of leverage
       2. Problems faced by financial managers

    B. The process of financial management
       1. The five-step financial planning process

    C. The sources and uses of funds
       1. Alternative sources of funds
       2. Types of financing needs

    D. The cost of capital
       1. What cost of capital is
       2. Risk
       3. Interest rates
       4. Mix of funding vehicles
          a. Internal versus external financing
          b. Short- versus long-term funding
             (1) The matching principle
          c. Debt versus equity
             (1) Advantages and disadvantages of debt financing

    E. Capital budgeting
       1. What capital investments are
       2. The capital budgeting process

II. Short-term financing

    A. Definition and categories of short-term debt

   B.   Trade credit
      1. Open-book credit
      2. Promissory notes

   C.   Loans
      1. Fixed- versus variable-rate loans
      2. Secured loans
        a. Types of collateral
          (1) Accounts receivable
          (2) Factoring
          (3) Pledging inventories
          (4) Chattel mortgages
      3. Unsecured loans
        a. Compensating balances
        b. Lines of credit
          (1) Revolving line of credit

   D.   Commercial paper
      1. What commercial paper is
      2. How commercial paper is used
      3. Commercial paper's appeal

III.   Long-term financing

   A.   Long-term loans and leases

   B.   Bonds
      1. Bond terminology
      2. Secured and unsecured bonds
      3. Bond interest rates
        a. Junk bonds
      4. Retirement of debt
        a. Serial bonds versus term bonds
        b. Sinking funds
        c. Callable bonds
        d. Convertible bonds

   C.   Equity
      1. What equity financing is
      2. Stock terminology
      3. Preferred stock
      4. Common stock
        a. Common stock dividends
        b. Stock splits
      5. New issues and the secondary market

IV.   Internal financial planning and control

   A.   Managing working capital

   B.   Managing cash and marketable securities
      1. Types of marketable securities

   C.   Managing receivables and payables
      1. Issues in accounts receivable management

   D.   Managing inventory
      1. Economic order quantity (EOQ)
      2. Just-in-time inventory control

MAJOR POINTS TO REMEMBER

1. How to obtain and use money is the concern of an extremely complex subject area known as **financial management.** Sometimes it takes money to make money, and the use of borrowed money is called **leverage.** A firm stays ahead by earning more profit on the borrowed money than it costs the company in interest.

2. A financial manager's job involves finding the combination of funding sources with the lowest cost, then making sure that these funds are used efficiently. The achievement of a positive cash flow and the efficient investment of excess cash flow to make the firm grow are the two objectives of a financial plan.

3. Sources of funds include a company's revenues (e.g., cash from sales, property rentals, and interest on investments), loans, and credit from suppliers. Large corporations may also raise funds by selling stocks and bonds. Monies raised from all sources are used to cover business expenses (e.g., payroll, rent, and advertising) and to acquire new assets.

4. The price a firm must pay to raise money is called the **cost of capital.** This cost fluctuates with the amount of risk associated with the company, the current interest rate, and the type of funding vehicle used. The reward to the lender or investor is expected to be greater if the business is risky. Time also plays a role; the longer it takes for an investor or lender to receive an expected return, the greater the risk. Blue-chip companies, therefore, tend to obtain funds more cheaply than higher-risk companies. Interest rates also vary over time, and a company forced to borrow when rates were high may be able to renegotiate the loan when rates drop.

5. Financial managers have a huge number of funding vehicles from which to select. Internal sources of financing include retained profits (money kept by the company after meeting expenses and taxes) and the sale of assets. Most firms do not rely entirely on internal sources but instead use a mix of debt and equity. This mix is the firm's **capital structure.**

6. A firm may use the **matching principle** to choose between short- and long-term financing. This principle states that the timing of borrowing should roughly match the timing of spending.

7. Yet another decision to be made involves choosing between debt (borrowing) and equity (selling shares of stock) financing. Interest payments on debt are tax deductible, but stock dividends, if paid, are not deductible. Additionally, the fact that bondholders and lenders must always be paid before shareholders usually means than a company can pay them a lower rate of return over time. This makes debt financing usually less expensive for a firm than equity financing. However, in bad times a company might omit dividends, but if it can't meet its loan and/or bond commitments it could be forced into bankruptcy.

8. By 1990, debt as a percentage of total capital for nonfinancial firms had soared to 49 percent, up from 34 percent ten years earlier. Interest payments ate into profits, and corporate debt became so widespread that it was a major cause of the economic recession at the start of the 1990s. This huge amount of debt canceled out the tax advantages of leveraging.

9. The advantage of issuing stock (i.e., equity financing) is that dividend payments can be omitted. However, it is a more expensive way of raising money because dividends are paid to stockholders with dollars remaining after the firm has paid its income tax.

10. **Capital budgeting** is the process of evaluating and comparing long-term investments (called **capital investments**). Such projects include new facilities, new equipment, or even major personnel training programs. The financial manager should consider investments whose cost is less than its projected rate of return. In some instances, the financial risks of all proposed investments may be greater than alternative uses for the money; under such conditions, the firm may decide to invest in short-term certificates of deposit rather than new equipment.

11. **Short-term debt** is debt that must be repaid within one year. The three major sources of short-term financing are trade credit, loans, and commercial paper. **Trade credit,** which means that the purchaser gets credit directly from the supplier, is the most widespread source of short-term funding and can take several forms.

Open-book credit is the informal arrangement whereby purchasers may obtain goods from suppliers and pay for them perhaps thirty or sixty days later. This arrangement is used in the majority of all business transactions that involve merchandise and helps to minimize the mismatch between cash outflows and inflows.

12. For business people who prefer the security of a written agreement, there is the **promissory note.** This is a note signed by the buyer agreeing unconditionally to pay the seller a specific amount of money (the value of the goods plus an interest charge) on a future date.

13. About 28 percent of all short-term financing is from commercial bank loans. The interest rate of the loan may be either fixed or floating (i.e., it increases and decreases with fluctuations in prevailing rates). Major banks loan money to their best customers at the prime rate. All other loan customers pay an interest rate higher than the prime.

14. **Secured loans** are loans from a bank that are backed by a pledge of some specific valuable item or items (known as **collateral**), which can be seized by the lender if the borrower fails to repay. For collateral, a business may pledge its accounts receivable (the amount due the business from customers with open-book accounts), engage in **factoring** accounts receivable (instruct customers to send their bills directly to a financial institution), or pledge other property like inventories or movable property like automobiles (the borrower is often asked to sign a **chattel mortgage**, giving the lender the legal right to take the property if payments are not made).

15. Banks that issue **unsecured loans** (i.e., loans that require no collateral) rely on the general credit record and earning power of the borrower. Many banks require the borrower to maintain some substantial portion of the loan in an account at the bank. This deposit, called a **compensating balance**, reduces the bank's risk and has the effect of raising the interest rate the borrower is paying for the unsecured loan. A bank may also establish a **line of credit** for a company, eliminating the need to negotiate each time a business needs a loan. This line of credit represents the maximum amount of money the bank will loan a business during a specific period of time. However, there is no guarantee that the bank will honor the line of credit up to the stated maximum amount. If a company needs the guaranty that a bank will honor its line of credit, a **revolving line of credit** (at a higher fee) is required.

16. Many large corporations with top credit ratings can raise short-term capital by selling **commercial paper** (the company's promise to pay back a stated amount of money on a given date within 3 to 270 days from the time it is issued). The market for commercial paper experienced rapid growth in the 1980s. During the second half of the 1980s there was a 70 percent increase in the number of firms issuing commercial paper, and a 115 percent increase in the nonbank financial companies issuing commercial paper. The appeal of commercial paper is that it does not require a compensating balance, it allows a borrower to lock in an interest rate for up to 270 days, and it is easier for a company to sell commercial paper for short-term financing than to receive a commercial loan at a bank.

17. Long-term financing is used for such purposes as major construction projects, acquisition of other companies, and research and development expenses. Most firms rely on a combination of internal and external funding sources.

18. The four main sources of long-term debt financing are loans, leases, bonds, and equity. **Long-term loans** may be secured or unsecured and are repaid over a period of at least five years. Interest rates on long-term loans tend to be higher than those on short-term loans because the longer time frame increases the lender's risk.

19. The most common type of long-term loan is a mortgage. The second source, a **lease**, allows the company to use property that belongs to another party and provides tax advantages for all. Creditors may be more willing to provide a lease than a loan since the leased item can be repossessed if the lessee defaults. Some companies use leases to finance up to 35 percent of their total assets.

20. A **bond** obligates a company to repay a certain amount of money, plus interest, to the bondholder. Every bond has a **denomination,** which is the amount of the loan represented by one bond. They are typically sold in $1,000 denominations, with each bond indicating the date (called the maturity date) when the full amount (the **principal**) is to be repaid (usually in ten years or more).

21. Bonds may be secured or unsecured (not backed by any specific collateral). **Secured bonds** are backed by specific property of one type or another (e.g., a real estate mortgage or a claim on assets like an airplane or plant equipment). **Unsecured bonds**, also called **debentures**, are backed only by the general good name of the issuing company.

22. The interest rate offered on bonds is a function of the risk the investor must take. Bonds of a company in a strong financial position and with excellent prospects for future earnings will carry a lower interest rate than bonds of a less financially secure firm. There are bond-rating agencies that rate bonds, based on the financial stability of the issuing company. Bonds rated investment grade or higher are safest for investors; below-investment grade bonds were called **junk bonds** in the 1980s.

23. The standard way for a corporation to repay its bondholders is on the bond's maturity date. However, if a large number of bonds mature at one time, the cost to the company could be huge. Therefore, companies sometimes issue **serial bonds**, which mature at different times (instead of **term bonds**, which all mature at the same time). A **sinking fund** is another way this problem can be handled. The company sets aside a sum of money each year to pay off the debt. The money can be used to retire a few bonds each year, or it can be allowed to accumulate until the bond issue matures.

24. **Callable bonds** (or redeemable bonds) are bonds that a corporation retains the right to pay off before maturity. If bond interest rates decline, a corporation may call in its high-interest bonds and pay them off by selling a new bond issue at a lower interest rate. Sometimes a company may wish to redeem its bonds prior to the call date. It tries to induce its bondholders to buy callable bonds by offering them a higher interest rate. Since the bond can be recalled, companies must offer investors a higher interest rate to get them to purchase callable bonds. The difference between the normal interest rate and this higher interest rate is referred to as the "call premium."

25. Bonds that may be repaid with stock instead of money are convertible bonds. The bondholder has the option of accepting stock or money. **Convertible bonds** generally carry lower interest rates because investors have two options for making money with them (i.e., they can accept cash or stock).

26. Unlike debt, which must be repaid, equity is "a piece of the action." When a firm raises money through equity financing, it is selling ownership in the company. In a small business, equity financing might mean that a new partner is brought in, while in a large corporation, stock is sold to investors on the open market.

27. Stocks are shares of ownership in a company. The shareholder receives a **stock certificate** listing his or her name, the number of shares owned, and the special characteristics of the stock. Many certificates also contain a **par value**, which is some arbitrary face value (typically less than the stock's market value). The number of shares a corporation will try to sell is based on the amount of equity capital required and the price of each share that it sells. **Authorized stock** is the maximum number of shares into which a company can be divided (as authorized by a corporation's board of directors). Usually, a corporation sells only part of its authorized stock. The part held by the shareholders is called **issued stock**; unsold shares are referred to as **unissued stock**. Most corporations distribute a part of their profits to shareholders in the form of **dividends**; although usually paid in cash, in rapidly growing companies they often take the form of stock.

28. A company may issue both **preferred stock** and **common stock**. Preferred stock is a class of stock that gives its owners special privileges. In general, all preferred stock dividends must be paid before dividends are paid to owners of common stock. If the corporation should fail, preferred stockholders receive their share of whatever assets the company has before common stockholders receive anything. However, unlike common stockholders, holders of preferred stock typically have limited voting rights or no voting rights at all.

29. The more usual way for a corporation to raise money is by selling shares of common stock. In fact, many corporations issue only common stock. Its owners are entitled to vote for the company's board of directors and to voice their opinions on important issues facing the firm. While preferred stock may be more dependable and stable, the value of the shares does not usually change much. Owners of common stock, on the other hand, may see their investment increase dramatically.

30. The board of directors decides whether the corporation will pay dividends to owners of common stock. Young, high-growth companies often omit dividends in order to plow the profits back into the business, and major corporations may cut or skip a dividend when profits fall.

31. A corporation can also offer its shareholders a **stock split**, a procedure that multiplies the number of shares of ownership each stock certificate represents. A stock split can benefit shareholders because the more shares the corporation has outstanding, the less affected it is by market fluctuations.

32. Corporations often issue new stock when their present **stock price** rises. After stock has been issued, it is bought and sold in secondary markets called **stock exchanges.**

33. When managing working capital, the goal is to minimize the amount of money tied up in excess cash, uncollected bills (receivables), and inventory. Firms sometimes temporarily have more cash on hand than they need. Part of the financial manager's job is to invest this money so that it earns interest. The investment should yield the highest possible return but must be liquid (i.e., the investment can be quickly converted into cash). There are many types of short-term investments, called **marketable securities**, that meet these requirements. For example, a firm may select large-denomination certificates of deposit (CDs), which are really time deposits at a bank, or securities issued by the federal government, which are called Treasury bills. These short-term debt instruments must be repaid less than a year after purchase. Many federal agencies borrow in the money market and issue securities known by such names as "Fannie Maes," "Freddie Macs," "Ginnie Maes," and "Sally Maes." Financial managers may also opt to buy securities in other corporations (commercial paper).

34. Because revenues do not always come in when bills have to be paid, a company's financial manager must manage working capital. Accounts receivable (money owed the firm by customers) must be monitored, and the firm has to decide who qualifies for credit and how long customers should be given to pay their bills. Payables must also be managed. Here the objective is to postpone paying bills until the last moment because they represent interest-free loans from suppliers. Sometimes, however, prompt payment may entitle the firm to cash discounts.

35. Financial managers must also use inventory management to properly control a firm's cash flow. Excess inventory represents money tied up and not earning interest. However, the company needs an adequate level of inventory to fill orders on time. Therefore, the financial manager may try to determine the **economic order quantity (EOQ)**, which is the quantity of raw materials that, when ordered regularly, results in the lowest ordering and storage costs.

36. Many firms today are turning to **just-in-time inventory control.** Under this system, businesses are linked via computers to their customers and their suppliers, thereby automatically ordering only as much inventory as is needed for a given period of time. Cost savings to the firm result from not having huge piles of inventory sitting in warehouses or in factory storage rooms.

KEY TERMS

financial management	principal
leverage	secured bonds
cost of capital	unsecured bonds
capital structure	debentures
capital budgeting	junk bonds
capital investments	serial bonds
short-term debt	term bonds
trade credit	sinking fund
open-book credit	callable bonds
promissory note	convertible bonds
secured loans	stock certificate
collateral	par value
factoring	authorized stock
chattel mortgage	issued stock
unsecured loans	unissued stock
compensating balance	dividends
line of credit	preferred stock
revolving line of credit	common stock
commercial paper	stock split
long-term loans	stock exchanges
lease	marketable securities
bond	economic order quantity
denomination	just-in-time inventory control

KEY TERMS EXERCISE

Directions: On the line provided, place the letter of the statement on the right that most closely defines the key term.

_____ 1. Financial management

_____ 2. Leverage

_____ 3. Cost of capital

_____ 4. Capital structure

_____ 5. Matching principle

_____ 6. Capital budgeting

_____ 7. Capital investments

_____ 8. Short-term debt

_____ 9. Trade credit

_____ 10. Open-book credit

_____ 11. Promissory note

_____ 12. Secured loans

_____ 13. Collateral

a. Bonds from a single issue that must be repaid at intervals.

b. Debt that must be repaid over a period of more than a year.

c. The financing mix of a firm.

d. An agreement that the movable property purchased through a loan belongs to the borrower, although the lender has a legal right to the property if payments are not made as specified in the loan agreement.

e. The optimal, or least-cost, quantity of inventory that should be ordered.

f. Money paid out to acquire something of permanent value in a business.

g. The effective acquisition and use of money.

h. An arbitrary value assigned to a stock.

i. Facilities where owners of stock can buy and sell their shares.

_____ 14.   Factoring

_____ 15.   Chattel mortgage

_____ 16.   Unsecured loan

_____ 17.   Compensating balance

_____ 18.   Line of credit

_____ 19.   Revolving line of credit

_____ 20.   Commercial paper

_____ 21.   Long-term loans

_____ 22.   Lease

_____ 23.   Bond

_____ 24.   Denomination

_____ 25.   Principal

_____ 26.   Secured bonds

_____ 27.   Unsecured bonds

_____ 28.   Debentures

_____ 29.   Junk bonds

_____ 30.   Serial bonds

_____ 31.   Term bonds

_____ 32.   Sinking fund

_____ 33.   Callable bonds

_____ 34.   Convertible bonds

_____ 35.   Stock certificate

_____ 36.   Par value

_____ 37.   Authorized stock

_____ 38.   Issued stock

_____ 39.   Unissued stock

_____ 40.   Dividends

_____ 41.   Preferred stock

j.   An unconditional written promise to repay a certain sum of money on a specified date.

k.   A guaranteed line of credit.

l.   Bonds that are not backed by specific assets.

m.   Payments to shareholders from a company's earnings.

n.   A tangible asset that a lender can claim if a borrower defaults on a loan.

o.   The face value of a single bond.

p.   Borrowed funds used to cover current expenses and generally repaid within a year.

q.   Bonds that offer the buyer the option of converting them into a stated number of shares of common stock.

r.   The average rate of interest a firm pays on its combination of debt and equity.

s.   The decision to increase the number of shares of ownership that each stock certificate represents.

t.   Payment terms that allow the purchaser to take possession of goods and pay for them later.

u.   Loans backed up with something of value that the lender can claim in case of default, such as a piece of property.

v.   A portion of an unsecured loan that is kept on deposit at the lending institution to protect the lender and increase the lender's return.

w.   Bonds backed only by the reputation of the issuer.

x.   Authorized shares that are to be released in the future.

y.   Shares that a corporation's board of directors has decided to sell eventually.

z.   The use of borrowed funds to finance a portion of an investment.

aa.   Sale of a firm's accounts receivable to a finance company known as a factor.

bb.   Stocks, bonds, and other investments that can be turned into cash quickly.

cc.   Bonds that a company can redeem before the stated maturity date.

_____ 42. Common stock

_____ 43. Stock split

_____ 44. Stock exchanges

_____ 45. Marketable securities

_____ 46. Economic order quantity

_____ 47. Just-in-time inventory control

dd. Shares that give their owners first claim on a company's dividends and assets.

ee. A process for evaluating proposed investments in select projects that provide the best long-term financial return.

ff. A legal agreement that obligates the user of an asset to make payments to the owner of the asset in exchange for using it.

gg. Credit obtained by the purchaser directly from the supplier.

hh. Bonds backed by specific assets.

ii. Shares whose owners have the last claim on distributed profits and assets.

jj. The concept of funding long-term projects with long-term sources of capital and short-term expenditures with current income.

kk. Agreement stating the amount of unsecured short-term loans the lender will make available to the borrower, provided the lender has the funds.

ll. A loan requiring no collateral, but a good credit rating.

mm. Bonds that pay high interest because they are below investment grade.

nn. A document that proves stock ownership.

oo. The amount of a debt, excluding any interest.

pp. An account into which a company makes annual payments for use in redeeming its bonds in the future.

qq. A computerized system of managing inventory more efficiently.

rr. Bonds from a single issue that must be repaid simultaneously.

ss. A certificate of indebtedness sold to raise funds.

tt. Authorized shares that have been released to the market.

uu. A short-term note issued by a company and backed by the company's good name.

ANSWERS TO KEY TERMS EXERCISE

1. g (p. 542)	13. n (p. 552)	25. oo (p. 557)	37. y (p. 560)
2. z (p. 542)	14. aa (p. 553)	26. hh (p. 558)	38. tt (p. 560)
3. r (p. 544)	15. d (p. 553)	27. w (p. 558)	39. x (p. 560)
4. c (p. 546)	16. ll (p. 553)	28. i (p. 558)	40. m (p. 560)
5. ff (p. 546)	17. v (p. 553)	29. mm (p. 558)	41. pp (p. 560)
6. ee (p. 549)	18. kk (p. 553)	30. a (p. 558)	42. ii (p. 560)
7. f (p. 549)	19. k (p. 554)	31. rr (p. 558)	43. s (p. 561)
8. p (p. 550)	20. nn (p. 554)	32. dd (p. 558)	44. i (p. 562)
9. gg (p. 550)	21. b (p. 556)	33. cc (p. 558)	45. bb (p. 562)
10. t (p. 550)	22. ff (p. 557)	34. q (p. 559)	46. e (p. 564)
11. j (p. 551)	23. ss (p. 557)	35. uu (p. 559)	47. qq (p. 564)
12. u (p. 552)	24. o (p. 557)	36. h (p. 559)	

SELF TEST

True-False Questions

_____ 1. The ultimate financial objective of a corporation is to increase the owner's wealth.

_____ 2. When loans are secured by accounts receivable, the amounts due the business from customers with promissory notes are used as collateral.

_____ 3. A line of credit guarantees the business that a loan will be available from the bank.

_____ 4. Debt capital and equity capital are both examples of external sources of capital.

_____ 5. Bonds may be either secured or unsecured.

_____ 6. A corporation is not permitted to pay off its bonds before maturity.

_____ 7. Par value is a set face value of the stock, based on the per share capitalization of the company.

_____ 8. Dividends, or payments to shareholders from a company's earnings, must be paid in the form of cash.

_____ 9. Preferred stockholders have preference over common stockholders in terms of dividends and assets.

_____ 10. Marketable securities are a place for firms to "park" their excess funds.

Multiple Choice Questions

_____ 1. A financial manager of a corporation tries to
    a. generate leverage.
    b. find the lowest-cost funding.
    c. use funds efficiently.
    d. all of the above.

_____. 2. The use of borrowed money to make more money is known as
    a. capital budgeting.
    b. leverage.
    c. cash flow.
    d. the matching principle.

_____ 3. Blue-chip companies
    a. should sell stock to raise capital.
    b. can obtain funds more cheaply than less-secure rivals.
    c. have little need to raise cash by selling bonds.
    d. should always use internal financing.

_____ 4. The matching principle states that
    a. a firm's debt should equal its equity.
    b. capital investments should equal long-term debt.
    c. leverage should equal short-term debt.
    d. the timing of borrowing should equal the timing of spending.

_____ 5. An unconditional written promise to pay a certain sum of money on a specific date in return for immediate credit is called
    a. an open account.
    b. a promissory note.
    c. factoring accounts receivable.
    d. a chattel mortgage.

_____ 6. An unsecured loan may require
    a. a chattel mortgage.
    b. collateral.
    c. a compensating balance.
    d. a sinking fund.

_____ 7. The type of short-term financing known as commercial paper
    a. represents only a very small fraction of all business debt in the United States.
    b. requires a compensating balance.
    c. locks in a given interest rate for a given period.
    d. has limited availability.

_____ 8. An appeal of commercial paper is that it
    a. locks in an interest rate for up to one year.
    b. requires only a small compensating balance.
    c. can be factored.
    d. can only be issued by blue-chip companies.

_____ 9. A corporation may retain the right to pay off bonds before they mature. These are known as
    a. sinking funds.
    b. callable bonds.
    c. convertible bonds.
    d. junk bonds.

_____ 10. Which of the following is not a marketable security?
    a. Treasury bill
    b. Fannie Mae
    c. chattel mortgage
    d. certificate of deposit

Completion Questions

1. Your text defines _____ as the price a business must pay to raise money.

2. A loan that requires no collateral is called _____.

3. If one business allows another business to use a good, in exchange for regular financial payments, that good is said to be _____.

4. Debt must be repaid, but _____ capital does not have to be repaid.

5. Stock is a relatively expensive way to raise capital because dividends are paid with _____ dollars.

6. When a corporation doubles the number of shares that each stock certificate represents, it is conducting a _____.

7. An agreed-on maximum amount of money a bank is willing to lend a business during a specific period of time is called a _____.

8. Another name for unsecured bonds is _____.

9. A _____ bond is one that may be repaid with stock, rather than with money.

10. Investments in new facilities, equipment, and machinery are known as _____.

PROJECT

Purchasing Bonds

You are still holding a considerable amount of cash in your investment portfolio after winning the Florida lottery. Krupin Corporation (a fictitious company) has just announced the purchase of Milvane Company (another fictitious company), which it plans to finance through the issue of bonds. Your broker has just called to tell you that Krupin is offering a convertible bond at 9.25 percent maturing in thirty years and recommends that you invest $10,000 in the offering. Before doing so, you want to consider whether this is a good bond for you to buy. To evaluate this offer, answer the following questions, using information from your book. Go to the library and use Moody's and Standard & Poor's to gain more information.

1. What are the advantages or disadvantages of a convertible bond?

2. Is 9.25 percent at, below, or above the current bond market?
    What does the difference, if any, tell you about the risk involved in this investment?

3. Would you be more interested if this offer was not only a 9.25 percent bond but also a "deep discount" bond? What would that tell you about the risk involved?

4. Why would Krupin be interested in offering a bond instead of stock? Why did it choose a convertible bond?

Chapter 20

Securities Markets

LEARNING OBJECTIVES

1. List five objectives that should be considered when choosing investments.

2. List five investment options available to the investor, and compare them in terms of safety and potential rate of return.

3. Describe asset allocation and how it's used during changing economic conditions.

4. Explain the efficient market hypothesis and its importance to institutional investors.

5. Describe two types of securities marketplaces.

6. Characterize six indexes that provide a broad indication of how the stock market is performing.

7. List at least four sources of information about investments.

8. Name two federal agencies involved in regulating the investment industry.

OUTLINE

I. Investors and investing

    A. Institutions and private investors
        1. Institutional investors
        2. Individual investors

    B. Investment objectives
        1. Differences between institutional and individual investor objectives
        2. Investment strategies and considerations
            a. Tax consequences

    C. The investment portfolio
        1. The benefits of diversification
        2. Asset allocation
        3. Efficient market theory
            a. The efficient market hypothesis (EMH)
            b. Market indexes

II. Investment choices

    A. Government securities
        1. Federal government issues
            a. Treasury bills, notes, and bonds
            b. U.S. savings bonds
            c. Other government agencies issuing debt
        2. Municipal bonds
            a. Types of municipal bonds

B. Corporate bonds
   1. Types of corporate bonds
   2. Corporate bond ratings

C. Stocks
   1. Shareholders and dividends
   2. Common stocks
      a. Blue-chip stocks
      b. Characteristics of common stock
   3. Preferred stocks
      a. Advantages of preferred stock
      b. Types of preferred stock
   4. Short selling
      a. What short selling involves
      b. The risks of short selling

D. Mutual funds
   1. How mutual funds operate
   2. Types of mutual funds

E. Other investments
   1. Options
      a. Types of options
   2. Financial futures
      a. Stock index futures
      b. Stock index options
   3. Commodities
      a. Types of trading contracts
      b. The role played by speculators

III. The mechanisms of investing

A. Securities marketplaces
   1. Auction exchanges
      a. The New York Stock Exchange (NYSE)
         (1) How the NYSE operates
      b. Program trading
      c. Commodity exchanges
   2. Dealer exchanges
      a. NASDAQ
      b. Auction exchanges versus dealer exchanges
      c. Foreign exchanges
         (1) Purchasing foreign securities

B. Trading procedures
   1. Selecting a broker
   2. The order to buy or sell
   3. Margin trading
      a. How margin trading works
   4. The cost of trading
      a. Types of brokerage houses

IV. Analysis of the financial news

A. Sources of financial information

B. Broad market indicators
1. Bull markets and bear markets
2. The Dow Jones Industrial Average
3. Standard & Poor's 500 Stock Index

C. Daily price quotations
1. Stock exchange listings
a. The information contained in the listing
(1) Price-earnings ratios
2. Listings of other investments

V. Regulation of securities trading

A. The Securities and Exchange Commission (SEC)
1. The job of the SEC
a. Insider trading
2. Protecting investors when a brokerage fails
a. Securities Investor Protection Corporation (SIPC)

MAJOR POINTS TO REMEMBER

1. There are two types of investors who buy and sell marketable securities in financial markets: institutional investors and private investors. **Institutional investors** (e.g., insurance companies, pension funds, investment companies, and universities) employ professional money managers and have large amounts of money to invest. They account for 82 percent of all trading on the New York Stock Exchange. Private investors are also important, although for the past twenty years there has been a trend for individuals to make indirect investments (i.e., rather than purchase securities directly, they invest instead in mutual funds, insurance products, and/or employee pension plans).

2. Because institutional investors seek the highest returns in the shortest possible time, they trade large amounts of securities frequently. In contrast, the majority of individual investors tend to make long-term investments. Most often, individuals make investment decisions based on the criteria of income, growth, safety, liquidity, and/or tax consequences.

3. If what is desired from the investment is a steady flow of cash, then the chief purpose of the investment is income. However, some investors are more concerned with growth and maximizing **capital gains** (money made from selling an investment at a higher price than they paid for it). Common stock is commonly known as **equity** because it represents an ownership position in the company.

4. To realize large capital gains, **speculators** often must take high risks. For example, although a savings account is safer, junk bonds pay a higher rate of return. If liquidity is a factor, it must be remembered that common stock is more liquid than real estate. Finally, with respect to tax considerations, dividend and interest income is heavily taxed, whereas capital gains are taxed at a lower rate (although in 1986 Congress eliminated the tax advantage associated with long-term gains).

5. In most instances, a single investment vehicle will not allow an investor to achieve all of his or her objectives. Therefore, investors typically assemble a collection of different investments—their **investment portfolio. Diversification** is generally recommended, so that if one investment turns sour, it will be offset by others that do well (e.g., a portfolio might contain stock in a number of companies and investment-grade corporate bonds). The portfolio might also be designed to provide a desired **rate of return** (the percentage gain or yield on investments).

6. The task of **asset allocation** is to manage an investment portfolio for the highest rates of return and the lowest risk. Consequently, the money manager must determine how much of the portfolio's total assets should be allocated to each type of investment (e.g., stocks, government bonds, and cash instruments).

7. The **efficient market hypothesis (EMH)** is a controversial theory which states that all securities are appropriately valued at all times because securities markets make quick and efficient price adjustments. The theory claims that since no individual can "beat" the market, a chimpanzee randomly pointing at stocks in the newspaper will be as successful in selecting the right investments as Wall Street's smartest money manager. Still further, individuals believing in EMH feel that a person can rarely beat the market by continually changing investments (as institutional investors often do). However, EMH's failure to explain the October 19, 1987, stock market crash has brought the theory under harsh criticism.

8. **Market indexes** use a selection of securities as a model to gauge the market. Standard & Poor's 500 is an example of such an index. To avoid wasting time trying to beat the market, many institutional investors tie the performance of their investments to the performance of the market. This is accomplished by **indexing,** which involves the creation of a portfolio of securities that are selected because together they reflect the profile of the market as a whole.

9. Federal government securities are the most risk-free investments possible. While some are backed by the U.S. Treasury, others are backed by agencies of the government. State and local governments also raise money through bond issues.

10. The three main types of federal government issues are **Treasury bills** (for short-term debt), **Treasury notes** (for one- to ten-year debt obligations), and **Treasury bonds** (for long-term debt). Treasury bills do not pay interest; they are sold at a discount to their face value and redeemed at full face value when they mature. In contrast, Treasury notes and bonds pay a fixed amount of interest twice a year (exempt from state and local income taxes) and are available for a minimum investment of $1,000, in contrast to the T-bill's $10,000 minimum investment. Small investors can also purchase **U.S. savings bonds** in denominations from $50 to $10,000.

11. Twenty other government agencies also issue debt. The two largest are the Government National Mortgage Association (Ginnie Mae) and the Federal National Mortgage Association (Fannie Mae). These agencies finance mortgages for U.S. homeowners.

12. **Municipal bonds** are issued by many state and local governments and are exempt from federal income taxes. The two basic types are **general obligation bonds**, which are backed by the municipality's taxing power, and **revenue bonds**, which guarantee repayment from revenues generated by the project being financed. Some municipal bonds are also free from state and local taxes. When the junk bond market burst in the 1980s, some corporations found themselves in **default** on their bond issues (i.e., they didn't have enough money to meet interest payments).

13. Although the financial news tends to pay more attention to the stock market, the bond market is actually several times larger. The three main types of bonds issued by corporations are mortgage bonds, debentures and convertible bonds. While **mortgage bonds** are backed by real property owned by the company, **debentures** are nothing more than the promise of the corporation to pay. Finally, **convertible bonds** can be exchanged by the investor for common stock in the corporation that issued them. Both Standard & Poor's and Moody's rate the "safety" of corporate bonds.

14. Not only do bondholders receive interest, but they also may realize capital gains by taking advantage of shifts in interest rates. A $1,000 bond with an interest rate of 8 percent, for example, will sell for more than $1,000 if interest rates fall to 7 percent.

15. A person owning stock in a company is called a **shareholder** and gets to vote on the members of the corporation's board of directors and on any major policies that will affect ownership. The stockholder also gets to share in the firm's profits or losses through capital gains (or losses) and through **dividends** (or the cancellation of dividends). Once expenses and taxes have been paid out of revenue, the company's board of directors can pay part of what remains to investors as dividends, although no law requires that dividends be paid.

16. Most stock that is issued by corporations is **common stock**. This class of stock carries no special privileges and is the last to be paid off when the company goes out of business. The stock of established companies

that have paid sizable dividends consistently for years are known as **blue-chip stocks**. In contrast, **growth stocks** are those issued by smaller and younger companies with strong growth potential. Such firms typically do not pay dividends because they reinvest their earnings to finance their rapid growth.

17. While most shareholders are primarily interested in growth, others want the income provided by dividends. An investor might also want to own a stock because of special situations regarding the issuing firm. For example, the company may be on the verge of a turnaround, or the company might be "in play" (i.e., it is rumored that it will be acquired by another company). Some investors also look for cyclical stocks—stocks issued by companies whose business reflects the cycles of the economy.

18. **Preferred stock** is most often purchased for the dividends they pay. Such stock offers two advantages over common stock: (1) owners of preferred stock are guaranteed to receive their dividends before shareholders of common stock, and (2) preferred stockholders will be paid off before owners of common stock if the firm goes out of business. Owners of cumulative preferred stock have the advantage that if dividends are suspended, the dividends on these shares will accumulate until shareholders have been paid in full. Shares of convertible preferred stock can be traded for a certain number of shares of the company's common stock (at the discretion of the shareholder).

19. An investor might engage in **short selling** if he or she believes that the price of the stock will fall. The shares of stock are borrowed from a broker, in the hope of buying it back later at a lower price.

20. A **mutual fund** pools money from small investors to buy stocks, bonds, government securities, gold, or other marketable securities. Some mutual funds specialize by investing only in particular industries; others might have income or growth as their objectives. A popular type of mutual fund today is the **money-market fund**, which invests in short-term securities such as commercial paper, certificates of deposit, and Treasury bills.

21. Mutual funds may be either open-ended or closed-ended. The size of an open-ended fund increases and decreases as investors put money in or take money out. In contrast, the closed-ended fund invests on behalf of a fixed number of investors; as soon as a certain number of shares are sold, the fund closes its books.

22. A **stock option** is the purchased right (but not the obligation) to buy a specified number of shares of a stock-ended at a predetermined price during a specified period of time. An investor who thinks the price of a stock is going to rise would invest in a **call option**; an investor selling a call option believes just the opposite. An individual believing that the price of a stock is going to decline will use a **put option**, while a person thinking the stock's value will rise would sell a put option.

23. Although options can be highly speculative, they can also be used to make an investor's stock portfolio a little safer. Investors can **hedge** their position (i.e., protect against a sudden loss) by selling a call option at the price of the underlying stock. If the stock's price should suddenly fall, the investor receives the premium from the call option to help offset the loss.

24. **Financial futures** are similar to stock options; however, they are legally binding contracts to buy or sell a financial instrument for a set price at a future date and are generally traded on margin. The types of financial futures include stock market index futures, in which the investor speculates on the behavior of a certain group of stocks, and stock index options, which is the right to sell or buy a hypothetical portfolio of stocks at a particular price and time.

25. The **commodities** market, which deals in raw materials and agricultural products, tends to be riskier than the stock market. **Spot trading** (or cash trading) is the trading of contracts for immediate delivery, while trading for future delivery (usually months in advance) is called trading **commodities futures**. The original purpose of futures trading was to allow a farmer to sell his crop before planting in order to obtain operating capital. But today, speculators play a major role in commodities trading.

26. Securities can be traded on **auction exchanges** (the traditional marketplace) and **dealer exchanges**. In an auction exchange, all buy and sell orders are funneled onto an auction floor, where a **stock specialist** matches buyers and sellers. The stock specialist is a member of a brokerage firm who has a post on the

trading floor and conducts all the trades in a particular stock. One of the most important duties of the specialist is to act as the buyer or seller if one can't be found. During the October 19, 1987, stock market crash, specialists were forced to buy many stocks for which there were no buyers.

27. In a dealer exchange, all buy and sell orders are executed through computers (there is no central facility) by **market makers**, who are registered stock and bond representatives who sell securities out of their own inventories.

28. Auction exchanges include the New York Stock Exchange (NYSE), also known as "The Big Board." While only one of eight stock exchanges in the United States, the NYSE dwarfs the other seven. The stocks and bonds of over 1,600 firms, with a market value of more than $2.6 trillion, are traded here. However, many believe that the auction process itself is becoming antiquated, due to advances in computerized trading. Additionally, while twenty years ago individual investors held 80 percent of equities in the United States, today that number has declined to 55 percent.

29. The use of **program trading**, in which institutional investors use computer programs to buy and sell huge numbers of shares, could become a major problem. Program traders do not realize their profit if prices change too much too quickly, and stock specialists might run out of capital and be unable to purchase stocks from program traders if the practice becomes too widespread. Additionally, one common variation of program trading is **arbitrage**, which is the practice of buying something in one market while at the same time selling its equivalent in another market at a higher price and pocketing the difference.

30. **Commodity exchanges** use their own variation of the auction, as crowds of dealers stand in auction "pits" to buy and sell contracts. Each exchange handles specific commodities.

31. The biggest threat to all auction exchanges comes from dealer exchanges, which are decentralized marketplaces where securities are bought and sold by dealers out of their own inventories. The largest and most important dealer exchange is the **over-the-counter market** (**OTC**), which consists of a network of 415,000 registered stock and bond representatives across the United States. Approximately 420 of these brokers are market makers (they buy and sell securities held in inventory); they are linked via a nationwide computer network called NASDAQ (National Association of Securities Dealers Automated Quotations). NASDAQ has grown to the point where its total market value is second only to the NYSE, and it is now international in operation (a branch in Great Britain was opened January, 1992).

32. Dealer exchanges offer the advantage of computerized trading as well as a cost advantage, because the commission structure of the auction exchange is not used.

33. Many cities of the world have their own stock exchanges (e.g., Tokyo, London, and Paris), with the Tokyo Stock Market being second in size only to the NYSE. Institutional investors from the United States are the major players in foreign stock markets, with significant investments being made by pension funds and international or global mutual funds.

34. An investor's first step is to select a brokerage firm. Next, he or she chooses or is assigned a commodities broker or stockbroker. This **broker** is an expert who has studied extensively in the area of investment practices and has passed a series of examinations on the buying and selling of securities. Large brokerage firms are registered with many exchanges.

35. An investor wishing to buy or sell stock could instruct the stockbroker to place a **market order**, meaning that the broker will instruct the member on the floor to make the trade almost immediately at the best price that can be negotiated at the moment. If a **limit order** is placed instead, the investor specifies the highest price he or she is willing to pay if buying, or the lowest price he or she will accept if selling. Limit orders are entered for one day only, unless otherwise specified. If the investor wants the order to be kept in on subsequent days until it is canceled, then an **open order** can be placed. When an investor has confidence in the stockbroker's ability to judge the trend of market prices, he or she might place a **discretionary order**, which gives the stockbroker the right to judge whether to have the order executed at once or to wait for a better price.

36. The technique of **margin trading** allows an individual to purchase stock partially with money borrowed from the stockbroker (leaving the stock with the broker as collateral). Margin requirements (i.e., the percentage of the total stock price that may be borrowed), which are set by the Federal Reserve Board, change periodically. Presently, the margin on most stock trades is 50 percent.

37. The stockbroker gets a commission for the tasks performed. The total **transaction costs** for the investor consist of the commission plus taxes on the sale. Trading in odd lots (fewer than 100 shares) results in higher percentage fees than trading in round lots. Other factors affecting the transaction costs include the nature of the brokerage house and the level of activity in the account. **Full-service brokerages**, like Merrill Lynch, provide a variety of services for clients (e.g., research). As a consequence, they charge higher commissions than **discount brokerages**, which provide nothing more than a service to buy or sell.

38. An excellent single source of financial news and information is a good newspaper, which contains daily reports on the many varied security markets. Additionally, there are newspapers aimed specifically at investors, such as *Investor's Daily* and *Barron's*. A number of general-interest business publications also contain a great deal of financial information; such sources include *The Wall Street Journal* (a national financial newspaper), *Forbes, Fortune*, and *Business Week*. Newsletters and special reports are published by Standard & Poor's, Moody's Investor Service, and Value Line, while computer owners can access the Dow Jones News Retrieval Service, Investor's Express, and The Source.

39. A **bull market** is when stock prices are rising, while a **bear market** indicates that prices of stocks are falling. Optimistic investors are said to be "bullish"; pessimistic ones are "bearish." The most common way to determine if the market is bullish or bearish is to watch indexes and averages. The Dow Jones Industrial Average (DJIA) is the most famous index; it tracks the prices of thirty blue-chip stocks traded on the NYSE. Some individuals, though, prefer to follow Standard & Poor's 500 Stock Index (S&P 500) because it uses many more stocks in its calculations.

40. Some investors limit their activities to a single type of security (e.g., stocks or bonds) or to a particular industry or type of commodity. In searching for a specific stock, the daily newspaper could be used to track stock performance. The listing for each would give high and low prices, volume traded, and **price-earnings ratio** (which usually ranges from 8 to 16).

41. Major newspapers also provide price information for bonds, mutual funds, commodities, options, and government securities.

42. Trading in stocks and bonds is monitored by the Securities and Exchange Commission (SEC); the Commodities Futures Trading Commission (CFTC) supervises trading in commodities. The SEC employs over 2,000 people to supervise the stock exchanges, OTC markets, brokerage houses, registered representatives, investment advisers, and public-utility holding companies. With this heavy workload and limited staff, the SEC must focus its efforts where they are likely to do the most good. One top priority is to crack down on insider trading, which is when a company's stock is bought or sold based on information not available to the public.

43. If a brokerage fails (and 228 have failed since 1970), investors are protected by the Securities Investor Protection Corporation (SIPC). This organization provides up to $500,000 worth of insurance against fraud or bankruptcy for an investor who buys and leaves securities with a brokerage house, and up to $100,000 worth of insurance for cash left with a brokerage house.

KEY TERMS

institutional investors
capital gains
equity
speculators
investment portfolio
diversification
rate of return
asset allocation
efficient market hypothesis
market indexes
indexing
Treasury bills
Treasury notes
Treasury bonds
U.S. savings bonds
municipal bonds
general obligation bonds
revenue bonds
default
mortgage bonds
debentures
convertible bonds
shareholder
dividends
common stock
blue-chip stocks
growth stocks
preferred stock
short selling
mutual fund

money-market fund
stock option
call option
put option
hedge
financial futures
commodities
spot trading
commodities futures
auction exchanges
dealer exchanges
stock specialist
market makers
program trading
arbitrage
commodity exchanges
over-the-counter market
broker
market order
limit order
open order
discretionary order
margin trading
transaction costs
full-service brokerages
discount brokerages
bull market
bear market
price-earnings ratio

KEY TERMS EXERCISE

Directions: On the line provided, place the letter of the statement on the right that most closely defines the key term.

_____ 1. Institutional investors

_____ 2. Capital gains

_____ 3. Equity

_____ 4. Speculators

_____ 5. Investment portfolio

_____ 6. Diversification

_____ 7. Rate of return

_____ 8. Asset allocation

_____ 9. Efficient market hypothesis

_____ 10. Market indexes

a. Payments made by companies to shareholders from earnings.

b. Costs of trading securities, including broker's commission and taxes.

c. Rising stock market.

d. Failure of issuers to meet their contractual principal and interest obligation.

e. Companies that invest money entrusted to them by others.

f. Short-term debt issued by the federal government.

g. Individual registered to sell securities.

h. An investment that protects the investor from suffering loss on another investment.

____ 11. Indexing

____ 12. Treasury bills

____ 13. Treasury notes

____ 14. Treasury bonds

____ 15. U.S. savings bonds

____ 16. Municipal bonds

____ 17. General obligation bonds

____ 18. Revenue bonds

____ 19. Default

____ 20. Mortgage bonds

____ 21. Debentures

____ 22. Convertible bonds

____ 23. Shareholder

____ 24. Dividends

____ 25. Common stock

____ 26. Blue-chip stocks

____ 27. Growth stocks

____ 28. Preferred stock

____ 29. Short selling

____ 30. Mutual fund

____ 31. Money-market fund

____ 32. Stock option

____ 33. Call option

____ 34. Put option

____ 35. Hedge

____ 36. Financial futures

____ 37. Commodities

____ 38. Spot trading

i. Selling stock borrowed from a broker with the intention of buying it back later at a lower price, repaying the broker, and pocketing the profit.

j. Method of shifting investments within a portfolio to adapt them to the current investment environment.

k. Market order that allows the broker to decide when to trade a security.

l. Equities issued by small companies with unproven products or services.

m. Decentralized marketplaces where securities are bought and sold by dealers out of their own inventories.

n. Simultaneous purchase in one market and sale in a different market with a profitable price or yield differential.

o. Investors who seek large capital gains through relatively risky investments.

p. Financial services companies that sell securities but that give no advice.

q. Network of dealers who trade securities that are not listed on an exchange.

r. Debt instruments in small denominations sold by the federal government.

s. Assembling investment portfolios by selecting securities that together reflect the profile of the market as a whole.

t. Contract allowing the holder to buy or sell a given number of shares of a particular stock at a given price by a certain date.

u. Borrowing money from brokers to buy stock, paying interest on the borrowed money, and leaving the stock with the broker as collateral.

v. Debt securities issued by the federal government that mature in ten to thirty years.

w. Corporate bonds backed by the company's good faith.

x. Raw materials used in producing other goods.

y. Difference between the price at which a financial asset is sold and its original cost (assuming the price has gone up).

z. Centralized marketplaces where securities are traded by specialists on behalf of investors in auctions.

aa. Comparison of a stock's market price with its earnings per share.

_____ 39. Commodities futures

_____ 40. Auction exchanges

_____ 41. Dealer exchanges

_____ 42. Stock specialist

_____ 43. Market makers

_____ 44. Program trading

_____ 45. Arbitrage

_____ 46. Commodity exchanges

_____ 47. Over-the-counter market

_____ 48. Broker

_____ 49. Market order

_____ 50. Limit order

_____ 51. Open order

_____ 52. Discretionary order

_____ 53. Margin trading

_____ 54. Transaction costs

_____ 55. Full-service brokerages

_____ 56. Discount brokerages

_____ 57. Bull market

_____ 58. Bear market

_____ 59. Price-earnings ratio

bb. Pools of money that are invested in stocks, bonds, or other marketable securities.

cc. Stock option giving the holder the right to sell shares at a given price.

dd. Market order that stipulates the highest or lowest price at which the customer is willing to trade securities.

ee. Dealers in dealer exchanges sell securities out of their own inventories so that a market is always available for buyers and sellers.

ff. Measures of security markets calculated from the prices of a selection of securities.

gg. Municipal bonds backed by the issuing agency's general taxing authority.

hh. Financial services companies with a full range of services, including investment advice, securities research, and investment products.

ii. Corporate bonds that can be exchanged at the owner's discretion into common stock of the issuing company.

jj. Intermediaries who trade in particular securities on the floors of auction exchanges; "buyers of last resort."

kk. Marketplaces where contracts for raw materials are bought and sold.

ll. Falling stock market.

mm. Assembling investment portfolios in such a way that a sudden loss in one investment won't affect the value of the entire portfolio.

nn. Equities issued by corporations, generally carrying no special privileges and usually the last to be paid off if a firm liquidates.

oo. Limit order that does not expire at the end of a trading day.

pp. Debt securities issued by the federal government that mature within one to ten years.

qq. Debt issued by a state or a local agency; interest earned is exempt from federal income tax and from taxes in the issuing jurisdiction.

rr. Theory that the market finds its true value quickly and efficiently.

ss. Legally binding agreements to buy or sell financial instruments at a future date.

tt. The stocks that represent a part ownership in a company's equity.

uu. Contracts for commodities that will be delivered at a future date.

vv. Municipal bonds backed by revenue generated from the projects financed with the bonds.

ww. Investment strategy using computer programs to buy or sell large numbers of securities, thereby taking advantage of price discrepancies between stock index futures or options and the actual stocks represented in those indexes.

xx. Hybrid of fixed-income instruments and equities; dividends always paid ahead of those on common stocks.

yy. Stock option giving the holder the right to sell shares at a given price.

zz. Percentage increase in the value of an investment.

aaa. Assortment of investment instruments.

bbb. Authorization for a broker to buy or sell securities at the best price that can be negotiated at the moment.

ccc. Mutual funds that invest in short-term securities.

ddd. Trading in commodities that will be delivered immediately.

eee. An owner of equities.

fff. Equities issued by large, well-established companies with consistent records of price increases and dividend properites.

ggg. Corporate bonds backed by real property, not by mortgages.

ANSWERS TO KEY TERMS EXERCISE

1. e (p. 572)	16. bb (p. 576)	31. ccc (p. 580)	46. kk (p. 584)
2. y (p. 573)	17. gg (p. 576)	32. t (p. 580)	47. q (p. 584)
3. tt (p. 573)	18. vv (p. 577)	33. yy (p. 580)	48. g (p. 585)
4. o (p. 573)	19. p (p. 577)	34. cc (p. 581)	49. bbb (p. 585)
5. aaa (p. 574)	20. ggg (p. 577)	35. h (p. 581)	50. dd (p. 586)
6. mm (p. 574)	21. w (p. 577)	36. ss (p. 581)	51. oo (p. 586)
7. zz (p. 574)	22. ii (p. 577)	37. x (p. 581)	52. k (p. 586)
8. j (p. 574)	23. eee (p. 578)	38. ppp (p. 582)	53. u (p. 586)
9. rr (p. 574)	24. a (p. 578)	39. nn (p. 582)	54. b (p. 587)
10. ff (p. 575)	25. nn (p. 578)	40. z (p. 582)	55. hh (p. 588)
11. s (p. 575)	26. fff (p.578)	41. m (p. 582)	56. d (p. 588)
12. f (p. 576)	27. l (p. 578)	42. jj (p. 582)	57. c (p. 588)
13. pp (p. 576)	28. xx (p. 579)	43. ee (p. 583)	58. ll (p. 588)
14. v (p. 576)	29. i (p. 579)	44. ww (p. 583)	59. aa (p. 591)
15. r (p. 576)	30. qq (p. 580)	45. n (p. 583)	

SELF TEST

True-False Questions

_____   1. Margin trading involves borrowing money from a broker to buy stock.

_____   2. People invest their money to make money, but the motives in terms of trade-offs between growth and income vary.

_____   3. Different investment options have traditionally been taxed at a different rate, thus altering the attractiveness of investment alternatives.

_____   4. The efficient market hypothesis holds that most securities are rarely valued appropriately.

_____   5. Selling stock short is illegal, since you don't really own the stock.

_____   6. Stock exchanges are able to perform efficiently because they hold an inventory of stocks for sale to interested parties.

_____   7. Commodity exchanges are like stock exchanges for raw materials.

_____   8. Brokers work on the floor of stock exchanges to buy and sell stock.

_____   9. Over-the-counter market dealers hold OTC securities in inventory, for sale to interested parties.

_____   10. The Dow Jones Industrial Average represents an index of all industrial stocks sold in the United States.

Multiple Choice Questions

_____   1. What sort of priority does an investor have who is interested in receiving a steady and predictable flow of cash from his or her investments?
         a. equity appreciation.
         b. income.
         c. risk maximization.
         d. tax minimization.

_____   2. A speculator might be most likely to invest in
         a. Treasury bills.
         b. mutual funds.
         c. common stocks.
         d. municipal bonds.

_____   3. A tax-free bond whose income is exempt from income taxes and that is backed by a city's taxing power is called a
         a. revenue bond.
         b. municipal bond.
         c. general obligation bond.
         d. business development bond.

_____   4. A common stock usually issued by a large, well-capitalized company that has consistently paid dividends is called a
         a. blue-chip stock.
         b. convertible stock.
         c. preferred stock.
         d. dividend guaranteed stock.

_____ 5. The right to sell or buy a specific number of stock shares at a given time and at a predetermined price is known as
  a. a stock option.
  b. selling short.
  c. selling long.
  d. margin trading.

_____ 6. A contract that calls for immediate delivery of a set amount of corn is
  a. a spot trade.
  b. a futures trade.
  c. a commodity swap.
  d. an investment that would be managed by a money-market fund.

_____ 7. The largest stock exchange in the United States is
  a. NASDAQ.
  b. the American Stock Exchange.
  c. the New York Stock Exchange.
  d. the Chicago Board of Trade.

_____ 8. An order to buy a security that dictates the highest price that you are willing to pay is known as
  a. a market order.
  b. a limit order.
  c. an open order.
  d. a discretionary order.

_____ 9. A useful source of information for the investor is
  a. business magazines.
  b. electronic data services.
  c. investment seminars.
  d. all of the above.

_____ 10. If a brokerage fails, investors are protected by the
  a. SIPC.
  b. FDIC.
  c. SEC.
  d. U.S. Treasury Department.

Completion Questions

1. Insurance companies, pension funds, and mutual funds are examples of _____ investors.

2. A bond issued by the U.S. government to finance short-term debt is a _____ .

3. Small investors are particularly fond of U.S. _____, which are sold at a discount from their face value.

4. _____ is when the bond issuer is unable to make the agreed-on payment on the bond.

5. A _____ fund invests only in short-term securities rather than stocks and bonds.

6. A mutual fund investing on behalf of a fixed number of investors is a _____ fund.

7. The right to sell 100 shares of AT&T in six months at a per share price of $150 is an example of a

_____ .

8. In a stock-exchange transaction, the trade is handled by a _____.

9. If you have a great deal of confidence in your stockholder's ability to judge the trend of market prices, you

   would place a _____ order.

10. An _____ is a general gauge of investment market activity.

PROJECT

Your Investment in the Stock Market

   Unfortunately, your Aunt Tillie passed away. Fortunately, since you were her favorite, she has left you $20,000 for your personal use, provided you put it into the securities market. You must now make several decisions. Before you do, talk to either a stockbroker or investment counselor, and review material on securities investment in the chapter.

1. What type of securities will you buy (stocks, bonds, commodities, mutual shares, etc.) and why? What are some of the trade-offs between the different forms of securities, and why are some people more attracted to different forms?

2. What should you buy? Place your $20,000 in those securities and follow them for one week in the newspaper. (Your library should have *The Wall Street Journal*.) After one week, answer the following questions:

   a. Did you lose or make money?
   b. How much?
   c. Why?

Chapter 21

Government Relations and Business Law

LEARNING OBJECTIVES

1. List three roles of government that affect business.

2. Name two general areas in which government regulates business.

3. List five revenue-raising taxes and two regulatory taxes.

4. Explain how business influences government.

5. Describe the three sources of law.

6. Name six areas of law related to business.

7. State the seven elements of a valid contract.

8. Distinguish among real, personal, and intellectual property.

OUTLINE

I.   Business and government

    A. Government as friend, partner, and customer
        1. Forms of government support for business

    B. Government as watchdog and regulator
        1. Government regulation of noncompetitive practices
            a. Interstate Commerce Act
            b. Sherman Antitrust Act
            c. Clayton Antitrust Act
            d. Federal Trade Commission Act
            e. Robinson-Patman Act
            f. Wheeler-Lea Amendment
            g. Celler-Kefauver Amendment
            h. Antitrust in the 1970s and 1980s
            i. Antitrust now
        2. Government regulation to protect the public
            a. Federal agencies that protect society
        3. Deregulation
            a. The move toward deregulation
            b. Problems produced by deregulation
            c. Cost-benefit analysis as a way to evaluate regulations
            d. Deregulation and the Bush administration

   C.   Government as tax collector
      1. The purposes of taxes
      2. Personal income taxes
      3. Corporate income taxes
      4. Property taxes
      5. Sales taxes
      6. Value-added taxes
      7. Excise taxes
      8. Customs duties

   D.   Business's influence on government
      1. Lobbies
      2. Political action committees (PACs)

II.   The U.S. legal system

   A.   Sources of law
      1. Statutory law
         a. The Uniform Commercial Code (UCC)
      2. Administrative law
         a. Consent orders
      3. Common law
         a. The doctrine of stare decisis

   B.   Business-related law
      1. Private law versus public law
      2. Torts
         a. Intentional torts
         b. Negligence
         c. Strict liability
      3. Product-liability law
         a. Negligence
         b. Breach of warranty
         c. Strict product liability
         d. Market-share liability
      4. Contracts
         a. What a contract is
            (1) Express versus implied contracts
         b. Elements of a contract
            (1) The factors that must be present for a contract to be valid
         c. Breach of contract
            (1) Options available
      5. Agency
         a. What "agency" means
         b. Power of attorney
      6. Property transactions
         a. Real property, personal property, and intellectual property
         b. Transfer of real property
            (1) Deeds and leases
         c. Transfer of personal property
      7. Bankruptcy
         a. What bankruptcy is
         b. Voluntary versus involuntary bankruptcy
         c. The scope of recent bankruptcies

MAJOR POINTS TO REMEMBER

1. Businesses may have to deal with federal, state, county, and local governments; some even do business with foreign governments. Although it often appears as if business and government are adversaries, the fact is that one of government's prime objectives is to ensure the prosperity of the business system.

2. Government support for business may take several forms. The various governments try to (1) promote economic growth; (2) support and subsidize business through activities such as loan guarantees, information, training, and subsidies; (3) maintain the infrastructure by building roads, airports, and so on; and (4) buy industry's products.

3. Another role of government is that of watchdog and regulator of business. Government regulation of noncompetitive practices began with the Interstate Commerce Act of 1887, which was aimed at curbing the abuses of the railroads. The act also established the Interstate Commerce Commission, the country's first regulatory body. Subsequently, other legislation was enacted.

4. The Sherman Antitrust Act of 1890 declared **trusts** (one company buying a controlling share of the stock of competing companies in the same industry) and conspiracies "in restraint of trade or commerce" illegal. In 1914, the Clayton Act amended the Sherman Act in order to make it more effective; it specifically prohibited **tying contracts** (forcing buyers to purchase unwanted goods along with goods actually desired) and **interlocking directorates** (members of the board of one company sitting on the board of a competing firm).

5. The Federal Trade Commission Act, also passed in 1914, declared unfair methods of competition illegal and established the Federal Trade Commission (FTC). The FTC Act was strengthened in the area of injury to the public by the Wheeler-Lea Act of 1938. This act also declared false advertising illegal. The Robinson-Patman Act of 1936 specifically prohibits a seller from reducing a price offered to any one buyer without giving all other buyers the same concession on a proportional basis. Furthermore, all quantity discounts must reflect decreased costs to the seller. The law also applies to advertising concessions. Finally, the Celler-Kefauver Act of 1950 forbade anticompetitive mergers.

6. Two other major antitrust laws were passed in the 1970s. The Antitrust Procedures and Penalties Act of 1974 increased the fines imposed for violation of the Sherman Act and made such violations a much more serious crime. And in 1976, the Antitrust Improvements Act made it necessary for firms to notify the FTC of their merger plans prior to the actual merger taking place, and empowered state attorneys general to institute a suit on behalf of injured consumers in their states.

7. New guidelines for determining the legality of mergers were issued during the 1980s by the Department of Justice. Rather than just using market share as the criterion for judging a merger, the new guidelines require a more sophisticated evaluation in terms of a merger's economic impact.

8. The Anti-Trust Amendments Act, which raised the ceiling on antitrust fines, was passed by Congress in 1990. Additionally, the Bush administration is increasing its antitrust enforcement efforts, especially when it comes to helping American companies compete globally.

9. Government regulation to protect the public includes a number of federal agencies that serve as watchdogs (e.g., the Consumer Product Safety Commission, the Equal Employment Opportunities Commission). But a move toward **deregulation** (i.e., the abandonment of existing regulations) was begun during the Nixon administration and gained momentum during the Carter presidency. Rather than trying to enforce rules to prevent "bad" behavior, the federal government is focusing instead on creating market incentives that will motivate firms to behave responsibly. However, deregulation has had some problems; for example, airline deregulation has resulted in a few airlines dominating the market and some small cities losing air service.

10. In 1981, President Reagan created the Task Force on Regulatory Relief. This group concluded that regulation simplification could save $150 billion in the next decade. Today, one popular way to evaluate regulations is **cost-benefit analysis**, which compares the cost of a regulation to its benefit.

11. With the Bush administration, "regulatory reform" is the favored terminology. Vice President Quayle has been assigned to oversee every regulation proposed by the government.

12. Taxes not only raise revenues for the government but also provide incentives or disincentives for certain behaviors through **tax credits** (i.e., an amount deducted from the income on which a person or business is taxed). For example, the purpose of the investment tax credit is to encourage firms to invest in capital equipment. Businesses are affected by personal and corporate income taxes, property taxes, sales taxes, value-added taxes, excise taxes, and customs duties.

13. Personal income taxes are the government's largest single source of revenue. Profits from partnerships and sole proprietorships are considered personal income and are taxable at personal-income-tax rates. Furthermore, all firms are required to withhold a percentage of each worker's earnings and forward this amount to the government as a "down payment" on the employee's personal income taxes.

14. Corporate income taxes are paid by corporations in much the same way individuals pay personal income taxes. The new tax-reform measures passed in 1986 lowered the top corporate rate from 46 percent to 34 percent and also imposed a minimum tax rate of 20 percent to ensure that large, prosperous companies pay their fair share. Many states and localities also tax corporate income, but at lower rates. Firms that do business abroad pay income taxes in foreign nations as well; however, the government allows tax credits for such payments (i.e., a deduction from the income on which the company pays U.S. income tax).

15. Companies that own property pay property taxes on their land and on structures on that land. Typically, commercial property is taxed at a higher rate than the property of individuals. Still further, retail stores often are required to collect sales taxes and must forward this money to the taxing locality (e.g., state, city).

16. Other types of taxes include **value-added taxes (VATs)**, which are assessed all along the distribution channel based on the cost of the inputs (e.g., raw materials) and the prices of the end products (outputs). Although not adopted in the United States, VATs do exist in other countries (e.g., the European Community). There are also **excise taxes**, which are designed to control potentially harmful practices ("sin taxes") or to pay for services used only by certain individuals (e.g., gasoline taxes, liquor taxes). The income from such taxes must be used for a purpose associated with the tax. Finally, **customs duties** may be imposed on products brought into the country. These are designed to protect U.S. firms from foreign competition. Customs duties have increasingly been used as a weapon in foreign policy (i.e., imports from friendly nations are taxed at a lower rate).

17. Because of the role that government plays in the business system, firms often respond by trying to influence government. This may take the form of **lobbies** (groups of people who attempt to persuade legislators to vote in the group's interest), which often involve industrywide associations (e.g., the American Bankers Association, the American Medical Association). Another possibility is that companies may funnel contributions through **political action committees (PACs)**. This method overcomes the present campaign laws that strictly limit the ability of a business to donate money directly to candidates. PACs control large sums of money today; through PACs, a company can solicit contributions from its employees.

18. Laws originate through legislative action (statutory law), through administrative rulings (administrative law), and through custom and judicial precedents (common law). **Statutory law** refers to laws created by government statutes, that is, laws written and enacted by local, state, or federal bodies. The **Uniform Commercial Code (UCC)** provides a nationwide standard in many areas of commercial law and overcomes some of the difficulties posed by laws that may vary from one state to another. Forty-nine states have adopted the entire UCC; Louisiana has adopted about half of it.

19. Regulations written by an administrative agency (e.g., the FTC) are known as **administrative law**. Agencies also have the power to investigate companies suspected of not adhering to such regulations. When a firm is found to be misbehaving, the company and the federal agency may agree to a **consent order**, in which it is agreed that the misbehavior will cease but the organization does not actually have to admit that anything illegal was done. As an alternative, the federal agency may start legal proceedings against the offending company.

20. The "unwritten law," **common law**, does not appear in legislative acts but is based on custom and the doctrine of **stare decisis**. This means that judges' decisions establish a precedent for deciding future cases of a similar nature.

21. In cases where one of the three types of law conflicts with another type, statutory law generally prevails.

22. Laws may also be categorized as either **private law** (deals with the relationships between individuals, between individuals and a business, or between businesses) or **public law** (deals with the relationship between the government and individual citizens). In business affairs, private law is generally of greater importance (e.g., a company fails to meet the terms in a contract).

23. A **tort** is a noncriminal act that results in injury to person or property. The victim is legally entitled to compensation. Tort law covers intentional torts, strict liability, and negligence. **Intentional torts** are purposeful acts that result in injury, like cutting down a neighbor's tree.

24. One of the most controversial aspects of tort law is **negligence**, which is a failure to use a reasonable amount of care to protect others from unreasonable risk of injury. To prove a case of negligence, five elements must be established: (a) duty of care, (b) breach of duty, (c) injury, (d) cause, and (e) proximate cause. The tort of **strict liability** applies when the defendant has used reasonable care and has committed no wrongdoing (e.g., engaging in an inherently dangerous activity, such as keeping wild animals).

25. A product-liability case is one in which a manufacturer is held libel for injuries caused by a defective product. **Product-liability law** developed from tort law and holds companies responsible for their wares on the grounds of negligence, strict liability, and warranty. Similar to tort law, the five elements of negligence must be established.

26. A guarantee or promise made for a product is a **warranty**. It may be express (a written or spoken promise made by the company about the product) or implied (not written or spoken, but created by operation of law when a seller enters into a contract). An implied warranty of merchantability guarantees that the product is suitable for the purposes for which it is to be used, whereas an implied warranty of fitness for a particular purpose guarantees to the buyer that the seller's judgment in selecting or furnishing goods may be relied upon.

27. Under **strict product liability**, a company may be held responsible for a defective product even if reasonable care was used in the product's manufacture and sale (i.e., liability can be assigned without assigning fault). Even greater potential liability problems stem from the concept of **market-share liability**, which makes it possible for a firm to be sued even if it did not manufacture the actual product that caused the injury. Today's large number of product-liability cases makes it difficult for some firms to obtain product-liability insurance at reasonable rates. Consequently, some companies are withdrawing from high-risk businesses. Several states, though, have instituted reforms to control excessive damage rewards.

28. A **contract** is an exchange of promises enforceable by law. An **express contract** is derived from words (i.e., it is either spoken or written), and an **implied contract** comes from the deeds or actions of the parties.

29. In order for a promise to be considered a contract, seven conditions must be met: (a) an offer must be made (i.e., one party must propose that an agreement be entered into); (b) an offer must be accepted; (c) **consideration** (an item of value) must be given by both parties, and this consideration must impose a **legal detriment** (the assumption of a duty or the forfeit of a right, to one or both parties); (d) both parties must give genuine assent (e.g., no fraud, duress, or undue influence); (e) both parties must be competent; (f) the contract must not involve an illegal act; and (g) the contract must be in proper form.

30. Most valid contracts are adhered to by both parties. But when there is a **breach of contract** (i.e., when one party, with no legal excuse, fails to live up to the terms of the contract), three options are available to the damaged party. The first option, discharge, frees one party from fulfilling a contractual obligation when the other party violates the contract. The second option, damages, allows the injured party to sue for damages resulting from the other party's failure to live up to the contract's terms. The last option, specific performance, permits the injured party to demand performance, that is, fulfillment of the contract's terms.

31. **Agency** exists when one party (the principal) authorizes another party (the agent) to act on his or her behalf. For example, a person who requests his or her stockbroker to buy stock is creating an agency relationship (empowering the stockbroker to act as an agent). When such authorization is in written form, the document is known as a **power of attorney**.

32. **Property** is the relationship between a person having rights with respect to any tangible or intangible object and all other persons. **Real property** is land and everything more or less permanently attached to it, whereas **personal property** is anything that is not real property. Personal property may be tangible (e.g., cars and jewelry) or intangible (e.g., bank accounts and insurance policies). Some intangible property is known as **intellectual property** and includes trademarks, patents, trade secrets, and copyrights.

33. **Deeds** are legal documents that transfer ownership of real property. Temporary transfer of interest in property is accomplished with a **lease**. The owner of the property, the landlord, grants a tenant the right to occupy the property for a specific time period and for a rental fee.

34. The transfer of personal property (both tangible and intangible) is technically a transfer of **title** (ownership of the property). Normally, title passes from seller to buyer when the buyer's money is accepted and the vendor hands over the goods. But when property is bought COD (cash on delivery), title is not transferred until the buyer accepts the merchandise and pays for it. With installment purchases, title typically passes when the purchaser takes possession of the property.

35. The legal procedure that provides relief for debtors (either businesses or individuals) is called **bankruptcy**; it is used by those unable to meet their financial obligations. When the debtor initiates the proceedings in court, the procedure is called **voluntary bankruptcy**. When the creditors initiate such proceedings, the procedure is called **involuntary bankruptcy**. Companies use voluntary bankruptcy to give them time to reorganize and cut costs, while at the same time relieving them of the need to make regular payments to creditors. Some firms emerge from bankruptcy as leaner, healthier companies. Due to the debt binge of the 1980s, approximately 60,000 U.S. businesses declared bankruptcy in 1990.

KEY TERMS

trusts
tying contracts
interlocking directorates
deregulation
cost-benefit analysis
tax credit
value-added taxes
excise taxes
customs duties
lobbies
political action committees
statutory law
Uniform Commercial Code
administrative law
consent order
common law
stare decisis
private law
public law
tort
intentional tort
negligence
strict liability

product-liability law
warranty
strict product liability
market-share liability
contract
express contract
implied contract
consideration
legal detriment
breach of contract
agency
power of attorney
property
real property
personal property
intellectual property
deeds
lease
title
bankruptcy
voluntary bankruptcy
involuntary bankruptcy

KEY TERMS EXERCISE

Directions: On the line provided, place the letter of the statement on the right that most closely defines the key term.

_____ 1. Trust

_____ 2. Tying contracts

_____ 3. Interlocking directorates

_____ 4. Deregulation

_____ 5. Cost-benefit analysis

_____ 6. Tax credit

_____ 7. Value-added taxes

_____ 8. Excise taxes

_____ 9. Customs duties

_____ 10. Lobbies

_____ 11. Political action committees

_____ 12. Statutory law

_____ 13. Uniform Commercial Code

_____ 14. Administrative law

_____ 15. Consent order

_____ 16. Common law

_____ 17. Stare decisis

_____ 18. Private law

_____ 19. Public law

_____ 20. Tort

_____ 21. Intentional tort

_____ 22. Negligence

_____ 23. Strict liability

_____ 24. Product-liability law

_____ 25. Warranty

_____ 26. Strict product liability

a. All property that is not real property.

b. A willful act that results in injury.

c. Groups formed under federal election laws to raise money for candidates.

d. The set of standardized laws governing business transactions that have been adopted by most states.

e. Bargained-for exchange necessary to make a contract legally binding.

f. Statute, or law, created by a legislature.

g. The written authorization for one party to legally act for another.

h. Law based on the precedents established by judges' decisions.

i. Bankruptcy proceedings initiated by the debtor.

j. The removal or relaxation of rules and restrictions affecting business.

k. The concept that extends strict product liability by dividing responsibility for injuries among all manufacturers in an industry according to their market share at the time of the injury.

l. An exchange of promises enforceable by law.

m. Legal ownership of property.

n. An amount deducted from the income on which a person or business is taxed.

o. The concept that assigns product liability even if the company used all reasonable care in the manufacture, distribution, or sale of its product.

p. Arrangement in which people owning stock in several companies give control of their securities to trustees who then gain control of and manage the companies; sometimes used to buy up or drive out smaller companies, thus giving monopolistic powers to the trusts.

q. A legal agreement that temporarily transfers the right to use an asset from the owner to another individual or business.

_____ 27. Market-share liability

_____ 28. Contract

_____ 29. Express contract

_____ 30. Implied contract

_____ 31. Consideration

_____ 32. Legal detriment

_____ 33. Breach of contract

_____ 34. Agency

_____ 35. Power of attorney

_____ 36. Property

_____ 37. Real property

_____ 38. Personal property

_____ 39. Intellectual property

_____ 40. Deed

_____ 41. Lease

_____ 42. Title

_____ 43. Bankruptcy

_____ 44. Voluntary bankruptcy

_____ 45. Involuntary bankruptcy

r.   Taxes intended to help control potentially harmful practices or to help pay for government services used only by certain people or businesses.

s.   A settlement in which an individual or organization agrees to discontinue some illegal activity without admitting guilt.

t.   The law that holds a manufacturer liable for injuries caused by a defective product.

u.   Contracts forcing buyers to buy unwanted goods along with goods actually desired.

v.   Failure to live up to the terms of a contract, with no legal excuse.

w.   Law that concerns itself with relationships between individuals, between an individual and a business, or between two businesses.

x.   Failure to observe a reasonable standard of care in order to protect others from unreasonable risk of injury.

y.   The concept of liability even in cases where the defendant has used reasonable care.

z.   Fees imposed on goods brought into the country from abroad.

aa. A noncriminal act that results in injury to person or property.

bb. The business relationship that exists when one party (the principal) authorizes another party (the agent) to act on her or his behalf, while controlling the agent's conduct.

cc. Land and everything permanently attached to it.

dd. A situation in which members of the board of one firm sit on the board of a competing firm.

ee. Bankruptcy proceedings initiated by a firm's creditors.

ff. Taxes paid at each step in the distribution chain on the difference between the cost of inputs and the price obtained for outputs at that step.

gg. The concept of using previous judicial decisions as the basis for deciding similar court cases.

hh. Rights held regarding any tangible or intangible object.

ii. Rules, regulations, and interpretations of statutory law set forth by administrative agencies and commissions.

jj. A comparison of the costs and benefits of a particular action for the purpose of assessing its desirability.

kk. Groups who try to persuade legislators to vote according to the groups' interests.

ll. · Law that concerns itself with relationships between the government and individual citizens.

mm. The legal procedure by which a person or a business that is unable to meet financial obligations is relieved of debt.

nn. A legal document by which an owner transfers the title to real property to a new owner.

oo. Intangible personal property such as ideas, songs, or any mental creativity.

pp. A contract derived from words, either oral or written.

qq. The assumption of a duty or the forfeit of a right, which is necessary to make a contract legally binding.

rr. A guarantee or promise.

ss. A contract derived from actions or conduct.

ANSWERS TO KEY TERMS EXERCISE

1.	p	(p. 606)	13.	d	(p. 615)	25.	rr	(p. 620)	37.	cc	(p. 624)
2.	n	(p. 606)	14.	ii	(p. 616)	26.	o	(p. 620)	38.	a	(p. 624)
3.	pp	(p. 606)	15.	s	(p. 616)	27.	k	(p. 620)	39.	oo	(p. 624)
4.	j	(p. 609)	16.	h	(p. 616)	28.	l	(p. 621)	40.	nn	(p. 624)
5.	jj	(p. 609)	17.	gg	(p. 616)	29.	dd	(p. 621)	41.	b	(p. 624)
6.	u	(p. 611)	18.	w	(p. 617)	30.	ss	(p. 621)	42.	m	(p. 624)
7.	ff	(p. 613)	19.	ll	(p. 617)	31.	e	(p. 621)	43.	mm	(p. 625)
8.	r	(p. 613)	20.	aa	(p. 617)	32.	bb	(p. 621)	44.	i	(p. 625)
9.	z	(p. 614)	21.	q	(p. 618)	33.	v	(p. 622)	45.	ee	(p. 625)
10.	kk	(p. 614)	22.	x	(p. 619)	34.	qq	(p. 623)			
11.	c	(p. 614)	23.	y	(p. 619)	35.	g	(p. 623)			
12.	f	(p. 615)	24.	t	(p. 619)	36.	hh	(p. 624)			

SELF TEST

True-False Questions

_____ 1. Although the U.S. government may provide support to businesses through loans or information, it does not directly bail out specific companies in trouble.

_____ 2. In the United States, government's main role in regulating business is to maintain balance, so that all competitors have an equal chance of success.

_____ 3. The Sherman Antitrust Act and the Clayton Act were successful in stopping abuses of the market system, since they specified legal and illegal actions.

_____ 4. The Federal Trade Commission can act on a possible antitrust activity only if its own investigators have discovered such activity.

_____ 5. The federal government looks not only at the size of firms involved in a potential merger but also at the number of firms in the same market.

_____ 6. Excise taxes, just like sales taxes, are paid by the consumer.

_____ 7. Under the concept of market-share liability, a company may be sued for a defective product, even if it did not actually produce the item that caused the injury.

_____ 8. In determining whether a contract is valid under the concept of consideration, the relative value of each party's consideration must be equal.

_____ 9. As a principal, your responsibility for the actions of your agent is limited if the agent does something illegal.

_____ 10. Title is transferred as soon as the buyer accepts the goods.

Multiple Choice Questions

_____ 1. The federal government tries to keep the economy growing at a steady pace and affects the economy through what policy(ies)?
   a. monetary
   b. fiscal
   c. tax
   d. all of the above

_____ 2. Interstate shipping rates and other standards for commerce are regulated by what federal agency?
   a. the Federal Trade Commission
   b. the Attorney General's Office
   c. the Interstate Rate Office
   d. the Interstate Commerce Commission

_____ 3. Which legislation outlaws discrimination against buyers as well as sellers?
   a. the Celler-Kefauver Act
   b. the Robinson-Patman Act
   c. the Wheeler-Lea Act
   d. the Antitrust Procedures and Penalties Act

_____ 4. Historically, what has been the rationale for taxes in the United States?
   a. to raise revenues and punish lawbreakers
   b. to provide disincentives for particular types of behavior
   c. to raise revenues and provide incentives and disincentives for particular types of behavior
   d. to raise capital for corporations

_____ 5. A tax that is assessed in the channel of distribution on the difference between the cost of the good and the end price is called
   a. a value-added tax.
   b. a sales tax.
   c. a channel services tax.
   d. an excise tax.

_____ 6. The document providing a nationwide standard in a number of areas of commercial law is known as
   a. a consent order.
   b. stare decisis.
   c. strict liability law.
   d. the Uniform Commercial Code.

_____ 7. When an administrative agency allows a company to promise to stop doing something without admitting any illegal behavior, the ruling is called
   a. a neutrality decree.
   b. an administrative opinion.
   c. a consent order.
   d. a cessation order.

_____ 8. If your roommate pours a soft drink on your stereo because "you were playing it too loud," then tells your best friend the spill was done on purpose, a(n) _____ has been committed.
   a. public law violation
   b. tort
   c. intentional tort
   d. white-collar crime

_____ 9. If your eleven-year-old sister signs a contract to buy a thousand Cabbage Patch dolls through the mail, it is probably not enforceable according to what conditions for a contract?
   a. consideration
   b. legality
   c. competency
   d. proper form

_____ 10. When the bank loaning funds to a company initiates bankruptcy proceedings, the action is called
   a. voluntary bankruptcy.
   b. involuntary bankruptcy.
   c. reorganization bankruptcy.
   d. cost minimization bankruptcy.

Completion Questions

1. When one company buys a controlling share of stock in competing companies, a(n) _____ is created.

2. The _____ Act makes it necessary for the FTC to be notified by companies of their merger plans before the merger.

3. The single largest source of revenue for the federal government comes from _____ taxes.

4. One way businesses try to influence government is by channeling political contributions through

   _____. This allows them to make larger and more important contributions.

5. If the Federal Trade Commission issues a regulation concerning the advertising of used cars, it has created

   a(n) _____ law.

6. The doctrine of _____ means that common law decisions establish a precedent for deciding similar future cases.

7. A _____ is an exchange of promises enforceable by law.

8. A _____ allows one person to act for another to the extent of the written authorization.

9. A _____ is used for a temporary transfer of interest in property.

10. A _____ protects the inventor of a new and useful process.

PROJECT

How Government Aids Business

The federal government supplies business with a great deal of aid. To get a better idea of the range of its assistance, write or visit the nearest Department of Commerce office and make a list of what aid the agency offers and how it might help business. Be sure to ask about assistance provided for companies interested in international business opportunities, such as the TOP program.

Chapter 22

RISK MANAGEMENT AND INSURANCE

LEARNING OBJECTIVES

1. Explain the difference between pure risk and speculative risk.

2. Discuss the risk-management techniques available to a risk manager.

3. Distinguish uninsurable risks from insurable risks.

4. Clarify how insurance companies decide the amount of income they need to generate from premiums.

5. List the two main government insurance programs.

6. Name four types of business risks that are often insured.

7. Identify the two main types of health insurance coverage.

8. Describe the five main forms of life insurance.

OUTLINE

I. Protection against risk

   A. The nature of risk

   B. Pure risk versus speculative risk
      1. Examples of pure and speculative risks

   C. Risk management
      1. Definitions of risk management and loss exposure
      2. Risk assessment
      3. Risk-management techniques
         a. Risk-control
            (1) Risk avoidance
            (2) Loss prevention
            (3) Loss reduction
            (4) Risk control transfer
         b. Risk financing
            (1) Risk retention
            (2) Risk transfer
         c. Implementing and monitoring risk management techniques
            (1) How to monitor results

   D. Insurable and uninsurable risks
      1. Uninsurable risks
      2. Insurable risks
         a. The conditions that make a risk insurable

II. The insurance industry
   A. Basic insurance concepts
      1. The jobs of actuaries and underwriters
      2. The law of large numbers

B. Insurance providers
    1. Government insurance programs
        a. Social Security
    2. Private insurance companies
        a. Stock companies
        b. Mutual companies
        c. International insurers
        d. Environmental insurers

C. Insurance-industry problems
    1. Insurance cycles

III. Types of business insurance

A. Loss of property
    1. Loss due to destruction or theft
        a. Types of property insurance
    2. Loss due to dishonesty or nonperformance
        a. Fidelity and surety bonds
        b. Credit life insurance and crime insurance

B. Loss of income
    1. Business-interruption insurance
    2. Extra-expense insurance

C. Liability
    1. What liability insurance covers
    2. Sources of liability
    3. Types of liability insurance
        a. Comprehensive general liability
            (1) Product liability coverage
            (2) Occurrence policies versus claims-made policies
        b. Automobile liability
            (1) No-fault insurance laws
        c. Workers' compensation
            (1) What this type of insurance covers
            (2) Trends in workers' compensation insurance
        d. Umbrella liability insurance
        e. Personal liability insurance
            (1) Malpractice insurance

D. Loss of key personnel
    1. Key-person insurance

IV. Types of employee insurance

A. Federal requirements

B. Health insurance
    1. Medical coverage
        a. Types of medical coverages
        b. The costs of medical care
        c. Cost-containment measures
            (1) Managed care
            (2) Health maintenance organizations
            (3) Preferred-provider organizations

      2. Disability coverage
         a. Disability income insurance
    C. Life insurance
      1. Types of life insurance
         a. Term insurance
         b. Whole life insurance
         c. Endowment insurance
         d. Variable life insurance
         e. Universal life insurance

MAJOR POINTS TO REMEMBER

1. Companies cannot guard against every conceivable form of **risk** and may at some time find themselves being sued by some individual or firm for **damages** (the amount a court awards a plaintiff in a successful lawsuit). The threat of loss without the possibility of gain is known as **pure risk** (e.g., fire), and insurance against such loss contributes nothing to a firm's profits. **Speculative risk**, the possibility of losing money in order to make money, is a type of risk people take when, for example, they start a business.

2. **Risk management** is the process of reducing the threat of loss due to uncontrollable events. Areas of risk where there is a potential for loss are called **loss exposures**. These areas include (a) loss of property, (b) loss of income, (c) legal liability to others, and (d) loss of services of key personnel. A single event may involve more than one type of loss.

3. Typically, it is the risk manager's job to prevent losses. In doing so, the risk manager must (1) assess the risk, (2) choose the risk-management techniques that ensure the proper mix of insurance and loss prevention methods, and (3) implement and monitor those techniques.

4. The two techniques available to a risk manager to deal with risk problems are risk control and risk financing. **Risk-control techniques** include risk avoidance, loss prevention, loss reduction, and risk control transfer (i.e., the transfer of the risk to some other person or group). The alternatives with respect to risk financing are risk retention (paying losses with company funds, i.e., self-insurance) and risk transfer (paying losses with outside funds). Under risk transfer, the company purchases insurance by paying a premium to an insurance company. Proper risk management usually requires a combination of at least one risk-control technique and one risk-financing technique.

5. The risk manager must implement the techniques that best suit the needs of the organization, which is often measured in terms of net cash flows. The risk-management program must also be constantly monitored to determine whether the choices made were the correct ones. Effective monitoring involves setting standards for acceptable performance, comparing actual results with these standards, then making any corrections that are deemed to be necessary.

6. **Uninsurable risks** are those that few, if any, insurance companies will agree to cover. Examples include drought, potential government actions, and general economic conditions. Some uninsurable risks eventually become insurable when data become available that help insurers estimate the actual risk. For example, insurers were reluctant to cover passengers on airplanes in the early days of commercial aviation.

7. An **insurable risk** is one that an insurance company will cover. Such risks generally meet the following requirements: (a) the peril insured against must not be under the control of the insured; (b) losses must be calculable, and the cost of insuring must be economically feasible; (c) there must be a large number of similar cases subject to the same peril; (d) the peril must be unlikely to affect all insured simultaneously; and (e) the possible loss must be financially serious. Because an insurance company could not afford the paperwork involved in handling huge numbers of small **claims**, most auto insurance policies have a **deductible** clause.

8. Private insurance companies are businesses. They must predict the amount they will have to pay in claims over a given period of time and base the premium on the probability of loss. Individuals who calculate the

likelihood of particular events occurring (e.g., fires, accidents) are called **actuaries**. They develop "actuarial tables" that are used to determine premiums. Then **underwriters** decide what risks to insure and under what terms. Actuaries rely on the **law of large numbers**, which assumes that out of a large number of insured people, most will never suffer a loss that requires payment.

9. The largest single source of insurance in the United States is the government, with Social Security being the largest public insurance program. Providing a minimum level of retirement income is the primary aim of Social Security, though it also provides hospital and medical payments (Medicare), as well as payments to surviving spouses, their dependents, and the disabled. The cost of this program is shared by employees and employers. Additionally, the Social Security Act of 1935 provides for federal and state cooperation to insure workers against unemployment.

10. About 5,000 private insurance firms operate in this country, the majority being either stock or mutual companies. A **stock company** is a profit-making organization that pays dividends to shareholders. **Mutual companies**, in contrast, are nonprofit cooperatives owned by policyholders, with any profits being returned to them either as dividends or as reduced insurance premiums. Stock companies tend to specialize in property and liability insurance; mutual companies specialize in medical and life insurance.

11. Some insurance companies classify as international insurers, even offering special insurance packages tailored to the needs of small exporters. The most famous international insurer is Lloyd's of London, which is an association of individuals who issue insurance on a cooperative basis. This firm takes on such risks as insuring racehorses, athletes, movie stars, and oil tankers operating in war zones.

12. The role of insurance companies with respect to certain types of environmental damage is still being debated. For example, insurance companies argue that the standard property insurance policy was never meant to cover damage stemming from a firm's long-term waste disposal practices.

13. The private insurance business typically goes through cycles of profit and loss. When interest rates are high, investment income supplements income from premiums. When interest rates fall, private insurance firms have to rely more heavily on income from premiums. Problems have also been compounded by the trend toward more lawsuits and higher awards for damages.

14. Businesses purchase **property insurance** to cover physical damage to or destruction of property, as well as its loss by theft. A buyer of property insurance must decide between **replacement cost** coverage (which pays the cost of purchasing new property to replace the old) or **depreciated value** coverage (which assumes that the lost property was worth less than new property because of use).

15. Criminals and dishonest employees pose another threat to business. A **fidelity bond** protects the insured against the dishonest acts of employees, and a **surety bond** protects companies against losses incurred through nonperformance of a contract (one party agrees to be responsible to a second party for the obligations of a third). Surety bonds are often required for municipal contracts, to insure that work is completed. Still other types of insurance against a loss due to nonperformance include **credit life insurance**, which guarantees repayment of a loan if a borrower dies, and **crime insurance**, which covers loss from theft.

16. A prolonged interruption of business could cost a company millions of dollars in lost income, and could even cause bankruptcy. Consequently, many firms carry (1) **business-interruption** insurance, which protects the insured when a fire or other disaster causes a company to shut down temporarily; (2) **extra-expense insurance**, which covers the additional costs of maintaining operations in temporary quarters; and/or (3) **contingent business-interruption insurance**, which protects against the loss of business due to an interruption in the delivery of essential supplies.

17. **Liability insurance** covers the insured for losses arising from injury (including death) to an individual and damage to the property of others. A company may take out liability insurance to protect itself in the event a consumer receives an injury caused by the company's product or is injured on the company's property. It also covers the firm's employees if they are hurt on the job. Malpractice insurance comes under this category of coverage and includes bodily injury due to treatment by doctors and dentists and loss of assets due to mishandling by lawyers and accountants.

18. There are different types of liability insurance. **Comprehensive general liability insurance** provides basic coverage against all forms of liability not specifically excluded by the policy. It also typically includes **product liability** coverage to protect a firm from being financially threatened when a person claims that one of its products caused damage. The purchaser of liability insurance can choose between occurrence policies, which cover losses only during the policy period regardless of when the claim is made, or claims-made policies, which cover claims made during the policy period for losses that occurred on or after some retroactive date. Another form of liability insurance is automobile liability. Many states presently have **no-fault insurance laws**, which limit lawsuits associated with car accidents.

19. **Workers' compensation insurance** (another form of liability coverage) is required by law throughout the United States. It pays the medical bills of employees who are hurt or become ill as a result of their work, pays rehabilitation expenses, and provides a death benefit for the survivors of any worker killed on the job. It has been estimated that premiums for this type of insurance will double every five years, because courts have expanded the definition of a work-related injury. Firms are therefore trying to develop less expensive alternatives, including self-insurance and better on-the-job safety programs.

20. **Umbrella policies** provide extra protection above and beyond that provided under other liability policies. However, many insurance companies have recently increased rates on these policies or have discontinued this form of insurance.

21. Doctors, lawyers, accountants, architects, and other professionals usually carry some form of **malpractice insurance**. As with other forms of insurance, premiums have been skyrocketing in recent years. Additionally, some businesses also carry **key-person insurance** to protect against the financial impact of the death of a key employee. The beneficiary is the business firm, not the executive's family.

22. Most companies buy coverage for risks to its employees; coverage generally includes health and life insurance. Health insurance coverage for workers generally covers both medical expenses and income in the event of a disabling illness or injury. Medical coverage may include **hospitalization insurance**, which pays for the major portion of a hospital stay (Blue Cross is the best-known plan); **surgical and medical insurance**, which pays the costs of surgery and of physicians' in-hospital care; and **major-medical insurance**, which provides for expenses that fall outside the coverage limits of hospitalization and surgical policies. Major-medical insurance often includes a **coinsurance** provision whereby costs are shared between the insured and the insurance company. The trend in recent years has been toward "comprehensive" medical insurance, often with a deductible as low as $25 to $50.

23. Other types of health insurance include **dental and vision insurance**, which covers a fixed percentage of a worker's expenses for eyeglasses and various forms of dental work, and **mental health insurance**, which provides for psychiatric care or psychological counseling.

24. While more than 75 percent of all employees are covered by employer-provided health insurance (with the employer typically paying 80 percent of the premium and the employee paying 20 percent), the rising costs of health care have made some firms ask their workers to pay a larger portion of their own premiums. Indeed, health care costs amounted to 26 percent of corporate profits in 1990. Factors leading to the escalating cost of health care include **cost shifting**, whereby hospitals and physicians boost their fees to cover the shortfall in government Medicare and Medicaid reimbursements, the costs of dealing with the AIDS epidemic, and the use of very expensive high-tech diagnostic equipment (e.g., magnetic resonance imaging scanners).

25. In an effort to contain health care costs, some firms have opted for a **managed care** approach, whereby employers (typically through an insurance carrier) set up their own networks of physicians and hospitals. These providers have agreed to discount the fees they charge in return for the flow of patients. Many firms have also instituted "wellness programs," or "wellcare."

26. An alternative to traditional health insurance coverage is the **health maintenance organization (HMO)**, a comprehensive, prepaid group-practice medical plan in which subscribers pay a set fee and in return receive all their health care at little or no additional cost. Because HMOs charge a fixed annual fee, they have an incentive to limit costs.

27. As an alternative to HMOs, **preferred-provider organizations (PPOs)** contract with employers, insurance companies, or other third-party payers to deliver health care services to an employee group at a reduced fee. They are less expensive to establish because they use existing facilities and permit the employer to control the quality and appropriateness of the services provided. However, they do restrict a worker's choice of hospitals and doctors. Furthermore, PPOs may be tempted to make up in quantity of service what they lose in reduced fees.

28. **Disability income insurance** protects a worker from the loss of income while disabled or partially disabled because of illness or accident. The insured receives monthly payments while disabled.

29. In midsize to large firms, almost all workers (96 percent) are offered life insurance policies. Individuals also purchase personal life insurance policies for their **beneficiaries**, who are paid by insurance companies if the policyholder dies. The most common forms of life insurance are term, whole life, endowment, variable life, and universal life.

30. **Term insurance** covers an individual for a specific time period (the term of the policy). In contrast, **whole life insurance** offers a combination of insurance and savings, with the policy staying in force until the holder's death if the premiums are paid. The third alternative, **endowment insurance**, is like whole life in that it combines savings and insurance but is written for a specified term. If the policyholder is alive when the term expires, he or she receives the full face value of the policy. **Variable life insurance** is also similar to whole life but allows the policyholder to decide how the policy's cash value should be invested (it is most often associated with a stock portfolio). Finally, universal life insurance uses its premiums to fund term insurance and a savings account, with the interest that accrues in the savings portion pegged to current money-market rates.

KEY TERMS

risk
damages
pure risk
speculative risk
risk management
loss exposures
risk-control techniques
risk financing
self-insurance
insurance
premium
uninsurable risks
insurable risk
claims
deductible
actuaries
underwriters
law of large numbers
stock company
mutual company
property insurance
replacement cost
depreciated value
fidelity bond
surety bond
credit life insurance
crime insurance
business-interruption insurance

extra-expense insurance
contingent business-interruption insurance
liability insurance
comprehensive general liability insurance
product liability
no-fault insurance laws
workers' compensation insurance
umbrella policies
malpractice insurance
key-person insurance
hospitalization insurance
surgical and medical insurance
major-medical insurance
coinsurance
dental and vision insurance
mental health insurance
cost shifting
managed care
health maintenance organizations
preferred-provider organizations
disability income insurance
beneficiaries
term insurance
whole life insurance
endowment insurance
variable life insurance
universal life insurance

KEY TERMS EXERCISE

Directions: On the line provided, place the letter of the statement on the right that most closely defines the key term.

_____ 1. Risk

_____ 2. Damages

_____ 3. Pure risk

_____ 4. Speculative risk

_____ 5. Risk management

_____ 6. Loss exposure

_____ 7. Risk-control techniques

_____ 8. Risk-financing techniques

_____ 9. Self-insurance

_____ 10. Insurance

_____ 11. Premium

_____ 12. Uninsurable risk

_____ 13. Insurable risk

_____ 14. Claims

_____ 15. Deductible

_____ 16. Actuaries

_____ 17. Underwriters

_____ 18. Law of large numbers

_____ 19. Stock company

_____ 20. Mutual company

_____ 21. Property insurance

_____ 22. Replacement cost

_____ 23. Depreciated value

_____ 24. Fidelity bond

_____ 25. Surety bond

_____ 26. Credit life insurance

a. Insurance that covers losses arising either from injury to an individual or from damage to other people's property.

b. Insurance against loss from theft.

c. Demands for payment by an insurance company due to some loss by the insured.

d. People named in a life insurance policy who are paid by the insurer if the policyholder dies.

e. Health insurance that pays for most of the costs of a hospital stay.

f. Insurance that covers losses arising from damages or injuries caused by the insured in the course of performing professional services for clients.

g. Life insurance that guarantees death benefits for a specified period, after which the face value of the policy is paid to the policyholder.

h. The amount a court awards a plaintiff in a successful lawsuit.

i. When employers (usually through an insurance carrier) set up their own networks of doctors and hospitals that agree to discount the fees they charge in return for the flow of patients.

j. A written contract that transfers to an insurer the financial responsibility for any losses.

k. A profit-making insurance company owned by shareholders.

l. Insurance that covers losses resulting from temporary business closings.

m. Health care providers offering reduced-rate contracts to groups that agree to obtain medical care through the providers' organization.

n. The fee that the insured pays the insurer for coverage against losses.

o. Laws limiting lawsuits connected with auto accidents.

p. Insurance that covers many medical expenses not covered by other health insurance plans.

_____ 27. Crime insurance

_____ 28. Business-interruption insurance

_____ 29. Extra-expense insurance

_____ 30. Contingent business-interruption insurance

_____ 31. Liability insurance

_____ 32. Comprehensive general liability insurance

_____ 33. Product liability

_____ 34. No-fault insurance laws

_____ 35. Workers' compensation insurance

_____ 36. Umbrella policies

_____ 37. Malpractice insurance

_____ 38. Key-person insurance

_____ 39. Hospitalization insurance

_____ 40. Surgical and medical insurance

_____ 41. Major-medical insurance

_____ 42. Coinsurance

_____ 43. Dental and vision insurance

_____ 44. Mental health insurance

_____ 45. Cost shifting

_____ 46. Managed care

_____ 47. Health maintenance organizations

_____ 48. Preferred-provider organizations

_____ 49. Disability income insurance

_____ 50. Beneficiaries

_____ 51. Term insurance

_____ 52. Whole life insurance

_____ 53. Endowment insurance

q. Paying to restore losses.

r. A mechanism that protects companies against losses incurred through nonperformance of a contract.

s. Insurance that protects a business from losses due to an interruption in the delivery of supplies.

t. Risk that involves the chance of both loss and profit.

u. The cost of replacing a lost or damaged item with a new one.

v. Insurance that protects an individual against loss of income while that individual is disabled as the result of an illness or accident.

w. The principle that the larger the group on which probabilities are calculated, the more accurate their predictive value.

x. A nonprofit insurance company owned by the policyholders.

y. Insurance that provides coverage for physical damage to, or destruction of, property.

z. The process of evaluating and minimizing the risks faced by a company.

aa. Persons employed by an insurance company to compute expected losses and calculate the cost of premiums.

bb. Liability insurance that covers a wide variety of losses, except certain losses specifically mentioned in the policy.

cc. Insurance that covers loss of a key employee.

dd. A risk that few, if any, insurance companies will assume because of the difficulty of calculating the probability of loss.

ee. Insurance that provides death benefits and savings for the policyholder's lifetime, provided that premiums are paid.

ff. Insurance that provides businesses with coverage beyond what is provided by other parts of a liability policy.

gg. Insurance that covers a portion of the costs of dental and eye care.

hh. Insurance that covers the added expense of operating the business in temporary facilities after an event such as a fire.

_____ 54. Variable life insurance

_____ 55. Universal life insurance

ii. An arrangement whereby a company insures itself by accumulating funds to pay for any losses, rather than buying insurance from another company.

jj. Insurance that partially replaces lost income, medical costs, and rehabilitation expenses for employees who are injured on the job.

kk. Prepaid medical plans in which consumers pay a set fee in order to receive a full range of medical care from a group of medical practitioners.

ll. The company's responsibility for injuries or damages that result from use of a product the company manufacturers or distributes.

mm. Areas of risk in which a potential for loss exists.

nn. Coverage that guarantees repayment of a loan or an installment contract if the borrower dies.

oo. Risk that involves the chance of loss only.

pp. Life insurance that provides death benefits for a specified period.

qq. A risk for which an acceptable probability of loss may be calculated and that an insurance company might therefore be willing to cover.

rr. The value of something after it has been in use for a time, which is less than its value when new.

ss. A mechanism that protects employers from dishonesty on the part of their employees.

tt. The amount of loss that must be paid by the insured before the insurer will pay for the rest.

uu. Combination of a term life insurance policy and a savings plan with flexible interest rates and flexible premiums.

vv. Insurance company employees who decide which risks to insure, for how much, and for what premiums.

ww. A whole life insurance policy that allows the policyholder to decide how to invest the cash value.

xx. Insurance that pays for the costs of surgery and physicians' fees while a person is hospitalized or recovering from hospitalization.

yy. Methods of minimizing losses.

zz.   Insurance that covers the costs of psychiatric care, psychological counseling, and substance abuse treatment programs.

aaa. The threat of loss.

bbb. The share of medical costs the patient picks up to supplement the remaining costs paid by the insurer.

ccc. When hospitals and doctors boost their charges to private paying patients to make up for the shortfall in government reimbursements.

ddd. Insurance that covers a portion of the costs of dental and eyecare.

ANSWERS TO KEY TERMS EXERCISE

1. aaa (p. 634)	15. tt (p. 639)	29. hh (p. 644)	43. ddd (p. 648)
2. h (p. 634)	16. aa (p. 639)	30. s (p. 644)	44. zz (p. 648)
3. oo (p. 634)	17. vv (p. 639)	31. a (p. 644)	45. ccc (p. 649)
4. t (p. 634)	18. w (p. 639)	32. bb (p. 644)	46. i (p. 650)
5. z (p. 635)	19. k (p. 641)	33. ll (p. 645)	47. kk (p. 650)
6. mm (p. 635)	20. x (p. 641)	34. o (p. 645)	48. m (p. 650)
7. yy (p. 636)	21. y (p. 643)	35. jj (p. 645)	49. v (p. 650)
8. q (p. 636)	22. n (p. 643)	36. ff (p. 646)	50. d (p. 651)
9. ii (p. 636)	23. rr (p. 643)	37. f (p. 647)	51. pp (p. 651)
10. j (p. 637)	24. ss (p. 643)	38. cc (p. 647)	52. ee (p. 651)
11. u (p. 637)	25. r (p. 643)	39. e (p. 648)	53. g (p. 651)
12. dd (p. 637)	26. uu (p. 644)	40. xx (p. 648)	54. ww (p. 651)
13. bb (p. 638)	27. b (p. 644)	41. p (p. 648)	55. nn (p. 651)
14. c (p. 639)	28. l (p. 644)	42. bbb (p. 648)	

SELF TEST

True-False Questions

_____ 1. Proper risk management nearly always requires a combination of at least one risk-control technique and at least one risk-financing technique.

_____ 2. Once a risk is classified as uninsurable, it will never become insurable.

_____ 3. Because of the need to predict probability of loss, insurance companies will not issue policies that give protection except for specified liability risks.

_____ 4. The premium charged is based largely on the probability that the loss being insured will occur.

_____ 5. When interest rates are high, insurance companies actually lose money as people buy less insurance.

_____ 6   The general guideline in buying business insurance is to protect property and assets against loss.

_____ 7. Most of the various solutions to the liability insurance crisis involve government action to limit damages.

_____ 8. Psychiatric care is not an insurable health risk.

_____ 9. As medical expenses climb, businesses are beginning to cover less of the employees' health insurance needs.

_____ 10. Life insurance is the closest thing there is to a universal employee benefit.

Multiple Choice Questions

_____ 1. Improving quality control in order to lower the probability of a lawsuit based on unsafe products is an example of which approach to risk management?
    a. avoiding risk
    b. reducing risk
    c. assuming risk
    d. transferring risk

_____ 2. Many insurance policies have a clause which says that the insurance company will pay only part of a loss, that part greater than an amount known as a
    a. self-absorbed insurance premium.
    b. net loss to the company.
    c. coinsurance clause.
    d. deductible.

_____ 3. The basic purpose of the Social Security program is to provide a
    a. uniform amount of unemployment insurance funded by the federal government.
    b. full level of retirement income.
    c. minimum level of income for retirees only.
    d. minimum level of income for retirees, among others.

_____ 4. An insurance policy that provides protection against all forms of liability not specifically excluded under the terms of the policy is called
    a. umbrella malpractice liability.
    b. comprehensive general liability.
    c. workers' compensation.
    d. comprehensive property insurance.

_____ 5. Insurance in which one party agrees to be responsible to a second party for the obligations of a third is known as
    a. a fidelity bond.
    b. a surety bond.
    c. a nonperformance contract.
    d. all of the above.

_____ 6. With which type of insurance policy does an insurance company agree to repay the amount due on a loan if you should die?
    a. loss of earning power
    b. credit life
    c. pension plan
    d. a surety bond

_____ 7. Which type of liability insurance covers losses that occur during the policy period, no matter when the claim is made?
    a. occurrence policies
    b. claims-made policies
    c. no-fault policies
    d. contingent business policies

_____ 8. Of the following kinds of insurance coverage, companies must offer
   a. dental and vision insurance.
   b. life insurance.
   c. major-medical coverage.
   d. workers' compensation.

_____ 9. An insurance plan that covers medical expenses beyond the coverage limits of hospitalization insurance is known as
   a. surgical insurance.
   b. mental health insurance.
   c. dental and vision insurance.
   d. major-medical insurance.

_____ 10. Providing an injured worker a partial income while he or she is injured and unable to work is an example of
   a. injured worker income guarantee plans.
   b. disability income insurance.
   c. union income guarantee negotiations.
   d. employer income protection planning.

COMPLETION QUESTIONS

1. In a lawsuit, one party sues another for _____, or the estimated value of the loss.

2. People going into business accept _____ risks, or the possibility of losing money in order to make money.

3. Management's task of reducing the threat of loss due to uncontrollable events is called _____

   _____ management.

4. A(n) _____ risk is one that few, if any, insurance companies will agree to cover.

5. When an insured company files a _____ with the insurance company, it is asking for money related to a loss.

6. People who calculate what the probability of a loss is are called _____.

7. A nonprofit cooperative that is in the insurance business and is owned by the policyholders is called a _____

   _____ company.

8. A type of insurance that covers the insured from losses stemming from injury to an individual, or damage to

   someone else's property, is known as _____ insurance.

9. Professionals such as stockbrokers and architects carry _____ insurance in case their clients are dissatisfied and sue.

10. A prepaid group-practice medical plan in which consumers pay a set fee and little or no additional fees when

   they receive treatment is called a _____.

PROJECT

Buying Business Insurance

Insurance is an important part of good risk management for businesses. It is important for you to know what insurance can and cannot do for you as a manager. Visit an insurance agent and find out about business insurance. Be sure to cover the following points:

1. For what kind of risks would you buy business insurance?

2. When would self-insurance be appropriate?

3. What type of liability insurance does the agent recommend and why?

4. If all companies incur insurable losses—and most do—how can the insurance company make any money?

CHAPTER 1

True-False

1. F (p. 4)	13. F (p. 19)
2. F (p. 4)	14. F (p. 19)
3. T (p. 8)	15. T (p. 22)
4. T (p. 8)	16. T (p. 22)
5. T (p. 10)	17. T (p. 20)
6. F (p. 10)	18. T (p. 21)
7. T (p. 7)	19. F (p. 21)
8. T (p. 13)	20. F (p. 22)
9. T (p. 13)	21. F (p. 24)
10. T (p. 13)	22. T (p. 26)
11. T (p. 4)	23. T (p. 9)
12. T (p. 19)	

Multiple Choice

1. d (p. 4)	10. b (p. 14)
2. c (p. 4)	11. b (p. 14)
3. b (p. 5)	12. d (p. 19)
4. a (p. 4)	13. b (p. 20)
5. c (p. 4)	14. c (p. 18)
6. b (p. 8)	15. e (p. 24)
7. e (p. 7)	16. d (p. 9)
8. a (p. 11)	17. c (p. 23)
9. c (p. 14)	18. e (p. 23)

Completion

1. one's own effort (p. 4)	9. multiplier effect (p. 17)
2. entrepreneurs (p. 4)	10. public goods (p. 18)
3. growing (p. 5)	11. pure (p. 19)
4. underground economy (p. 5)	12. recession (p. 19)
5. communism; socialism; capitalism (p. 4)	13. increase; decrease (p. 13)
6. pure capitalism (p. 7)	14. imports; exports (p. 21)
7. mixed (p. 7)	15. environmental (p. 25)
8. innovation (p. 11)	

CHAPTER 2

True-False

1. F (p. 35)	10. F (p. 45)
2. T (p. 36)	11. T (p. 46)
3. T (p. 35)	12. F (p. 48)
4. T (p. 41)	13. F (p. 49)
5. T (p. 44)	14. T (p. 49)
6. T (p. 45)	15. T (p. 52)
7. T (p. 45)	16. T (p. 52)
8. F (p. 43)	17. F (p. 53)
9. F (p. 45)	18. F (p. 35)

Multiple Choice

1. b (p. 37)	
2. c (p. 40)	
3. e (p. 41)	
4. b (p. 41)	
5. b (p. 46)	
6. e (p. 44)	
7. a (p. 49)	
8. b (p. 53)	

Completion

1. goods; service (p. 34)	6. partnership (p. 43)
2. general; limited (p. 43)	7. life span (p. 45)
3. sole proprietorship; corporations (p. 40)	8. board of directors (p. 48)
4. sole proprietorship (p. 41)	9. acquisition (p. 51)
5. small; low (p. 41)	10. cooperative (p. 52)

CHAPTER 3

True-False

1. F (p. 67)
2. T (p. 63)
3. T (p. 69)
4. F (p. 72)
5. T (p. 76)
6. F (p. 86)
7. T (p. 83)
8. F (p. 62)
9. F (p. 77)
10. T (p. 78)
11. F (p. 73)
12. T (p. 81)
13. F (p. 82)
14. T (p. 78)
15. F (p. 83)

Multiple Choice

1. a (p. 62)
2. a (p. 71)
3. a (p. 69)
4. d (p. 72)
5. c (p. 74)
6. e (p. 72)
7. a (p. 72)
8. e (p. 78)
9. e (p. 83)

Completion

1. business plan (p. 72)
2. lifestyle (p. 62)
3. deciding on a legal structure; obtaining financing (p. 69)
4. business plan (p. 72)
5. debt; equity (p. 72)
6. fortress complex (p. 77)

CHAPTER 4

True-False

1. T (p. 90)
2. F (p. 90)
3. F (p. 90)
4. F (p. 90)
5. F (p. 92)
6. F (p. 108)
7. F (p. 99)
8. T (p. 108)
9. T (p. 95)
10. T (p. 100)
11. T (p. 99)
12. T (p. 108)
13. F (p. 108)
14. T (p. 110)
15. T (p. 114)
16. T (p. 111)
17. T (p. 93)
18. T (p. 103)

Multiple Choice

1. c (p. 90)
2. d (p. 108)
3. b (p. 90)
4. c (p. 92)
5. c (p. 94)
6. a (p. 94)
7. c (p. 108)
8. b (p. 101)
9. c (p. 100)
10. c (p. 112)

Completion

1. society at large (p. 90)
2. environmental protection; consumerism; civil rights; national defense (p. 91)
3. greenhouse (p. 94)
4. improved (p. 94)
5. be heard (p. 104)
6. Ponzi scheme (p. 112)
7. sexual (p. 108)

CHAPTER 5

True-False

1. F (p. 125)
2. T (p. 127)
3. F (p. 137)
4. F (p. 135)
5. F (p. 138)
6. F (p. 142)
7. F (p. 132)
8. T (p. 133)
9. F (p. 138)
10. T (p. 127)
11. F (p. 142)
12. T (p. 145)
13. T (p. 130)
14. T (p. 144)

Multiple Choice

1. a (p. 142)
2. d (p. 125)
3. a (p. 140)
4. c (p. 142)
5. c (p. 138)
6. a (p. 132)
7. b (p. 132)
8. c (p. 138)
9. d (p. 127)
10. c (p. 142)
11. e (p. 132)
12. e (p. 146)
13. e (p. 144)

Completion

1. multinational (p. 126)
2. absolute (p. 125)
3. balance of trade (p. 127)
4. franchising (p. 141)
5. free trade (p. 135)
6. trading blocks (p. 136)
7. macquiladoras (p. 130)
8. foreign sales corporation (p. 138)
9. protectionism (p. 132)
10. quota (p. 132)
11. dumping (p. 133)

CHAPTER 6

True-False

1. T (p. 154)
2. F (p. 155)
3. T (p. 157)
4. F (p. 157)
5. T (p. 160)
6. F (p. 162)
7. F (p. 164)
8. T (p. 165)
9. T (p. 165)
10. T (p. 166)
11. T (p. 157)
12. T (p. 160)
13. F (p. 164)
14. F (p. 155)
15. T (p. 164)
16. T (p. 157)
17. F (p. 154)

Multiple Choice

1. c (p. 155)
2. b (p. 155)
3. d (p. 155)
4. e (p. 158)
5. c (p. 160)
6. e (p. 164)
7. e (p. 168)
8. b (p. 157)
9. a (p. 154)
10. d (p. 154)
11. c (p. 154)
12. a (p. 162)
13. b (p. 162)
14. d (p. 165)
15. a (p. 165)
16. b (p. 165)
17. c (p. 165)
18. c (p. 158)
19. a (p. 158)

Completion

1. top; middle; operating (p. 155)
2. planning (p. 160)
3. goals and objectives (p. 161)
4. operational plans (p. 162)
5. certainty (p. 158)
6. strategic; operational (p. 162)
7. ambiguity (p. 158)
8. motivating; leading (p. 164)
9. decision maker (p. 154)
10. crisis management (p. 169)
11. strategic; tactical; operational (p. 162)

CHAPTER 7

True-False

1. T (p. 178)
2. T (p. 178)
3. F (p. 179)
4. T (p. 181)
5. T (p. 178)
6. T (p. 179)
7. F (p. 179)
8. T (p. 180)
9. F (p. 189)
10. T (p. 192)
11. T (p. 181)
12. T (p. 181)
13. F (p. 184)
14. T (p. 183)
15. F (p. 183)
16. T (p. 189)
17. T (p. 196)
18. T (p. 198)
19. T (p. 198)
20. T (p. 198)
21. T (p. 180)
22. T (p. 195)
23. T (p. 178)
24. T (p. 187)
25. T (p. 187)

Multiple Choice

1. d (p. 181)
2. e (p. 189)
3. b (p. 190)
4. c (p. 189)
5. a (p. 189)
6. b (p. 181)
7. e (p. 184)
8. c (p. 184)
9. e (p. 183)
10. d (p. 197)
11. d (p. 198)
12. a (p. 179)
13. e (p. 179)
14. e (p. 179)
15. e (p. 189)
16. d (p. 192)
17. d (p. 194)
18. d (p. 194)
19. c (p. 194)
20. d (p. 178)

Completion

1. above; below (p. 183)
2. responsible (p. 178)
3. formal (p. 179)
4. horizontal (p. 194)
5. wide (p. 184)
6. centralized; flat (p. 184)
7. advice; services (p. 183)
8. matrix (p. 193)
9. organizing (p. 178)
10. restructuring; downsizing (p. 186)
11. corporate culture (p. 198)

CHAPTER 8

True-False

1. T (p. 206)
2. T (p. 207)
3. T (p. 207)
4. T (p. 207)
5. T (p. 207)
6. F (p. 208)
7. T (p. 208)
8. T (p. 209)
9. T (p. 208)
10. F (p. 209)
11. F (p. 210)
12. F (p. 210)
13. T (p. 218)
14. T (p. 218)

Multiple Choice

1. e (p. 207)
2. e (p. 207)
3. d (p. 208)
4. c (p. 209)
5. a (p. 209)
6. d (p. 219)
7. e (p. 218)
8. b (p. 221)
9. d (p. 223)
10. c (p. 209)
11. b (p. 206)
12. c (p. 206)
13. a (p. 217)
14. e (p. 213)

Completion

1. conversion (p. 206)
2. breaking down; combining (p. 206)
3. routing; schedule (p. 219)
4. quality control (p. 214)
5. critical path (p. 224)
6. conversion (p. 206)
7. just-in-time (p. 213)

CHAPTER 9

True-False

1. T (p. 249)
2. F (p. 242)
3. T (p. 234)
4. T (p. 234)
5. F (p. 239)
6. F (p. 245)
7. T (p. 245)
8. T (p. 237)
9. F (p. 237)
10. F (p. 238)
11. T (p. 254)
12. F (p. 242)
13. T (p. 234)
14. T (p. 237)
15. F (p. 237)
16. T (p. 237)
17. T (p. 242)
18. T (p. 244)
19. T (p. 249)
20. T (p. 251)
21. T (p. 254)
22. F (p. 252)
23. T (p. 254)

Multiple Choice

1. e (p. 234)
2. d (p. 234)
3. a (p. 243)
4. e (p. 244)
5. d (p. 245)
6. a (p. 237)
7. b (p. 238)
8. c (p. 234)
9. b (p. 236)
10. d (p. 237)
11. a (p. 241)
12. e (p. 241)
13. b (p. 239)
14. d (p. 239)
15. a (p. 252)
16. b (p. 250)
17. e (p. 251)
18. e (p. 254)
19. c (p. 254)

Completion

1. leadership; communication; motivation (p. 234)
2. "If I do it, what will I get?" (p. 239)
3. cultural diversity (p. 244)
4. money (p. 236)
5. Hawthorne effect (p. 237)
6. safety (p. 237)
7. environment; human relations (p. 238)
8. authority; human growth (p. 241)
9. rewarding; punishing (p. 249)
10. job (p. 251)
11. job enrichment (p. 251)
12. work sharing; job sharing (p. 253)
13. telecommuting (p. 252)
14. confidence; criteria; credibility; compensation (p. 239)
15. work teams (p. 254)

CHAPTER 10

True-False

1. T (p. 262)
2. T (p. 262)
3. F (p. 263)
4. T (p. 266)
5. F (p. 267)
6. T (p. 274)
7. F (p. 284)
8. F (p. 286)
9. F (p. 287)
10. T (p. 288)
11. F (p. 277)
12. F (p. 276)
13. F (p. 278)
14. F (p. 280)
15. T (p. 283)
16. T (p. 270)
17. T (p. 283)

Multiple Choice

1. e (p. 262)
2. e (p. 262)
3. a (p. 265)
4. c (p. 265)
5. e (p. 266)
6. e (p. 269)
7. e (p. 267)
8. d (p. 266)
9. e (p. 273)
10. b (p. 277)
11. a (p. 277)

Completion

1. demand; supply (p. 263)
2. job description; job specification (p. 265)
3. recruiting (p. 266)
4. applications; reference (p. 267)
5. orientation (p. 272)
6. layoffs; fired (p. 285)
7. worker buyout (p. 288)
8. commission (p. 277)
9. fringe benefit (p. 279)

CHAPTER 11

True-False

1. T (p. 296)
2. T (p. 296)
3. F (p. 296)
4. T (p. 296)
5. F (p. 296)
6. F (p. 297)
7. F (p. 297)
8. T (p. 297)
9. T (p. 299)
10. T (p. 303)
11. T (p. 303)
12. T (p. 304)
13. F (p. 309)
14. F (p. 314)
15. T (p. 307)
16. T (p. 305)
17. F (p. 305)
18. T (p. 303)
19. F (p. 317)
20. T (p. 314)
21. T (p. 314)
22. T (p. 314)
23. F (p. 297)

Multiple Choice

1. b (p. 296)
2. e (p. 297)
3. c (p. 315)
4. a (p. 303)
5. c (p. 303)
6. b (p. 303)
7. a (p. 314)
8. e (p. 309)
9. a (p. 310)
10. e (p. 305)
11. c (p. 305)
12. b (p. 303)
13. b (p. 303)
14. a (p. 305)
15. e (p. 305)
16. e (p. 317)
17. c (p. 314)

Completion

1. profits (p. 296)
2. labor federations (p. 300)
3. shop steward (p. 314)
4. 30 (thirty) (p. 300)
5. certification (p. 300)
6. closed; union; agency (p. 310)
7. two-tier wage plan (p. 310)
8. cost-of-living adjustment, or COLA (p. 310)
9. lockout (p. 308)
10. ratification (p. 304)
11. grievance mediation (p. 314)
12. mutual assistance pacts (p. 309)

CHAPTER 12

True-False

1. T (p. 329)
2. T (p. 333)
3. T (p. 344)
4. T (p. 336)
5. F (p. 330)
6. T (p. 331)
7. T (p. 335)
8. F (p. 335)
9. T (p. 337)
10. T (p. 337)
11. T (p. 341)
12. F (p. 342)
13. T (p. 343)
14. T (p. 343)
15. T (p. 341)

Multiple Choice

1. b (p. 332)
2. a (p. 333)
3. d (p. 333)
4. d (p. 338)
5. a (p. 345)
6. b (p. 331)
7. d (p. 331)
8. d (p. 332)
9. e (p. 337)
10. e (p. 341)
11. c (p. 342)
12. c (p. 342)
13. a (p. 347)
14. c (p. 350)
15. c (p. 335)

Completion

1. competitive advantage (p. 332)
2. utility (p. 329)
3. time (p. 329)
4. market (p. 333)
5. needs; wants (p. 329)
6. economic (p. 342)
7. target market; marketing mix (p. 332)
8. challenger (p. 337)
9. multiple buying influence (p. 343)
10. long-term (p. 331)

CHAPTER 13

True-False

1.	F	(p. 361)	7.	F (p. 374)
2.	T	(p. 372)	8.	T (p. 377)
3.	F	(p. 363)	9.	T (p. 358)
4.	F	(p. 365)	10.	T (p. 371)
5.	T	(p. 358)	11.	T (p. 376)
6.	T	(p. 378)		

Multiple Choice

1.	c	(p. 361)	11.	a (p. 361)
2.	b	(p. 358)	12.	b (p. 361)
3.	c	(p. 369)	13.	b (p. 371)
4.	b	(p. 370)	14.	a (p. 376)
5.	d	(p. 365)	15.	c (p. 376)
6.	c	(p. 374)	16.	c (p. 361)
7.	c	(p. 378)	17.	b (p. 365)
8.	d	(p. 377)	18.	a (p. 370)
9.	d	(p. 361)	19.	b (p. 376)
10.	c	(p. 362)	20.	e (p. 360)

Completion

1. convenience (p. 361)
2. equity (p. 364)
3. product mix (p. 372)
4. product life cycle (p. 370)
5. brand (p. 363)
6. national (p. 363)
7. trademark (p. 363)
8. return on investment (p. 374)
9. skimming (p. 374)
10. markup (p. 378)
11. shopping products; convenience products (p. 361)
12. inelastic; elastic (p. 376)

CHAPTER 14

True-False

1.	T	(p. 396)	7.	T (p. 408)
2.	T	(p. 391)	8.	F (p. 408)
3.	F	(p. 392)	9.	F (p. 408)
4.	T	(p. 393)	10.	T (p. 391)
5.	F	(p. 404)	11.	F (p. 397)
6.	F	(p. 406)	12.	T (p. 409)

Multiple Choice

1.	c	(p. 388)	8.	c (p. 401)
2.	a	(p. 394)	9.	c (p. 402)
3.	d	(p. 396)	10.	d (p. 406)
4.	b	(p. 390)	11.	b (p. 408)
5.	b	(p. 392)	12.	c (p. 398)
6.	a	(p. 393)	13.	d (p. 397)
7.	d	(p. 398)		

Completion

1. distribution channel (p. 388)
2. channel conflict (p. 394)
3. vertical marketing system (p. 396)
4. channel captain (p. 396)
5. retailers (p. 398)
6. rack jobber (p. 398)
7. scrambled merchandising (p. 399)
8. wheel of retailing (p. 400)
9. nonstore (p. 404)
10. intensive (p. 392)
11. reverse (p. 391)
12. factory outlets (p. 402)

CHAPTER 15

True-False

1. F (p. 418)
2. F (p. 420)
3. T (p. 421)
4. T (p. 422)
5. T (p. 430)
6. F (p. 419)
7. F (p. 439)
8. F (p. 419)
9. T (p. 423)
10. T (p. 423)
11. T (p. 425)
12. F (p. 428)
13. T (p. 430)
14. T (p. 432)
15. T (p. 433)
16. T (p. 420)

Multiple Choice

1. b (p. 418)
2. e (p. 419)
3. d (p. 418)
4. a (p. 429)
5. d (p. 430)
6. b (p. 438)
7. d (p. 422)
8. a (p. 436)
9. d (p. 420)
10. a (p. 423)
11. a (p. 441)
12. d (p. 423)
13. a (p. 425)
14. d (p. 428)
15. c (p. 430)
16. e (p. 432)
17. e (p. 435)

Completion

1. Federal Trade Commission (FTC) (p. 419)
2. television (p. 438)
3. direct mail (p. 438)
4. market (p. 422)
5. media (p. 435)
6. continuity (p. 436)
7. sales support (p. 423)
8. outbound; inbound (p. 424)
9. trade allowance (p. 441)
10. prospecting; approaching the prospect; follow-up (p. 425)
11. copy; artwork (p. 435)
12. database (p. 438)

CHAPTER 16

True-False

1. T (p. 452)
2. T (p. 454)
3. F (p. 454)
4. F (p. 456)
5. T (p. 457)
6. T (p. 458)
7. T (p. 463)
8. T (p. 467)
9. T (p. 470)
10. F (p. 470)
11. T (p. 474)
12. T (p. 474)

Multiple choice

1. d (p. 454)
2. a (p. 455)
3. b (p. 455)
4. b (p. 456)
5. c (p. 458)
6. a (p. 458)
7. a (p. 460)
8. b (p. 461)
9. a (p. 463)
10. e (p. 467)
11. b (p. 470)
12. c (p. 471)

Completion

1. chief information (p. 452)
2. management information (p. 456)
3. artificial intelligence (p. 457)
4. mainframe (p. 461)
5. hardware; software (p. 462)
6. database management (p. 469)
7. network (p. 472)
8. Do organizations know more about you than they need to? Are they telling anyone else? (p. 474)

CHAPTER 17

True-False

1.	T (p. 482)	11.	F (p. 496)
2.	F (p. 482)	12.	T (p. 497)
3.	T (p. 483)	13.	T (p. 501)
4.	T (p. 486)	14.	T (p. 501)
5.	F (p. 486)	15.	T (p. 504)
6.	F (p. 487)	16.	T (p. 505)
7.	T (p. 487)	17.	T (p. 505)
8.	T (p. 489)	18.	T (p. 498)
9.	T (p. 492)	19.	T (p. 498)
10.	T (p. 496)		

Multiple Choice

1.	b	(p. 482)	8.	a	(p. 489)
2.	e	(p. 486)	9.	c	(p. 503)
3.	d	(p. 487)	10.	a	(p. 504)
4.	e	(p. 487)	11.	d	(p. 505)
5.	b	(p. 487)	12.	c	(p. 505)
6.	c	(p. 487)	13.	e	(p. 497)
7.	d	(p. 489)	14.	b	(p. 498)

Completion

1. the outside world (p. 482)
2. objective (p. 482)
3. certified public accountant (p. 484)
4. corporate (p. 486)
5. two (p. 487)
6. retained earnings (p. 487)
7. balance sheet (p. 489)
8. net income (p. 492)
9. accrual (p. 492)
10. cash (p. 492)
11. net sales (p. 494)
12. trend analysis; ratio analysis (p. 501)

CHAPTER 18

True-False

1.	T	(p. 516)	6.	F	(p. 525)
2.	F	(p. 516)	7.	T	(p. 522)
3.	F	(p. 516)	8.	F	(p. 531)
4.	F	(p. 516)	9.	T	(p. 525)
5.	T	(p. 517)	10.	F	(p. 533)

Multiple Choice

1.	c	(p. 515)	6.	a	(p. 523)
2.	b	(p. 516)	7.	b	(p. 521)
3.	a	(p. 517)	8.	b	(p. 527)
4.	a	(p. 520)	9.	d	(p. 530)
5.	b	(p. 521)	10.	b	(p. 532)

Completion

1. money (p. 514)
2. currency (p. 516)
3. time deposits (p. 516)
4. national (p. 517)
5. finance company (p. 518)
6. NOW (p. 521)
7. automated teller machines (p. 523)
8. monetary policy (p. 531)
9. M2 (p. 515)
10. Fed (p. 531)

CHAPTER 19

True-False

1. T (p. 542)	6. F (p. 558)
2. F (p. 553)	7. F (p. 559)
3. F (p. 553)	8. F (p. 560)
4. T (p. 546)	9. T (p. 560)
5. T (p. 558)	10. T (p. 562)

Multiple Choice

1. d (p. 542)	6. c (p. 553)
2. b (p. 542)	7. c (p. 554)
3. b (p. 545)	8. a (p. 555)
4. d (p. 546)	9. b (p. 558)
5. b (p. 551)	10. c (p. 562)

Completion

1. cost of capital (p. 544)	6. stock split (p. 561)
2. unsecured (p. 553)	7. line of credit (p. 553)
3. leased (p. 571)	8. debentures (p. 558)
4. equity (p. 559)	9. convertible (p. 559)
5. after-tax (p. 549)	10. capital investments (p. 549)

CHAPTER 20

True-False

1. T (p. 586)	6. F (p. 584)
2. T (p. 573)	7. T (p. 581)
3. T (p. 573)	8. F (p. 582)
4. F (p. 574)	9. T (p. 584)
5. F (p. 579)	10. F (p. 589)

Multiple Choice

1. b (p. 573)	6. a (p. 582)
2. c (p. 573)	7. c (p. 583)
3. c (p. 576)	8. b (p. 586)
4. a (p. 578)	9. d (p. 588)
5. a (p. 580)	10. a (p. 595)

Completion

1. institutional (p. 572)	6. closed-end (p. 580)
2. Treasury bill (p. 576)	7. put option (p. 581)
3. savings bonds (p. 576)	8. stock specialist (p. 582)
4. default (p. 577)	9. discretionary (p. 586)
5. money market (p. 580)	10. index (p. 589)

CHAPTER 21

True-False

1.	T	(p. 605)	6.	T (p. 613)
2.	T	(p. 605)	7.	T (p. 620)
3.	F	(p. 606)	8.	F (p. 621)
4.	F	(p. 606)	9.	F (p. 623)
5.	T	(p. 607)	10.	F (p. 624)

Multiple Choice

1.	d	(p. 604)	6.	d (p. 615)
2.	d	(p. 605)	7.	c (p. 616)
3.	b	(p. 606)	8.	c (p. 618)
4.	c	(p. 611)	9.	c (p. 622)
5.	a	(p. 613)	10.	b (p. 625)

Completion

1. trust (p. 606)
2. Antitrust Improvements (p. 607)
3. personal income (p. 612)
4. political action committees (p. 614)
5. administrative (p. 616)

6. stare decisis (p. 616)
7. contract (p. 621)
8. power of attorney (p. 623)
9. lease (p. 624)
10. patent (p. 626)

CHAPTER 22

True-False

1.	T	(p. 637)	6.	T (p. 642)
2.	F	(p. 637)	7.	T (p. 644)
3.	F	(p. 638)	8.	F (p. 649)
4.	T	(p. 639)	9.	T (p. 649)
5.	F	(p. 641)	10.	F (p. 651)

Multiple Choice

1.	b	(p. 636)	6.	b (p. 644)
2.	d	(p. 639)	7.	b (p. 645)
3.	d	(p. 640)	8.	d (p. 645)
4.	b	(p. 645)	9.	d (p. 648)
5.	b	(p. 643)	10.	b (p. 650)

Completion

1. damages (p. 634)
2. speculative (p. 634)
3. risk (p. 635)
4. uninsurable (p. 637)
5. claim (p. 639)

6. actuaries (p. 639)
7. mutual (p. 641)
8. liability (p. 644)
9. malpractice (p. 644)
10. health maintenance organization (p. 650)

CHAPTER 1

1. Which of the following would be considered a factor of production?
   a. natural resources
   b. labor
   c. capital
   d. entrepreneurs
   e. all of the above

2. Which of the following is *not* considered part of the factor of production known as capital?
   a. machines and tools
   b. minerals and timber
   c. money used to buy other resources
   d. buildings

3. Which of the following is a basic question asked by all economic systems?
   a. How should the country's limited economic resources be used to satisfy society's needs?
   b. What goods and services should be produced?
   c. Who should produce goods and services?
   d. How should goods and services be divided among the population?
   e. All of the above are basic economic questions.

4. Which of the following would be an example of a country having a communistic economic system?
   a. Sweden
   b. United States
   c. China
   d. France

5. Which of the following is *not* true of communist countries?
   a. Unemployment and inflation can more easily be controlled.
   b. Many incentives exist to develop more efficient and productive ways of doing thing.
   c. There is less of a gap between the wealthy and the poor.
   d. They have a planned economy.

6. Which of the following industries are most likely to be controlled by the government in a socialist economy?
   a. transportation, utilities, medicine, communications
   b. clothing, furniture, housewares
   c. watches, shoes, automobiles, beer
   d. all of the above

7. Which of the following countries does *not* have a socialist economy?
   a. India
   b. Britain
   c. France
   d. China

8. Which of the following is a limiting force in the American economy?
   a. technological forces
   b. social forces
   c. economic forces
   d. government policy
   e. all of the above

9. Opportunity cost is
   a. the value placed on time.
   b. the foregoing of some potential benefit by using a resource for some other activity.
   c. the cost involved in developing a new product or opportunity.
   d. the price paid in order to be entitled to do business.

10. Which of the following is an appropriate means of competing?
    a. price
    b. quality
    c. innovation
    d. all of the above

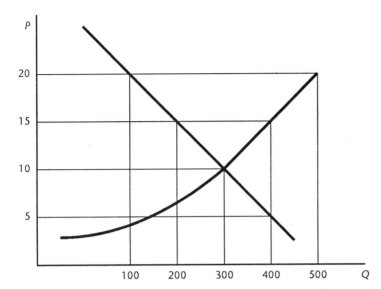

11. For the above graph, what will the market price be?
    a. $50
    b. $75
    c. $100
    d. $125

12. What will the amount supplied at the market price be?
    a. 300
    b. 400
    c. 500
    d. 600

13. Which of the following is *not* one of the "flows" of the circular flow?
    a. goods and services from businesses to households in exchange for money
    b. goods and services from government to households and businesses in exchange for taxes
    c. labor from households in exchange for wages
    d. All of the above are flows within the circular flow.

14. Which of the following is *not* one of the major economic roles of government in a capitalistic society?
    a. enforcing rules and regulations
    b. manufacturing and distributing products
    c. fostering competition
    d. contributing to economic stability
    e. providing public goods and transfer payments

15. Social Security benefits, food stamps, welfare, and unemployment compensation are all examples of
    a. transfer payments.
    b. public goods.
    c. welfare payment programs.
    d. private benefit programs.

16. The competitive situation in which no single buyer or seller can control the market is known as
    a. pure competition.
    b. oligopoly.
    c. monopoly.
    d. dualopoly.

17. The competitive situation in which a single company controls the market is known as
    a. pure competition.
    b. oligopoly.
    c. monopoly.
    d. dualopoly.

18. The competitive situation in which a few producers control the market is known as
    a. pure competition.
    b. oligopoly.
    c. monopoly.
    d. dualopoly.

19. The government's use of revenue collection and spending to control the business cycle, employment, and inflation is known as
    a. tax policy.
    b. business planning control.
    c. circulation control.
    d. fiscal policy.

20. Disinflation in the economy during the 1980s is a result of
    a. deregulation of industry.
    b. a decline in power of labor unions.
    c. restrictions on the amount of money circulated.
    d. weakening of oil cartels.
    e. All of the above have helped reduce the rate of inflation.

21. Which of the following is *false* concerning business activity in the future?
    a. There will be more emphasis on goods and less emphasis on services.
    b. There will be accelerating technological development.
    c. There will be more consumer-driven marketing.
    d. There will be a more global economy.

22. Modified capitalism differs from pure capitalism in that modified capitalism
    a. does not use price as a means of determining supply and demand.
    b. has some government intervention to change prices or allocate resources.
    c. allows for price fixing among producers.
    d. allows consumers to have complete and perfect information about market prices.

23. The demand curve basically states that
    a. consumers demand greater quantities of a product at higher prices.
    b. consumers demand greater quantities of a product at lower prices.
    c. consumers demand the same amount, regardless of the product's price.
    d. individual companies set their own price without any consideration of the market price.

24. The supply curve basically states that
    a. producers supply greater quantities of a product at higher prices.
    b. producers supply greater quantities of a product at lower prices.
    c. producers supply the same quantities regardless of price.
    d. producers attempt to set prices at an artificially high level.

25. The United States is considered to have full employment when _____ percent of the people who are willing and able to work are employed.
    a. 100
    b. 95
    c. 75
    d. 65

26. When the value of the U.S. dollar is high,
    a. exports out of the United States will increase.
    b. the cost of American goods to foreigners is relatively inexpensive.
    c. imports into the United States will increase.
    d. All of the above are true.

27. Which of the following is one of the major changes occurring within the United States?
    a. Companies are becoming more international in scope.
    b. Services have a more important role within our society and economy.
    c. The rate of technological development is accelerating.
    d. Use of participative management is increasing.
    e. All of the above are occurring.

CHAPTER 2

1. Which of the following comprise the two major sectors of the economy?
   a. goods-producing businesses and service businesses
   b. goods-producing businesses and retail businesses
   c. goods-producing businesses and governments
   d. profit organizations and nonprofit organizations

2. Which of the following is *not* a part of the goods-producing sector?
   a. agriculture
   b. mining
   c. finance and insurance
   d. construction
   e. manufacturing

3. The growth of the service sector can be attributed to
   a. increased productivity within the goods-producing sector.
   b. increased manufacturing from foreign nations with inexpensive labor forces.
   c. increased acceptance of computers.
   d. all of the above.

4. Which subsector of the goods-producing sector is currently experiencing the most difficult time?
   a. mining
   b. construction
   c. agriculture
   d. manufacturing

5. Which of the following is *not* an advantage of sole proprietorship?
   a. autonomy and personal satisfaction
   b. easy entrance
   c. limited liability
   d. flexibility of organization and management.

6. Partnerships are *most* common in which of the following?
   a. commercial or industrial firms
   b. professional and financial services
   c. retail stores
   d. discount houses

7. Company A purchases Company B, with Company A remaining dominant. This form of business combination is called
   a. an acquisition.
   b. joint venture.
   c. a conglomerate.
   d. a cooperative.

8. The form of combination in which a company involved in one phase of business absorbs or joins a company in another phase to guarantee a supplier or customer is called a
   a. horizontal merger.
   b. vertical merger.
   c. conglomerate.
   d. cooperative

9. An organization or a small group of companies or people with similar products, services, or interests banded together for greater bargaining power is called a
   a. partnership.
   b. cooperative.
   c. franchise.
   d. corporation.

10. A corporation that carries on business to make a profit for its owners, the shareholders, is a
    a. public corporation.
    b. private corporation.
    c. single-person corporation.
    d. government-owned corporation.

11. Top officers of a corporation are elected by and can be removed by
    a. shareholders.
    b. the board of directors.
    c. the chairman of the board.
    d. none of the above.

12. Under what type of partnership is a person's liability limited to his or her own personal investment?
    a. limited partnership
    b. general partnership
    c. corporate partnership
    d. every partnership

13. The owners of a corporation are known as the
    a. board of directors.
    b. chief executive officers.
    c. shareholders.
    d. creditors.

14. Success in a sole proprietorship generally requires
    a. individual initiative.
    b. hard work.
    c. self-reliance.
    d. all of the above.

15. Which of the following is *true* concerning corporations?
    a. To be incorporated, an organization must be designed to make a profit.
    b. A corporation must sell its shares on the open market.
    c. A corporation must make public reports on its financial condition.
    d. Corporations have limited liability.

16. Unlimited liability means that any damages or debt attributed to the business can be attached to the
    a. stockholders.
    b. board of directors.
    c. owners.
    d. creditors.

17. A legal association of two or more persons in a business as co-owners is call a
    a. cooperative.
    b. corporation.
    c. sole proprietorship.
    d. partnership.

18. The board of directors of a corporation is elected by the
    a. company officers.
    b. voting stockholders.
    c. employees.
    d. chief executive officers.

19. As a practical matter, the entity that has ultimate authority in guiding corporate affairs and making general policy is the
    a. company president or chief executive officer.
    b. stockholders.
    c. board of directors.
    d. company lawyer.

20. Conflict among the owners in a business is most likely to occur in
    a. sole proprietorship.
    b. partnerships.
    c. public corporations.
    d. nonprofit corporations.

21. The owners of a business can sell their interest in a business with the least amount of trouble in a
    a. sole proprietorship.
    b. partnerships.
    c. public corporation.
    d. nonprofit corporation.

22. Which of the following is an advantage of a partnership over a sole proprietorship?
    a. limited financial liability for the partners
    b. ease of entry
    c. greater borrowing power
    d. unlimited life span

23. Which form of business ownership accounts for the most money and has the most power?
    a. sole proprietorship
    b. partnership
    c. corporation
    d. They are all about equal.

24. Which of the following is *not* one of the major reasons for increased merger activity?
    a. desire of corporations to increase [operational operations]
    b. greater profit potential
    c. more lenient attitude by government toward mergers
    d. deregulation in certain industries
    e. All of the above *are* reasons.

CHAPTER 3

1. Success in a small business requires
    a. being well organized.
    b. being able to communicate with customers and employees.
    c. being willing to work hard.
    d. having a "love" for the field in which the business is.
    e. all of the above.

2. Which of the following is a benefit of small businesses in our society?
    a. They create new jobs.
    b. They introduce new products.
    c. They meet the needs of large businesses and customers by providing specialized products.
    d. All of the above are benefits.

3. Which of the following is a way of getting into business for yourself?
    a. start a new business from scratch
    b. buy an existing business
    c. obtain a franchise
    d. all of the above

4. The best form of organization for a new business is
    a. sole proprietorship.
    b. partnership.
    c. corporation.
    d. any of the above, depending on the financial position, number of employees, risk involved, tax position, and so on.

5. The most common source for funding a lifestyle company is
    a. personal savings and loans from friends.
    b. equity financing.
    c. bank loans.
    d. debt financing.

6. State and local venture capital programs are a good source of financing a start-up company if the business
    a. will boost employment in the area.
    b. has a high potential for success.
    c. has 85 percent collateral.
    d. needs between $75,000 and $500,000 and expects to employ at least twenty people.

7. "Going public" by selling stock in the company allows the company to
    a. reduce risk.
    b. raise money.
    c. raise money and generate profits for early investors
    d. produce profits.

8. Success for a small business requires
   a. promising business opportunity.
   b. management ability.
   c. adequate financing.
   d. modern business practices.
   e. all of the above.

9. Entrepreneurs tend to
   a. be willing to work hard and learn from mistakes.
   b. be self-confident.
   c. regard difficulty as a challenge.
   d. take risks.
   e. do all of the above.

10. Which of the following is a benefit of small businesses in our society?
    a. They create new jobs.
    b. They introduce new products.
    c. They meet the needs of large businesses and customers by providing specialized products.
    d. All of the above are benefits.

11. The major advantage of franchising for a business is the
    a. ability to expand quickly with limited funds.
    b. receipt of high return of sales.
    c. elimination of competition.
    d. minimization of training requirements.

12. The major advantage of purchasing a franchise is
    a. having control over the business.
    b. having low initial start-up costs.
    c. receiving a proven business system and training from the franchiser.
    d. having no competition.

*13. The business plan should provide information on
    a. the company and industry.
    b. products and markets.
    c. marketing strategy and management team.
    d. financial status and critical risks.
    e. all of the above.

*14. Which of the following characteristics are desirable if you are to own your own small business?
    a. follower; easily discouraged; poor health
    b. dislike people; dishonest; hate responsibility
    c. well organized; leader; self-starter
    d. poor decision maker; irresponsible; lazy

*15. Most successful small business owners would be described as
    a. being self-starters and persistent.
    b. friendly and capable of leading others.
    c. responsible, well organized, and hard working.
    d. being good decision makers and honest in their dealings.
    e. all of the above.

CHAPTER 4

1. In operating a business, whose needs must be served and met if the business is to survive?
   a. consumers
   b. employees
   c. owners
   d. society at large
   e. all of the above

2. During the 1960s activists were concerned about
   a. civil rights.
   b. environmental protection.
   c. consumerism.
   d. all of the above.

3. The greatest amount of progress in cleaning up the environment has been made in which of the following areas?
   a. air pollution
   b. water pollution
   c. toxic waste disposal
   d. Progress has been about the same in all of the above.

4. The philosophy that stresses producing the greatest good for the greatest number of people is
   a. individual rights.   c. justice.
   b. utilitarianism.   d. egalitarianism.

5. Which philosophy would reject an alternative simply because it violates the rights of a single person, even though it provides the greatest benefit for the greatest number of people?
   a. individual rights   c. justice
   b. utilitarianism   d. egalitarianism

6. The philosophy that feels people should be treated equally is
   a. individual rights.   c. justice.
   b. utilitarianism.   d. egalitarianism.

7. The United States has _____ pollution problems.
   a. air   c. land
   b. water   d. all of the above

8. Which of the following is *not* one of the consumer's basic rights?
   a. right to return merchandise   d. right to choose
   b. right to safety   e. right to be heard
   c. right to be informed

9. Which of the following groups of people have been discriminated against?
   a. women   c. handicapped
   b. racial minorities   d. all of the above

10. Discrimination against women in the workplace has taken the form of
    a. not hiring women for certain types of positions.
    b. not paying women as much as men for the same job.
    c. sexual harassment.
    d. all of the above.

11. A company's major responsibility to investors is to
    a. manage resources efficiently.   c. maximize social benefit.
    b. make money on their behalf.   d. maximize market share.

12. Ponzi schemes and "creative accounting" techniques are examples of cheating investors by
    a. mismanaging the resources so as to reduce the return on investment.
    b. misrepresenting the potential of the investment.
    c. legal activities to maximize a firm's profit.
    d. illegal activities to maximize a firm's sales.

13. A Ponzi scheme is
    a. a form of fraud in which money received from later investors is used to pay off early investors.
    b. a form of fraud in which stock to a phony company is sold.
    c. a legal means of acquiring funds.
    d. a legal, though unethical, business practice.

14. Using the company resources for personal gain, cheating on expense accounts, and insider trading are examples of cheating investors by
    a. mismanaging the resources so as to reduce the return on investment.
    b. misrepresenting the potential of the investment.
    c. legal activities to maximize a firm's profit.
    d. illegal activities to maximize a firm's sales.

CHAPTER 5

1. Changing conditions in world trade are influencing the way U.S. companies are doing business. One of these changes is
    a. lower foreign investment in the United States.
    b. cooperative efforts between former U.S. and foreign competitors.
    c. U.S. companies are dominating almost every aspect of world trade.
    d. world trade is experiencing a slow but steady decline.

2. U.S. foreign aid
    a. represents an economic drain on our country.
    b. has failed to help any nation rebuild after World War II.
    c. has flowed back to American companies supplying goods and services in countries we helped to rebuild.
    d. has proven to be highly effective, especially in helping developing countries restructure their economies.

3. The growth of multinational corporations, whether in the United States, Europe, or Japan, is reflected in
    a. an increasing variety in the world's wants.
    b. increasing opportunities for market segmentation across national boundaries.
    c. an increasing similarity in the world's wants.
    d. the nations involved generating a common trade policy.

4. An individual or company that sells products to a customer who is located in a foreign country is
    a. importing.   c. involved in countertrading.
    b. adding to the trade deficit. d. exporting.

5. The balance of payments, or the current account,
    a. measures the total flow of money into a country, minus the flow out of that country.
    b. does not include foreign investment.
    c. has been positive for the United States since 1982.
    d. all of the above.

6. An agreement between businesses in two countries in which one company obtains the rights to duplicate a product of the other company is a(n)
    a. export or import.   c. franchise.
    b. licensing arrangement.   d. joint venture.

7. Why would a company be interested in a joint venture with a company from another country?
    a. Investment costs might be shared, lowering risks.
    b. Each might bring a special skill to the partnership.
    c. Local restrictions may demand a joint venture.
    d. All of the above.

8. The expansion of world trade means that
    a. consumers will have access to fewer products, at higher prices.
    b. understanding of people from other cultures may increase.
    c. a country's own producers will experience lessened foreign competition.
    d. all of the above.

9. An organization that is concerned with reducing tariffs and encouraging free trade among member nations is
   a. an economic union.
   b. the General Agreement on Tariffs and Trade.
   c. an economic summit meeting.
   d. all of the above.

10. Which of the following is an example of a cultural or language difference that might affect international business?
    a. employee motivation
    b. labeling or packaging requirements
    c. advertising slogans
    d. all of the above

11. An example of a political or legal barrier to conducting business internationally is
    a. protectionism.
    b. a poorly translated advertising slogan.
    c. a floating exchange rate.
    d. all of the above.

12. Countries subsidize producers so that
    a. their products will have lower prices than those produced elsewhere.
    b. a long-term gain in international trade will be realized.
    c. tariffs will be reinforced.
    d. all of the above.

13. Perhaps the most important policy change the federal government can make to help U.S. companies compete more successfully internationally is to
    a. lower the value of the dollar relative to foreign currencies.
    b. impose strong import barriers.
    c. impose quotas on Japanese goods.
    d. provide credit assistance to American sellers of consumer products.

14. The ratio of one country's currency that is traded for the currency of another country is known as
    a. the exchange rate.
    b. the floating exchange rate.
    c. foreign exchange.
    d. a blocked currency.

15. What is the impact on U.S. importers if the dollar is strong in comparison to foreign currencies?
    a. Import sales will suffer.
    b. Import sales will increase.
    c. There is no impact, since the demand for imports is not price sensitive.
    d. Importers will not be allowed to increase sales, as that would lead to a negative balance of trade.

16. The governments of the United States, Japan, West Germany, France, and Great Britain have been working together to bring down the value of the U.S. dollar. What impact will that decline have?
    a. U.S. exports should be more price competitive.
    b. Inflation may increase in the United States.
    c. Interest rates may be lowered in other countries.
    d. All of the above.

17. Why have European marketers been interested in increasing exports to the United States?
    a. The traditional weak dollar has made their imports more expensive, hence more profitable.
    b. European markets are expanding so fast that they are generating too much competition.
    c. Transportation costs have declined due to deregulation.
    d. All of the above.

18. In the discussion of avoiding business blunders abroad, what element was mentioned in the text as being highly important in ensuring success in international business?
    a. packaging
    b. local customs
    c. language and translation
    d. all of the above

19. Which of the following statements accurately describes the assistance provided by the U.S. government to firms interested in engaging in international trade?
    a. No legislation or agency of the U.S. government provides assistance of any kind.
    b. More assistance is provided by the U.S. government than by any other nation.
    c. Both legislation and agency support is provided, but less than in most other major trading countries.
    d. The U.S. government is in the middle of establishing a comprehensive foreign trade policy and will soon announce what assistance it will start to provide.

20. Agricultural products tend to use which form of import protection?
    a. tariffs
    b. quotas
    c. subsidies
    d. restrictive standards

21. Requiring licenses before importing, mandating special tests, and establishing difficult standards are examples of what type of import protective measures?
    a. tariffs
    b. quotas
    c. subsidies
    d. restrictive standards

CHAPTER 6

1. The level of management with the most power and overall responsibility is
   a. top management.
   b. middle management.
   c. supervisory management.
   d. mega management.

2. The level of management primarily responsible for implementing the broad goals established by others is
   a. top management.
   b. middle management.
   c. supervisory management.
   d. mega management.

3. A manager's ability to understand others and interact effectively with them is a(n)
   a. technical skill.
   b. human skill.
   c. conceptual skill.
   d. administrative skill.

4. A manager's ability to gather information, analyze data, plan, and organize would be classified as a(n)
   a. administrative skill.
   b. human skill.
   c. conceptual skill.
   d. mechanical skill.

5. Decision making requires which skill?
   a. technical
   b. human
   c. conceptual
   d. communicational

6. The four functions of management are
   a. systemizing, utilizing, operating, and assigning.
   b. maximizing, centralizing, controlling, and leading.
   c. planning, organizing, controlling, and directing.
   d. motivating, socializing, cajoling, and entertaining.

7. Goals and objectives are needed for
   a. level of desired profitability.
   b. level of manager performance and development.
   c. worker performance and attitude.
   d. amount of social responsibility.
   e. all of the above.

8. The process of managers establishing personal goals consistent with the organization's overall goals and being evaluated by those goals is known as
   a. management by objective.
   b. contingency management.
   c. situational management.
   d. strategic management.

9. Which of the following statements concerning planning is *false*?
   a. Top managers are primarily responsible for long-range planning.
   b. Supervisory managers are mostly involved with short-range planning.
   c. Strategies are plans to accomplish short-range goals.
   d. Top managers face more complex problems and planning than do lower level managers.

10. The answer to the question "What business are we in?" is usually formulated in the
    a. company objectives.
    b. mission statement.
    c. budget.
    d. company policies.
    e. company procedures.

11. The process of arranging resources to carry out organizational plans is known as
    a. planning.
    b. organizing.
    c. arranging.
    d. directing.

12. Matching the right people with the right jobs defines the management task of
    a. motivating.
    b. leading.
    c. controlling.
    d. staffing.

13. The management function that consists of getting people to work effectively and willingly is called
    a. organizing.
    b. controlling.
    c. planning.
    d. directing.

14. A leader who delegates little authority and exercises much direct control over employees exhibits leadership that may be termed
    a. autocratic.
    b. democratic.
    c. laissez-faire.
    d. socialistic.

15. Which of the following styles of leadership is used *most* often in emergency situations that call for quick decisions?
    a. autocratic
    b. democratic
    c. laissez-faire
    d. socialistic

16. Which leadership style involves putting problems into the group's hands and letting members proceed?
    a. autocratic
    b. democratic
    c. laissez-faire
    d. socialistic

17. Where is the laissez-faire style most likely to be found?
    a. in retail businesses
    b. in highly creative organizations
    c. in the automotive industry
    d. in the construction industry

18. The process of taking corrective action when goals are *not* being met is called
    a. controlling.
    b. directing.
    c. leading.
    d. organizing.

19. The process of coordinating resources to meet an objective is called
    a. organizing.
    b. managing.
    c. systemizing.
    d. controlling.

20. Managers exercise the management controlling function when they
    a. keep close, direct supervision over subordinates.
    b. compare where they are with where they should be and take necessary corrective action.
    c. exercise authority over subordinates to assure observation of rules and regulations.
    d. make sure subordinates don't take advantage of the company.

21. Technical skills are usually needed *most* at which of the following job levels?
    a. first-line supervisor
    b. middle-line manager
    c. top management
    d. board of directors

CHAPTER 7

1. Which of the following statements concerning authority is *correct*?
    a. To be effective, authority need only be given.
    b. To be effective, authority must be given and received.
    c. To be effective, authority must be given, received, and acknowledged.
    d. Authority cannot be given, only responsibility accepted.

2. The pathway for the flow of authority from one level of an organization's employees to the next is known as
    a. chain of command.
    b. authority.
    c. formal organization.
    d. span of control.

3. The *most* common error in delegation is failing to give the recipient
    a. enough authority to carry out assigned responsibilities.
    b. complete authority.
    c. proper compensation.
    d. adequate training to accomplish duties.

4. An organization with most of the authority and responsibility at the top would be an example of
    a. a flat structure.
    b. an organization with no planning.
    c. a tall structure.
    d. an organization with extensive delegation.

5. In contrast to a centralized company, a decentralized company would more likely
    a. have a flat structure.
    b. engage in extensive delegation.
    c. contain more middle management positions.
    d. have or do all of the above.

6. According to management theory, which of the following statements is *true*?
    a. There is no "best" type of organization.
    b. Decentralized management is best.
    c. Centralized management is best.
    d. A wide span of control gets the best results.

7. The simple chain of command system is represented by
    a. line organization.
    b. a line-and-staff organization.
    c. a staff-assisted organization.
    d. a staff organization.

8. In practice, the person who is held fully accountable for the mistakes or poor performance of the production worker is the
    a. middle manager.
    b. chairman of the board.
    c. president.
    d. foreman or supervisory manager.

9. The number of people a manager directly supervises is called that person's
   a. department.
   c. division.
   b. span of management.
   d. group of employees.

10. In a flat structure with a broad span of management, authority and decision making tend to be
    a. centralized.
    c. unclear.
    b. decentralized.
    d. routine matter.

11. In a tall structure with a narrow span of management, authority tends to be
    a. centralized.
    c. dictatorial.
    b. decentralized.
    d. a routine matter.

12. A line organization is so called because
    a. it establishes a clear line of authority flowing from the top downward through every subordinate position.
    b. there is one top executive who has the last word.
    c. every employee knows who his or her superior or boss is.
    d. All of the above conditions are the case.

13. In a line-and-staff organization, the staff people are necessary because they
    a. take over for their counterpart line member when the latter has to be away.
    b. provide advice and specialized services.
    c. make the policies of the company.
    d. are responsible for the financial part of the company and operation.

14. "Office politics" is
    a. the attempt to become chairman of the board.
    b. the complex struggle for dominance that takes place in an organization.
    c. running for a position in the informal organizational structure.
    d. communicating through the grapevine.

15. The art of making and using contacts is known as
    a. networking.
    c. positioning.
    b. office politics.
    d. one-upmanship.

CHAPTER 8

1. The sequence of events that transforms resources into products is the
   a. transformation process.
   c. utility process.
   b. conversion process.
   d. output process.

2. Which of the following statements is *false*?
   a. Services do not require a conversion process.
   b. The conversion process can involve breaking down a raw material into one or more different products.
   c. The conversion process can involve combining two or more materials to form a single product.
   d. The conversion process involves taking inputs and transforming them into outputs.

3. The production of goods in very large quantities is called
   a. standardization.
   c. mass production.
   b. utilization.
   d. mass marketing.

4. Mechanization is best described as the
   a. use of animals to do the work previously performed by people.
   b. use of standardization to eliminate duplication of effort.
   c. use of machines to do the work previously performed by people.
   d. process of performing a mechanical operation without any human involvement at all.

5. The production of uniform or identical goods is called
   a. mechanization.
   b. standardization.
   c. automation.
   d. mass production.

6. The process of performing a mechanical operation without any human involvement at all is called
   a. mechanization.
   b. standardization.
   c. automation.
   d. dehumanization.

7. Flexible manufacturing is particularly desirable for
   a. mass production.
   b. job shops.
   c. repetitive manufacturing processes.
   d. producing long runs of a single product.

8. Focused factors
   a. produce all of a company's product at one central location.
   b. employ hard manufacturing processes.
   c. deal with only one narrow set of products.
   d. tend to make firms less efficient but more competitive.

9. Determining the available quantity of various items and keeping track of their movement and use within the plant is called:
   a. material sighting.
   b. inventory support.
   c. inventory control.
   d. material availability.

10. The delivery of materials to where they are needed precisely when they are needed is known as
    a. inventory control.
    b. materials requirement planning.
    c. just-in-time delivery.
    d. manufacturing resource planning.

11. Attempting to do it right the first time, by designing tools, machinery, and production processes to produce high-quality products and using quality materials and workers, is known as
    a. quality control.
    b. quality assurance.
    c. manufacturing resource planning.
    d. statistical quality control.

12. The coordination of labor, materials, and machinery in making a finished product and maintaining a smooth work flow so that orders can be filled efficiently and economically is called
    a. PERT control.
    b. zero-based budgeting.
    c. CPM control.
    d. production control.

13. Planning, routing, scheduling, dispatching, follow-up, and control are basic steps in
    a. production control.
    b. purchasing.
    c. accounting.
    d. inventory control.

14. Important factors that a manager must consider in locating a plant include
    a. energy, labor, raw materials, and market.
    b. land cost, taxes, and community.
    c. educational institutions, suppliers, and transportation facilities.
    d. all of the above.

15. The issuing of orders to department heads and supervisors to specify the work to be done and the schedule for its completion is known as
    a. planning.
    b. routing.
    c. scheduling.
    d. dispatching.

16. The production routing process in which production tasks are carried out in discrete locations that contain specialized equipment and personnel is
    a. process layout.
    b. service-line layout.
    c. assembly-line layout.
    d. fixed-position layout.

17. Automobiles and personal computers are best suited for which type of production routing process?
    a. process layout
    b. service-line layout
    c. assembly-line layout
    d. fixed-position layout

18. The control procedure that divides a large project into many different steps and analyzes the time requirements for completion of each step and the entire project is called
    a. PERT.
    b. the Gantt production chart system.
    c. the zero-based budgeting system.
    d. materials requirement planning.

19. The use of computer-aided design and computer-aided manufacture allows
    a. faster changes in product setups.
    b. more customized products.
    c. shorter production runs.
    d. higher-quality products.
    e. all of the above.

20. Accidents, mechanical breakdowns, or supplier failures are all good reasons for industries to develop
    a. good routing procedures.
    b. follow-up and control systems.
    c. dispatching techniques.
    d. a perpetual inventory system.

21. Which of the following is an advantage of utilizing computer technology in the production process, such as in GM's Saturn project?
    a. savings in labor costs
    b. increased efficiency
    c. faster production and quicker deliveries
    d. savings in transportation and warehousing costs
    e. all of the above

CHAPTER 9

1. Which of the following is *not* one of the basic ingredients of a good human relations program?
   a. good leadership
   b. excellent compensation programs
   c. effective communications
   d. effective motivation program

2. Baby boomers
   a. tend to perceive work in the same way as their parents.
   b. find it easier to get jobs and promotions due to a lack of competition.
   c. tend to be less responsive to authority.
   d. have caused the average age of workers to decrease.

3. Which of the following is *true* concerning the impact of women in the work force?
   a. Employment decisions must be made in light of how they will impact other family members as well as the employee.
   b. Transferring workers to others parts of the country is easier.
   c. Getting employees to work overtime is easier.
   d. Child care is not as important.

4. The view that money is the sole motivator of a person in the work force is known as
    a. Hawthorne theory of management.
    b. greed principle of motivation.
    c. classical theory of motivation.
    d. Maslow's theory.

5. A sense of personal worth and integrity is an example of a
    a. physiological need.
    b. safety need.
    c. social need.
    d. esteem need.
    e. self-realization need.

6. Achievement, recognition, and responsibility would be classified as
    a. hygiene factors.
    b. motivators.
    c. dissatisfiers.
    d. formal compensators.

7. Which of the following statements is *false* concerning the motivational hygiene theory?
    a. Hygiene factors are associated with dissatisfying experiences.
    b. Motivators are associated with satisfying experiences.
    c. Improving hygiene factors increases employee satisfaction.
    d. Improving motivator factors increases productivity.

8. Which of the following statements is *false*?
    a. Human relations is concerned with the way people in organizations behave toward one another.
    b. Contemporary management theory has moved away from the concept of meshing the needs of the individual with the needs of the organization.
    c. The classical theory of motivation holds that money is the sole motivator in the workplace.
    d. McGregor's Theory Y states that work is as natural as play or rest and that workers will work toward objectives to which they are committed and will seek responsibility.

9. Which of the following statements is *false*?
    a. Money is the only motivation that can be used by management to increase satisfaction.
    b. Good company management can increase the amount of worker satisfaction.
    c. Workers are likely to be motivated if they feel they have something to gain by doing the job the way the organization wants it done.
    d. The informal organization, by exerting social pressure, can motivate workers.

10. Which of the following statements is *false*?
    a. A Theory X manager feels that the average worker must be forced or threatened with punishment to be motivated.
    b. The most satisfying forms of work are those in which the worker has full control over a finished product.
    c. The most important resource of an organization is its equipment.
    d. Employees involved in piecework quotas are rewarded for each unit produced if the quota is obtained.
    e. Managers once thought that money was the only way to motivate workers.

11. According to Maslow, the highest level of needs that people seek to fulfill are
    a. social needs.
    b. esteem needs.
    c. self-realization needs.
    d. status needs.

12. The Hawthorne studies found that
    a. social or peer pressure was a strong motivating force.
    b. participation in some management functions was a strong motivating factor.
    c. new worker enthusiasm and confidence provided a stronger incentive than the paycheck.
    d. all of the above.

13. Which of the following is *false* concerning Theory Y management?
    a. It basically treats employees like family.
    b. Employment is guaranteed for life.
    c. Workers are highly specialized for their work.
    d. Everyone participates in decision making.
    e. All of the above are true.

14. Which of the following is a technique that can be used to stimulate unmotivated employees?
    a. goal setting
    b. behavior modification
    c. retraining
    d. all of the above

15. Rewarding desirable actions and punishing undesirable acts is known as
    a. goal setting.
    b. behavior modification.
    c. retraining.
    d. operant learning theory.

16. Increased motivation through job structure can be achieved by
    a. quality circles.
    b. job enrichment and redesign.
    c. flextime.
    d. work and job sharing.
    e. all of the above.

17. Increasing a worker's job to include more responsibility for the entire process is an example of
    a. quality circle.
    b. job sharing.
    c. job enrichment.
    d. flextime.

18. Flextime would most likely be used by which of the following?
    a. workers on production lines
    b. clerks in retail stores
    c. receptionists in offices
    d. white-collar workers in offices

19. Two employees sharing the same job for their own convenience is an example of
    a. job sharing.
    b. work sharing.
    c. temporary employees.
    d. split-time working.

20. Which of the following is *not* one of the principles of the one-minute manager?
    a. setting clear goals
    b. praising right behavior
    c. devaluing people for wrong behavior
    d. reprimanding poor behavior

CHAPTER 10

1. Human resource managers are responsible for
    a. hiring and training personnel to staff the organization.
    b. developing and managing a compensation and fringe benefits program.
    c. developing programs that will help retain good employees.
    d. dismissing and laying off employees.
    e. all of the above.

2. The determination of what a particular job involves (duties, responsibilities, skills required) is made through a job
    a. analysis.
    b. description.
    c. specification.
    d. evaluation.

3. Which of the following consists of a list of the tasks a job involves and the conditions under which the tasks are performed?
    a. a job study
    b. a job analysis
    c. a job description
    d. a job specification

4. A statement describing the kind of person best suited for the job is the
   a. job analysis.
   b. job description.
   c. job specification.
   d. job evaluation.

5. The member of the human resources staff who is responsible for obtaining new candidates is the
   a. trainer.
   b. personnel specialist.
   c. job analyzer.
   d. recruiter.

6. Which of the following is a source for recruiting applicants?
   a. pirating employees from other companies
   b. referrals from employees or colleagues
   c. employment agencies
   d. union hiring halls
   e. all of the above

7. In selecting job applicants, a company's personnel department should be careful to screen applicants by
   a. sex.
   b. race.
   c. job skills.
   d. national origin.
   e. all of the above.

8. Job discrimination cases are handled by the
   a. FTC.
   b. EEOC.
   c. TDD.
   d. U.S. Civil Service Commission.
   e. Justice Department.

9. Which of the following is *not* an advantage of the performance appraisal system over subjective evaluations of employees?
   a. It is fairer to the employee in that job-related factors are evaluated.
   b. Evaluative criteria and evaluations are in writing.
   c. The employee is rated by several people.
   d. The system is easily implemented.
   e. All of the above are advantages.

10. An alternative to layoffs is
    a. reducing expenses.
    b. freezing wages.
    c. encouraging early retirement.
    d. postponing new hiring.
    e. all of the above

11. A worker buyout involves
    a. employees buying all of the company's stock.
    b. employees providing financial incentives to leave the company.
    c. employees from a competing company being given financial incentives to work for you.
    d. employees being given special incentives if they increase their productivity.

12. Compensation includes which of the following?
    a. wages
    b. salaries
    c. fringe benefits
    d. all of the above

13. When a blue-collar worker's output is always related to the number of hours worked, the best method of compensation is
    a. a wage.
    b. profit sharing.
    c. goal sharing.
    d. a salary.

14. The type of compensation to which employees are paid extra money based on a company's growth statistics is known as
   a. a bonus plan.
   b. a performance plan.
   c. profit sharing.
   d. goal sharing.

15. Fringe benefits include
   a. unemployment benefits.
   b. insurance plans.
   c. paid holidays.
   d. pension plans.
   e. all of the above.

16. What are cafeteria benefits?
   a. the fringe benefits of a food service catering lunch for employees
   b. the total package of fringe benefits provided to employees
   c. a package that allows employees to select the fringe benefits they want, up to a certain dollar amount
   d. a compensation plan that gives the employees a choice over the mixture of salary and fringe benefits

17. Which of the following is *not* one of the major functions of the human resource department?
   a. planning employment needs
   b. training and developing employees
   c. accommodating changes in employee status
   d. developing compensation plans
   e. All of the above are major functions.

18. Changes in an employee's status can be a result of
   a. promotions, reassignments, or demotions.
   b. terminations.
   c. retirements.
   d. all of the above.

19. Compensation based on the number of hours worked is a
   a. wage.
   b. salary.
   c. bonus.
   d. fringe benefit.

20. Which of the following provides an incentive for employees to cut costs?
   a. bonuses
   b. profit sharing
   c. goal sharing
   d. perks

21. Which of the following distributes a portion of the company's profits to employees?
   a. bonuses
   b. profit sharing
   c. goal sharing
   d. perks

22. Bonuses are provided for
   a. doing your regular job.
   b. not making errors.
   c. doing something extra.
   d. achieving sales quotas.

23. Which of the following provides a way of preserving jobs by setting aside stock in the company so the employees become part-owners?
   a. employee stock ownership plan
   b. employment insurance
   c. pension plan
   d. profit sharing

*24. Which of the following is the best position for a company to take concerning employee privacy?
   a. The rights of the company should prevail over the rights of the employee.
   b. The rights of the employee should prevail over the rights of the company.
   c. The company should develop formal policies, clearly specifying the rights of both the company and the employee.
   d. The company should handle each issue on a case-by-case basis.

*25. Being a good employee requires
   a. doing more than you are asked to do.   d. being truthful.
   b. being familiar with what others do.   e. all of the above.
   c. encouraging those above and below you.

CHAPTER 11

1. Labor unions alter the supply and demand equation when they represent most or all of the workers by creating
   a. monopolistic control.
   b. pure competition.
   c. oligopolistic control.
   d. more supply than demand.

2. Which of the following statements is *true?*
   a. Labor unions flourished in the administration of Franklin D. Roosevelt.
   b. Worker interest in unions declined during the high-employment period of World War II.
   c. Union membership increased substantially during the 1970's.
   d. Service industries traditionally are highly unionized.

3. Which of the following statements is *false?*
   a. Professional workers who have not unionized in the past are beginning to associate and use union tactics to gain their objectives.
   b. Foreign competition has had an impact on the number of unions.
   c. Since World War II, union membership has declined during a time when the work force has increased substantially.
   d. The success of unions does not fluctuate with the business cycle because unions are not affected by the success or failure of businesses.

4. Which of the following is responsible for the decline in labor union membership?
   a. increase of foreign competition
   b. increase of high technology and service industries
   c. antiunion administrations in government
   d. poor leadership in the unions
   e. All of the above are factors leading to the decline.

5. During the high-employment period of World War II, union membership
   a. increased.   c. remained static.
   b. decreased.   d. fluctuated.

6. Which of the following *best* explains why workers are interested in forming unions?
   a. They seek higher wages.
   b. They feel that they are being treated unfairly and management is not willing to listen.
   c. They hope to obtain safe working conditions.
   d. They want to receive better benefits.

7. The AFL-CIO is an example of a
   a. local union.   d. industrial union.
   b. national union.   e. craft union.
   c. labor federation.

8. Which of the following is not a step in the negotiating process?
   a. preparing to meet   d. grievances
   b. reaching agreement   e. union ratification
   c. negotiating

9. In negotiations, decisions made by _____ are binding:
    a. a mediator
    b. an arbitrator
    c. a union negotiator
    d. grievances
    e. union ratification

10. A worker's grievances are handled by the _____.
    a. shop stewards.
    b. local union president.
    c. national union president.
    d. worker's supervisor.

11. Unions bargain with management to obtain
    a. better safety and health conditions for members.
    b. a better quality of work life for members.
    c. job security for members.
    d. more compensation for members.
    e. all of the above.

12. Nonunion workers who have to pay dues if they benefit from a union agreement belong to
    a. a closed shop.
    b. a union shop.
    c. a right-to-work shop.
    d. an open shop.
    e. an agency shop.

13. A guarantee that worker's pay will keep pace with inflation is known as a(n)
    a. inflation clause.
    b. COLA clause.
    c. guaranteed wage clause.
    d. fringe benefit.

14. All of the following tactics are used by unions to bring about favorable agreements *except*
    a. strikes.
    b. boycotts.
    c. political pressure.
    d. lockouts.

15. A court order that directs a union and/or management to do something or refrain from doing something is called a(n)
    a. legislative order.
    b. executive order.
    c. injunction.
    d. cease-and-desist order.

16. Management preventing workers from entering a struck business in order to pressure a union to accept management's last contract proposal is known as a(n)
    a. lockout.
    b. boycott.
    c. injunction.
    d. strike.

17. Large numbers of union members and other sympathizers forming an enormous block of negative purchasing power is an example of a(n)
    a. lockout.
    b. boycott.
    c. injunction.
    d. strike.

18. If a deadlock is reached between an employer and a union, a request for a ruling may be sought from the
    a. National Labor Relations Board.
    b. National Business Protection Agency.
    c. National Assessment and Arbitration Board.
    d. National Workers' Protection Agency.

19. Which of the following gives the correct order of personnel who are successively involved in handling a grievance?
    a. business agent, shop steward, arbitrator
    b. shop steward, business agent, arbitrator
    c. arbitrator, shop steward, business agent
    d. shop steward, arbitrator, business agent
    e. arbitrator, business agent, shop steward

20. Which of the following is the *most* powerful weapon that labor unions can use on management to achieve demands?
    a. a strike
    b. picketing
    c. a boycott
    d. political influence

21. To provide a united front in combating unions, some industries have formed _____, in which they agree temporarily to abandon competition against the company that is being struck.
    a. counter-strike alliances
    b. strike-breaking alliances
    c. mutual assistance pacts
    d. lockouts

22. The general term for the negotiation process between unions and management is
    a. a strike.
    b. mediation.
    c. collective bargaining.
    d. arbitration.

23. The two main types of unions are
    a. open and closed.
    b. worker controlled and management controlled.
    c. craft and industrial.
    d. industrial and service.

CHAPTER 12

1. Competitive advantage is the strategy of
    a. offering the lowest possible price for a product.
    b. offering a different product for every buyer.
    c. offering a unique benefit that justifies a higher price.
    d. maintaining a similar product as the market changes.

2. Distributing the product through retailers, instead of just having the product stay at the manufacturer's, adds
    a. form utility.
    b. place utility.
    c. time utility
    d. possession utility.

3. Developing a marketing strategy involves
    a. defining a target market.
    b. developing a marketing mix.
    c. defining a target market and developing a marketing mix.
    d. defining a target market and developing market segmentation.
    e. developing a marketing mix and developing market segmentation.

4. Which of the following is *not* a step involved in the marketing planning process?
    a. setting goals
    b. analyzing external environments
    c. analyzing internal capabilities
    d. selecting a strategy
    e. All of the above are steps in the marketing planning process.

5. Identifying potential customers and settling on a marketing program designed to satisfy their needs is known as
   a. product differentiation.
   b. customer manipulation.
   c. marketing strategy.
   d. sales-oriented marketing.

6. An example of an organization market would be
   a. your personal purchase of a typewriter for writing term papers for this class.
   b. the purchase of a ballpoint pen by a doctor.
   c. your buying a ticket from a travel agent who normally deals with IBM.
   d. your buying a personal computer.

7. Focusing on a specific market segment to avoid spreading organizational resources too thin allows businesses to concentrate on the needs and wants of a specific
   a. adopter category.
   b. utility receiver.
   c. supplier.
   d. target market.

8. The marketing mix is a blend of
   a. product, price, promotion, and utility.
   b. promotion, advertising, price, and place.
   c. product, price, promotion, and place.
   d. place, promotion, product, and need satisfaction.

9. Informing a potential customer about the products offered by an organization is which part of the marketing mix?
   a. promotion
   b. product offering
   c. pricing
   d. place of distribution

10. Which of the following is an outside environmental factor that may influence the way a marketing mix is put together?
    a. an economic force
    b. a social trend
    c. a technology force
    d. all of the above

11. Discovering what size and color consumers will prefer in the car models to be offered next year is an example of
    a. market research.
    b. market segmentation.
    c. reaction to technology.
    d. product differentiation.

12. Which of the following is an example of an external environmental variable?
    a. economic conditions
    b. social and legal climate
    c. technology
    d. competition
    e. all of the above

13. A simple formula that sums up the decision-making process nearly all consumer and industrial buyers go through when making a decision about a purchase is
    a. choice = need + want + ability to recall name brand.
    b. choice = need + want + ability to buy.
    c. choice = want + ability to buy + attitude toward brand name.
    d. choice = want + attitude toward brand name.

14. Analyzing internal capabilities informs a company about
    a. a competitor's strategies and customers.
    b. its strengths and weaknesses.
    c. changes in legislation and regulations influencing the company.
    d. changes occurring in consumer behavior.
    e. the marketing goals to set.

15. Grouping potential customers according to some useful characteristic that will help the organization make more effective marketing decisions is known as
    a. buyer behavior analysis.
    b. market segmentation.
    c. industrial versus consumer market targeting.
    d. all of the above.

16. Challenges usually follow a strategy of
    a. assaulting the leader.
    b. taking a "me too" approach.
    c. trying to differentiate by carving out a niche.
    d. all of the above.

17. Educational level, occupation, and family history determine a person's
    a. culture.
    b. social class.
    c. reference group.
    d. subculture.

18. Segmenting a market on the basis of a customers' age, sex, and income is known as _____ segmentation.
    a. demographic
    b. geographic
    c. behavioristic
    d. psychographic

19. Describing consumers in terms of their social roles, opinions, lifestyles, and interests is an example of_____ segmentation.
    a. demographic
    b. geographic
    c. behavioristic
    d. psychographic

20. Family members, friends, coworkers, and other people whom we use as benchmarks for decision making in purchasing products are known as
    a. culture.
    b. social class.
    c. reference groups.
    d. subcultures.

CHAPTER 13

1. Marketers divide consumer products into subgroups based on the
   a. approach people take in shopping.
   b. brand name of the product.
   c. price of the product.
   d. channel of distribution the consumer uses.

2. A Coca-Cola shirt that your friend went to three stores before finding is probably an example of what type of consumer product?
   a. convenience
   b. shopping
   c. specialty
   d. emergency

3. A consumer will probably consult the greatest variety of information sources for what type of product?
   a. convenience
   b. shopping
   c. specialty
   d. emergency

4. In developing a product mix, a company may choose to
   a. offer a single product.
   b. present a product line to a similar market.
   c. offer a widely diverse set of product lines.
   d. all of the above.

5. The stage of the product life cycle in which the producer makes little or no profit and is trying to inform the market about the availability of the product is the _____ stage.
   a. introductory
   b. growth
   c. maturity
   d. decline

6. In managing the new product development process, which of the following statements will provide accurate guidance to the marketing manager?
   a. A good decision might be to focus on new products with high growth potential.
   b. All new products must be true innovations.
   c. New products can be guaranteed market successes through careful research and planning.
   d. All of the above are true.

7. A brand owned by a manufacturer or retailer is
   a. illegal.
   b. a national brand.
   c. a private brand.
   d. a generic product.

8. Brand loyalty
   a. is equally applicable across all types of products.
   b. may cost more to generate than it is worth.
   c. cannot be measured.
   d. cannot result in sufficient product identification to ever be worth the time and effort.

9. If a consumer will not purchase a competitive product, he or she has reached what stage of brand loyalty?
   a. brand recognition
   b. brand preference
   c. brand insistence
   d. brand loyalty

10. Labeling serves an important role in the packaging of a product because
    a. it offers a misleading image to the customer, as part of an international manufacturer's strategy.
    b. a manufacturer can say whatever it wants on the label without fear or regulation.
    c. it helps a manufacturer monitor product performance.
    d. it forces consumers to buy in supermarkets.

11. A company can determine how many units of a product it must sell at a given price to keep from losing money through
    a. rate of return pricing.
    b. markup pricing.
    c. breakeven analysis.
    d. profit maximization analysis.

12. Offering products at a limited number of set process is an example of
    a. pricing at below the market.
    b. price lining.
    c. odd-even pricing.
    d. suggest pricing.

13. A price discount, offered by the producer to a wholesaler, is what type of pricing?
    a. illegal bait and switch
    b. suggest pricing
    c. trade discount
    d. psychological pricing

14. Which of the following is an example of a discount price?
    a. a cash discount
    b. a quantity discount
    c. a trade discount
    d. all of the above

CHAPTER 14

1. An organization must make a decision about the best combination of channels to use in the marketing of its product. That combination is called the
   a. distribution mix.
   b. marketing mix.
   c. wholesaler mix.
   d. physical distribution planning.

2. To be helpful to both producer and consumer, intermediaries perform which of the following functions?
    a. providing market information   c. assuming risks
    b. sorting, standardizing, and dividing   d. all of the above

3. By consolidating a variety of goods in one place, intermediaries provide which other service to the buyer?
    a. offering promotional support   c. delivering the product
    b. buying   d. all of the above

4. Which of the following is an example of horizontal conflict within a distribution system?
    a. A manufacturer wanting retailers to perform services the retailers do not want to perform.
    b. Wholesalers not stocking merchandise the retailers want to carry.
    c. One retailer being upset with another over the prices charged to consumers.
    d. A retailer being unhappy with the margin it is earning from the manufacturer.
    e. All of the above are examples of horizontal conflict.

5. In which type of vertical marketing system does one channel member own the other members?
    a. contractual   c. corporate
    b. administered   d. franchise

6. The dominant company within the administered vertical marketing system is the
    a. manufacturer.   d. channel captain.
    b. wholesaler.   e. sales branch.
    c. retailer.

7. In making a decision about a distribution mix, what question must the company answer?
    a. Should we sell directly to end users or use intermediaries?
    b. Which intermediaries should we select?
    c. Would more than one channel be employed?
    d. All of the above should be answered.

8. For a shopping good, where the buyer is likely to compare features and prices, the best market coverage strategy is _____ distribution.
    a. selective   c. exclusive
    b. intensive   d. extensive

9. Limiting the number of outlets for products in a particular geographic area is an example of _____ distribution.
    a. selective   c. exclusive
    b. intensive   d. extensive

10. Wholesalers sell primarily to
    a. retailers.
    b. other wholesalers and industrial users.
    c. retailers, other wholesalers, and end users.
    d. retailers, other wholesalers, and industrial users.

11. A wholesaler who takes title to merchandise and then resells it is called a(n)
    a. merchant wholesaler.   c. sales representative.
    b. agent.   d. branch office.

12. Shops that offer mostly relatively inexpensive items, but that also carry some national brands sold at discount, are known as _____ stores.
    a. discount   c. off-price
    b. department   d. bargain

13. The latest form of bargain shopping, which offers an annual membership to customers who in turn get low prices, is the
    a. catalog showroom.
    b. variety store.
    c. office-price store.
    d. warehouse club.

14. The type of store that maximizes time and place utility, while often charging a price premium, is a
    a. supermarket.
    b. convenience store.
    c. specialty store.
    d. mail-order firm.

15. One form of retailing that has declined in recent years due to changing lifestyles is
    a. door-to-door sales.
    b. vending machines.
    c. department stores.
    d. mail-order firms.

16. A warehouse that serves as a command post for moving products to customers is known as a
    a. full-service warehouse.
    b. distribution center.
    c. materials handling center.
    d. bonded agency.

17. The tradeoff between adequate levels of inventories and the minimization of holding costs is the process of
    a. warehousing.
    b. materials handling.
    c. containerization.
    d. inventory control.

CHAPTER 15

1. The combination of advertising, personal selling, publicity, and sales promotion that a firm uses to communicate with its target market is the _____ mix.
    a. marketing
    b. promotion
    c. industrial communication
    d. media

2. A strategy in which a company promotes a product by persuading wholesalers and retailers to carry it, then having retailers in turn promote the product to end users, is a(n)
    a. pull strategy.
    b. channel promotion strategy.
    c. push strategy.
    d. illegal act under antitrust legislation.

3. Trying to get buyers to purchase a particular brand of product is what type of advertising?
    a. generic
    b. product
    c. cooperative
    d. institutional

4. Which producers of national brands share the cost of local advertising with local merchants is what type of advertising?
    a. generic
    b. shared media expense
    c. cooperative
    d. advocacy

5. Each medium has its own strengths and weaknesses for specific advertising applications. Which of the following statements correctly describes newspapers as a media type?
    a. Newspapers are an effective and efficient media for a national campaign.
    b. Newspapers are not effective at all in reaching specific subgroups of the population.
    c. Newspapers are among the most "gripping" of all media types.
    d. Newspapers are particularly useful to local business.

6. Which of the following is *not* one of the major objectives of promotion?
    a. informing
    b. entertaining
    c. persuading
    d. reminding
    e. All of the above are major objectives.

7. In designing a media buy for a product that must have very good photography to illustrate its appeal to consumers, which medium is preferable?
   a. radio
   b. magazines
   c. telephone directories
   d. newspapers

8. Product complexity, price, and stage of the life cycle are _____ factors influencing the promotional mix.
   a. market
   b. competition
   c. product
   d. company
   e. environmental

9. The promotional mix for industrial products tends to emphasize
   a. advertising.
   b. personal selling.
   c. publicity.
   d. sales promotion.

10. Promotions are regulated by
   a. the FTC.
   b. industry and company self-regulation.
   c. both the FTC and self-regulation.
   d. Promotions are not regulated.

11. In business and industrial selling, either to wholesalers or retailers, salespeople find
   a. this form of selling relatively easy, as buying specialists approach the process from a rational framework.
   b. that they must have detailed understanding of the product and each buyer's needs.
   c. that they must function as order takers but do not have to have a great deal of skill in sales techniques.
   d. all of the above

12. A local bank giving away calendars with its name printed on them is an example of
   a. a demonstration.
   b. couponing.
   c. a refund offer.
   d. specialty advertising.

13. Attempting to increase sales by offering a price discount to consumers is an example of
   a. specialty advertising.
   b. a point-of-purchase display.
   c. a sweepstakes.
   d. couponing.

CHAPTER 16

1. Information is
   a. facts.
   b. data.
   c. relevant data.
   d. statistics.

2. To be useful, information must be
   a. accurate and timely.
   b. complete and relevant.
   c. concise.
   d. all of the above.

3. A computerized information system that processes the daily flow of customer, supplier, and employee transactions, including inventory, sales, and payroll records, is a _____ system.
   a. transaction-processing
   b. office automation
   c. management information
   d. decision support
   e. executive information

4. Office automation systems allow people to
   a. use word processing.
   b. produce reports.
   c. prepare budgets.
   d. prepare graphs.
   e. do all of the above.

5. A computer system that can supply periodic, predefined reports to assist in managerial decision making is a
    _____ system.
    a. transaction-processing
    b. office automation
    c. management information
    d. decision support
    e. executive information

6. A manager who must solve highly unstructured and nonroutine problems would use a _____
    system.
    a. transaction-processing
    b. office automation
    c. management information
    d. ·decision support
    e. executive information

7. Artificial intelligence computer systems
    a. replace human problem solving.
    b. mimic human thought processes.
    c. create new biological life forms.
    d. are the first generation of computer systems.

8. Personal computers, such as desktops and laptops, are examples of
    a. microcomputers.
    b. workstations.
    c. minicomputers.
    d. mainframes.
    e. supercomputers.

9. Individuals needing fast computing and powerful graphics capabilities to solve mathematically intense
    problems would most likely use
    a. microcomputers.
    b. workstations.
    c. minicomputers.
    d. mainframes.
    e. supercomputers.

10. Minicomputers have the same general capabilities as, but are smaller, cheaper, and less powerful than,
    a. microcomputers.
    b. workstations.
    c. mainframes.
    d. supercomputers.

11. The most complex processing tasks, such as seismic analyses, weather forecasting, and genetic research,
    require
    a. microcomputers.
    b. workstations.
    c. minicomputers.
    d. mainframes.
    e. supercomputers.

12. Which of the following would *not* be considered part of a computer's hardware?
    a. input devices
    b. computer program
    c. central processing unit
    d. output devices
    e. storage

13. The arithmetic, logic, and control/communication functions of a computer are performed in the
    a. input devices.
    b. computer program.
    c. central processing unit.
    d. output devices.
    c. storage.

14. Application software
    a. gives the computer specific functions to perform, such as word processing.
    b. controls the computer's overall operation.
    c. directs the flow of data into, around, and out of the system.
    d. stores data.

15. Which of the following is a category for applications software?
    a. drafting and CAD
    b. production and process control
    c. publishing
    d. communications
    e. all of the above

16. Multiple computers are able to communicate with each other through
    a. mainframes.
    b. distributed processing.
    c. networks.
    d. open systems.

17. A decentralized computer communication network is an example of
    a. micro-to-mainframe link.
    b. distributed processing.
    c. open system.
    d. work group computing.

18. Which type of computer language uses single commands to accomplish several commands?
    a. machine
    b. assembly
    c. high-level
    d. fourth-generation

19. Which type of computer language allows users to give instructions from their perspective rather than the functions the computer is to perform?
    a. machine
    b. assembly
    c. high-level
    d. fourth-generation

20. Which of the following represents a potential problem brought on through computerization?
    a. unethical sharing of databases
    b. lack of security on sensitive databases
    c. invasion of personal privacy
    d. All of the above are problems.

CHAPTER 17

1. Which type of business accounting is concerned with providing information for the outside world?
   a. financial accounting
   b. managerial accounting
   c. public accounting
   d. certified accounting

2. Investors and shareholders examine a company's financial accounting records to determine
   a. creditworthiness.
   b. profit potential.
   c. tax liabilities.
   d. market share.

3. The controller is responsible for
   a. keeping basic records.
   b. conducting financial audits.
   c. certifying a company's records as being accurate.
   d. overseeing all the financial aspects of a company.

4. Which of the following is an advantage of public accountants over corporate accountants?
   a. They are more familiar with the company.
   b. They have a more objective viewpoint.
   c. They communicate better.
   d. They work faster.

5. Accounting information is needed to
   a. evaluate and interpret past performance.
   b. evaluate and interpret present conditions.
   c. develop future plans.
   d. do all of the above.

6. The accounting equation can be expressed as follows:
   a. liabilities = assets + owners' equity.
   b. assets = liabilities + owners' equity.
   c. owners' equity = assets + liabilities.
   d. assets + owners' equity = profits.

7. Double-entry bookkeeping
   a. is an accounting system requiring two entries for every transaction to keep the accounting equation in balance.
   b. is an accounting system in which two sets of books are maintained, one for stockholders and one for the IRS.
   c. can be expressed as assets = liabilities + owners' equity.
   d. is an accounting system in which two sets of books are maintained in order to detect mistakes.

8. Which of the following lists represents the proper order in which assets can be turned into cash (from easiest to most difficult)?
   a. current, fixed, intangible
   b. fixed, current, intangible
   c. intangible, fixed, current
   d. current, intangible, fixed

9. Equipment, machinery, and furniture would all be examples of
   a. current assets.
   b. fixed assets.
   c. intangible assets.
   d. liabilities.

10. Patents, copyrights, trademarks, and goodwill are all examples of
    a. current assets.
    b. fixed assets.
    c. intangible assets.
    d. liabilities.

11. Accounts payable, notes payable, and accrued expenses are examples of
    a. current assets.
    b. current liabilities.
    c. long-term liabilities.
    d. owners' equity.

12. Long-term loans and mortgages are examples of
    a. fixed assets.
    b. current liabilities.
    c. long-term liabilities.
    d. owners' equity.

13. The process of comparing financial data from year to year to see how they have changed is known as
    a. accounting.
    b. bookkeeping.
    c. trend analysis.
    d. ratio analysis.

14. Comparing two elements from the same year's financial figures is known as
    a. accounting.
    b. bookkeeping.
    c. trend analysis.
    d. ratio analysis.

15. Which of the following would be the best means of measuring a firm's profitability?
    a. inventory turnover
    b. liquidity ratios
    c. return on investment
    d. current ratio

16. Liquidity measures are used to determine
    a. a firm's profitability.
    b. a company' ability to pay its short-term debts.
    c. how well a firm is managing its assets.
    d. a company's ability to pay its long-term debts.

17. Activity ratios measure
    a. a firm's profitability.
    b. a company's ability to pay its short-term debts.
    c. how well a firm is managing its assets.
    d. a company's ability to pay its long-term debts.

18. Which of the following ratios would indicate that a firm is in trouble?
    a. a debt-to-equity ratio of 1.5
    b. a current ratio of 2
    c. a quick ratio of less than 1
    d. a debt-to-total-assets ratio of 1 to 2

19. Accountants can exercise discretion in
    a. the timing of revenue recognition.
    b. their choice of depreciation method.
    c. their choice of inventory evaluation.
    d. the determination of allowance amounts.
    e. all of the above.

20. The ability of a firm to pay its short-term debts with cash, marketable securities, and receivables on hand is measured by the
    a. return-on-equity ratio.
    b. current ratio.
    c. acid-test ratio.
    d. owners' debt-to-equity ratio.

21. The ability to repay long-term loans is best measured by the
    a. return-on-equity ratio.
    b. current ratio.
    c. acid-test ratio.
    d. owners' debt-to-equity ratio.

22. If a firm has liabilities of $400,000 and owners' equity of $300,000, then the assets must be
    a. $700,000.
    b. $100,000.
    c. $400,000.
    d. $300,000.

23. If a firm has assets of $800,000 and owners' equity is $600,000, then its liabilities must be
    a. $1,400,000.
    b. $600,000.
    c. $200,000.
    d. $800,000.

24. Compared to the current ratio, which of the following is *not* included in the calculation of the acid-test ratio (or quick ratio)?
    a. accounts receivable
    b. cash
    c. inventories
    d. marketable securities
    e. notes receivable

CHAPTER 18

1. A token of wealth, or money, functions as
    a. a measure of exchange.
    b. a measure of value.
    c. a store of value.
    d. all of the above.

2. The ability to convert money into other forms of wealth relatively quickly illustrates which characteristic of money?
    a. medium of exchange
    b. liquidity
    c. legitimacy
    d. durability

3. The narrowest commonly used measure of money, which consists of currency and demand deposits, is
    a. M1.
    b. M2.
    c. bills and coins.
    d. currency, demand deposits, and time deposits.

4. A checking account is known as a demand deposit because the
    a. bank can demand you make a deposit to the account at any time.
    b. customer can demand that money be added to the account.
    c. bank will release on demand a specified amount from the account.
    d. interest paid on the account is set by supply and demand.

5. The member of the banking system that accepts deposits and uses those deposits to make loans for a profit is a
   a. thrift institution.
   b. credit union.
   c. commercial bank.
   d. limited-service bank.

6. A member-owned cooperative that functions as a bank is a
   a. thrift institution.
   b. limited-service bank.
   c. credit union.
   d. state bank.

7. Another name for nonbank banks is
   a. credit unions.
   b. investment banks.
   c. finance companies.
   d. limited-service banks.

8. Although they may vary in the services they offer, all financial institutions operate with what basic principles?
   a. Generate money supply for the Fed.
   b. Attract deposits, then invest them in the stock market.
   c. Borrow money from other banks, then make loans.
   d. Attract deposits, then lend some of that money to customers.

9. How can banks and financial institutions attract depositors?
   a. by offering interest on deposit accounts
   b. by providing convenient locations
   c. by providing premiums for opening high-value accounts
   d. all of the above

10. An account that usually pays a higher interest than any type of checking account but offers limited liquidity is
   a. a certificate of deposit.
   b. an Individual Retirement Account.
   c. a Keogh account.
   d. all of the above.

11. A financial institution may legally provide what services for its customers?
   a. kiting checks
   b. helping them use the "cheapest money in town"
   c. electronic funds transfer
   d. all of the above

12. Finance companies increasingly have
   a. experienced financial difficulties.
   b. come under federal regulation.
   c. dealt only with consumers.
   d. taken market share from banks.

13. During the 1980s
   a. an increasing number of banks failed.
   b. bank profits rose steadily.
   c. the number of banks increased dramatically.
   d. banks became more willing to make commercial loans.

14. All deposits in nationally chartered banks are insured up to $100,000 per account by the
   a. FDIC.
   b. FSLIC.
   c. NCUIF.
   d. state insurance programs.

15. The Federal Reserve System is a network of twelve regional banks that
   a. permit only national banks to belong.
   b. have no regulatory authority over savings and loan associations.
   c. have great influence over the economic and political environments in the United States.
   d. establish economic guidelines that include high inflation to help the economy grow quickly.

16. As the official banker of the federal government, the U.S. Department of the Treasury
    a. competes with business borrowing when it borrows from the public, pushing up interest rates.
    b. prefers to borrow money from the Fed, as that only increases the money supply and will not lead to inflation.
    c. does not get involved in monetary transactions (it leaves that to the Fed).
    d. raises money only when the federal budget is in surplus.

17. If the Fed wishes to cool off inflation, it may increase the amount of money that member banks are required to keep on hand as a percentage of deposits. This is a change in the
    a. reserve requirement.
    b. discount rate.
    c. open-market operations.
    d. selective credit control.

18. If the Fed believes that inflation is about to increase rapidly, it will undertake what open-market operation?
    a. It will buy government bonds back from the public.
    b. It will sell government bonds to the public.
    c. It will lower the prime interest rate.
    d. It will raise the prime interest rate.

19. The interest rate that banks charge each other for overnight loans is called the
    a. reserve rate.
    b. discount rate.
    c. Fed funds rate.
    d. prime interest rate.

20. The Fed can encourage banks to make loans by
    a. raising the prime rate.
    b. lowering the discount rate.
    c. raising the Fed funds rate.
    d. lowering margin requirements.

CHAPTER 19

1. Magnifying the power of the borrower, or using money to make money, is known as
    a. profit minimization.
    b. leverage.
    c. equity debt.
    d. financial debt structure.

2. The step in the financial planning process in which the financial manager predicts surplus or shortfall of funds is known as
    a. estimating outflow of funds.
    b. estimating inflow of funds.
    c. comparing inflows and outflows.
    d. all of the above.

3. A possible source of money for the operation of a firm is
    a. the firm's suppliers.
    b. loans from financial institutions.
    c. funds from outside investors.
    d. cost accounting.

4. The financial manager must keep a sharp eye on
    a. accounts receivable.
    b. inventories.
    c. accounts payable.
    d. all of the above.

5. One of the most basic principles of finance is that
    a. short-term debt should be accumulated so that it covers long-term debt.
    b. long-term debt, which is cheaper than short-term debt, should be used to cover short-term needs.
    c. either short- or long-term debt may be used to cover medium-term needs.
    d. the length of debt should roughly match the need it is to cover.

6. A major source of short-term financing is
   a. trade credit.
   b. selling assets.
   c. selling stock.
   d. bonds.

7. An informal arrangement in which a purchaser obtains merchandise before paying for it is known as
   a. a promissory note.
   b. a trade draft.
   c. open-book credit.
   d. commercial paper.

8. Which of the following may be used as collateral to secure a loan?
   a. accounts payable
   b. inventories
   c. future sales predictions
   d. All of the above may be used as collateral to secure a loan.

9. Selling accounts receivable to a financial institution as a form of financing business activity is
   a. an excellent idea, because accounts receivable are sold at full face value with no loss of income to the seller.
   b. of not much value since the seller has to collect the bills anyway.
   c. known as pledging inventories.
   d. referred to as factoring accounts receivable.

10. A compensating balance has the effect of
    a. raising the real rate of interest paid on the loan.
    b. acting as a secured loan.
    c. tying the borrower to the lending bank for all future financial transactions.
    d. all of the above.

11. In order for a business to be able to draw on its line of credit whenever it wants, it usually must pay an extra fee to secure a
    a. commercial paper guarantee.
    b. factor agreement.
    c. revolving line of credit.
    d. marketable security.

12. A business that temporarily has excess cash to invest might consider the purchase of
    a. accounts receivables.
    b. commercial paper.
    c. junk bonds.
    d. preferred stock.

13. A corporate IOU that obligates a company to repay a given sum plus interest to the holder of that IOU is called
    a. commercial paper.
    b. equity capital.
    c. a bond.
    d. a chattel mortgage.

14. If a company uses bonds to raise capital,
    a. each bond will have a denomination, or the amount of the loan represented by one bond.
    b. the bond will also provide for interest payments.
    c. the full amount of the bond will be referred to as the principal.
    d. all of the above.

15. What accounts for the differences in interest rates offered on bonds?
    a. Unsecured bonds are always a riskier investment than secured bonds.
    b. A company in a stronger financial position represents less risk to the investor.
    c. Junk bonds are popular but low-risk investments.
    d. Debentures, as secured bonds, will have lower interest rates.

16. Bonds that all mature at the same time are called _____ bonds.
   a. junk
   b. serial
   c. term
   d. sinking fund

17. Investors are attracted to convertible bonds, which means that a corporation may be able to offer lower interest rates because
   a. sinking funds guarantee they will be paid off.
   b. they are convertible to higher interest rates if the prime interest rate increases.
   c. an investor may be paid off in either stock or money.
   d. they are convertible from term to serial bonds, which means the investor can "roll over" the investment.

18. The part of a corporation's stock that is sold and held by shareholders is called
   a. preferred stock.
   b. authorized stock.
   c. par value stock.
   d. issued stock.

19. Stocks are purchased from individuals through secondary markets known as
   a. stock exchanges.
   b. common stock trading corporations.
   c. new issue agencies.
   d. over-the-counter markets.

20. Marketable securities, or securities that are relatively low in risk and standardized in order to increase their liquidity, include
   a. Treasury bills.
   b. factored accounts.
   c. leases.
   d. all of the above.

CHAPTER 20

1. The investment system of the United States may be described as
   a. providing benefits to companies because it enables them to attract needed capital.
   b. not being beneficial to individuals, since only institutions make money through investing.
   c. being composed only of major institutional investors.
   d. all of the above.

2. An investor who is concerned with investing to achieve capital gains would probably invest in
   a. Treasury bills and high-grade corporate bonds.
   b. preferred stocks and certificates of deposit.
   c. common stocks.
   d. money market funds.

3. If you compare corporate bonds to common stocks, you would say that
   a. corporate bonds have a higher risk.
   b. corporate bonds have a higher chance of capital gains.
   c. corporate bonds are more income-oriented.
   d. common stocks are more income-oriented.

4. In general, as an investment guideline, the higher the risk, the higher the potential return on the investment. This is the concern for
   a. risk/return minimization.
   b. safety.
   c. capital liquidity.
   d. all of the above.

5. Which of the following is the most liquid investment?
   a. common stock
   b. real estate
   c. municipal bonds
   d. commercial paper

6. An investor who accepts high risks in order to realize possible high capital gains is
   a. a bear-market specialist.
   b. a speculator.
   c. selling long.
   d. selling short.

7. To finance long-term debt, the U.S. government sells
   a. Treasury bills.
   b. Treasury bonds.
   c. tax-free municipal bonds.
   d. general obligation bonds.

8. The most risk-free investments possible are
   a. real estate purchases.
   b. U.S. government securities.
   c. blue-chip stocks.
   d. mutual funds.

9. Bonds backed by real property owned by the issuing corporation are known as
   a. convertible bonds.
   b. debentures.
   c. corporate bonds.
   d. mortgage bonds.

10. Selling a stock short is something done by an investor who is
    a. looking for long-term income.
    b. optimistic.
    c. pessimistic.
    d. in need of immediate cash.

11. Selling stock you don't own in hopes of buying it back later at a lower price is
    a. illegal.
    b. selling long.
    c. selling futures.
    d. selling short.

12. The ratio of a stock's market price to its earnings per share is
    a. the single best indicator of whether a stock is a good buy or not.
    b. a good indicator of whether or not the earnings are significantly below the industrial norm.
    c. known as the profit-to-earnings ratio.
    d. referred to as the price-earnings ratio.

13. Investors may pool their money to buy stocks or bonds through participation in a
    a. corporate bond.
    b. buying club.
    c. stock index option.
    d. mutual fund.

14. Mutual funds invested entirely in short-term securities are called _____ funds.
    a. money-market
    b. pooled
    c. cash management
    d. growth

15. A stock option that gives you the right to buy is a
    a. put option.
    b. call option.
    c. futures option.
    d. purchase on sight.

16. The ability to bet that the price of a financial instrument will rise or fall is available through a
    a. financial future.
    b. stock index future.
    c. stock index option.
    d. all of the above.

17. The biggest threat to all auction exchanges comes from
    a. high interest rates.
    b. the state of the U.S. economy.
    c. dealer exchanges.
    d. foreign exchanges.

18. What influences the size of the broker's commission and the taxes on a sale, or transaction costs, that you have to pay?
    a. the size of the transaction
    b. if you are buying odd versus round lots
    c. the nature of the brokerage house
    d. all of the above

19. A stock market that is characterized by rising share values is called a(n)
    a. bear market.
    b. bull market.
    c. inflation pull market.
    d. margin trading motivated market.

20. Trading in stocks and bonds is monitored by which agency of the federal government?
    a. the Federal Reserve Board
    b. the Securities and Exchange Commission
    c. the Commodities Futures Trading Commission
    d. the New York Stock Exchange Regulatory Agency

21. The best-known stock market index is the
    a. Dow Jones Industrial Average.
    b. Standard & Poor's 500 Stock Average.
    c. New York Stock Exchange Index.
    d. Wilshire Index.

CHAPTER 21

1. A business organization's management of government relations is best described as
    a. fairly straightforward, since governmental policy is laid out in laws and regulations.
    b. usually adversarial.
    c. complicated by the need to deal with several different levels of government.
    d. usually mutually supportive, since government and business are both interested in achieving the same objectives.

2. In addition to direct governmental support of business,
    a. the government is also a major customer.
    b. the government provides little indirect support.
    c. business can manipulate government to provide whatever support it wants through lobbying.
    d. all of the above.

3. The Interstate Commerce Act and the Sherman Antitrust Act were passed for what purpose?
    a. mainly to reduce business activity that may endanger society
    b. mainly to reduce noncompetitive practices
    c. to guarantee that businesses would make a profit
    d. to give the federal government total control over all business practices

4. Which of the following forbids tying contracts?
    a. the Interstate Commerce Act
    b. the Sherman Antitrust Act
    c. the Federal Trade Commission Act
    d. the Clayton Act

5. The legislation that established a federal agency charged with defining, detecting, and enforcing compliance with federal antitrust acts is known as the
    a. Sherman Antitrust Act.
    b. Interstate Commerce Act.
    c. Federal Trade Commission Act.
    d. Wheeler-Lea Act.

6. Which of the following is a provision of the Robinson-Patman Act?
    a. Sellers must provide all buyers with exactly equal prices or promotional assistance.
    b. There are no permissible quantity discounts.
    c. The FTC has the authority to approve mergers before they take place.
    d. Quantity discounts which reflect decreased costs are legal.

7. What is the theory that underlies the current trend of deregulation?
   a. Governmental regulation is anticompetitive in itself.
   b. The government is concerned with public interests, not private ones.
   c. Market forces are more efficient than government intervention.
   d. Businesses are capable of regulating themselves.

8. The tax-reform legislation discussed in the text has what objective?
   a. to reduce individual taxpayer burden
   b. to obtain more taxes from business
   c. to eliminate tax loopholes
   d. all of the above

9. Taxes imposed on land and the buildings on that land are called _____ taxes.
   a. land use
   b. property
   c. sales
   d. value-added

10. Income from federal excise taxes
    a. is used for any general purpose, just like income from sales taxes.
    b. is set aside in a fund, to be used for an as-yet-undetermined activity.
    c. must be used for national defense.
    d. must be used for a purpose related to the tax.

11. Which of the following statements correctly describes customs duties, or import taxes?
    a. They vary according to the product and country of origin.
    b. They are used strictly to generate revenue.
    c. They are consistent across product and country of origin.
    d. They are absorbed by the company paying them, not passed along to the consumer.

12. The Uniform Commercial Code is an example of what type of law?
    a. common
    b. administrative
    c. statutory
    d. federal

13. The type of law that is concerned with the relationships between the government and individual citizens is called
    a. public law.
    b. private law.
    c. social law.
    d. a tort.

14. If a company unknowingly makes a product that later proves to be defective, it may be responsible for damages through the concept of
    a. public law.
    b. negligence.
    c. market-share liability.
    d. strict product liability.

15. In order to have a legal contract,
    a. the offer must be made in writing.
    b. the acceptance of the offer must be voluntary.
    c. consideration must be given by one party, but not necessarily by both.
    d. all of the above.

16. If one party to a contract is in breach and the other party wishes for the contract to be carried out anyway, which option is being pursued?
    a. discharge
    b. damages
    c. specific performance
    d. breach fulfillment

17. A building, which can be bought and sold, is an example of what basic type of property?

    a. personal property
    b. transactional property
    c. contract negotiation
    d. real property

18. An interest in real property must be transferred through a

    a. property transfer.
    b. bill of sale.
    c. title.
    d. deed.

19. For installment purchases, title generally passes from the seller to the buyer when

    a. the buyer pays the final installment.
    b. the buyer takes possession.
    c. when more than 50 percent of the purchase price has been paid.
    d. one year after the date of the transaction.

20. Which of the following may be a benefit to a firm that enters voluntary bankruptcy?

    a. It gains time to reorganize.
    b. It eliminates all costs.
    c. Although it may not reorganize, it still benefits by having to delay lawsuits.
    d. All of the above are benefits.

CHAPTER 22

1. A disaster such as a fire is an example of a threat of a loss without the possibility of gain, or a(n)

    a. pure risk.
    b. speculative risk.
    c. uninsurable risk.
    d. unacceptable risk.

2. A risk that an insurance company will cover is called a(n)

    a. uninsurable risk.
    b. speculative risk.
    c. insurable risk.
    d. self-insurable risk.

3. Which of the following correctly describes the general requirements a risk must meet in order to be insurable?

    a. The peril insured must be under the control of the insured.
    b. There must be a small number of similar cases subject to the same peril.
    c. The peril must be unlikely to affect all insured parties at the same time.
    d. The possible loss must not be financially serious.

4. The people working for insurance companies who decide which risks to insure, and under what terms, are called

    a. actuaries.
    b. underwriters.
    c. agents.
    d. brokers.

5. In calculating probability of loss, actuaries rely on

    a. the law of random occurrence.
    b. the law of large numbers.
    c. co-insurance risk reduction.
    d. premium calculation tied to inflation rates.

6. Social Security benefits include

    a. payments to spouses of deceased workers.
    b. hospital and medical payments.
    c. income for retirees.
    d. all of the above.

7. What are the two sources of income for insurance companies?
   a. premiums and fees
   b. investment income and interest income
   c. premiums and investment income
   d. deductible rebates and interest income

8. An insurance policy that covers the insured for physical damage to property and theft of property is an example of what type of insurance?
   a. property insurance
   b. liability insurance
   c. employee liability
   d. umbrella insurance

9. A three-party contract in which one party agrees to be responsible to a second party for the obligations of a third is known as
   a. a surety bond.
   b. a fidelity bond.
   c. crime insurance.
   d. an umbrella policy.

10. An individual purchasing a new home and wanting to obtain a policy that would pay off the mortgage in the event he or she dies would be asking for _____ insurance.
    a. term
    b. whole life
    c. credit life
    d. endowment

11. Insurance against loss of earning power is represented by
    a. business-interruption insurance.
    b. extra-expense insurance.
    c. contingent business-interruption insurance.
    d. all of the above.

12. Malpractice insurance is usually carried by
    a. doctors.
    b. lawyers.
    c. architects.
    d. all of the above.

13. In which type of life insurance policy does the insured get to decide how to invest the cash value?
    a. endowment
    b. variable life
    c. universal life
    d. whole life

14. Insurance that protects companies from lawsuits by people who are injured by the companies' products is called
    a. workers' compensation.
    b. automobile liability.
    c. product liability.
    d. product protection insurance.

15. When no-fault auto insurance is in effect,
    a. there is no liability coverage available.
    b. the insurance company is not obligated to pay claims.
    c. drivers need not purchase liability coverage.
    d. the size of lawsuits that can be brought is limited.

16. Which of the following is growing in popularity as a method of managing workers' compensation insurance claims?
    a. lowering insurance premiums, since claims are getting smaller
    b. eliminating workers' compensation insurance programs
    c. restricting workers' compensation claims to those related only directly to an employee's work
    d. improving safety programs to lower accidents

17. One of the three types of employee insurance that guarantees income in the event of a disabling injury is
    a. health insurance.
    b. life insurance.
    c. pension plans.
    d. all of the above.

18. Which form of medical coverage pays the costs of in-hospital care by a physician?
    a. hospitalization insurance
    b. major-medical insurance
    c. surgical and medical insurance
    d. mental health insurance

19. What is an advantage of using a preferred-provider organization instead of a health maintenance organization?
    a. Although more expensive, it provides superior treatment.
    b. It provides a wider choice of hospitals and doctors.
    c. It is less expensive to set up.
    d. It may include employers with doctors in a malpractice action.

20. Life insurance that provides a combination of insurance and savings and is in force until the policyholder dies is called _____ insurance.
    a. term
    b. whole life
    c. endowment
    d. key-person